D1105356

WAGING NONVIOLENT STRUGGLE

Selected Publications in English by the Author

Books

Civilian-Based Defense: A Post-Military Weapons System. Princeton, New Jersey: Princeton University Press, 1990

Making Europe Unconquerable. London: Taylor & Francis, 1985 and Cambridge, Massachusetts: Ballinger, 1986

Social Power and Political Freedom. Boston, Massachusetts: Porter Sargent, 1980

Gandhi as Political Strategist, with Essays on Ethics and Politics. Boston, Massachusetts: Porter Sargent, 1979, and New Delhi: Gandhi Media Centre, 1999

The Politics of Nonviolent Action. Boston, Massachusetts: Porter Sargent, 1973 and in three volumes, *Power and Struggle, The Methods of Nonviolent Action,* and *The Dynamics of Nonviolent Action,* 1974 and later

Co-authored and co-edited books

Nonviolent Action: A Research Guide (second editor). New York: Garland. 1997

Resistance, Politics, and the American Struggle for Independence, 1765-1775 (co-editor). Boulder, Colorado: Lynne Rienner, 1986

Booklets and pamphlets

From Dictatorship to Democracy: A Conceptual Framework for Liberation. Boston, Massachusetts: Albert Einstein Institution, 2002 and 2003. Earlier edition: Bangkok: Committee for the Restoration of Democracy in Burma, 1993

There Are Realistic Alternatives. Boston, Massachusetts: Albert Einstein Institution, 2003

The Anti-Coup (co-author). Boston, Massachusetts: Albert Einstein Institution, 2003

Self-Reliant Defense Without Bankruptcy or War. Cambridge, Massachusetts: Albert Einstein Institution, 1992

The Role of Power in Nonviolent Struggle. Cambridge, Massachusetts: Albert Einstein Institution, 1990

Encyclopedia articles

"Nonviolent Struggle and the Media" in Donald Johnston (ed.). *The Encyclopedia of International Media and Communications.* vol. 3, pp. 363-370. San Diego: Academic Press, 2003

"Nonviolent Action" in Lester Kurtz (ed.), *The Encyclopedia of Violence, Peace, and Conflict,* Vol. 2. San Diego: Academic Press, 1999

"Civil Disobedience" and "Nonviolent Action" in Joel Krieger, *et. al.,* (eds.), *The Oxford Companion to the Politics of the World,* Second Edition, pp. 137-138, and 603-605. New York and Oxford: Oxford University Press, 2001

Full listing of publications

Dr. Sharp is the author of dozens of additional publications, including articles, pamphlets, chapters, and books, in English and translations. His writings have been published in over thirty languages. For the most recent listing, see the Albert Einstein Institution website: *www.aeinstein.org* The Albert Einstein Institution is located at 427 Newbury St., Boston, MA 02115, USA.

WAGING NONVIOLENT STRUGGLE

20th Century Practice and 21st Century Potential

by Gene Sharp

with the collaboration of Joshua Paulson

and the assistance of Christopher A. Miller
and Hardy Merriman

Extending Horizons Books

PORTER SARGENT PUBLISHERS, INC.

BOSTON

Copyright 2005 by Hardy Merriman
Published 2005 by
Extending Horizons Books
an imprint of
Porter Sargent Publishers, Inc.
11 Beacon St., Ste. 1400, Boston, MA 02108
www.extendinghorizons.com

Paperback cover and jacket design: Kirsten Macdonald
Text design: Leslie A. Weston

Printed in Canada

10 9 8 7 6 5 4 3 2 1

Library of Congress Cataloging-in-Publication Data

Sharp, Gene.
  Waging nonviolent struggle : 20th century practice and 21st century potential / by Gene Sharp ; with the collaboration of Joshua Paulson and the assistance of Christopher A. Miller and Hardy Merriman.
    p. cm.
  Summary: "Instructs how to strategically plan nonviolent action, a technique of waging conflict that uses protest, noncooperation and intervention. Draws parallels between nonviolent and military strategy. Documents twenty-three cases showing how nonviolent action has been applied to conflicts throughout the world in the twentieth century"-- Provided by publisher.
  Includes index.
  ISBN-13: 978-0-87558-161-3 (cloth)
  ISBN-10: 0-87558-161-7 (cloth)
  ISBN-13: 978-0-87558-162-0 (pbk.)
  ISBN-10: 0-87558-162-5 (pbk.)
  1. Nonviolence. I. Paulson, Joshua, 1974- II. Title.
  HM1281. S53 2005
  303.6'1--dc22
                                    2004027014

CONTENTS

PART THREE
THE DYNAMICS OF NONVIOLENT STRUGGLE

AUTHOR'S PREFACE

LEARNING FROM A CENTURY OF NONVIOLENT STRUGGLES

An alternative type of power

Although we live in a world of many grave problems, oppression, and violence, we also live in a world of much good and great potential for a better future. While we are unable to transform this world overnight, we can take important steps to change it, to solve its problems, lift its oppression, and minimize the many applications of violence.

Violence shapes our societies in many ways, through wars, dictatorships, social oppression, genocide, political assassinations, and terrorism. However, violence in organized and institutionalized forms is not used only for purposes that are widely recognized to be "bad." Violence is also employed to oppose those purposes and in favor of causes believed to be "good." Although problems are often recognized in these "good" uses of violence, it is widely believed that there is no realistic alternative.

As we enter the twenty-first century, it is beginning to be more widely understood that there is in fact an alternative. This alternative is not a simple moral injunction against the use of violence. This alternative is a means of struggle to apply power in acute conflicts. It is called nonviolent struggle.

In the past, this technique has often been poorly understood, and frequently it has been misrepresented. However, on the basis of past improvised applications, it has often served as a realistic alternative to the use of violence. This has been especially important in conflicts where serious issues have been at stake and violence was threatened or applied for unacceptable purposes. Today, if understood accurately and applied intelligently, wisely, and courageously, this alternative type of struggle in fact offers great hope for a better future for our world.

The Parts of this book

This book is organized into four Parts. Part One is introductory. It explains what nonviolent struggle is and offers crucial insights into political power. The sources of political power, as well as the potential to sever those sources, are explored. Those chapters open the way for consideration of noncooperation, the technique of nonviolent action, and its many methods.

Part Two contains 23 cases of the application of nonviolent struggle in the twentieth century. These cases have often been more successful than is usually recognized, even in extreme situations. Part Three of this book examines the dynamics of how this technique operates. Ways in which wise strategies can be developed are presented in Part Four. A major contention of this final Part is that future nonviolent conflicts can now be made more effective than the improvised struggles of the past by means of careful preparations, and especially by strategic planning. If groups facing serious conflicts find the guidelines for strategic planning presented in Part Four to be useful, this could be significant.

The accounts in Part Two of the 23 cases of applications of nonviolent struggle in the twentieth century are intended to be factual and purely descriptive. Most of these have been researched and drafted by persons other than myself, as stated in the Acknowledgements. The cases have been identified by the type of action employed, not on the basis of moral or doctrinal criteria. The simple act of bringing together these descriptive accounts corrects some of the widespread misconceptions of this type of struggle. These misconceptions are mentioned in Chapter Twenty-eight on "Assessing These Diverse Cases."

As is explained in that chapter, the described cases in Part Two are, unfortunately, not representative of all cases of nonviolent struggle, or even of the cases of the twentieth century. Due to the historical neglect of past applications of this alternative technique, there is no comprehensive record from which representative cases could be selected. Nonetheless, the cases presented in this book are still highly significant.

A few of them are known to be important and simply had to be included. These include Russia 1905, Germany 1920, India 1930-31, the North-West Frontier Province 1930-1934, Norway 1942, Czechoslovakia 1968, Poland 1980-1989, Burma 1988-

1990, China 1989, the Soviet Union 1991, Thailand 1992, and Serbia 2000.

Some other cases are here partly because I knew the researchers. These include Berlin 1943, Guatemala 1944, France 1961, Namibia 1971-1972, and Latvia 1991. Other cases are here in part because I personally learned something about the case by being present in the country not long after the events (as in Norway 1942 and Serbia 2000), or, even during them (as in China 1989 and Latvia 1991). In one case, a colleague argued for the importance of the case and knew the sources of information (the U.S. grape workers' strikes and boycotts 1965-1970). The issue of representativeness is further discussed in Chapter Twenty-eight.

The aim of this book

The aim of this book is to advance knowledge and understanding of the technique of nonviolent struggle and its potential. It does this by offering information and new insights and interpreting their significance. The ways nonviolent struggle operates are complex and variable. No two cases of the use of this technique are identical.

It is hoped that *Waging Nonviolent Struggle* will be useful to diverse individuals and groups that seek more knowledge and understanding of this alternative to both passivity and violence. My intent in writing this volume was to make a significant scholarly contribution to the deliberate refinement and development of nonviolent struggle. This is especially true of the role of strategic planning in increasing its effectiveness. Also, I hope this book will stimulate serious investigation of the potential of nonviolent struggle if applied in conflicts in which violence had been considered the only realistic option.

A growth of understanding

This book was not born fully developed. My serious studies of this phenomenon began in 1949. My master's thesis in sociology at Ohio State University in 1951 opened my exploration of this field. However, conclusions presented in this volume were reached slowly and incrementally, as a result of more than fifty years of study, observation, and reflection about the practice of nonviolent struggle and thought about its relevance and potential in a world of major violence used for political purposes. Some of my earlier perceptions about nonviolent action have over the years been modified, enriched, rejected and even reversed.

A careful study of M. K. Gandhi's thinking on power, strategy, and nonviolent struggle was exceptionally important and continues to influence my insights into this type of conflict. Equal or greater influence, however, has come from learning more about the practice of pragmatic nonviolent struggle in other parts of the world, especially Europe.

My studies of political theory while at St. Catherine's College, Oxford, focusing heavily on political power, authority, and political obligation, were extremely enriching. So, too, were the studies of totalitarianism, including the Nazi system.

Major parts of conclusions from my studies of power and nonviolent struggle were contained in my 1973 book *The Politics of Nonviolent Action*, which can be beneficially studied along with this volume. This volume does not replace that book, but instead, builds on and expands it. This is especially true of the topic of strategic planning, which was merely introduced in that earlier book.

Robert Helvey, a retired U.S. Army colonel, stimulated both thinking about strategic planning and effective consulting about the potential of nonviolent struggle among groups that were committed at the time to using violent resistance. Other contacts with military officers and institutions from several countries were also useful.

Reading books on military strategy, as by Carl von Clausewitz and Sir Basil Liddell Hart, were also important, as were personal conversations with Sir Basil at his home in the early 1960s.

Reality against extreme violence

Much additionally has been learned by attempts to grapple with issues related to how nonviolent struggle can be applied practically in facing extreme situations. These situations included its possible role against foreign aggression and coups d'état by civilian-based defense planning from the early 1960s. Later, attention was required to the potential and problems of incorporating a nonviolent resistance component into a predominantly military defense policy, as in Sweden, Norway, and Lithuania in the 1980s and 1990s.

My understanding of the requirements for effective anti-dictatorship struggles arose not only from anti-Nazi resistance movements, but also from meeting with Burmese opposition groups on the Thai-Burma border areas and in Thailand in the 1990s. I met with Panamanian democrats protesting against Noriega in 1987. I met with students and opposition leaders in Beijing in parts of May and June 1989, and was in Tiananmen Square as the troops first entered. I also met with ministers of the independence-minded governments of Latvia, Estonia, and Lithuania as they were struggling to secede from the Soviet Union in 1991. Brutal political reality can focus the mind on the difficulties of applying nonviolent struggle against extreme dictatorships.

One thing that is clear from these experiences is that nonviolent struggle has operated in situations of much violence and often in societies where at least some of the nonviolent resisters had great faith in the power and necessity of violence, although they still chose and effectively used nonviolent struggle.

It is also clear that nonviolent struggle is an important part of political reality. It has often been belittled or ignored by persons, movements, or governments that "know" that the "real" power derives from violence. However, nonviolent struggle is another very powerful form of force.

Of course, this book is only one contribution among the many studies that are needed in developing this alternative to both passivity and violence. Much new work is merited into the potential of nonviolent struggle in applications against political oppression as well as in undermining extreme economic and social oppression, and blocking attempts to perpetrate genocide.

It is my hope that this book offers some significant information, understanding, and ideas that will facilitate the consideration of a realistic alternative. We need to press forward with this exploration.

ACKNOWLEDGEMENTS

This book has grown in response to expressed needs from people in countries facing acute conflicts, some of which I have visited. I hope that this book will help people in acute conflicts to make wise decisions and to act effectively on behalf of humane objectives.

This work has been in the process of development for several years. I am grateful to the diverse people and groups who have stimulated me to find ways to share knowledge of nonviolent struggle with them.

This book is intended to contribute to meeting the widespread hunger in various countries for greater knowledge and understanding about ways to act to enable people to triumph over immense problems that often seem to be overwhelming.

Awareness of these situations has prodded me to continue to develop this volume. This is a kind of hybrid book. It is partly a product of multidisciplinary scholarship on the nature of nonviolent struggle. This includes both the studies that produced *The Politics of Nonviolent Action* (1973) and later studies by myself and others. Additional important contributions to this book have come from studies in political theory, especially insights into political power. The tools of sociological, political, and strategic analysis have also been important.

The assistance of several other researchers was needed to produce this text. This help is most evident in the 23 historical accounts of the practice of the technique. These cases are further discussed in the Preface and in Chapter Twenty-eight on assessing these cases.

Some of these descriptive accounts I have researched and drafted myself, such as those on the Russian 1905 revolution, India's 1930-1931 independence campaign, and the resistance by Norway's teachers in 1942.

However, the majority of these case accounts were drafted by other researchers, as is acknowledged in each chapter. Joshua Paulson produced the majority of these, working both part-time for many months elsewhere and for eight months here in the offices of the Albert Einstein Institution. He researched and drafted the chapters on the Montgomery, Alabama, bus boycott of 1955-

1956, the Czech and Slovak resistance of 1968, the mothers of the Plaza de Mayo, Argentina 1977-1983, Poland's Solidarity struggle of 1980-1989, the South African school boycotts in 1984-1987, the Philippine people power removal of Marcos in 1986, the Burmese defiance of the military dictators from 1988-1990, the uprising in China in 1989, the blocking of the hard-line coup in the Soviet Union in 1991, and the 2000 Serbian struggle that ousted Milosevic as a dictator.

Joshua Paulson also assisted in other important ways, especially in consulting and making decisions about the development of the whole book, and in evaluating and editing other chapters that I had drafted. He was for many months a genuine collaborator in the planning and development of this book.

Dr. Mohammad Raqib, a Pashtun scholar, did the research and writing for the chapter on the Muslim movement in the North-West Frontier Province of British India. I regard this case as especially important. Dr. Nathan Stoltzfus merits great gratitude for his remarkable research on the successful struggle by women of Berlin to save their Jewish husbands from the Holocaust.[1] Hardy Merriman researched and wrote the important chapter on the strikes by California grape workers and the boycotts to support them. The Namibia chapter is based on much earlier research by Dr. Suzanne Wedel and Curt Goering about indigenous resistance while under South African rule. The chapter on Czechoslovakia in 1968-1969 is based on research by Carl Horne and Christopher A. Miller. Christopher A. Miller also ably researched and drafted the chapter on Thailand in 1992. I am also grateful to Professor Kasian Tejapira of the Political Science Department of Thammasat University in Bangkok for consultation and advice. The Guatemala chapter has been drafted on the basis of previous original research by Dr. Chris Clamp. The account of the Latvian resistance to the Soviet Union is heavily based on the knowledge and writing of Olgerts Eglitis.[2] The chapter on the French resistance to the 1961 coup d'état in French-ruled Algeria is based on earlier research by Professor Sir

---

[1] This chapter is based on his book: Nathan Stoltzfus, *Resistance of the Heart: Intermarriage and the Rosenstrasse Protest in Nazi Germany,* New York and London: W. W. Norton, 1996.
[2] Olgerts Eglitis, *Nonviolent Action in the Liberation of Latvia,* Cambridge, Massachusetts: Albert Einstein Institution, 1993.

Adam Roberts. Without the skilled assistance of these persons, these chapters could not have been prepared without several years of additional work.

Robert Helvey has always been available for his insights and judgment at many points in the preparation of this manuscript. I am very pleased to be able to include an appendix based on his work on preparing, prior to planning a nonviolent struggle, a strategic estimate of the characteristics, strengths, and weaknesses of the contending sides of a conflict.

These modest credits make it clear that it has been possible to prepare this manuscript only because of the contributions and the assistance of others over several years.

This book is a major expansion of my earlier book *The Power and Practice of Nonviolent Struggle,* translated into Tibetan by Pema Tsewang Shastri and published by the Tibetan Parliamentary and Policy Research Center in New Delhi in 1999, with a Foreword by the Dalai Lama.

The chapters in Part Three on the dynamics of nonviolent struggle are a major revision and expansion of an extreme condensation of *The Politics of Nonviolent Action,* which was prepared in Spanish by Jaime Gonzales Bernal in the 1980s. This condensation was published privately in Mexico as *La Lucha Política Noviolenta* in several printings by groups that were preparing to resist electoral fraud, and one edition was published in Chile during the struggle against Pinochet. The text in this book, however, while closely following the format of *La Lucha Política Noviolenta,* is considerably different and was drafted in English.

During the preparation of this book, I have fortunately had the assistance of several very talented individuals in the evaluation of content and writing of my draft chapters and in helping to edit them for readability. In addition to Joshua Paulson, these persons are Christopher A. Miller and, most recently, Hardy Merriman. Their contributions have been of great importance. In particular, Hardy Merriman's proofreading and final review of the text, as well as his preparation of the index, has been a great help.

For several years, my work has been supported by the Albert Einstein Institution in Boston, Massachusetts, its staff members, and, above all, its donors. I remain very grateful.

In past years, staff members of the Albert Einstein Institution have included Bruce Jenkins and Christopher A. Miller. At present, in addition to Hardy Merriman, Jamila Raqib has been very helpful in several ways, including providing research assistance on the important Muslim nonviolent struggle movement in the North-West Frontier Province of British India. Latifa Raqib secured research materials.

I am grateful also to the staff of Porter Sargent Publishers for making this publication possible in a timely way, especially to John Yonce, President, and to Dan McKeever for his skilled editing. I am also grateful to Cornelia Sargent for her evaluation of the manuscript and encouragement during the production period.

This book is intended to provide readers not only with solid information and understanding about nonviolent struggle, but also with insights into necessary steps in planning strategies for future use of this technique.

The past practice of nonviolent struggle is very important. It establishes that this technique has been widely used. It also illustrates something of how nonviolent struggle has operated and some of the problems that can occur with it, while also showing that it has often been successful. However, the past does not impose a limit on the future of this technique. It is now possible to go beyond past experiences to make nonviolent struggle more effective in the future as an alternative to both violence and submission. This technique can be adopted and adapted to operate in place of violence in many acute conflicts of the future with increasing effectiveness. This merits full exploration.

PART ONE

EMPOWERMENT BY CAPACITY TO STRUGGLE

Chapter One

FACING ACUTE CONFLICTS

All conflicts are not equal

We live in a world of many conflicts, and we have a responsibility to face many of them.

Not all conflicts are equal. Some are much more important than others, and in some conflicts the issues at stake are more difficult to resolve in acceptable ways than are those in other conflicts.

Where the issues are of only limited importance, the difficulties in reaching a resolution are often small. Potentially, we can split the difference, agree on a third option, or postpone dealing with some issues until a later time. Even in these lesser conflicts, however, the group with a grievance requires effective means of pressing its claims. Otherwise, there is little reason for one's opponents to consider those claims seriously.

There are, however, many other conflicts in which fundamental issues are, or are believed to be, at stake. These conflicts are not deemed suitable for resolution by any methods that involve compromise. These are "acute conflicts."

Waging acute conflicts

In acute conflicts, at least one side regards it as necessary and good to wage the conflict against hostile opponents because of the issues seen to be at stake. It is often believed that the conflict must be waged in order to advance or protect freedom, justice, religion, one's civilization, or one's people. Proposed settlements that involve basic compromises of these fundamental issues are rarely acceptable. Likewise, submission to the opponents, or defeat by them, is regarded as disastrous. Yet, compromise or submission is often believed to be required for peaceful solutions to acute conflicts. Since these are not acceptable options for the parties involved, people therefore believe that it is necessary to wage the conflict by applying the strongest means available to them. These means often involve some type of violence.

There are alternatives

Violence, however, is not the only possibility. War and other forms of violence have not been universal in the waging of acute conflicts. In a great variety of situations, across centuries and cultural barriers, another technique of struggle has at times been applied. This other technique has been based on the ability to be stubborn, to refuse to cooperate, to disobey, and to resist powerful opponents powerfully.

Throughout human history, and in a multitude of conflicts, one side has instead fought by psychological, social, economic, or political methods, or a combination of them. Many times this alternative technique of struggle has been applied when fundamental issues have been at stake, and when ruthless opponents have been willing and able to apply extreme repression. This repression has included beatings, arrests, imprisonments, executions, and mass slaughters. Despite such repression, when the resisters have persisted in fighting with only their chosen "nonviolent weapons," they have sometimes triumphed.

This alternative technique is called nonviolent action or nonviolent struggle. This is "the other ultimate sanction." In some acute conflicts it has served as an alternative to violent struggle.

In the minds of many people, nonviolent struggle is closely connected with the persons of Mohandas K. Gandhi and

Dr. Martin Luther King, Jr. The work and actions of both men and the movements that they led or in which they played crucial roles are highly important. However, those movements are by no means representative of all nonviolent action. In fact, the work of these men is in significant ways atypical of the general practice of nonviolent struggle during recent decades and certainly throughout the centuries. Nonviolent struggles are not new historically. They have occurred for many centuries, although historical accounts frequently give them little recognition.

Widespread nonviolent struggle

Nonviolent struggle has occurred in widely differing cultures, periods of history, and political conditions. It has occurred in the West and in the East. Nonviolent action has occurred in industrialized and nonindustrialized countries. It has been practiced under constitutional democracies and against empires, foreign occupations, and dictatorial systems. Nonviolent struggle has been waged on behalf of a myriad of causes and groups, and even for objectives that many people reject. It has also been used to prevent, as well as to promote, change. Its use has sometimes been mixed with limited violence, but many times it has been waged with minimal or no violence.

The issues at stake in these conflicts have been diverse. They have included social, economic, ethnic, religious, national, humanitarian, and political matters, and they have ranged from the trivial to the fundamental.

Although historians have generally neglected this type of struggle, it is clearly a very old phenomenon. Most of the history of this technique has doubtless been lost, and most of what has survived has been largely ignored.

Many cases of the use of nonviolent action have had little or nothing to do with governments. Modern cases include labor-management conflicts and efforts to impose or resist pressures for social conformity. Nonviolent action has also been used in ethnic and religious conflicts and many other situations, such as disputes between students and university administrations. Important conflicts between the civilian population and governments where one side has employed nonviolent action have also occurred very widely. The following examples are often of this type.

Cases of nonviolent struggle

From the late eighteenth century through the twentieth century, the technique of nonviolent action was widely used in colonial rebellions, international political and economic conflicts, religious conflicts, and anti-slavery resistance.[1] This technique has been aimed to secure workers' right to organize, women's rights, universal manhood suffrage, and woman suffrage. This type of struggle has been used to gain national independence, to generate economic gains, to resist genocide, to undermine dictatorships, to gain civil rights, to end segregation, and to resist foreign occupations and coups d'état.

In the twentieth century, nonviolent action rose to unprecedented political significance throughout the world. People using this technique amassed major achievements, and, of course, experienced failure at times. Higher wages and improved working conditions were won. Oppressive traditions and practices were abolished. Both men and women won the right to vote in several countries in part by using this technique. Government policies were changed, laws repealed, new legislation enacted, and governmental reforms instituted. Invaders were frustrated and armies defeated. An empire was paralyzed, coups d'état thwarted, and dictatorships disintegrated. Nonviolent struggle was used against extreme dictatorships, including both Nazi and Communist systems.

Cases of the use of this technique early in the twentieth century included major elements of the Russian 1905 Revolution. In various countries growing trade unions widely used the strike and the economic boycott. Chinese boycotts of Japanese products occurred in 1908, 1915, and 1919. Germans used nonviolent resistance against the Kapp *Putsch* in 1920 and against the French and Belgian occupation of the Ruhr in 1923. In the 1920s and 1930s, Indian nationalists used nonviolent action in their struggles against British rule, under the leadership of Mohandas K. Gandhi. Likewise, Muslim Pashtuns in what was the North-West Frontier Province of British India (now in Pakistan) also used

---

1 For bibliographic references to books in English on many of these cases, see Ronald M. McCarthy and Gene Sharp, with the assistance of Brad Bennett, *Nonviolent Action: A Research Guide*, New York and London: Garland Publishing, 1997.

nonviolent struggle against British rule under the leadership of Khan Abdul Ghaffar Khan.

From 1940 to 1945 people in various European countries, especially in Norway, Denmark, and The Netherlands, used nonviolent struggle to resist Nazi occupation and rule. Nonviolent action was used to save Jews from the Holocaust in Berlin, Bulgaria, Denmark, and elsewhere. The military dictators of El Salvador and Guatemala were ousted in brief nonviolent struggles in the spring of 1944. The American civil rights nonviolent struggles against racial segregation, especially in the 1950s and 1960s, changed laws and long-established policies in the U.S. South. In April 1961, noncooperation by French conscript soldiers in the French colony of Algeria, combined with popular demonstrations in France and defiance by the Debré-de Gaulle government, defeated the military coup d'état in Algiers before a related coup in Paris could be launched.

In 1968 and 1969, following the Warsaw Pact invasion, Czechs and Slovaks held off full Soviet control for eight months with improvised nonviolent struggle and refusal of collaboration. From 1953 to 1991, dissidents in Communist-ruled countries in Eastern Europe, especially in East Germany, Poland, Hungary, Estonia, Latvia, and Lithuania, repeatedly used nonviolent struggles for increased freedom. The Solidarity struggle in Poland began in 1980 with strikes to support the demand of a legal free trade union, and concluded in 1989 with the end of the Polish Communist regime. Nonviolent protests and mass resistance were also highly important in undermining the apartheid policies and European domination in South Africa, especially between 1950 and 1990. The Marcos dictatorship in the Philippines was destroyed by a nonviolent uprising in 1986.

In July and August 1988, Burmese democrats protested against the military dictatorship with marches and defiance and brought down three governments, but this struggle finally succumbed to a new military coup d'état and mass slaughter. In 1989, Chinese students and others in over three hundred cities (including Tiananmen Square, Beijing) conducted symbolic protests against government corruption and oppression, but the protests finally ended following massive killings by the military.

Nonviolent struggle brought about the end of Communist dictatorships in Poland and Czechoslovakia in 1989 and in

East Germany, Estonia, Latvia, and Lithuania in 1991. Noncooperation and defiance against the attempted "hard line" coup d'état by the KGB, the Communist Party, and the Soviet Army in 1991, blocked the attempted seizure of the Soviet State.

In Kosovo, the Albanian population between 1990 and 1999 conducted a widespread noncooperation campaign against repressive Serbian rule. When the de facto Kosovo government lacked a nonviolent strategy for gaining de jure independence, a guerrilla Kosovo Liberation Army initiated violence. This was followed by extreme Serbian repression and massive slaughters by so-called ethnic cleansing, which led to NATO bombing and intervention.

Starting in November 1996, Serbs conducted daily parades and protests in Belgrade and other cities against the autocratic governance of President Milosevic and secured correction of electoral fraud in mid-January 1997. At that time, however, Serb democrats lacked a strategy to press the struggle further and failed to launch a campaign to bring down the Milosevic dictatorship. In early October 2000, the Otpor (Resistance) movement and other democrats rose up again against Milosevic in a carefully planned nonviolent struggle and the dictatorship collapsed.

In early 2001, President Estrada, who had been accused of corruption, was ousted by Filipinos in a "People Power Two" campaign.

There were many other important examples this past century, and the practice of nonviolent struggle continues.

The many methods of nonviolent struggle

A multitude of specific methods of nonviolent action, or nonviolent weapons, exist. Nearly two hundred have been identified to date, and without doubt, scores more already exist and others will emerge in future conflicts. These methods are detailed in Chapter Four.

Methods of nonviolent action include protest marches, flying forbidden flags, massive rallies, vigils, leaflets, picketing, social boycotts, economic boycotts, labor strikes, rejection of legitimacy, civil disobedience, boycott of government positions, boycott of rigged elections, strikes by civil servants, noncooperation by police, nonobedience without direct supervision, mutiny, sit-ins, hunger strikes, sit-downs on the streets, establishment of alternative institutions, occupation of offices, and creation of parallel governments.

These methods may be used to protest symbolically, to put an end to cooperation, or to disrupt the operation of the established system. As such, three broad classes of nonviolent methods exist: *nonviolent protest and persuasion, noncooperation,* and *nonviolent intervention.*

Symbolic protests, though in most situations quite mild, can make it clear that some of the population is opposed to the present regime and can help to undermine its legitimacy. Social, economic, and political noncooperation, when practiced strongly and long enough, can weaken the opponents' control, wealth, domination, and power, and potentially produce paralysis. The methods of nonviolent intervention, which disrupt the established order by psychological, social, economic, physical, or political methods, can dramatically threaten the opponents' control.

Individuals and groups may hold differing opinions about the general political usefulness and the ethical acceptability of the methods of nonviolent struggle. Yet everyone can benefit from more knowledge and understanding of their use and careful examination of their potential relevance and effectiveness.

A pragmatic choice

Nonviolent struggle is identified by what people do, not by what they believe. In many cases, the people using these nonviolent methods have believed violence to be perfectly justified in moral or religious terms. However, for the specific conflict that they currently faced they chose, for pragmatic reasons, to use methods that did not include violence.

Only in rare historical instances did a group or a leader have a personal belief that rejected violence in principle. Nevertheless, even in these cases, a nonviolent struggle based on pragmatic concerns was often still viewed as morally superior.

However, belief that violence violates a moral or religious principle does not constitute nonviolent action.[2] Nor does the simple absence of physical violence mean that nonviolent action is occurring. It is the type of activity that identifies the technique of nonviolent action, not the belief behind the activity.

The degree to which nonviolent struggle has been consciously chosen in place of violence differs widely among historical examples. In many past cases, nonviolent action appears to have been initiated more or less spontaneously, with little deliberation. In other cases, the choice of a certain nonviolent method—such as a labor strike—was made on grounds specific to the particular situation only, without a comparative evaluation of the merits of nonviolent action over violent action. Many applications of nonviolent action seem to have been imitations of actions elsewhere.

There has been much variation in the degree to which people in these conflicts have been aware of the existence of a general nonviolent technique of action and have had prior knowledge of its operation.

In most of these cases, nonviolent means appear to have been chosen because of considerations of anticipated effectiveness. In some cases, there appear to have been mixed motives, with practical motives predominating but with a relative moral preference for nonviolent means.

What words to use?

The type of action in these cases and others has been given various names, some of which are useful and others of which are inappropriate. These names include "nonviolent resistance," "civil resistance," "passive resistance," "nonviolence," "people power," "political defiance," and "positive action." The use of the term "nonviolence" is especially unfortunate, because it confuses these forms of mass action with beliefs in ethical or religious nonviolence ("principled nonviolence"). Those beliefs, which have their merits, are different phenomena that usually are unrelated to mass struggles conducted by people who do not share

---

[2] It is worth noting that some believers in "principled nonviolence" have even *rejected* nonviolent struggle because it was a way to wage conflict (in which they did not believe).

such beliefs. To identify the technique, we here use and recommend the terms *nonviolent action* or *nonviolent struggle*.

Because of the continuing imprecision and confusion about which words to use, it has been necessary over recent decades to refine existing terminology to describe and discuss such action, and even to develop new words and phrases. Therefore, a short glossary has been included for reference at the end of this book.

Exposing misconceptions

In addition to misconceptions conveyed by unfortunate terminology, there are other areas of confusion in the field of nonviolent struggle as well. Despite new studies in recent decades, inaccuracies and misunderstandings are still widespread. Here are corrections for some of them:

(1) Nonviolent action has nothing to do with passivity, submissiveness, or cowardice. Just as in violent action, these must first be rejected and overcome before the struggle can proceed.

(2) Nonviolent action is a means of conducting conflicts and can be very powerful, but it is an extremely different phenomenon from violence of all types.

(3) Nonviolent action is not to be equated with verbal persuasion or purely psychological influences, although this technique may sometimes include action to apply psychological pressures for attitude change. Nonviolent action is a technique of struggle involving the use of psychological, social, economic, and political power in the matching of forces in conflict.

(4) Nonviolent action does not depend on the assumption that people are inherently "good." The potentialities of people for both "good" and "evil" are recognized, including the extremes of cruelty and inhumanity.

(5) In order to use nonviolent action effectively, people do *not* have to be pacifists or saints. Nonviolent action has been predominantly and successfully practiced by "ordinary" people.

(6) Success with nonviolent action does not require (though it may be helped by) shared standards and principles, or a high degree of shared interests or feelings of psychological closeness between the contending sides. If the opponents are emotionally unmoved by nonviolent resistance in face of violent repression, and therefore unwilling to agree to the objectives of the nonvio-

lent struggle group, the resisters may apply coercive nonviolent measures. Difficult enforcement problems, economic losses, and political paralysis do not require the opponents' agreement to be felt.

(7) Nonviolent action is at least as much of a Western phenomenon as an Eastern one. Indeed, it is probably more Western, if one takes into account the widespread use of strikes and economic boycotts in the labor movements, the noncooperation struggles of subordinated European nationalities, and the struggles against dictatorships.

(8) In nonviolent action, there is no assumption that the opponents will refrain from using violence against nonviolent resisters. In fact, the technique is capable of operating against violence.

(9) There is nothing in nonviolent action to prevent it from being used for both "good" and "bad" causes. However, the social consequences of its use for a "bad" cause differ considerably from the consequences of violence used for the same "bad" cause.

(10) Nonviolent action is not limited to domestic conflicts within a democratic system. In order to have a chance of success, it is *not* necessary that the struggle be waged against relatively gentle and restrained opponents. Nonviolent struggle has been widely used against powerful governments, foreign occupiers, despotic regimes, tyrannical governments, empires, ruthless dictatorships, and totalitarian systems. These difficult nonviolent struggles against violent opponents have sometimes been successful.

(11) One of the many widely believed myths about conflict is that violence works quickly, and nonviolent struggle takes a long time to bring results. This is *not* true. Some wars and other violent struggles have been fought for many years, even decades. Some nonviolent struggles have brought victories very quickly, even within days or weeks. The time taken to achieve victory with this technique depends on diverse factors—including the strength of the nonviolent resisters and the wisdom of their actions.

What about human nature?

Despite the widespread occurrence of this type of conflict, many people still assume that nonviolent struggle is contrary to "human nature." It is often claimed that its widespread practice would require either a fundamental change in human beings or the acceptance of a powerful new religious or ideological belief system. Those views are not supported by the reality of past conflicts that have been waged by use of this technique.

In fact, the practice of this type of struggle is not based on belief in "turning the other cheek" or loving one's enemies. Instead, the widespread practice of this technique is more often based on the undeniable capacity of human beings to be stubborn, and to do what they want to do or to refuse to do what they are ordered, whatever their beliefs about the use or nonuse of violence. Massive stubbornness can have powerful political consequences.

In any case, the view that nonviolent struggle is impossible except under rare conditions is contrary to the facts. That which has happened in the past is possible in the future.

The extremely widespread practice of nonviolent struggle is possible because the operation of this technique is compatible with the nature of political power and the vulnerabilities of all hierarchical systems. These systems and all governments depend on the subordinated populations, groups, and institutions to supply them with their needed sources of power. Before continuing with the examination of the technique of nonviolent struggle, it is therefore necessary to explore in greater depth the nature of the power of dominant institutions and all governments. This analysis sheds light on how it is that nonviolent struggle can be effective against repressive and ruthless regimes. They are vulnerable.

Chapter Two

TAPPING THE ROOTS OF POWER

Human problems and the distribution of power

Important progress has been made over the past century to meet human needs more adequately and to advance freedom and justice throughout the world. However, grave problems remain for which there are no easy solutions. Long-standing conflicts, injustices, oppression, and violence continue and even take new forms.

Many of these problems are created or maintained by the actions of those persons and groups that control the State apparatus of their society, using its vast resources, bureaucracy, police, and military forces, to implement and enforce their will. In many States, the dominant group is seen to be so powerful that it can ignore the good of those it dominates in order to gain its objectives. In other cases, certain elites have created their own means of con-

---

For fuller analyses of power and sources of the thinking in this chapter, see Gene Sharp, *The Politics of Nonviolent Action* (Boston: Porter Sargent, 1973), pp. 7-62, and Gene Sharp, *Social Power and Political Freedom* (Boston: Porter Sargent, 1980), pp. 21-67 and 309-378.

trol and repression and have imposed their will by violence outside of the State apparatus.

The concentration of power and control in the State can under certain circumstances be applied with great cruelty against an apparently helpless population. Such a State can impose tyranny, wage wars, establish or maintain oppression, indoctrinate the population, and commit genocide. It is the machinery of combined central controls and institutionalized violence that makes modern tyranny possible.[1]

Against opponents with strong means of control and repression, people who see themselves as victims of oppression, injustice, and dictatorship often feel weak and powerless, unable to challenge the forces that dominate them. These dominated groups may include exploited economic classes, harassed religious minorities, populations of attacked or occupied countries, victims of attempted genocide, people living under dictatorships, nations under foreign domination, or despised ethnic or racial groups, among others. In all such cases the problem exists because one group has the power to impose its will on a weaker group.

When faced with such a strong State, power is seen to derive from the few who command the administrative system and the institutions capable of applying violence for political purposes. The population is therefore believed to be fully vulnerable to rulers who may aim to sweep aside democratic institutions and human rights and to become tyrants. They never dream that they could possess sufficient power to improve their lives and to change those relationships.

Political power viewed as derived from violence

If the population widely believes that the real power in politics derives from violence, that it "comes out of the barrel of a gun," then whoever has the most and biggest guns will find it much easier to control the population.

Most such populations then passively submit. Sometimes, however, people who reject the current regime as oppressive and who see the power of violence arrayed against them conclude that

---

[1] For further discussion of this analysis see Gene Sharp, *Social Power and Political Freedom,* pp. 285-308.

they must use whatever violence they can muster against their oppressors. This may take the form of violent rebellions, assassinations, terrorism, or guerrilla warfare. The results of these actions for the oppressed population have often been far from positive. Violent rebels are unlikely to succeed against extreme odds and the general population most likely will suffer massive casualties.

In the unlikely case that violent rebels succeed in defeating oppressive rulers, the rebels will probably have simply established themselves as a new ruling elite in control of the State apparatus. Violence may on occasion remove the previous rulers or dominant elite and replace them with other persons or groups. However, the actual relationship between the dominant elite and the dominated population is unlikely to be fundamentally altered by use of violence. In fact, the violence will likely contribute to a still greater concentration of power and an increased use of violence for political objectives.

Real and lasting liberation requires significant changes in the power relationships within the society, not merely replacement of personnel. Liberation should mean that the members of the previously dominated and weak population obtain greater control over their lives and greater capacity to influence events.

If we wish to create a society in which people really shape their own lives and futures, and in which oppression is impossible, then we need to explore alternative ways to meet the society's basic need for means of wielding power. We also need to explore the origins of political power at a much more basic level.

Political power as variable

The views that power derives primarily from the capacity to wield violence and that the power of rulers is monolithic and relatively permanent are not correct. Power relationships are not fixed and unchangeable. Instead, the power capacities of the State and the other institutions of the society are variable and are derived from the interplay of

- the varying degrees of power wielded by the respective groups in the society;

- the degree to which these various groups have mobilized their power potential into effective power;

- the degree to which the social, economic, and political institutions of the State and other powerful institutions are flexible and responsive to the will of the various sections of the population.

The existing distribution of power in a society is very real, but it is not permanent and will not be maintained under all conditions. Indeed, that distribution can at times change dramatically and rapidly.

A major change in the distribution of power happens when the sources of power at the disposal of the rulers are weakened or withdrawn, thereby drastically reducing their effective power. The power relationships also change if formerly weak groups mobilize their unused power potential into effective power.

Unless the sources of power of dominant groups are restricted or severed, or the sources of power of weaker groups are mobilized or strengthened, or unless both happen, the subordinated and oppressed groups inevitably remain in essentially the same relative power position. This is true despite any other specific changes that may be made in the society or whether or not changes occur in the persons of the rulers.

A fuller understanding of the nature of political power will help us to understand how power relationships can be fundamentally changed. In contrast to the monolithic view that political power is solid and highly durable and can only be weakened or destroyed by major destructive violence, the following insight is more accurate. It also allows for an understanding of how effective control can be exercised over rulers who are, or could become, oppressors.

The social view of power

The social view of power sees rulers or other command systems, despite appearances, to be dependent on the population's goodwill, decisions, and support. As such, power rises continually from many parts of the society. Political power is therefore fragile. Power always depends for its strength and existence upon a replenishment of its sources by the cooperation of numerous institutions and people—cooperation that does not have to continue.

In order to control the power of rulers, those sources of power that are provided by the society's groups and institutions must first be identified. Then the population will be able, when needed, to restrict or sever the supply of those sources.

Sources of political power

The persons who are at any point the rulers do not personally possess the power of control, administration, and repression that they wield. How much power they possess depends on how much power society will grant them. Six of these sources of political power are:

(1) *Authority:* This may also be called legitimacy. It is the quality that leads people to accept a right of persons or groups to lead, command, direct, and be heard or obeyed by others. Authority is voluntarily accepted by the people and therefore is present without the imposition of sanctions (or punishments). The authority figures need not necessarily be actually superior. It is enough that the person or group be perceived and accepted as superior. While not identical with power, authority is clearly a main source of power.

(2) *Human resources:* The power of rulers is affected by the number of persons who obey them, cooperate with them, or provide them with special assistance, as well as by the proportion of such assisting persons in the general population, and the extent and forms of their organizations.

(3) *Skills and knowledge:* The rulers' power is affected by the skills, knowledge and abilities of such cooperating persons, groups, and institutions, and the relation of their skills, knowledge, and abilities to the rulers' needs.

(4) *Intangible factors:* Psychological and ideological factors, such as habits and attitudes toward obedience and submission, and the presence or absence of a common faith, ideology, or sense of mission, contribute to the rulers' power.

(5) *Material resources:* The degree to which the rulers control property, natural resources, financial resources, the economic system, communication and transportation, and the like, helps to determine the extent or limits of the rulers' power.

(6) *Sanctions:* These have been described as "an enforcement of obedience." The type and extent of sanctions, or punishments,

at the rulers' disposal, both for use against their own subjects and in conflicts with other rulers, are a major source of power. Sanctions are used by rulers to supplement voluntary acceptance of their authority and to increase the extent of obedience to their commands. The sanctions may be violent or nonviolent. They may be intended as punishment or deterrence against future disobedience. Violent domestic sanctions, such as imprisonment or execution, are commonly intended to punish disobedience or to prevent it in the future, not to achieve the objective of an original command. Military sanctions may be intended for defense or deterrence against foreign enemies or for combating strong internal opposition.

The presence of some or all of these six sources of power at the disposal of the rulers is always a matter of degree. Only rarely are all of them completely available to rulers, or completely absent.

Power relationships similar to those in political societies with State structures exist in other hierarchical institutions as well, which also derive their power from the cooperation of many persons and groups. Consequently various forms of dissent, noncooperation and disobedience may have important roles to play when members of such institutions have grievances against the people who direct or control those institutions.

The sources of power depend on obedience and cooperation

These six sources of political power are necessary to establish or retain power and control. Their availability, however, is subject to constant variation and is not necessarily secure.

The more extensive and detailed the rulers' control over the population and society, the more such assistance they will require from individuals, groups, organizations, and branches of the government. If these needed "assistants" reject the rulers' authority, they may then carry out the rulers' wishes and orders inefficiently, or may even flatly refuse to continue their usual assistance. When this happens, the total effective power of the rulers is reduced.

Because the rulers are dependent on other people to operate the system, the rulers are continually subject to influence and restriction by both their direct assistants and the general population. The potential control of these groups over the rulers will be greatest where the rulers depend on them most.

Let us, for example, consider *authority* and *sanctions* from this point of view. The other four sources of power are highly dependent on these two.

Authority is necessary for the existence and operation of any regime. All rulers require an acceptance of their authority: their right to rule, command and be obeyed. *The key to habitual obedience is to reach the mind. Obedience will scarcely be habitual unless it is loyal, not forced.* In essence, authority must be voluntarily accepted.

The weakening or collapse of authority inevitably tends to loosen the subjects' predisposition towards obedience. Then the decision to obey or not to obey will be made consciously. Obedience may even be refused. *The loss of authority sets in motion the disintegration of the rulers' power. Their power is reduced to the degree that their authority is repudiated.*

Sanctions may be applied to enforce obedience and cooperation. However, the rulers require more than reluctant outward compliance. Sanctions will be inadequate as long as acceptance of the rulers' authority is limited. Despite punishments, the population may still not obey or cooperate to the needed extent.

A special relationship exists between sanctions and submission. First, the capability to impose sanctions derives from the obedience and cooperation of at least some subjects. Second, whether these sanctions are effective or not depends on the response of the subjects against whom they are threatened or applied. *The question is to what degree people obey without threats, and to what degree they continue to disobey despite punishments.*

Even the capacity of rulers to detect and punish disobedience depends on the existing pattern of obedience and cooperation. The greater the obedience of the rulers' subjects, the greater the chances of detection and punishment of disobedience and noncooperation. The weaker the obedience and cooperation of the subjects, the less effective the rulers' detection and enforcement will be.

The rulers' power depends on the continuous availability of all the needed forms of assistance. This assistance comes not only from individuals, officials, employees and the like, but also from the subsidiary organizations and institutions that compose the system as a whole. These may include departments, bureaus, branches, committees, and the like. Just as individuals and independent groups may refuse to cooperate, so too these unit organizations may refuse to provide sufficient help to effectively maintain the rulers' position and to enable them to implement their policies. No complex organization or institution, including the State, can carry out orders if the individuals and unit organizations that compose such an institution do not enable it to do so.

The internal stability of rulers can be measured by the ratio of the strength of the social forces that they control and the strength of the social forces that oppose them.

Obedience is the heart of political power

The relationship between command and obedience is always one of mutual influence and some degree of interaction. That is, command and obedience influence each other. Without the expected obedience by the subordinates (whether in the form of passive acquiescence or active consent) the power relationship is not complete, despite the threat or infliction of sanctions.

The reasons why people obey rulers are multiple, complex, variable, and interrelated. These reasons include the following:

- Habit
- Fear of sanctions
- Moral obligation
- Self-interest
- Psychological identification with the ruler
- Indifference
- Absence of self-confidence to disobey

All rulers use the obedience and cooperation they receive from part of the society in order to rule the whole. The part of the population that administers and enforces the rulers' policies is most likely to obey and cooperate in those duties because of feelings of moral obligation and of personal self-interest, especially motives related to economic gain, prestige, and status.

Most people in the general population obey from habit. Yet, the degree of obedience among the general population, even among these administrators and enforcers, is never fixed, nor automatic, nor uniform, nor universal. Because the reasons for obedience are always variable, the degree of obedience is also variable, depending on the individuals concerned and on the social and political situation. In every society there are boundaries within which rulers must stay if their commands are to be obeyed and if the population is to cooperate.

Disobedience and noncooperation by the general populace are rarely undertaken lightly. Noncompliance usually is followed by punishments. However, under certain circumstances, members of the population will become willing to endure the consequences of noncooperation and disobedience, including inconvenience, suffering, and disruption of their lives, rather than continue to submit passively or to obey rulers whose policies and actions can no longer be tolerated.

When the reasons for obedience are weak, the rulers may seek to secure greater obedience by applying harsher sanctions or by offering increased rewards for obedience. However, even then, the results desired by the rulers are not guaranteed. A change in the population's will may lead to its withdrawing its service, cooperation, submission and obedience from the rulers.

This withdrawal of cooperation and obedience under certain circumstances may also occur among the rulers' administrators and agents of repression. Their attitudes and actions are especially important. Without their support, the oppressive system disintegrates.

Being accustomed to widespread obedience and cooperation, rulers do not always anticipate generalized noncompliance and therefore often have difficulties handling strong disobedience and noncooperation.

Consent and withdrawal of consent

Each reason for obedience, whether it is free consent or fear of sanctions (intimidated consent), must operate through the will or volition of the individual person to produce obedience. The present reasons for obeying must be seen by the population as sufficient grounds to obey. However, the will or volition of the individual may change with new influences, events, and forces. In varying degrees, the individual's own will can play an active role in producing obedience or disobedience. This process can happen with large numbers of people.

The personal choice between obeying and disobeying will be influenced by an evaluation of either the short-term or the long-term consequences of obeying or disobeying, or of a combination of the two, depending on the individual. If the subjects perceive the consequences of obedience to be worse than the consequences of disobedience, then disobedience is more likely.

Obedience only exists when one complies with the command. If you are sentenced to imprisonment and walk to jail willingly, you have obeyed. If you are dragged there, you have not obeyed.[2]

Physical compulsion may yield some results, but since it affects only the body, it does not necessarily produce obedience. Only certain types of objectives can be achieved by direct physical compulsion of disobedient subjects—such as moving them physically, preventing them from moving physically, seizing their money or property, or killing them. But these actions do not necessarily result in obedience. The overwhelming majority of rulers' commands and objectives can be achieved only by inducing the subject to be willing for some reason to carry them out. (The ditch remains undug even if the men who refuse to dig it are shot.) *It is not the sanctions themselves that produce obedience, but the fear of them.*

However, people generally seek to avoid severe penalties for disobedience and noncooperation, except for special cases in which feelings are very intense. In such cases, disobedience and noncooperation sometimes occur despite repression.

In summary, the rulers' power depends upon the availability of its six sources, as reviewed previously. This availability is determined by the degree of obedience and cooperation given by the subjects. Despite inducements, pressures, and even sanctions, such obedience and cooperation are, however, not inevitable. Obedience remains essentially voluntary. Therefore, all government is based upon consent.

This does not mean that the subjects of all rulers prefer the established order. Consent is at times granted because of positive

---

[2] David Austin, *Lectures on Jurisprudence or the Philosophy of Positive Law* (Fifth edition, rev. and ed. by Robert Campbell; 2 vols. London: John Murray, 1911), vol. I, pp. 295-297.

approval. However, it is also often granted because people are at times unwilling to suffer the consequences of the refusal of consent. The latter is consent by intimidation. Refusal of consent requires self-confidence, motivation to resist, and knowledge of how to act to refuse, and often involves considerable inconvenience and suffering.

The structural basis of resistance

The answer to the problem of uncontrolled political power, that is to oppression, therefore may lie in learning how to carry out and maintain withdrawal of obedience and cooperation despite repression. This will not be easy.

Greater confidence and ability to practice noncooperation and disobedience can usually be achieved when members of the population are able to act as members of groups or institutions. This is also a requirement for effective restriction or severance of the sources of political power that were discussed above. At times, individuals may protest or resign and barely be noticed, but if all persons in a government department refuse to implement a policy, their actions can create a major crisis.

Very importantly, in order to have a significant political impact, the disobedience and noncooperation often need to take the form of mass action. While individual acts may at times not have much impact, the defiance of organizations and institutions—for example, trade unions, business organizations, religious organizations, the bureaucracy, neighborhoods, villages, cities, regions, and the like—can be pivotal. Through these bodies people can collectively offer disobedience and noncooperation. Organizations and institutions such as these, which supply the necessary sources of power to the opponent group, are called "pillars of support."[3]

The ability of the population to wield effective power and to control the power of their rulers will be highly influenced by the condition of these organizations and institutions. It is these "places" (or *loci*) where power can be mobilized and where it operates. Such "places" provide the structural basis for the control of the rulers, whether or not they wish to be controlled. Where

---

[3] The term was introduced by Robert Helvey.

these independent bodies are weak, the controls over the rulers' power will be weak. Where those bodies are strong, the capacity to control the rulers will be strong.[4]

Factors in controlling political power

Three of the most important factors in determining to what degree rulers' power will be controlled or uncontrolled are

- the relative desire of the populace to control the rulers' power;
- the relative strength of the society's independent organizations and institutions;
- the population's relative ability to withhold their consent and cooperation by concrete actions.

Freedom is not something that rulers "give" the population. The degree of freedom within a society is achieved through the interaction between society and government.

According to this social insight into the nature of political power, people have immense power potential. It is ultimately their attitudes, behavior, cooperation, and obedience that supply the sources of power to all rulers and hierarchical systems, even oppressors and tyrants.

The degree of liberty or tyranny in any government is, therefore, in large part, a reflection of the relative determination of the population to be free and their willingness and ability to resist efforts to enslave them. "For the tyrant has the power to inflict only that which we lack the strength to resist," wrote the Indian sociologist Krishnalal Shridharani.[5]

Self-liberation and the mobilization of power potential

Without the direct participation of the population itself in the efforts to make changes, no major changes are likely to occur in the relative power positions between the population and whoever

---

[4] For further discussion of this analysis, see Gene Sharp, "Social Power and Political Freedom," in *Social Power and Political Freedom*, pp. 21-67.
[5] Krishnalal Shridharani, *War Without Violence: A Study of Gandhi's Method and its Accomplishments* (New York: Harcourt, Brace and Co., 1939; reprinted: New York & London: Garland Publishing, 1972), p. 305.

occupies the position of rulers. At most, a new group will replace the old one as rulers. The new rulers may or may not, at their own discretion, behave with restraint and concern towards the welfare and liberties of the people.

If the liberation of oppressed people is to happen and be genuine and durable, it must therefore be essentially self-liberation. That liberation needs to be achieved by means that ensure a lasting capacity of people to govern themselves, to shape their own society, and to act to ensure their freedoms and rights. Otherwise, the people will face the likelihood of new, potentially even more oppressive, rulers, merely waving a different flag or espousing a different doctrine.

The great Indian Gandhian socialist Rammanohar Lohia once wrote that he was tired of hearing only of the need to change the hearts of the oppressors. That was fine, but far more important was the effort to change the hearts of the oppressed. They needed to become unwilling to continue accepting their oppression, and to become determined to build a better society. Weakness in people's determination, and very importantly in their ability to act, makes possible their continued oppression and submission. Strengthen that determination and increase that ability to act, and these people need never again be oppressed. Such self-liberation can be achieved only through an increase in the power of the subordinates by their own efforts.

Indian independence leader Mohandas K. Gandhi emphasized the importance of a change of will and a change of attitude as prerequisites for a change in patterns of obedience and cooperation. There was, he argued, a need for

- a psychological change away from passive submission to self-respect and courage;

- recognition by the subjects that their assistance makes the existing regime possible;

- the building of a determination to withdraw cooperation and obedience.[6]

Gandhi was convinced that these changes could be consciously influenced.

---

[6] See Gene Sharp, *Gandhi as a Political Strategist, with Essays on Ethics and Politics* (Boston: Porter Sargent, 1979), pp. 43-59.

Once the dominated population wishes to make changes, it needs to be able to mobilize and wield effective power. Once the population is *willing* to disobey and noncooperate, it requires means of strong *action*. It then needs a technique of action through which it can maintain and strengthen its existing independent institutions, create and defend new ones, and, resist, confront, and undermine the power of oppressive rulers.

The population needs to be able to restrict and sever the sources of power of its oppressors. The power of the rulers is weakened to the degree that the population

- repudiates the moral right of the current rulers to rule;

- disobeys, noncooperates, and refuses to assist the rulers;

- declines to supply the skills and knowledge required by the rulers;

- denies the rulers control over administration, property, natural resources, financial resources, the economic system, communication, and transportation.

Additionally, if the rulers' punishments against a defiant population are not available because of disaffection in the military or police forces, or if popular defiance continues and even grows despite harsh penalties, then the power of the rulers will shrink or even dissolve.

A technique of action capable of accomplishing those controls over the power of rulers and of mobilizing the power potential of the population should also be one that will give the populace a lasting capacity to control any rulers, and to defend the population's capacity to rule itself. A type of action with the potential to achieve such controls is the technique of "nonviolent action" or "nonviolent struggle." Let us, therefore, examine in greater depth the nature of this type of struggle.

Chapter Three

AN ACTIVE TECHNIQUE
OF STRUGGLE

A simple insight

Nonviolent action, or nonviolent struggle, is a technique of action by which the population can restrict and sever the sources of power of their rulers or other oppressors and mobilize their own power potential into effective power. This technique is based on the understanding of political power presented in the previous chapter.

That understanding showed that the power of rulers and of hierarchical systems, no matter how dictatorial, depends directly on the obedience and cooperation of the population. Such obedience and cooperation, in turn, depend on the willingness of the population and a multitude of assistants to consent by their actions or inaction to support the rulers. People may obey and cooperate because they positively approve of the rulers or their orders, or

---

For fuller analysis of nonviolent struggle and the thinking in this chapter, see Gene Sharp, *The Politics of Nonviolent Action,* Boston: Porter Sargent, 1973.

they may obey and cooperate because they are intimidated into submission by the fear of punishment.

Yet, despite such punishments, acts of protest, disobedience, and noncooperation have occurred frequently in many societies. Sometimes, these have been of major significance, as noted in Chapter One.

Nonviolent struggle does not require acceptance of a new political doctrine or of a new moral or religious belief. In political terms, nonviolent action is based on a very simple insight: people do not always do what they are told to do, and sometimes they do things that they have been forbidden to do. Subjects may disobey laws they reject. Workers may halt work, which may paralyze the economy. The bureaucracy may refuse to carry out instructions. Soldiers and police may become lax in inflicting repression or even mutiny. When all these events happen simultaneously, the power of the rulers weakens and can dissolve.

The technique of nonviolent struggle has been applied against a wide variety of opponents. The term "opponents" is used here to refer to the adversary, whether a group, institution, regime, invader, or, rarely, an individual, against whom nonviolent struggle is being waged. Usually, the most difficult of these conflicts are those against the current rulers of the State or groups that have State backing. However, the technique is also applicable in conflicts against less formidable opponents. The issues in these conflicts vary from case to case. They may include not only political but also social, economic, religious, and cultural ones.

When people repudiate their opponents' authority, refuse cooperation, withhold assistance, and persist in disobedience and defiance, they are denying to their opponents the basic human assistance and cooperation that any government or hierarchical system requires. If the opponents are highly dependent on such assistance, and if the resisters refuse cooperation and disobey in sufficient numbers for enough time and persist despite repression, the persons who have been the "rulers" or dominant elite become just another group of people. This is the basic political assumption of this type of struggle.

A way to wage conflict

Nonviolent action is a generic term covering dozens of specific methods of *protest, noncooperation* and *intervention.* In all of these, the resisters conduct the conflict by doing—or refusing to do—certain acts by means other than physical violence.

Nonviolent action may involve acts of *omission*—that is, people may refuse to perform acts that they usually perform, are expected by custom to perform, or are required by law or regulation to perform. Or, people may commit acts of *commission*—that is, people may perform acts that they do not usually perform, are not expected by custom to perform, or are forbidden to perform. Or, this type of struggle may include a *combination* of acts of omission and commission. In no way is the technique of nonviolent action passive. It is action that is nonviolent.

Although nonviolent means of conducting conflicts have been widely used in the past, they have not been well understood, or they have been confused with other phenomena. This misunderstanding and confusion have often reduced the effectiveness of attempts to use this technique. This has thereby benefited the opponents against whose regime or policies the struggle was directed. If this type of struggle is falsely identified with weakness and passivity, confused with pacifism, lumped with rioting or guerrilla warfare, or viewed as a type of action that does not require careful preparations, then nonviolent struggle may not even be attempted, or, if it is, the effort may well be ineffective.

Classes of methods of action

At least 198 specific methods of nonviolent struggle have been identified. These constitute three main types of activity. The first large class is called nonviolent protest and persuasion. These are forms of activity in which the practitioners are expressing opinions by symbolic actions, to show their support or disapproval of an action, a policy, a group, or a government, for example. Many specific methods of action fall into this category. These include written declarations, petitions, leafleting, picketing, wearing of symbols, symbolic sounds, vigils, singing, marches, mock funerals, protest meetings, silence, and turning one's back, among many others. In many political situations these methods are quite mild, but under a highly repressive regime such actions may be dramatic challenges and require great courage.

The second class of methods is noncooperation, an extremely large class, which may take social, economic, and political forms. In these methods, the people refuse to continue usual forms of cooperation or to initiate new cooperation. The effect of such noncooperation by its nature is more disruptive of the established relationships and the operating system than are the methods of nonviolent protest and persuasion. The extent of that disruption depends on the system within which the action occurs, the importance of the activity in which people are refusing to engage, the specific type of noncooperation used, which groups are refusing cooperation, how many people are involved, and how long the noncooperation can continue.

The methods of social noncooperation include, among others, social boycott, excommunication, student strike, stay-at-home, and collective disappearance.

The forms of economic noncooperation are grouped under (1) economic boycotts and (2) labor strikes. The methods of economic boycott include, among others, consumers' boycotts, rent withholding, refusal to let or sell property, lock outs, withdrawal of bank deposits, revenue refusals, and international trade embargoes. Labor strikes include: protest strikes, prisoners' strikes, slowdown strikes, general strikes, and economic shutdowns, as well as many others.

Political noncooperation is a much larger subclass. It includes withholding or withdrawal of allegiance, boycotts of elections, boycotts of government employment or positions, refusal to dissolve existing institutions, reluctant and slow compliance, disguised disobedience, civil disobedience, judicial noncooperation, deliberate inefficiency, and selective noncooperation by enforcement agents, noncooperation by constituent government units, and severance of diplomatic relations.

The methods of nonviolent intervention all actively disrupt the normal operation of policies or the system by deliberate interference, either psychologically, physically, socially, economically, or politically. Among the large number of methods in this class are the fast, sit-ins, nonviolent raids, nonviolent obstruction, nonviolent occupation, the overloading of facilities, alternative social institutions, alternative communication systems, reverse strikes, stay-in strikes, nonviolent land seizures, defiance of blockades, seizures of assets, selective patronage, alternative economic institutions, the overloading of administrative systems, the seeking of imprisonment, and dual sovereignty and parallel government.

These and many additional similar methods of nonviolent protest and persuasion, noncooperation, and nonviolent intervention constitute the technique of nonviolent action.

Success has requirements

Nonviolent struggle does not work through magic. Although nonviolent resisters have succeeded many times, they have not done so every time, and certainly not without cost. The simple choice to conduct a conflict by nonviolent action does not guarantee success.

Many past struggles were only partially successful. Sometimes a victory was short-lived because people did not use it well to consolidate their gains, nor did they effectively resist new threats to their liberties. In other cases, victory in a single campaign won concessions, but new struggles were still required to gain the full objectives. Nevertheless, in some cases, major victories were achieved that many people would have expected to be impossible through nonviolent resistance.

However, some of the past cases of nonviolent struggles failed to accomplish their objectives. Such failure has occurred for a variety of reasons. If the resisters are weak, if the specific methods used are poorly chosen, or if the resisters become frightened and intimidated into submission, then they are unlikely to win. If the resisters lack a strategy by which to wage the struggle with maximum effectiveness, their chances of succeeding are greatly diminished. There is no substitute for genuine strength and wise action in the conduct of nonviolent struggle.

Participating in a nonviolent struggle does not make an individual immune from imprisonment, injury, suffering, or death. As in violent conflicts, the participants often suffer harsh penalties for their defiance and noncooperation. Yet, victories by nonviolent struggle with few casualties, and even none, also have occurred, and commonly the casualties in nonviolent struggles are significantly fewer than those in comparable violent struggles for similar objectives.

Much greater consideration of this technique will assist us in assessing its potential relevance and potential effectiveness. Let us, therefore, survey the operation of nonviolent struggle.

Uses and effects of nonviolent struggle

Nonviolent struggle can be employed as a substitute for violence against other groups in one's society, against groups in another society, against one's own government, or against another government.

Many times, only the methods of nonviolent protest and persuasion may be used in attempts to influence opinions of the opponents and others. Such actions may affect the moral authority or legitimacy of the opponents. However, these methods are the weaker ones.

Many of the methods of noncooperation are much more powerful because they can potentially reduce or sever the supply of the opponents' sources of power. These methods require significant numbers of participants and usually the participation of groups and institutions in the refusal of cooperation.

The methods of nonviolent intervention may be applied by groups of various sizes. Some of the methods—as a sit-in in an office—require fewer numbers of participants to make a major impact than do methods of noncooperation. In the short run at least, these methods are generally more disruptive of the status quo than noncooperation. However, some of these methods may often be met with extreme repression. In order to make their impact, the resisters must be prepared to withstand this, while persisting in their nonviolent defiance. Unless the numbers of participants are extremely large—as in massive sit-downs on central city streets—it may not be possible to maintain the application of these methods for long periods of time. Casualties may be severe.

It is very important that those who plan to engage in a nonviolent struggle choose the methods they will use with extreme care. The methods chosen should strike at the opponents' vulnerabilities, utilize the resisters' strengths, and be used in combination with other methods in ways that are mutually supportive. To be most effective, the methods will also need to be chosen and implemented in accordance with a grand strategy for the overall struggle. The grand strategy needs to be developed before the specific methods are selected. The development of grand strategies and strategies for limited campaigns will be discussed in Part Four.

The effects of the use of the diverse methods of nonviolent action vary widely. Such effects depend on the nature of the system within which they are applied, the type of the opponents' regime, the extent of their application, the normal roles in the operation of the system of the persons and groups applying them, the skill of the groups in using nonviolent action, the presence or absence of the use of wise strategies in the conflict, and, finally, the relative ability of the nonviolent resisters to withstand repression from the opponents and to persist in their noncooperation and defiance without falling into violence.

Repression and mechanisms of change

Since these methods of nonviolent action, especially those of noncooperation, often directly disturb or disrupt the supply of the needed sources of power and "normal" operations, the opponents are likely to respond strongly, usually with repression. This repression can include beatings, arrests, imprisonments, executions, and mass slaughters. Despite repression, the resisters have at times persisted in fighting with only their chosen nonviolent weapons.

Past struggles have only rarely been well planned and prepared and have usually lacked a strategic plan. Resistance was often poorly focused, and the resisters often did not know what they should or should not do. Consequently, it is not surprising that, in the face of serious repression, nonviolent struggles have at times produced only limited positive results or have even resulted in clear defeats and disasters. Yet, amazingly, many improvised nonviolent struggles have triumphed. There is now reason to believe that the effectiveness of this technique can be greatly increased with improved understanding of the requirements of this technique, and with development of strategic planning.

When nonviolent struggles succeed in achieving their declared objectives, the result is produced by the operation of one of four mechanisms—conversion, accommodation, nonviolent coercion, or disintegration—or a combination of two or three of them.

Rarely, the opponents have a change of view; that is, a conversion takes place. In this case, as a result of the nonviolent persistence and the willingness of the people to continue despite suffering, harsh conditions, and brutalities perpetrated on them, the opponents decide that it is right to accept the claims of the nonviolent group. Although religious pacifists frequently stress this possibility, it does not occur often.

A much more common mechanism is called accommodation. This essentially means that both sides compromise on issues and receive, and give up, a part of their original objectives. This can operate only in respect to issues on which each side can compromise without seeing themselves to be violating their fundamental beliefs or political principles. Accommodation occurs in almost all labor strike settlements. The final agreed working conditions and wages are usually somewhere between the originally stated objectives of the two sides. One must remember that these settlements are highly influenced by how much power each side can wield in waging the conflict.

In other conflicts, the numbers of resisters have become so large, and the parts of the social and political order they influence or control are so essential, that the noncooperation and defiance have taken control of the conflict situation. The opponents are still in their former positions, but they are unable any longer to control the system without the resumption of cooperation and submission by the resisters. Not even repression is effective, either because of the massiveness of the noncooperation or because the opponents' troops and police no longer reliably obey orders. The change is made against the opponents' will, because the supply of their needed sources of power has been seriously weakened or severed. The opponents can no longer wield power contrary to the wishes of the nonviolent struggle group. This is nonviolent coercion.

This is what occurred, for example, in the Russian 1905 Revolution. As a result of the Great October Strike, Tsar Nicholas II issued the constitutional manifesto of October 17, 1905, which granted a *Duma* or legislature, thereby abandoning his claim to be sole autocrat.

In more extreme situations, the noncooperation and defiance are so vast and strong that the previous regime simply falls apart. There is no one left with sufficient power even to surrender.

In Russia in February 1917, the numbers of strikers were massive; all social classes had turned against the tsarist regime; huge peaceful street demonstrations were undermining the loyalty of the soldiers; and troop reinforcements dissolved into the protesting crowds. Finally, Tsar Nicholas II, facing this reality, quietly abdicated, and the tsarist government was "dissolved and swept away." This is disintegration.

In Serbia in October 2000, the Otpor-initiated defiance and noncooperation campaign met almost all the characteristics of the disintegration campaign, with one notable exception. Milosevic had clearly lost his power capacity and faced nonviolent coercion. However, he retained enough power to go on television to capitulate. He had suddenly discovered that, contrary to earlier claims, his electoral rival Vojislav Kostunica had actually won the election and Milosevic had not. He had only enough remaining power to claim television time to surrender. This was almost disintegration. This mechanism, however, remains a rare ending of nonviolent struggles.

Additional elements of nonviolent struggle

While noncooperation to undermine compliance and to weaken and sever the sources of the opponents' power are the main forces in nonviolent struggle, one other process sometimes operates. This is "political ju-jitsu." In this process, brutal repression against disciplined nonviolent resisters does not strengthen the opponents and weaken the resisters, but does the opposite.

Widespread revulsion against the opponents for their brutality operates in some cases to shift power to the resisters. More people may join the resistance. Third parties may change their opinions and activities to favor the resisters and act against the opponents. Even members of the opponents' usual supporters, administrators, and troops and police may become unreliable and may even mutiny. The use of the opponents' supposedly coercive violence has then been turned to undermine their own power capacity. Political ju-jitsu does not operate in all situations, however, and instead heavy reliance must therefore be placed on the impact of large scale, carefully focussed noncooperation.

The importance of strategy

Effective nonviolent struggle is not the product of simple application of the methods of this technique. A struggle conducted by nonviolent means will, generally, be more effective if the participants first understand what the factors are that contribute to greater success or to likely failure, then act accordingly.

Another important variable in nonviolent struggles is whether they are or are not conducted on the basis of a wisely prepared grand strategy and strategies for individual campaigns. The presence or absence of strategic calculations and planning, and, if present, their wisdom, will have a major impact on the course of the struggle and on determining its final outcome. At this point in the historical practice of nonviolent struggle we can project that a very significant factor in its future practice and effectiveness will be its increasing application on the basis of strategic planning.

Competent strategic planning requires not only an understanding of the conflict situation itself, but also an in-depth understanding of why this technique can wield great power, the major characteristics of nonviolent struggle, the many methods that may be applied, and the dynamics and mechanisms at work in actual struggles of this technique when applied against repressive regimes.

The topics and themes of this chapter are all presented more extensively and in greater depth in the remaining chapters of this book.

We will examine the multitude of individual methods encompassed by this technique in the next chapter.

Chapter Four

THE METHODS OF
NONVIOLENT ACTION

The weapons of nonviolent struggle

The technique of nonviolent action consists of numerous specific "methods," or forms of action. Such methods serve as the weapons of nonviolent struggle. They are used to conduct the conflict by psychological, social, economic, or political pressure, or a combination of these.

Methods of nonviolent action were introduced in Chapters One and Three and some examples were cited. These included protest marches, flying forbidden flags, massive rallies, vigils, social boycotts, economic boycotts, labor strikes, civil disobedience, boycott of phony elections, strikes by civil servants, sit-ins, hunger strikes, occupation of offices, and creation of a parallel government. Such methods may be used to protest symbolically, end cooperation, or disrupt the operation of the established system.

These and similar methods collectively constitute the overall technique of nonviolent action. Familiarity with their diversity and characteristics is crucial to understanding nonviolent struggle as a whole and its variations in action.

Understanding the methods of nonviolent action

The many specific methods, or weapons, of nonviolent action are classified into three groups:

1. Protest and persuasion

2. Noncooperation

3. Nonviolent intervention

The following list of 198 methods is intended only to show the range of options available to groups that are using or considering the use of nonviolent struggle. The list is far from complete. Full definitions of each method and historical examples of its use are provided in *The Politics of Nonviolent Action*.[1] Many additional methods doubtless exist, and many new ones could certainly be invented or learned from other groups. Scholars studying this technique, as well as resisters contemplating how they can most effectively conduct a future struggle, are strongly encouraged to study Part Two of the above volume, which is published separately as *The Methods of Nonviolent Action*.

This chapter is not intended as a guide to the selection and application of the methods, but only as a survey of the various types of available methods. Factors to be considered in the selection of methods for a particular conflict will be discussed in Chapter Thirty-seven.

The wise selection of specific methods for use requires knowledge not only of the whole range of possible methods of action but also of the strategy that has been developed for the waging of the conflict.

As we will discuss in Part Four, careful strategic planning is very important *before* the selection of specific methods in a given conflict. Strategic calculation and planning are required to identify what kinds of pressure the resisters need to apply against

---

[1] See Gene Sharp, *The Politics of Nonviolent Action,* Part Two, *The Methods of Nonviolent Action,* Boston: Porter Sargent Publisher, 1973.

their opponents, and therefore what specific methods the resisters need to employ.

I. ACTIONS TO SEND A MESSAGE

NONVIOLENT PROTEST AND PERSUASION

Nonviolent protest and persuasion include numerous methods that are mainly symbolic acts of peaceful opposition or attempted persuasion. These extend beyond verbal expressions of opinion but stop short of noncooperation or nonviolent intervention. The use of these methods shows that the resisters are against or in favor of something, the degree of opposition or support, and, sometimes, the number of people involved.

The impact of these methods on the attitudes of others will vary considerably. It is possible that where a particular method is common, its influence in a single instance may be less than in locations where the method has hitherto been rare or unknown. The political conditions in which the method occurs are also likely to influence its impact. Dictatorial conditions make an act of nonviolent protest less common and more dangerous. Hence, if it does occur, the act may be more dramatic and may receive greater attention than it would where the act is common or carries no penalty.

The message may be intended to influence the opponents, the public, the grievance group[2], or a combination of the three. Attempts to influence the opponents usually focus on convincing them to correct or halt certain actions, or to do what the grievance group wants. The methods of nonviolent protest and persuasion may also be selected to facilitate a concurrent or later application of other methods, especially the forms of noncooperation. Fifty-four methods of nonviolent protest and persuasion are included in this listing, grouped here in ten subclasses.

Formal statements

1.   Public speeches

---

[2] The grievance group is the general population group whose grievances are issues in the conflict and are being championed by the nonviolent resisters.

2. Letters of opposition or support
3. Declarations by organizations and institutions
4. Signed public statements
5. Declarations of indictment and intention
6. Group or mass petition

Communications with a wider audience

7. Slogans, caricatures, and symbols (written, painted, drawn, printed, gestures, spoken, or mimicked)
8. Banners, posters, and displayed communications
9. Leaflets, pamphlets, and books
10. Newspapers and journals
11. Recordings, radio, television, and video
12. Skywriting and earthwriting

Group presentations

13. Deputations
14. Mock awards
15. Group lobbying
16. Picketing
17. Mock elections

Symbolic public acts

18. Displays of flags and symbolic colors
19. Wearing of symbols (advocacy buttons, patches)
20. Prayer and worship
21. Delivering symbolic objects
22. Protest disrobings
23. Destruction of own property (homes, documents, credentials, etc.)
24. Symbolic lights (torches, lanterns, candles)
25. Displays of portraits

26. Paint as protest
27. New signs and names and/or symbolic names
28. Symbolic sounds ("symbolic tunes" with whistles, bells, sirens, etc.)
29. Symbolic reclamations (takeover of lands or buildings)
30. Rude gestures

Pressure on individuals

31. "Haunting" officials (may involve constantly following them, or reminding them, or may be silent and respectful)
32. Taunting officials (mocking or insulting them)
33. Fraternization (subjecting persons to intense direct influence to convince them that the regime they serve is unjust)
34. Vigils

Drama and music

35. Humorous skits and pranks
36. Performance of plays and music
37. Singing

Processions

38. Marches
39. Parades
40. Religious processions
41. Pilgrimages
42. Motorcades

Honoring the dead

43. Political mourning
44. Mock funerals

45.   Demonstrative funerals

46.   Homage at burial places

Public assemblies

47.   Assemblies of protest or support

48.   Protest meetings

49.   Camouflaged meetings of protest

50.   Teach-ins with several informed speakers

Withdrawal and renunciation

51.   Walk-outs

52.   Silence

53.   Renunciation of honors

54.   Turning one's back

All these are symbolic actions. Greater power is wielded by the methods of noncooperation and nonviolent intervention.

II. ACTIONS TO SUSPEND COOPERATION AND ASSISTANCE

METHODS OF NONCOOPERATION

Overwhelmingly, the methods of nonviolent struggle involve noncooperation with the opponents. "Noncooperation" means that the resisters in a conflict either deliberately withdraw some form or degree of existing cooperation with the opponents or the resisters refuse to initiate certain forms of new cooperation. Noncooperation involves the deliberate discontinuance, withholding, or defiance of certain existing relationships—social, economic, or political. The action may be spontaneous or planned, and it may be legal or illegal.

The impact of the various forms of noncooperation hinges heavily on the number of people participating in the use of these methods and the degree to which the opponents are dependent on the persons and groups that are refusing cooperation. The classes of noncooperation are social, economic, and political noncooperation.

A. Actions to suspend social relations

The methods of social noncooperation

Social noncooperation is the refusal to carry on normal social relations, either particular or general, with persons or groups regarded as having perpetrated some wrong or injustice, or refusal to comply with certain behavior patterns or practices. Fifteen methods are listed in three subgroups of social noncooperation:

Ostracism of persons

55. Social boycott
56. Selective social boycott
57. Lysistratic nonaction (sexual boycott)
58. Excommunication (religious boycott)
59. Interdiction (suspension of religious services)

Noncooperation with social events, customs, and institutions

60. Suspension of social and sports activities
61. Boycott of social affairs
62. Student strike
63. Social disobedience (of social customs or rules)
64. Withdrawal from social institutions

Withdrawal from the social system

65. Stay-at-home
66. Total personal noncooperation
67. Flight of workers (fleeing elsewhere)
68. Sanctuary (withdrawal to a place where you cannot be touched without violation of religious, moral, social, or legal prohibitions)

69.   Collective disappearance (the inhabitants of a small area abandon their homes and villages)

70.   Protest emigration (hijrat: a deliberate permanent emigration)

B. Actions to suspend economic relations

The methods of economic noncooperation

These methods involve the suspension or refusal to initiate specific types of economic relationships. This noncooperation takes many forms that are grouped under the subclasses of economic boycotts and labor strikes.

(1) Economic boycotts

An economic boycott is the refusal to buy, sell, handle, or distribute specific goods and services, and often also includes efforts to induce others to withdraw such cooperation. In this list are twenty-five methods divided into six subgroups of economic boycotts.

Action by consumers

71.   Consumers' boycott of certain goods or firms

72.   Nonconsumption of boycotted goods (those already in one's possession)

73.   Policy of austerity (reducing consumption to an absolute minimum)

74.   Rent withholding (rent strike)

75.   Refusal to rent

76.   National consumers' boycott (refusal to buy products or use services from another country)

77.   International consumers' boycott (operating in several countries against the products of a particular country)

Actions by workers and producers

78. Workmen's boycott (refusal to work with products or tools provided by the opponents)

79. Producers' boycott (refusal by producers to sell or otherwise deliver their products)

Action by middlemen

80. Suppliers' or handlers' boycott (refusal by workers or middlemen to handle or supply certain goods)

Action by owners and management

81. Traders' boycott (refusal by retailers to buy or sell certain goods)

82. Refusal to let or sell property

83. Lockout (the employer initiates the work stoppage by temporarily shutting down the operation)

84. Refusal of industrial assistance

85. Merchants' "general strike"

Action by holders of financial resources

86. Withdrawal of bank deposits

87. Refusal to pay fees, dues, and assessments

88. Refusal to pay debts or interest

89. Severance of funds and credit

90. Revenue refusal (refusal to provide the government with revenue voluntarily)

91. Refusal of a government's money (demand alternative ways of payment)

Action by governments

92. Domestic embargo

93. Blacklisting of traders

94. International sellers' embargo

95.   International buyers' embargo

96.   International trade embargo

(2) Labor strikes

The methods of the strike involve the refusal to continue economic cooperation through work. Strikes are collective, deliberate, and normally temporary suspensions of labor designed to impose pressure on others. While the unit within which a strike is applied is usually an industrial one, it may also be political, social, agricultural, or cultural, depending on the nature of the grievance. Twenty-three types of strikes are listed here in seven subgroups.

Symbolic strikes

97.   Protest strike (for a pre-announced short period)

98.   Quickie walkout (lightning strike: short, spontaneous protest strike)

Agricultural strikes

99.   Peasant strike

100.   Farm workers' strike

Strikes by special groups

101.   Refusal of impressed labor

102.   Prisoners' strike

103.   Craft strike

104.   Professional strike

Ordinary industrial strikes

105.   Establishment strike (in one or more plants under one management)

106.   Industry strike (suspension of work in all the establishments of an industry)

107. Sympathetic strike (solidarity strike to support the demands of fellow workers)

Restricted strikes

108. Detailed strike (worker by worker, or area by area; piecemeal stoppage)

109. Bumper strike (the union strikes only one firm in an industry at a time)

110. Slowdown strike

111. Working-to-rule strike (the literal carrying out of regulations in order to retard production)

112. Sick-in (reporting "sick")

113. Strike by resignation (a significant number of workers resign individually)

114. Limited strike (workers refuse to perform certain marginal work or refuse to work on certain days)

115. Selective strike (workers refuse to do certain types of work)

Multi-industry strikes

116. Generalized strike (several industries are struck simultaneously)

117. General strike (all industries are struck simultaneously)

Combination of strikes and economic closures

118. Hartal (economic life temporarily suspended on a voluntary basis)

119. Economic shutdown (workers strike and employers simultaneously halt economic activities)

C. Actions to suspend political submission and assistance

The methods of political noncooperation

This class consists of methods that withhold or withdraw co-operation in political matters. The aim may be to achieve a particular limited objective or to change the nature or composition of a government, or even to produce its disintegration. This list consists of thirty-seven methods divided into six subgroups.

Rejection of authority

120. Withholding or withdrawal of allegiance
121. Refusal of public support (for the existing regime and its policies)
122. Literature and speeches advocating resistance

Citizens' noncooperation with government

123. Boycott of legislative bodies by its members
124. Boycott of elections
125. Boycott of government employment and positions
126. Boycott of government departments, agencies, and other bodies
127. Withdrawal from government educational institutions
128. Boycott of government-supported organizations
129. Refusal of assistance to enforcement agents
130. Removal of own signs and placemarkers
131. Refusal to accept appointed officials
132. Refusal to dissolve existing institutions

Citizens' alternatives to obedience

133. Reluctant and slow compliance
134. Nonobedience in absence of direct supervision
135. Popular nonobedience (not publicized, discreet)

136. Disguised disobedience (looks like compliance)

137. Refusal of an assemblage or meeting to disperse

138. Sit-down

139. Noncooperation with conscription and deportation

140. Hiding, escape, and false identities

141. Civil disobedience of "illegitimate" laws

Action by government personnel

142. Selective refusal of assistance by government aides (as refusal to carry out particular instructions; informing superiors of the refusal)

143. Blocking lines of command and information

144. Stalling and obstruction

145. General administrative noncooperation

146. Judicial noncooperation (by judges)

147. Deliberate inefficiency and selective noncooperation by enforcement agents

148. Mutiny

Domestic governmental action

149. Quasi-legal evasions and delays

150. Noncooperation by constituent governmental units

International governmental action

151. Changes in diplomatic and other representation

152. Delay and cancellation of diplomatic events

153. Withholding of diplomatic recognition

154. Severance of diplomatic relations

155. Withdrawal from international organizations

156. Refusal of membership in international bodies

157. Expulsion from international organizations

III. METHODS OF DISRUPTION

THE METHODS OF NONVIOLENT INTERVENTION

In contrast to the methods of protest and persuasion and of noncooperation, these are methods that intervene directly to change a given situation. Negative interventions may disrupt, and even destroy, established behavior patterns, policies, relationships, or institutions. Positive interventions may establish new behavior patterns, policies, relationships, or institutions.

Certain methods of nonviolent intervention can pose a more direct and immediate challenge to the opponents than the methods of protest and noncooperation, and may thereby produce more rapid changes. These methods may include sit-ins, nonviolent invasion, nonviolent interjection, nonviolent obstruction, nonviolent occupation, nonviolent land seizure, seeking imprisonment, and dual sovereignty and parallel government.

The methods of nonviolent intervention are, however, usually both harder for the resisters to sustain and harder for the opponents to withstand. Use of these methods may bring speedier and more severe repression than the methods of nonviolent protest and persuasion and the forms of noncooperation.

The methods of intervention may be used defensively: to maintain behavior patterns, institutions, independent initiatives, etc., or they can be used offensively to carry the struggle for the resisters' objectives into the opponents' own camp, even without any immediate provocation.

This list includes forty methods divided into five subgroups, according to the dominant means of expression of the intervention itself.

Psychological intervention

158. Self-exposure to the elements
159. The fast
160. Reverse trial (defendants become unofficial "prosecutors")
161. Nonviolent harassment

Physical intervention

162. Sit-in
163. Stand-in
164. Ride-in
165. Wade-in
166. Mill-in (gather in some place of symbolic significance and remain mobile)
167. Pray-in
168. Nonviolent raids (march to designated key point and demand possession)
169. Nonviolent air raids (perhaps bringing leaflets or food)
170. Nonviolent invasion
171. Nonviolent interjection (placing one's body between a person and the objective of his work or activity)
172. Nonviolent obstruction (generally temporary)
173. Nonviolent occupations

Social intervention

174. Establishing new social patterns
175. Overloading of facilities
176. Stall-in
177. Speak-in
178. Guerrilla theater (improvised dramatic interruptions)
179. Alternative social institutions
180. Alternative communication systems

Economic intervention

181. Reverse strike (working to excess)
182. Stay-in strike (occupation of work site)

183. Nonviolent land seizure
184. Defiance of blockades
185. Politically motivated counterfeiting
186. Preclusive purchasing
187. Seizure of assets
188. Dumping
189. Selective patronage
190. Alternative markets
191. Alternative transportation systems
192. Alternative economic institutions

Political intervention

193. Overloading of administrative systems
194. Disclosing identities of secret agents
195. Seeking imprisonment
196. Civil disobedience of "neutral" laws
197. Work-on without collaboration
198. Dual sovereignty and parallel government

The impact of the use of any of these methods depends on the adequacy and competency of their application, as well as important other factors in the conflict.

Learning from the past practice of such methods

Nonviolent struggles using these methods have occurred throughout human history. While the twentieth century was one of great violence and extreme dictatorships, genocide, nuclear weapons, massive slaughters, terrorism, and world wars, it was also a century of a multitude of nonviolent struggles.

The following chapters offer brief accounts of some of these important but highly imperfect struggles. They are intended to illustrate the historical scope of the practice of this technique in the twentieth century, the variety of opponents confronted by it, and the differing results of these conflicts. These accounts also offer examples of the application of many of these specific methods.

Much can be learned from these cases of nonviolent struggle, both positively and negatively. These cases also can give us important insights into both the potential of this technique and the problems of waging nonviolent struggle.

PART TWO

IMPROVISED NONVIOLENT STRUGGLES IN THE TWENTIETH CENTURY

INTRODUCTION TO THE CASES

The cases of nonviolent struggle described in the chapters of this Part are offered here primarily to show that nonviolent struggle has been a reality in a world of much violence and oppression. These cases also show how nonviolent struggle has operated and illustrate the diverse applications of this technique, as well as the diverse conditions under which it has been used.

Chapter Five

THE RUSSIAN REVOLUTION OF 1905

Prelude to revolution

At the turn of 1900, the Russian Empire ranged from Western Europe down to the Caucasus and east across Siberia to the Bering Sea. The Empire had long been ruled by tsars who believed in their divine right to rule as autocrats, as did the then-tsar, Nicholas II.

Much of the society of the Empire was in the process of change. Three-quarters of the population lived on the land, but many peasants were moving to the cities and industry was growing. With that growth came labor discontent and significant strikes. Because of social and political conditions, there had also been dissatisfaction among the peasants, the students, and the intelligentsia. Illegal newspapers had been founded to express political discontent. Although elected bodies of local government, called *zemstvos,* existed on the district and provincial levels, and

A list of sources for this case appears at the end of this chapter.

similar bodies, called *dumas,* operated on the municipal level, voting was highly restricted.

Ferment during 1904

A Union of Liberation representing liberals was founded in January 1904. Its declaration demanded a constituent assembly elected on the basis of universal, direct, equal, and secret suffrage, the incorporation of human and civil rights into the Fundamental Law, and the equality of all before the law, regardless of sex, religion, or nationality. That summer the government permitted a degree of public expression of dissenting opinions.

Among the many illegal opposition parties was the Party of Socialist Revolutionaries, which favored the peasants and often conducted assassinations of prominent officials. The Russian Social Democratic Labor Party (Social Democrats) included the Mensheviks, who were relatively moderate Marxists, and the Bolsheviks, led by Vladimir Lenin, who had a distinctive view of the elite role of the party, its mission, and the responsibility to seize the State with violence and to use it to restructure the society. The tsarist regime sought to repress these parties.

The year opened with the start of a war. Russian and Japanese imperial interests in Northeast Asia clashed, and in January 1904 the Japanese navy attacked the Russian city of Port Arthur. Most Russian troops, however, remained in European Russia and were used to quell strikes and demonstrations.

In February 1904, a workers organization was permitted to organize in the capital of St. Petersburg. The government hoped that if it was prohibited from becoming a trade union and from tackling political issues, this new organization would prevent the establishment of more radical organizations. Soon, the new Assembly of St. Petersburg Factory Workers had 100,000 members.

The war against Japan was bloody, going poorly for the Russians, and losing support at home. This contributed to unrest among the population. Some reservists even rioted. Despite the war, the regime could not ignore serious domestic problems. The government sought to control the *zemstvos* and prevent them from expanding their powers. The dominated non-Russian nationalities were resisting efforts to turn them into pseudo-Russians in language and culture, and demanded greater freedoms. Dissenting liberals held meetings, disguised as banquets, to agitate for a democratic constitution. Major violence against Jews occurred.

The middle and upper classes, except for the clergy and merchants, made unprecedented anti-government declarations. Students did so also, and held demonstrations as well. The Liberationists organized professional unions, and as a political group became stronger than the socialists. The barriers between the educated and the uneducated, and between the anti-government intelligentsia and the pro-monarchist masses, were weakening. Workers' calls for higher wages and shorter hours caused them to listen to the liberals and socialists. Conditions near open revolt existed in some parts of the Empire.

The various socialist groups concentrated on organizing workers, propagandizing, controlling strikes when they happened, and penetrating the military forces. They had no plan for overthrowing the monarchist government in the near future, however. In far away Baku on the Caspian Sea, strikers won a nine-hour day and wage increases, but they failed to gain a constituent assembly and civil rights. The war continued to go poorly for the Russians, and on December 20 they surrendered Port Arthur.

Strikes, petition, and a march

A week later, 350 workers from the Putilov ironworks in St. Petersburg, the capital, demanded reinstatement of four dismissed workers. When that failed, virtually the entire workforce of 13,000 quietly walked out. The news spread rapidly. The Putilov strikers were joined by others and a new method, the general strike, was launched. The strikers were reluctant to use violence. By the middle of the week, 25,000 workers were on strike.

At a strike meeting on January 6, 1905, Father Georgii Gapon announced it was time to appeal to the Tsar for both political and economic changes. He circulated a petition based on the view that political change was the precursor of economic change. The petition was not anti-monarchist. It asked the Tsar for an eight-hour working day, improved wages, human rights, universal secret suffrage, popular representation, an elected constituent assembly, and other demands. By January 7, 85% of the 175,000 workers in the capital were on strike.

Bloody Sunday

A march to deliver the petition to the Tsar was planned for January 9. The workers and their families were to gather for the march in the different Assembly halls in the city. Then, they would march in columns to converging points, eventually to join together in Palace Square, in front of the Tsar's Winter Palace. Father Gapon would there present the petition, signed by many thousands, to Tsar Nicholas II in person.

Father Gapon informed the government of the peaceful march. Orders from the Minister of the Interior, Svyatatopolk-Mirsky, for the St. Petersburg Prefect to have Gapon and his aides arrested were not carried out. The attempt by the famous writer Maxim Gorky and ten others to persuade the government to allow the march failed. Twenty thousand troops, eight major generals, and the police prepared to halt the marchers.

Despite the cold, the marchers were orderly and patient. Priests, icons, religious standards, the Russian national flag, and portraits of the Tsar and Tsarina headed the processions. After a mile and a half, at the Narva Triumphal Arch, in front of important government buildings, police and troops blocked the marchers' way. When the marchers refused orders to disperse, the horse guard galloped into them. They reformed and eight volleys were fired into the crowd. Essentially the same thing happened to the other processions. Later, thousands of marchers and others assembled in the Palace Square. After warning shots, the troops fired directly into the crowd both there and in nearby Nevsky Square. At Vasilievsky Island, a section of the city, a group of students, who had previously failed in their attempt to induce the marchers to use violence, then attached themselves to the march, set up barricades, and provoked the police.

Official figures reported 95 dead and 333 wounded, of whom 34 died. Many additional wounded and dead were taken away privately. Father Gapon spoke the next day to the liberals and sent a message to workingmen to continue the struggle.

The nineteenth century Russian revolutionaries of various types had faced an unsolved major problem: how to destroy the peasants' naïve faith in the Tsar. Bloody Sunday destroyed that alliance of the poor with the Tsar, and all classes turned against the tsarist system.

Strikes and struggle

A predominantly nonviolent revolt followed spontaneously. There was no plan, no strategy. The means of struggle used were mostly strikes and other noncooperation, as well as symbolic protests such as marches. However, there were secondary acts of scattered but significant violence. The strikes often involved many people and continued for weeks, while the violence usually involved fewer participants and was briefer.

Both the liberals and the social democrats were taken by surprise by the massive popular revolt. The Minister of Finance on January 11, 1905 warned that the events of Bloody Sunday had lowered Russia's credit abroad. St. Petersburg was placed under martial law on January 12, but after a few days, military paroles were removed and strikes ended. In Riga, in what is now Latvia, violent clashes killed seventy during a march of 15,000.

After Bloody Sunday, the Putilov original strikers declared they would continue the strike and were joined by others, including gas and electricity workers. Students, faculty, and lawyers also went on strike. Various professional associations denounced the government and called for a constituent assembly. *Zemstvos* and *dumas* throughout the country lodged strong protests. Nationalist and economic grievances were aired among the nationalities on the borderlands of Russia proper and where the Socialist Revolutionaries were active. When workers ran out of money and food, they returned to work in order to eat, but remained ready to strike again. Generally, the peasants remained calm, but in some places there was significant violence.

In the Transcaucasus, strikes, especially by railworkers, began on January 18. Existing strikes encouraged new strikes. Seeing the example, peasants engaged in other resistance. A faith in the possibility of change was strengthened.

That month, almost every institution of higher learning was closed by strikes or by government orders, in order to disperse protesting students, and remained so all year. The students could thus participate in the struggle full-time.

National minorities established their own organizations and issued publications in their own languages.

Socialists of all types were unprepared for these events and were unable to provide leadership. Many of the socialists had no confidence in the workers, although they attempted to organize some of them and to propagandize the soldiers. The soldiers were hostile to the students. The defiant liberals were better organized. Historian Sidney Harcave reported the liberals approved of methods that did not "injure either persons or property." By the end of January, even monarchists called for an elected assembly.

In imperial acts on February 18, the Tsar rebuked participants in the demonstrations and reaffirmed the autocracy. But he also granted the right of petition and, rather vaguely, ordered planning of some kind of elected group. The unrest continued. Schools and homes of the wealthy were used for anti-government meetings. Unplanned but powerful strikes were always occurring somewhere. Russian-ruled minorities, including Jews, Muslims, and Mongols, made demands. The peasants, usually independently but sometimes with participation of the Socialist Revolutionaries, demanded reforms and sometimes talked of violent redistribution of the land. Some estates were burned.

Meanwhile, the war with Japan became extremely bloody. Social Democrats began distributing leaflets and organizing among the troops at home. Resentment among soldiers about the war and their conditions were growing.

Organizational strengthening

Liberals used eased controls to advance their proposed reforms, and among the masses new or revitalized organizations were emerging. During the spring and summer, organizations based on professions, occupations, or political views were widely established. The Union of Liberation in March pressed for a constituent assembly based on universal suffrage, separation of church and state, increased rights for national minorities, the right to strike, an eight-hour working day, and government-provided insurance (health, old age, and life).

In April, at least 80,000 strikers were out and in May at least 220,000. One of the longest strikes, conducted by 70,000 textile workers, occurred in Ivano-Voznesensk, northeast of Moscow. Conditions there were often harsh, and political demands were later added to the initial economic demands. The first *soviet,* a grass roots extra-legal organization that often took on political powers, also began there. (This *soviet* was very different from the later Communist Party-controlled institutions of the Soviet Union.)

The organization of trade unions—which was expressly illegal—began in January and continued into the spring with the long-term hope of establishing a union of unions. Both professional and working class people formed unions and found that they could operate more or less openly. The Union of Unions became a reality.

Various counteractions to all these events were organized by different groups collectively known as the Black Hundreds. These included strong supporters of the monarchy and of the domination of the national minorities by the Great Russians, as well as people hurt economically by the strikes, and simple hooligans.

In May, 50 people meeting in Moscow made plans to organize Russia's first peasants' union. It grew in strength in August and September. The urgings of Socialist Revolutionaries for violent action appealed to the peasants, as they faced very meager harvests and possible starvation.

After the defeat of the Russian fleet by the Japanese on May 14, the Tsar sought the aid of the United States in making peace, which was achieved on August 23, 1905 at Portsmouth, New Hampshire. Due to the vast physical separation, the Russian soldiers in the Far East encountered revolutionary propaganda later than the rest of the population. Nearly a million troops came home slowly. They were not to be trusted by the government.

Spring and summer strikes and violence

During the spring and summer, there were numerous railroad strikes, often accompanied by political demands and sometimes by violence. There were clashes between workers and troops in the province of Congress Poland. There was also violence in Kharkov and between Muslims and Armenians in Baku.

In the Black Sea, the crew of the battleship *Potemkin* mutinied June 15 and killed, threw overboard, or imprisoned their officers. Only one other ship attempted to mutiny, but the entire Black Sea fleet was inactivated.

Agrarian violence was significant in the Baltic provinces and in Georgia. In Poland, rural strikes were more common. Illegal cutting of landlord-owned timber, hay, and grain often occurred in

European Russia, with only limited looting and burning of estates.

On August 6, the Tsar issued legislation to establish a State *Duma*. However, there were significant problems. There was no election date. The *Duma* would only discuss proposals to be sent to the Tsar, voting rights were strictly limited, elections were to be very indirect by a complicated procedure, and the *Duma* was to be dominated by Russians and rural populations. This was far short of what had been demanded. Opponents formed into three groups: those who favored participation anyhow; those who boycotted it while continuing peaceful action; and those who favored only a violent uprising. There were no preparations for either a violent uprising or what was seen to be its alternative, a general strike. Repression against anti-government forces intensified.

The growth of trade unions and university autonomy

Although illegal, trade unions operated openly, including not only bakers, jewelers, sales clerks, printers, and pharmacists, but also the extremely important Union of Railroad Workers. This was partly a political organization and partly a trade union. Both Mensheviks and Bolsheviks participated. Aware of its potential power, the government threatened to conscript the rail workers into the army and tried to placate them with reduced working hours and a government-sponsored congress of railroad employees. Despite a boycott of the election to that congress, radicals intent on using the new association against the government were elected. In September, several left-wing lawyers and union representatives in Moscow formed a strike committee to call for a general strike to disrupt elections for the new "Bulygin *Duma*."

Without planning or preparations, a printers' strike aimed for a wage increase began in Moscow on September 19. The new Moscow Printers Union then called on all printers to strike, and within ten days many workers in other industries and occupations also struck. Strike meetings were held often in the university and the Surveying Institute. Students, organized into the Central University Organization, participated. Such meetings were possible because of the restored autonomy of the universities, which protected the institutions of higher learning from police interference.

Labor unrest continued, and when most of the strikers suffered economically, they gradually returned to work. As a result of violent clashes in Moscow, 110 workers were killed during the strike and 50 from government forces.

The respected liberal Rector of Moscow University, Prince Sergei Trubeskoi, died unexpectedly in October. Although not a radical, he had several times acted to promote representative government in Russia. His death and funeral were used by more radical groups to promote their more extreme objectives, and the funeral was attended by thousands of workers, students, and members of the intelligentsia.

A political strike or a violent uprising?

Printers in St. Petersburg went on a new three-day strike in sympathy with striking printers in Moscow and were joined by shipbuilders and others. All the demands were political. They resorted to violence, denounced the Bulygin *Duma*, and erected barricades in the streets. Twelve thousand striking workers, intellectuals, and students crowded into the university buildings in the capital. Despite the enthusiasm, the Bolsheviks opposed a great strike, arguing that it might eclipse the idea of a violent uprising. Workers at the Naval Ministry plant walked out, demanding universal, equal, secret, and direct suffrage.

Some railroad workers already on strike were joined on October 4 by a call for all rail workers to strike. By October 8, all railroad lines were paralyzed except the train to St. Petersburg.

The unplanned Great October Strike

The action by the Moscow railroad workers on October 4 began the Great October Strike. Although unplanned and uncoordinated, and without preconceived strategy, it became the first countrywide general strike in Russia's history. Unlike previously, conscious efforts were made to press the strike to continue and to expand with the aim of bargaining with the government for both economic and political demands. More and more strikes ensued, and meetings at universities went on all night. Within a week, Moscow was virtually isolated and all public activities were halted. The strike situation was similar elsewhere. This included, for example, Kharkov, where there were workers' militias and violence. In St. Petersburg, the strike movement revived. On October 11, about 10,000 strikers and students met in the university. Socialist Revolutionaries pressed for violent methods.

In St. Petersburg, strikes spread to factories, stores, offices, schools, and, within two days, to the government itself. On October 13, 50,000 strikers and supporters crowded into the halls of the university and the Academy of Arts in the capital. Political groups vied for attention. Often following railroad lines, the strike spread throughout the country, from Congress Poland in the West, down the Caucasus, east to Siberia, and back west to Finland. Except in Kiev, newspapers ceased publication. In some places, clashes occurred between strikers and the Black Hundreds. The demands were for a constituent assembly, political amnesty, an eight-hour workday, and the lifting of legal discrimination against minorities, but all strikers were not united. Property was sometimes destroyed, and at times crowds intimidated people to enforce the strike. Some raids were conducted against estates in the countryside.

At its height, about 1,000,000 factory workers, 700,000 railroad workers, 50,000 government employees, and many thousands of professionals, students, and clerks were on strike. A minority of workers did not support the strike, and among the strikers some favored and used violent methods. Municipal *dumas* generally supported the strike or took a position of neutrality.

No organizations or individuals served as leaders of the general strike. Some strike leadership operated only locally and was often isolated. In some places, strike committees acted to maintain order and provide necessities, by opening bakeries and other stores, for instance. In some places, students and workers militias were organized to handle disorder. At times, newly organized *soviets* assumed functions for which there was no legal basis.

Power and concessions

Everything the government did to stop the spread of the strike failed. As the workers realized the power they wielded due to the strike, they became convinced that this action had great potential to change the political situation. The central government administration was practically powerless. The Tsar ordered General Trepov to use soldiers with live ammunition if necessary in St. Petersburg to quell resistance, but the order was never carried out.

After consultations, the Tsar on October 17 signed an imperial decree known as the October Manifesto. It pledged civic and personal freedoms and immediately gave some groups, previously completely deprived of rights, the right to participation in the State *Duma,* while leaving the principle of equal suffrage to be decided by the new legislature. The manifesto also asserted that no law could go into effect without the consent of the State *Duma,* and that the people's representatives had to be allowed participation in the supervision of the actions of the appointed officials. The Tsar had sworn he would never go that far.

On the other hand, the new *Duma* was to be responsible only to the Tsar. He had to approve all Council decisions and executive department personnel appointments. A constituent assembly, one of the main demands of the Liberationists, was not part of the October Manifesto.

There were crowd celebrations and processions in many cities, but also caution. Most of the population viewed the manifesto as inadequate, and continued struggle was viewed as necessary. A newly released political prisoner was killed in Moscow by a member of the Black Hundreds, and students in his funeral march were attacked by government Cossacks. The students then seized and held a university building in Moscow. However, for three days many demonstrations were held without government repression, except at Minsk. Soldiers demanded the right to organize and to attend meetings, and soldiers and sailors in uniform joined to demand release of mutinous sailors from the *Potemkin.* Minority groups asserted their rights, without hostility to Russians. There was every indication there was readiness for continued struggle that from all parts of the Empire.

There were three days of inaction and apparent helplessness by government forces. However, monarchist nongovernment groups engaged in violence, attacking revolutionary demonstrators. Five hundred persons were also killed in a three-day anti-Jewish pogrom.

Days of freedom

The people and organizations involved in the general strike did not wait for government permission to do what they believed they had the right to do. They just did it. These weeks following the Tsar's October 17 Manifesto became the "days of freedom." The strike was called off out of economic necessity, but only temporarily. The St. Petersburg *soviet* continued to operate. It decreed an end to censorship and ordered printers to refuse to print newspapers that had been submitted to the censors.

Throughout the Empire, by autumn, there were 50 workers' *soviets,* several peasants' *soviets,* and even, temporarily, some military *soviets.* The Moscow *soviet* had 80,000 members. *Soviets* began maintaining contact with each other and, for about two months after October 17, exerted governmental powers extralegally. Illegal organizations held public meetings, and trade unions began planning for a national congress. Liberal party organizations operated openly. Socialists of the three parties, however, were still hunted and thus continued to operate secretly or had gone into exile. Finland's rights were restored by the Tsar on October 22, following years of nonviolent resistance.

Peasant groups and organizations grew in strength in various provinces and had 200,000 members in 26 provinces. There was also significant peasant violence. However, at the Second Congress of the Peasants Union in Moscow in early November, most delegates opposed individual acts of violence and favored peaceful pressure to redistribute the land. No resolution favored a violent uprising.

Military disaffection and popular resistance

All sections of the military forces displayed disorderly or mutinous conduct during these weeks, including at the Kronstad Naval Base in the west, Vladivostock in Siberia, and crews of some ships in the Black Sea. During November alone, the army had to deal with 26 mutinies or near mutinies, although it was less affected than the navy. Soldiers returning from the war often fraternized with civilian radicals.

On November 24, new press rules ended pre-censorship, although if the censors were displeased with what was published, they still closed down publications and jailed editors. Previously underground publications were now issued openly. Suppressed newspapers reappeared with new names.

During November, mass movements grew of their own accord, forcing more radical resistance. The St. Petersburg *soviet* advised workers not to wait for an official eight-hour day, but just to go home after eight hours. The employers countered by closing their businesses.

In late November in Chita, north of Mongolia, soldiers and Cossacks demanded an eight-hour day and the right to organize for all men in uniform. In Kharkov, a citywide general strike upheld insubordinate activities of the local military garrison.

The October Manifesto clearly had not pacified the country. This was a semi-revolutionary situation. Yet, there was no single organization or leadership for a revolution, except for the St. Petersburg *soviet*. There was no plan and no unifying program except the goal of a constituent assembly, to be obtained by whatever means. Most of the rebellious population were not socialists of any party, but because of the socialists' vigorous tactics and a lack of alternatives, they received a great deal of sympathy and support.

Arrests and executions

On November 18, three days after a telegraph and postal strike began, the Minister of the Interior, Peter Durnovo, ordered the arrest of all those who had agitated for the strike and dismissed those on strike. This repression led to new railroad strikes and nationalist agitation, especially in the Baltic provinces. The same day, the Union of Railroad Workers voted to strike in response to the court martial order to execute several rail workers on the Central Asia Railroad. On November 25, Durnovo ordered the arrest of the members of the Central Bureau of the Congress of the Union of Railroad Workers. The St. Petersburg *Soviet* was considering what further resistance to take when Durnovo ordered the arrest of the *Soviet*'s Chairman, George Khrustalev-Nosar, the next day. There was no immediate response, but the ideas of both a general strike and of a violent uprising had been gaining supporters.

Financial war and military unreliability

Finally, on December 2, the St. Petersburg *Soviet*—supported by the Peasants Union, the Social Democrats, the Socialist Revolutionaries, and the Polish Socialist Party—issued the "Financial Manifesto." This was a plan for financial war against the tsarist government. The aim was to deprive the government of "its last strength" by refusing taxes, demanding gold for payment of all except minor transactions, and withdrawing in gold all deposits in government banks. Also, no government loans would be paid while the government "was openly at war with its own people."

Minister Durnovo closed eight newspapers that printed the Financial Manifesto. Their editors were prosecuted, the meeting place of the *soviet* was surrounded by troops, and 250 members of the *soviet*'s executive committee were arrested. The members of the executive committee still at liberty called for a general strike to begin December 8.

The Moscow *soviet* endorsed the strike, but could not agree whether or not to endorse the Bolshevik proposal for a simultaneous violent uprising. The *soviet* adopted the Menshevik proposal for the strike to begin on December 7 and to be developed into a violent uprising.

There had already been limited mutinies among soldiers and sailors, and the loyalty of troops still wavered. Their obedience or large-scale mutiny would determine in part the continued life or complete collapse of the regime. About two-thirds of the government troops were considered unreliable at this point.

Government and Bolshevik options

The Moscow Bolsheviks' call for a violent uprising was not an irresponsible independent act of the local group. On November 27, there had been a meeting of the Central Committee of the Russian Social Democratic Labor Party (Social Democrats) in St. Petersburg, attended by Lenin, at which preparations for a violent uprising were discussed.

The loyalty of the government troops still hung in the balance, and the chances of mutiny were high, while those of military victory on the streets of Moscow were very small. Michael Prawdin writes that "the real purpose of the Bolsheviks was to bring it home to the workers that they could not do without military organization and arms."[1] Of course, this could not happen if the general strike remained peaceful and was successful. Additionally, a successful peaceful revolution would most likely block the Bolsheviks from having a serious chance to "seize power," which was necessary in Lenin's view to implement their program. From that perspective, violence by the revolutionaries and its defeat, predictable in part because it was so ill prepared, were therefore necessary. This interpretation is consistent with Lenin's comments on the need for violence, which he had written before the Moscow uprising and with his comments on the uprising written afterwards. In fact, the Bolsheviks' view of the defeat of the Moscow uprising has been described as "beneficial."[2]

Henry W. Nevinson, a special correspondent in Moscow of the London *Daily Chronicle,* on December 6, the day before the general strike began, wrote ". . .the Government was only longing for disturbances as an excuse for military assassination." Two days later, he reported that the revolutionaries ". . . had only eighty rifles as yet, a good many revolvers, certainly, but not enough arms." "But the Government had determined that neither delay nor opportunity should be given." The government needed money, and military success was the perceived route to money. "Their one hope was to stir up an ill-prepared rebellion, to crush it down, and stand triumphant before the nations of Europe, confidently inviting new loans in the name of law and order" to pay the interest on old loans and maintain the value of the ruble. "For this object it was essential that people should be killed in large numbers. . . . The only alternative was national bankruptcy. . . . At all costs the people must be goaded into violence, or the Government's strategy would have failed."[3]

---

[1] Michael Prawdin, *The Unmentionable Nechaev,* p. 148.
[2] On these points, see J. L. H. Keep, *The Rise of Social Democracy in Russia,* pp. 245-246; Louis Fischer, *The Life of Lenin,* p. 236; Henry W. Nevinson, *The Dawn in Russia or Scenes in the Russian Revolution,* pp. 198-199; Adam Ulam, *The Bolsheviks,* p. 236; V. I. Lenin, *Selected Works,* vol. III, *The Revolution of 1905-1907,* pp. 313 and 315; Lenin, "The Boycott of the Bulygin *Duma* and the Insurrection," in Lenin, *Selected Works,* vol. III, p. 327; Lenin, "Lecture on the 1905 Revolution," in Lenin, *Selected Works,* vol. I, p. 795; and Lenin, "Lessons of the Moscow Uprising," in Lenin, *Selected Works,* vol. I, pp. 579-582.
[3] Henry W. Nevinson, *The Dawn in Russia or Scenes in the Russian Revolution,* pp. 123 and 136-138.

The strike began in Moscow on December 7 and in St. Petersburg on December 8. Within 24 hours, Moscow was nearly paralyzed. Almost all trains were halted, municipal services suspended, and schools closed. The St. Petersburg *soviet* was able only to support the strike, not to lead it widely, as its experienced leaders were jailed and it was operating underground. However, within a week almost all cities of the Empire were on strike. It stirred the spirit of rebellion.

At first, the Moscow *soviet* seemed to be master of the city, and the strike was clearly supported by the population, which often filled the streets. The strike leaders hoped that the Moscow garrison would join the strike, and this was exactly what the governor-general feared. The soldiers had recently displayed mutinous sentiments, and only a few days earlier the Second Genadier Rostov Regiment had mutinied. As it happened, the violent uprising ensured that the Moscow garrison did not join the uprising.

In the weeks prior to the Moscow strike, there had been considerable and widely scattered unrest in the military forces, involving a clear change toward unreliability, disobedience, and mutiny, even in the interior of the Empire. There had been several mutinies of both sailors and soldiers. The government was rightly concerned, because in a crisis it would have to rely on its military forces to maintain its control.

'Provoking the working class'

The government had good grounds for wanting the revolution to turn violent in order to defeat it. The Menshevik P. A. Garvi noted its efforts: ". . . [T]he tsarist government was deliberately provoking the working class. . . ."[4] A complicated system of interlocking organizations was established through the Moscow *soviet* to ensure Bolshevik control of the uprising. Yet, there was no reason to believe that a violent uprising in Moscow had a serious chance of success. The militia of the Social Democratic Party in Moscow numbered only about 1,000. They were poorly organized and were armed with fewer than twenty handmade bombs and grenades. The head of the Social Democratic Party militia

---

[4] J. L. H. Keep, *The Rise of Social Democracy in Russia,* p. 250.

himself opposed a violent uprising, and others doubted that the soldiers would support such an insurrection.

Historian J. L. H. Keep reports that workers, party revolutionaries, and even Bolsheviks were all uneasy about the plan. They lacked enthusiasm and even believed that defeat was inevitable. A violent uprising might damage the Government's prestige, Keep continued, but had "no chance of bringing about its overthrow. . ."[5] The Socialist Revolutionary Party leader V. M. Zenzinov later wrote that "in the depth of our hearts we were all convinced of the inevitability of defeat."[6]

The violent insurrection then developed on December 10, and lasted a week. This included partisan warfare tactics, street barricades, and sniper fire against the soldiers patrolling the city. In contrast to the earlier disaffection, disobedience, and mutiny, the troops now obeyed orders. Historian Hugh Seton-Watson wrote, "The army's loyalty was now ensured."[7]

Other cities did not respond to the call from Moscow for them to join in the violent uprising. However, Government authority did collapse in four significant cities, sometimes without opposition and sometimes with assistance from the use of violence.

Once it was clear that the various centers of strikes and violent uprisings were not uniting their resistance, the government initiated a counteroffensive, especially to suppress the violent uprising in Moscow. On December 15, reliable troops were sent to Moscow. Rebels fought on even after it was clear they could not win. Men who surrendered or were captured with weapons were simply shot. The Moscow *soviet* recognized its defeat and set December 19 for the end of the strike.

About 1,000 civilians had been killed, and many thousands were arrested and often sent to Siberia. Despite the defeat in Moscow, the struggle bravely continued in some places outside of Moscow, but not for long. Strikes were formally called off or ended by gradual resumption of work. Arrests spread and radical newspapers were closed. The "freedom days" came to an end.

---

[5] Keep, *The Rise of Social Democracy in Russia,* p. 243.
[6] Keep, *The Rise of Social Democracy in Russia,* p. 250.
[7] Hugh Seton-Watson, *The Decline of Imperial Russia, 1855-1914,* pp. 224-225.

The revolution dies

The defeat of the violent uprising in Moscow had its predictable consequences. Nevinson wrote, "The failure of Moscow fell like a blight upon all Russia, and all hope withered."[8] Even the strongly pro-violence Lenin honestly reported the result: "In October 1905, Russia was at the peak of the revolutionary upsurge. . . the period of decline set in after the defeat of December 1905. . . ." "The turning point in the struggle began with the defeat of the December uprising. Step by step, the counter-revolution passed to the offensive as the mass struggle weakened."[9]

The revolution gradually died out. At most, the spirit of the struggle survived, but without continuing resistance. Yet, certain forms of nonviolent struggle persisted into 1906. The downfall of the tsarist autocracy was, however, postponed until the predominantly nonviolent revolution of February 1917—which, as in 1905, took the political parties espousing revolution by surprise.

---

[8] Nevinson, *The Dawn in Russia or Scenes in the Russian Revolution,* p. 198.
[9] Lenin, "Revolution and Counter-Revolution," pp. 114 and 116.

Sources

Fischer, Louis, *The Life of Lenin*, New York: Harper & Row and London: Collier-Macmillan, 1963.

Harcave, Sidney, *First Blood: The Russian Revolution of 1905*, New York: Macmillan, 1964.

Keep, J. L. H., *The Rise of Social Democracy in Russia*, Oxford: Clarendon Press, 1963.

Lenin, V. I., "What Is To Be Done?," "Lecture on the 1905 Revolution," "Lessons of the Moscow Uprising," in *Selected Works in Three Volumes*, vol. I, New York: International Publishers and Moscow: Progress Publishers, 1967.

———— , "The Boycott of the Bulygin *Duma* and the Insurrection," in *Selected Works*, vol. III, *The Revolution of 1905-1907*, Moscow and Leningrad: Co-operative Publishing Society of Foreign Workers in the U.S.S.R., 1934[?].

———— , "Revolution and Counter-Revolution," in Lenin, *Collected Works*, vol. 13, *June 1907-April 1908*, Moscow: Foreign Languages Publishing House, 1962.

Nevinson, Henry W., *The Dawn in Russia or Scenes in the Russian Revolution*, London and New York: Harper & Bros., 1906.

Prawdin, Michael, *The Unmentionable Nechaev: A Key to Bolshevism*, London: George Allen and Unwin, 1961.

Schwartz, Solomon M., *The Russian Revolution of 1905*, Chicago: University of Chicago Press, 1967, esp. pp. 129-195.

Seton-Watson, Hugh, *The Decline of Imperial Russia, 1855-1914*. London: Methuen & Co., 1952, New York: Frederick A. Praeger, 1952.

Ulam, Adam, *The Bolsheviks*, New York: Macmillan and London: Collier-Macmillan, 1965.

Yarmolinsky, Avrahm, *Road to Revolution*, New York: Macmillan, 1959 and London: Cassell, 1957.

Chapter Six

DEFENSE AGAINST A MILITARY COUP, GERMANY—1920

Post-war conflicts in Germany

At the end of the First World War, Germany was beset by intense domestic unrest. Leftist workers went on strike at munitions factories. Battleship crews, knowing the war was lost, mutinied and refused to put to sea. In November 1918, the Crown Prince and the Kaiser were presented with an ultimatum: abdicate, or face the wrath of a general strike. Kaiser Wilhelm II fled to Holland, thus averting the strike, and the Weimar Republic was established.

Internal strife continued, constituting virtual civil war. In January 1919, revolutionary outbreaks spread throughout the country. Workers not satisfied with the limited gains for the working class promised by the interim government proclaimed a general strike in Berlin. In other parts of the country, they created

---

A list of sources for this case appears at the end of this chapter.

workers' and soldiers' councils (räte), and from Munich declared the establishment of a workers' Bavarian Republic.

The revolution was brutally put down by private mercenary armies known as Freikorps, created by officers of the old German Army and ordered by the government into service against the workers. In Berlin, the strike was crushed within ten days. Two months later, Berlin was paralyzed by yet another general strike, with this one intended to force the government to act more rapidly on promised social reforms. Once again, the workers' campaign was brutally suppressed by the Freikorps. Reprisals began soon afterward, and it is estimated that as many as 1,500 workers were rounded up and executed in the following weeks.

By the summer of 1919, the internal situation of the Weimar Republic had stabilized and the Treaty of Versailles was signed, officially ending the war. The treaty itself, however, soon led to new domestic problems, with threats against the government now coming from the extreme right. Issues surrounding the extradition of accused German war criminals raised a nationalist outcry throughout the country. The wrath of the army was aroused by a looming deadline for the demobilization of approximately 300,000 soldiers and the incorporation of the remainder into a new, much smaller Reichswehr.

The situation was further complicated in December, when a number of Freikorps units were ordered by the Allies to withdraw from Latvia, where they had been stationed in order to fight the Soviet advance in the Baltics. After holding off the Red Army in Riga, they had intended to stay and create a new landed (German) aristocracy to rule over the Latvians. When they were then forced to return to Germany, with their dreams of conquest and plunder vanquished, they expressed extreme hostility toward the government of the Republic.

Plans for a coup d'état

Right-wing and monarchist elements supported by the Freikorps had been planning a military coup d'état since July 1919. Several important generals were included in the plot, including old-guard General Walther von Lüttwitz, who had played an important role in the suppression of earlier strikes and revolutionary revolts. Other key figures included Captain Waldemar Pabst,

Colonel Max Bauer, and only one important civilian, ultra-nationalist Dr. Wolfgang Kapp. Kapp was a rather obscure provincial bureaucrat and a founder of the defunct Fatherland Party. He was slated to become the new Chancellor once the putsch was successful.

The revolt was scheduled for April 1920. But in late February, the Allied Commission of Control ordered the immediate demobilization of two Freikorps units, one of which was under the command of Captain Ehrhardt, a loyalist of General von Lüttwitz. Lüttwitz knew that if Ehrhardt's brigade was dissolved, he would lose one of the key groups he was counting on for the putsch to be successful. So when the Freikorps were moved to Döberitz, just outside Berlin, prior to their dismissal, Lüttwitz arrived to assure them he would not permit their demobilization.

Shortly thereafter, Lüttwitz approached representatives of the ultra-right Nationalist Party and the People's Party in order to gauge their support for a coup. Although both parties sympathized with the goals of the rebellious officers, they insisted that such a move was likely to fail, and that it would jeopardize their own efforts to force the National Assembly to dissolve itself, call new elections, and elect a new Reichstag and a president—moves they felt were sure to result in a nationalist victory. On March 9, the two parties introduced a motion in the Assembly to do just that, but it failed overwhelmingly. Lüttwitz then met with the parties' leaders again, in a final attempt to convince them to back the coup. Once again, they claimed the time simply was not right, and refused to offer support to the conspirators.

Meanwhile, Defense Minister Gustav Noske began to suspect the brewing plot. Noske, a right-wing Social Democrat, was considered a staunch ally of most of the officers involved. He had been personally responsible for drawing the Freikorps into government service the year before in order to fight striking workers and left-wing rebellions. At one time, his name had even been suggested by the putschists as a future chancellor. But Noske did not believe in the wisdom of a coup, and on March 9 he ordered the withdrawal of Ehrhardt's brigade from Lüttwitz's overall command.

On March 10, General von Lüttwitz met with Noske and President Friedrich Ebert. Lüttwitz presented the government representatives with an ultimatum that included all the demands made by the Nationalists and the People's Party that had been voted down in the Assembly. He also made a number of military demands, including a cessation of dismissals from the army and the reinstatement of Ehrhardt's brigade under Lüttwitz's command.

Ebert and Noske interpreted these demands as a threat, and informed the General that he either must obey orders or resign. Lüttwitz did neither, and on the following day Noske relieved him of his command. Arrest warrants were simultaneously issued for other coup plotters, including Dr. Kapp, Colonel Bauer, and Captain Pabst, but all were forewarned by the police and escaped arrest.

No military defense

On the night of March 12, the Ehrhardt brigade began its march toward Berlin. Preparations were sloppy. Dr. Kapp was not even informed that the putsch had begun. Ehrhardt sent a messenger to Noske and Ebert with a new ultimatum, basically echoing the demands presented earlier by Lüttwitz. The ultimatum was rejected out of hand by Noske.

Noske then called an emergency meeting of the cabinet and loyal military leaders. He informed them that Ehrhardt would reach Berlin in the morning, and suggested that the generals immediately prepare for the military defense of Berlin. The generals, however, were disturbed by such a suggestion. Only two concurred with the desire to use troops to defend the government. The rest agreed with General Hans von Seeckt, who quietly stated, "Reichswehr does not fire on Reichswehr."

For the generals, nothing was more important than the unity of the Army. Thus, while most did not side with the putschists, neither did they choose to defend the government. They simply declared neutrality and took a short vacation. The police forces, meanwhile, had for the most part already joined the Kappists. Berlin was left without a military option for its defense.

In the early morning of March 13, the Ebert cabinet abandoned Berlin without a fight, fleeing first to Dresden and then to Stuttgart. Less than an hour after their departure, Ehrhardt's troops arrived at the Brandenburg Gate. Wolfgang Kapp proclaimed himself Chancellor of the Reich, and General von Lüttwitz assumed command of the Ministry of Defense. A proclamation was issued announcing the formation of "a new government of order, liberty, and action." As the day went on, Ehrhardt's troops were joined by thousands of other Freikorps soldiers-of-fortune, as well as by hundreds of troops previously scheduled for demobilization.

Beginnings of noncooperation

At the Chancellery, it soon became clear that the putschists had no idea how to govern and had made frighteningly few preparations for such an eventuality. Their new constitution was only half-finished. No typewriters could be found on which to compose new proclamations and decrees because the typists had locked them away. Most importantly, it had not occurred to anyone that a government needed finances to carry out its activities (and, in the case of a coup, to pay its soldiers). When Kapp eventually drafted a request to the Reichsbank for ten million marks, the request was turned down. The officers of the bank insisted they could only honor requests signed by an "authorized official," and all the undersecretaries who remained in the ministries had refused to sign. Captain Ehrhardt then refused Kapp's suggestion that he take his soldiers to rob the Reichsbank at gunpoint, and the putschists were left without finances.

On the afternoon of March 13, the first day of the coup, many workers went out on strike against the new regime. They were promptly supported in their actions by a proclamation issued by the Social Democratic Party, which closed with the words:

> Workers, comrades! . . . Use every means to prevent this return of bloody reaction. Strike, stop working, strangle this military dictatorship, fight with every weapon for the preservation of the Republic, forget all dissension! There is only one way to block the return of Wilhelm II: to cripple the country's economic life! Not a hand must move, not a single worker must help the military dictatorship. General strike all along the line! Workers, unite![1]

By Sunday, March 14, the general strike was in full swing. For the first time, it united the centrist parties with the leftist

---

[1] Halperin, *Germany Tried Democracy*, p. 178 and Crook, *The General Strike*, p. 513.

Independent Socialists and, eventually, with the Communists as well. Civil servants struck or otherwise refused to head ministries under Kapp, who was unable to obtain cooperation from the bureaucracy. The right-wing Nationalist Party and the People's Party, meanwhile, did nothing to help the putschists.

Defiant resistance

The strike spread around the country. In Berlin, everything stopped. Hotels and restaurants were closed. Industry shut down. Lights were shut off and power stations abandoned. Trams and buses ceased to run. Newspapers did not appear. On March 15, Kapp grew desperate and issued a decree stating that all strike pickets were to be executed on the spot. However, when a specific order to that effect was given to troops later in the day by General von der Goltz, it was countermanded by General von Lüttwitz, to the dismay of many in the Freikorps who felt that the situation could be resolved in the same violent fashion as during previous strikes.

Kapp then began to seek negotiations with the legal government in Stuttgart, which, sensing Kapp's weakness, rejected all proposals for compromise. A number of important Reichswehr generals announced or resumed their loyalty to the Ebert government. Nationalist Party and People's Party leaders also began to pressure Kapp to give up the fight, primarily out of concerns for where the strike was heading. In many areas of Berlin without a heavy troop presence, workers not only went on strike but were also busy creating revolutionary councils (räte). On the night of March 15, reports came in to Berlin of heavy fighting in Frankfurt, and of a complete paralysis of the industrial Ruhr region. Conservative opinion even within the army was rapidly turning against the coup, not in defense of the old government, but rather to prevent revolution.

On March 16, Vice-Chancellor Schiffer of the constitutional government met in Berlin with leaders of the various political parties represented in the coalition government. They hastily promised to approve the demands of the far right that had been rejected in the Assembly: a date for new elections would be set, a popular election of the president would be guaranteed, and the cabinet would soon be reorganized. That evening, a unit of guards engineers mutinied in Berlin, arrested their officers, and declared their support for the constitutional government. On the following day, the security police, previously neutral, demanded Kapp's resignation.

Collapse of the coup

On March 17, one hundred hours after the coup had begun, Kapp responded to Schiffer's move by announcing that since the Ebert government had "resolved to fulfill the basic political demands whose rejection led on March 13 to the establishment of the Kapp government, Chancellor Kapp regards his mission as accomplished and is resigning."[2] Kapp handed full executive authority to Lüttwitz, who was still not prepared to give up. However, the legitimate government, then based in Stuttgart, refused to have anything to do with Lüttwitz. In the afternoon, top army commanders met to discuss the situation, and decided that the coup was a failure and must end immediately. Lüttwitz was asked to present his resignation, and at six o'clock in the evening he fled into exile behind Kapp. The constitutional government declared victory, and by the end of the week the last Freikorps troops had departed from Berlin, though not before turning their machine guns on civilians who jeered them as the troops marched out of the city.

The general strike continued for several more days, however, even after the return of the Ebert government, in the hope of winning new concessions for organized labor and the working classes. Such concessions were promised but were never fulfilled. The strike was officially lifted on March 22, 1920, the same day that President Ebert finally accepted the resignation of Noske. The replacement as Minister of Defense was Otto Gessler, who quickly came under the influence of the military, which had become the strongest power in the State.

Despite action by the trade unions and the Independent Socialists to terminate the strike, the Communists pressed for continuation of the general strike. The workers in Berlin returned to their jobs on March 23, despite the strong opposition of the Communists.

---

[2] Halperin, *Germany Tried Democracy,* p. 181.

In the industrial Ruhr, certain left-wing groups aiming for so-cial revolution formed a Red army. They gained control of several cities, and waged several bloody conflicts with the German army until quelled in early April, often with extreme brutalities.

Many factors contributed to the success of the strike in defeat-ing the Kapp putsch. The call to strike was heeded not only by the workers, but also by the government bureaucracy and the middle class. Hundreds of people had lost their lives during the putsch.

The important German historian Erich Eych wrote:

> The putsch was defeated by two principal forms of resistance: the general strike of the workers and the refusal of the higher civil servants to collaborate with their rebel masters.[3]

Furthermore, the strike had the support of nearly all political parties and tendencies, from the extreme left to the extreme right. The fact that important elements of the military forces refused to collaborate with Kapp, even while doing nothing actively against him, was also crucial.

An authority on the coup d'état, Lieutenant Colonel D. J. Goodspeed, has pointed out that in order for a coup to succeed, the conspirators must not only seize the machinery of govern-ment, but also "obtain the required minimum of consent for their own administration."[4] In the case of the 1920 coup, the unyield-ing general strike of the populace—strengthened by the noncoop-eration of the bureaucracy and the refusal of important military elements to participate in the putsch—did not allow the Kappists to obtain such consent. The coup collapsed in only four days and the Republic was preserved.

---

[3] Eych, *A History of the Weimar Republic,* vol. I, p. 151.
[4] See Goodspeed, *The Conspirators,* pp. 211-213.

Sources

Crook, Wilfred Harris, *The General Strike: A Study of Labor's Tragic Weapon in Theory and Practice* (Chapel Hill: University of North Carolina Press, 1931), pp. 496-527.

Eyck, Erich, *A History of the Weimar Republic* (Cambridge, Massachusetts: Harvard University Press, 1962), vol. I, pp. 129-160.

Goodspeed, D. J., *The Conspirators: A Study of the Coup d'Etat* (New York: The Viking Press, 1961), pp. 108-143 and 211-213.

Halperin, S. William, *Germany Tried Democracy: A Political History of the Reich from 1918 to 1933* (New York: Thomas Y. Crowell Co., 1946), pp. 168-188.

Wheeler-Bennett, John W., *The Nemesis of Power: The German Army in Politics 1918-1945* (New York: St. Martin's Press, 1954), pp. 60-82.

Chapter Seven

INDIAN INDEPENDENCE
CAMPAIGN—1930-1931

India struggles for independence

At the December 1928 meeting in Calcutta of the Indian National Congress, the largest nationalist political party, some of the younger pro-independence leaders, including Subas Chandra Bose and Jawaharlal Nehru, wanted the Congress to declare independence from the British Empire to be followed by a violent war of liberation. Mohandas Gandhi favored a two-year warning to the British before a declaration of independence and a nonviolent campaign to achieve it. Gandhi knew India was not yet ready to conduct an effective campaign. Under pressure, Gandhi agreed to a one-year warning that would expire December 31, 1929. He declared, "England will never make any real advance so as to satisfy India's aspirations till she is forced to it."[1]

A list of sources for this case appears at the end of this chapter.
[1] Sharp, *Gandhi Wields the Weapon of Moral Power*, p. 41.

The year 1929 witnessed increased British harassment of independence-minded Indians with raids on offices, house searches, suppression of publications, arrests, long prison sentences, and banning of books. Gandhi encouraged "constructive program" work of social and economic self-help activities to strengthen Indian society. The Congress strengthened its organization, and its members pressed for action and Gandhi's leadership. The Viceroy, Lord Irwin, in late October 1929 spoke of the possibility of a Round Table Conference and the possibility of Dominion Status for India, home rule under the Empire. A conciliatory response by senior Indian leaders, both some members of Congress and some Liberals, brought protests from others in India, including the younger Jawaharlal Nehru, then-President of the Indian National Congress.

On the morning of December 23, Lord Irwin's train was bombed outside New Delhi station. The Congress denounced the bombing.[2]

Generating power to end the Empire

That afternoon, in a meeting at the Viceroy's house with five Indian National Congress leaders, including Gandhi, the Viceroy refused to give assurances that a Round Table Conference would draft a constitution giving India full Dominion status. At the Indian National Congress meeting on December 31 in Lahore, Gandhi introduced a motion declaring complete independence to be the goal of the Congress. Despite opposition, resolutions in favor of independence and endorsing a campaign of civil disobedience were passed on December 31, 1929 with Gandhi's support. The resolution endorsing nonviolent struggle called for a campaign of boycott of elections, resignations of Congress members from legislatures and government committees, constructive program work, and a program of civil disobedience including tax refusal. Authority to plan such a campaign was given to the All-India Congress Committee, which in effect meant Gandhi would be the planner of the campaign.

In late January 1930, Gandhi wrote, "The British people must realize that the Empire is to come to an end. This they will not

---

[2] Gopal, *The Viceroyalty of Lord Irwin 1926-1931*, pp. 52-53.

realize unless we in India have generated power within to enforce our will. . . ."[3] Gandhi reasoned that there was no way to persuade advocates of violence for independence to desist without implementation of a program of nonviolent struggle.

On January 26, massive public meetings throughout India passed a resolution on complete independence, which was drafted by Gandhi and passed by the Working Committee of the Indian National Congress. The resolution denounced British rule but rejected violence as a means to achieve independence. Instead, the Congress adopted noncooperation and civil disobedience as means to gain freedom. Arrests and imprisonments by the British continued.

Gandhi sought to identify specific issues symbolizing British oppression against which Indian noncooperation and civil disobedience could be focused. Gandhi identified the British monopoly and tax on salt as an example of British oppression, a tax that even the then-British Prime Minister Ramsay MacDonald had earlier criticized.

At Gandhi's request, the All-India Congress Committee agreed that civil disobedience should be conducted and controlled by those who believed in principled nonviolence. A program of resistance by various population groups was developed, pledging noncooperation and disobedience. New persons were to be selected to replace resisters when they were arrested.

Gandhi sought to make "independence" concrete by identifying eleven specific demands, including abolition of the salt tax and release of political prisoners.

Showing India her power

On March 2, Gandhi wrote a letter to Lord Irwin, the Viceroy, appealing for concessions that might make civil disobedience unnecessary. The letter recounted Indian grievances and stated that "India must consequently evolve force enough to free herself from that embrace of death." Consequently, Gandhi continued, he would lead a campaign of civil disobedience. When the Viceroy's

---

[3] Sharp, *Gandhi Wields the Weapon of Moral Power,* p. 52.

secretary sent a perfunctory reply, Gandhi wrote, The "English Nation responds only to force. . . ."[4]

Rules for the conduct of civil disobedience were distributed and endorsements sought. The rules covered behavior for individuals, prisoners, and groups, and included guidelines for dealing with communal conflicts. The objective of nonviolent struggle was to show India the power latent within the nation.

On March 12, Gandhi began a 26-day march from his ashram—a residential center for discipline and social service—near Ahmedabad. The destination was the beach at Dandi where he intended to pick up salt from the seashore, thereby disobeying the British Salt Law. "Ours is a nonviolent battle," Gandhi said. Thousands lined the path and many joined the march. The British prohibited nationalist speeches for one month from March 7. Indian officials working for the British government were urged to resign. Gandhi taunted the British for being afraid to arrest him.

During the more than 200-mile march, elsewhere in India many acts of preparations, protest and defiance occurred. These included demonstrations by school boys. The national flag was hoisted. The mayor of Calcutta was arrested for making a seditious speech in Rangoon. A war council of nonviolent leaders was organized in Poona. Provincial committees were organized to lead civil disobedience. A short pledge of nonviolent discipline was recommended by Jawaharlal Nehru (who only recently had favored violence). Indian nationalist legislators resigned their positions. Plans were laid for mass civil disobedience to the Salt Law on April 6, when Gandhi would initiate the defiance.

Gandhi reached the isolated beach at Dandi on the Gulf of Cambay on April 5. The morning of April 6, Gandhi left the bungalow to meet 4,000 followers who had arrived, and spent an hour in silent prayer and nationalist songs. After a brief swim in the sea, he scooped up salt and saltwater in his hands and 82 volunteers with spades dug salt from nearby deposits and carried them off in bags. The Salt Act was broken.

---

[4] Sharp, *Gandhi Wields the Weapon of Moral Power*, p. 67.

Widespread defiance

A nonviolent struggle broke out all over India. All along the seacoast, villagers dug salt illegally. Mass meetings were held. Very large parades took place. Students in government schools withdrew. Liquor shops were picketed. "Illegal" salt was sold openly in the streets. Social boycotts were launched against Indians working for the British. In response, Indians making salt illegally were beaten. Prominent Indian National Congress leaders were arrested. Mass arrests occurred and replacement leaders stepped into position. In some areas, the defiance was so widespread that it appeared as though the salt law did not exist.

In certain places, the police seemed to be provoking violence by committing brutalities, but nonviolent discipline was generally maintained. Massive parades were held in many cities. Sellers of foreign cloth and liquor were picketed. Many businessmen supported the struggle. In some areas, people refused to pay the land tax.

In the city of Peshawar in the North-West Frontier Province, well-known as a violent region, prominent Muslim leaders of the nonviolent struggle were arrested. English soldiers fired into crowds of demonstrators. The Muslim "Frontier Gandhi," Khan Abdul Ghaffar Khan, and his co-workers were arrested. Martial law was declared. After two platoons of the Royal Garhwal Rifles refused orders to enter Peshawar to help maintain British control, the British Chief Commissioner ordered all troops withdrawn on the night of April 24. The British therefore had only limited control of the city until troops supported by aircraft re-entered the city at dawn on May 4.[5] Meanwhile, censorship was tightened throughout India.

Gandhi wrote a second letter to the Viceroy informing him of his intent to march to a government salt depot at Dharasana and to demand possession of it. It was the fifth week of the struggle. The night of May 4-5, 30 Indian policemen under British command arrested Gandhi. When this news became known, there were spontaneous demonstrations of sympathy, with mass meetings, short strikes (*hartals*), international protests, and massive parades.

---

[5] Gopal, *The Viceroyalty of Lord Irwin 1926-1931,* p. 69.

Police responded by killing 27 people, and in some places banned meetings of more than five participants. Speakers were arrested for sedition, strict censorship was imposed, newspapers were suppressed, and Congress organizations were declared unlawful.

The raid on the salt depot at Dharasana was pursued by new leaders and volunteers. Disciplined resisters, at one point as many as 2,500, led by the prominent poetess Sarojini Naidu, marched forward to demand the salt and were brutally beaten on their heads by heavy steel-shod bamboo rods (*lathis*) day after day. At times, the volunteers marched in groups of 25 and sat waiting to be beaten. Many were taken to an improvised hospital camp. Some of the Indian police seemed at times reluctant to strike.

Violence broke out in eight cities. The worst case was in Solapur, where after provocations a crowd threw stones and killed one soldier.

More boycotts and civil disobedience

The boycott movement continued. In some areas, autonomous village courts were organized, separate from the British courts. Some arrested resisters refused to pay fines. Salt raids were also conducted at Sankiatta salt stores in Karantak by between 10,000 and 15,000 people. Thousands of mounds of salt were taken away, and at the Shiroda salt depot in Maharashtra two groups of 75 volunteers raided the salt depot and 90 were arrested. Near Bombay and elsewhere, similar raids resulted in hundreds of arrests and massive amounts of salt seized.

On June 3, a mile-long procession of Muslims paraded through Bombay to demonstrate their sympathy with the civil disobedience movement. After the parade, the crowd passed a resolution to support the campaign and to boycott British cloth. Prohibited literature was read publicly in defiance of new restrictions. Sikhs and Hindu women, dressed in orange robes of sacrifice while facing mounted police in Bombay, were among the bravest nonviolent volunteers in the conflict. Many men were beaten to the ground by the mounted police.

On June 27, the All-India Working Committee urged the population to expand the resistance campaign, and added other British goods to the continuing foreign cloth boycott. The Working

Committee also launched a social boycott against persons responsible for atrocities, called on students to leave schools, recommended conversion of money into gold, and urged all Congress organizations to continue to function. They also recognized the increased role of women in the campaign.

One young man in Bombay was killed when he lay down to halt a truck carrying foreign cloth. A few days later, a procession of about 30,000 men, women, and children sat down on the street after being stopped by police. Other people provided the protesters with food, water, and blankets, some of which were passed to the blockading police. Despite hours in the rain, the people remained sitting until the police gave in and the procession concluded with a triumphal midnight march.

Mass action: "dangerously subversive"

On July 9, Viceroy Lord Irwin made an important speech to both houses of the legislature in New Delhi. He denounced the nonviolent rebellion:

> In my judgment and in that of my Government it is a deliberate attempt to coerce established authority by mass action, and for this reason, as also because of its natural and inevitable developments, it must be regarded as unconstitutional and dangerously subversive. Mass action, even if it is intended by its promoters to be non-violent, is nothing but the application of force under another form, and, when it has as its avowed object the making of Government impossible, a Government is bound either to resist or abdicate. . . . So long as the Civil Disobedience Movement persists, we must fight it with all our strength.[6]

Limited steps toward negotiations took place in June and July. Gandhi stated that no constitutional scheme was acceptable that did not contain a clause for the right of secession from the Empire and another clause that would give India the right and power to act on the 11 points he had presented as demands at the beginning of the campaign.

Leading Congressman Rajendra Prasad, later President of India, declared that in face of repression every home must be a Congress office, and every soul a Congress organization.

---

[6] Gopal, *The Viceroyalty of Lord Irwin 1926-1931,* p. 168.

The Working Committee of the Congress met in Bombay from July 30-August 1, under Acting President Vallabhbhai Patel. The Committee congratulated the people on their progress and restraint and reminded them of the need to maintain strict nonviolent discipline. The Working Committee directed all Congress organizations to take steps to carry out a 14-point program of boycott, disobedience, alternative institutions, economic resistance, and support of Indian products.

Special days were observed, sometimes once every month, for such purposes as honoring Gandhi and political prisoners and hoisting the national flag. Prisons were full and new detention camps were established. People saluted the Indian national flag and it appeared over public buildings. Prisoners defied regulations and others disobeyed restraining orders. Attempts were made to reoccupy Congress offices that had been closed. New leaders sprang up to replace imprisoned ones. Prison conditions were often terrible and beatings and torture occurred. The British seized property—land, houses, moveable property—totally out of proportion to the amount of taxes that had been refused.

Nationalist meetings, mutiny, and repression

On August 14, imprisoned members of the Working Committee were taken to meet with Gandhi, while he was still imprisoned. The government hoped that a settlement might be reached. However, despite an exchange of letters with the Viceroy, it was clear by the end of August that the negotiations had failed.

Two committees investigating police excesses in Gujarat were arrested. Photographs of national leaders were widely sold and displayed. In October, Jawaharlal Nehru was released from prison and rearrested a week later, then sentenced to two more years. New repressive decrees banned protests by closings of shops, singing national songs, raising the national flag, or urging boycotts of foreign cloth or liquor, with punishments of six months imprisonment.

The Secretary of State for India reported to the British House of Commons that 18 percent of the British decline in world trade was directly due to the Indian boycott.

The Indians organized a boycott of the coming British census. The sale of illegal salt continued. Several people, usually political prisoners, engaged in long hunger strikes. No-tax movements spread.

The Garhwali soldiers who had refused to enter Peshawar were court-martialed, and then sentenced to 10- to 14-year prison terms.

Houses of persons who had left an area because of harsh repression were broken into and their goods seized by persons opposed to the resistance struggle. Sometimes, the houses were burned.

In the face of extreme repression in British-controlled Gujarat, 80,000 people moved across the border into the Indian state of Baroda, which the British did not control. Repression continued elsewhere with beatings, declarations that certain groups were unlawful, and arrests.

In England, the important *Manchester Guardian* newspaper reported on January 12, 1931, that beatings and shootings helped to discredit the British Government during a crucial time.

Prisoners released

Members of the Working Committee of the Indian National Congress who were not in prison met. On January 25, Lord Irwin declared the Working Committee now legal, and Gandhi and all imprisoned members and their wives were unconditionally released on Independence Day, January 26. On January 31, the Working Committee resolved that civil disobedience should continue until further instructions, and picketing and boycotts should continue indefinitely. The illegal making and selling of salt also was to continue. On February 6, private instructions were given that the movement should continue but no new campaigns were to be organized or new situations developed.

Several provinces experienced serious declines in revenues. Marches and repression continued. More Congress organizations were declared illegal.

The negotiated settlement

Following a short letter from Gandhi to the Viceroy requesting an interview, the two met on February 17. Winston Churchill was revolted at the "nauseating and humiliating spectacle" of Gandhi negotiating "on equal terms with the representative of the King-Emperor."[7] The Indian movement had proved that when India refused to cooperate, Britain could not continue to rule India as she had done. Talks continued for three days.

Negotiations resumed on February 27. After consultations and debates within the Working Committee and changes in the government draft, the Gandhi-Irwin Pact, also called the Delhi Settlement, was signed. The text was published on March 5 in the official *Gazette of India Extraordinary*. It was to be regarded as a temporary truce. Political independence was still for the future.

Between March 12, 1930 and March 5, 1931, 100,000 Indians had been placed in prisons, detention camps, and improvised jails. At least 17,000 of these detainees were women.

Although concessions were made to the nationalists, the actual terms favored the government more than the nationalists. The Congress was to participate in future talks about India's status. Civil disobedience was to be cancelled. The boycott of British goods was to halt. Unobstructive picketing could continue. Enquiries into police conduct would not be pressed. Some repressive measures would be lifted. Government prosecutions of police or soldiers for disobedience of orders would not be withdrawn, nor would those who had already been convicted receive amnesty. Some fines and seized properties would be returned. Some resigned officials could be reinstated. No substantial changes in the Salt Acts would be made, but the making and selling of salt locally would be permitted. If Congress failed to live up to the agreement, the government would take such action as it deemed to be necessary.

The terms were far from a clear victory for the Indian National Congress, and later critics have argued that Gandhi failed to press for concessions proportionate to the demonstrated Indian power. In Gandhi's view, it was more important, however, that the strength generated in the Indians by the struggle meant that independence could not long be denied. He also thought that by having to participate in direct negotiations with the nonviolent rebels, the British government had recognized India as an equal with whose representatives it had to negotiate.

---

[7] Gopal, *The Viceroyalty of Lord Irwin 1926-1931,* p. 206.

Jawaharlal Nehru, who was later to become Prime Minister of independent India, was no believer in an ethic of nonviolence, nor in Gandhi's philosophy or frequent religious explanations. However, like many other Indians, he became a supporter of Gandhi's nonviolent "grand strategy" for obtaining a British withdrawal from India. He spent years in prison in that struggle. Nehru wrote in his autobiography:

> We had accepted that method, the Congress had made that method its own, because of a belief in its effectiveness. Gandhiji had placed it before the country not only as the right method but as the most effective one for our purpose. In spite of its negative name it was a dynamic method, the very opposite of a meek submission to a tyrant's will. It was not a coward's refuge from action, but a brave man's defiance of evil and national subjection.[8]

The struggle for independence for India was not yet over in 1931. However, in the difficult years ahead it was clear to everyone that the future of India would be determined in the end by the will of the Indians. Independence for India and Pakistan finally came on August 15, 1947.

---

[8] Jawaharlal Nehru, *Toward Freedom* (Boston: Beacon Press, 1961), p. 80.

Sources

Gopal, S., *The Viceroyalty of Lord Irwin 1926-1931* (London: Oxford University Press, 1957), pp. 54-122.

Sharp, Gene, *Gandhi Wields the Weapon of Moral Power,* Ahmedabad: Navajivan, 1957.

Chapter Eight

THE MUSLIM PASHTUN MOVEMENT OF THE NORTH-WEST FRONTIER OF INDIA—1930-1934

Dr. Mohammad Raqib

The land of the Pashtuns

After a violent and tumultuous history, the Pashtuns[1] of the North-West Frontier Province of British India adopted nonviolent struggle to resist oppression and win freedom for their homeland during India's struggle for independence. The Pashtuns, who live predominantly in Afghanistan and on the North-West Frontier area of the Indo-Pakistani subcontinent, are Muslim, and have been often characterized as a brutal, backward, and tribal people.

A list of sources for this case appears at the end of this chapter.
[1] Also called the *Pushtuns* or *Pathans*.

113

In 1848, when this area[2] was taken over by the British, they divided it into two parts: the settled districts, which were under strict government control, and the tribal area, where the people lived their traditional lives with less outside interference, under the tribal *Jirga* (council). Later, the danger of Russia's approach to India and internal unrest in the Frontier concerned the British, and in 1893 they established the Durand Line[3] to separate their Empire from Russian influence. The settled districts were under the administrative authority of the Governor of Punjab, while the tribal areas were semi-independent.

British administration and repression

In 1902, the British Viceroy Lord Curzon brought the settled districts and tribal areas into one administrative unit and called it the North-West Frontier Province in an attempt to counter the internal and external challenges in the Frontier. A series of measures was taken to suppress and counter anti-government actions taking place there. The Frontier Crimes Regulation, a set of laws widely seen as repressive and unfair, was adopted to fight anti-government activities in the settled districts. The police were given the authority to destroy buildings that were used by anti-British elements. Authority to inflict collective punishment was also given to police to punish families, villages, or even whole communities for the acts of one person. In addition, the Tranquility Act was enacted in order to strictly control the people's right to assemble. The British undertook major expenses to build roads and railways to increase and assure the mobility of its strong military forces in order to control the Frontier.

Oppressive measures were taken by the government to counter the introduction of unwelcome political ideas and to bestow favors on particular religious leaders and others who were helping to improve the British image among the people. The expense of a large scale police and army force in the Frontier was an unbearable burden on the settled districts, since the tribal areas did not pay taxes. As most of the Province's budget was centered on fi-

---

[2] The Pashtuns themselves refer to the region as *Pashtunistan,* or *The Land of the Pashtuns.*
[3] The border between Afghanistan and British India.

nancing the huge military, police, and other projects, social assistance, education, and sanitation did not receive enough attention. Only 25 out of 1,000 men were literate in 1911 and a far lower percentage of women.

This served the interests of the colonial authorities, and they intentionally paralyzed political growth in the province. Political, social, and economic reforms that the British applied in other provinces of India were denied to the Frontier.

Ghaffar Khan's early work

Khan Abdul Ghaffar Khan, the son of a well-respected landowner in a village near Peshawar, started his mission as a reformer in 1912. He opened schools throughout the districts of Mardan and Peshawar, seeking to educate the villagers and prepare them to understand the reforms that he intended to introduce. Soon this education movement spread to all parts of the Frontier. The British authorities resented these activities and warned Ghaffar Khan to cease his work, even pressuring his family to stop him. In 1919, when he ignored the warning, the government arrested him, his 95-year-old father—who was released after three months—and other members of his family. After serving a six-month sentence, Ghaffar Khan was released later that same year and received a warm welcome from his people.

Upon his release, Ghaffar Khan joined the *Khalifat* movement, which began as a Muslim protest against British conduct in Turkey after the First World War, but later became a popular anti-British resistance struggle with Hindu participation.[4]

Ghaffar Khan soon returned to the Frontier to carry on with his work. Upon his return, he founded the organization *Anjuman-Islah-e-Afaghina* (Afghan Reform Society) to increase education and reform in the Province. The organization developed rapidly, and soon established branches throughout the Frontier. Ghaffar Khan himself frequently traveled on foot to villages in the Province, educating the rural population. His reforms touched on various social problems in the Province. He appealed to his peo-

---

[4] Mukulika Banerjee, *The Pathan Unarmed*, p. 49. In 1920, Abdul Ghaffar Khan participated in the *Khalifat Flight* to Afghanistan, where he met Afghan King Amanullah Khan.

ple to become involved in other kinds of work besides farming. To set an example, Ghaffar Khan opened a commission shop in his home village. He took these actions to convince the Pashtuns to live peaceful, productive lives, free from dependence on the British occupiers.

Imprisonment and persistence

The government, however, did not approve of Ghaffar Khan's work and the Chief Commissioner of the North-West Frontier Province (NWFP), Sir John Maffy, warned him to cease his activities or be responsible for the outcome. Ghaffar Khan ignored the warning and continued with his mission even more rigorously. By 1921, before being arrested once again and sentenced to a three-year term in one of the most notorious prisons in India, he had toured every village in the Province and completed his goal of spreading his ideas to the villages surrounding Peshawar.

In 1924, when Ghaffar Khan was released from jail, a huge gathering was summoned in his home village. Prominent workers and thousands of people from all districts of the province participated in the assembly and resolved to start a strong popular movement. During this meeting, in appreciation for his sacrifices, the people gave him the title of *Fakhr-i-Afghan* (Pride of the Afghans).

A new strategy of struggle

After attending the Grand Conference in Mecca in 1926,[5] Ghaffar Khan changed the strategy of his activities. With the sup-

---

[5] The conference was organized by the King of Saudi Arabia, Sultan Ibn-Saud, during the *Hajj* to discuss problems facing the Muslim nations. On this occasion he spoke to the delegations of many nations, whose views greatly increased his understanding of the dilemma of colonized nations.

After performing *Hajj*, Ghaffar Khan visited other parts of the Middle East, including Iraq, Lebanon, Egypt, Syria, and Palestine. During meetings with the subjects of these nations, he found that it was the vast resources of India that enabled the British to keep these nations under control. He concluded that independence of India from the British would also free other nations from the grip of this colonial power. Indian soldiers not only fought for the British in the First World War and the Second World War, but they also fought many wars in the Middle East, the Far East, Africa, and China. He stated: "Therefore, at the same time we are slaves ourselves, we are the means of enslaving others as well, from this point we should develop our strategy of non-cooperation with our alien ruler, to free ourselves from its oppression and also

port of his contemporaries, he founded the *Pashtun Jirga* (Pashtun Council). This body had a program centered on education, social, and political matters. Most of the members of the new organization were educated in schools run by Ghaffar Khan and others who were his longtime associates. The *Pashtun Jirga* also began publishing a journal called *Pashtun.* The new organization quickly gained momentum and, in 1929, a new contingent of volunteer members was added. This body was called the *Khudai Khidmatgar* (Servants of God). This group was designed to be the most efficient and orderly force among the Pashtuns. It later developed into a disciplined nonviolent army to fight for the independence of India from the British.

A pledge of service

Before getting accepted into the *Khudai Khidmatgars,* the new recruits had to take the following pledge:

"In the presence of God I solemnly affirm that:

1. I hereby honestly and sincerely offer myself for enrollment as a *Khudai Khidmatgar.*

2. I shall be ever ready to sacrifice personal comfort, property and even life itself to serve the nation and for the attainment of my country's freedom.

3. I shall not participate in factions, nor pick up a quarrel with or bear enmity towards anybody. I shall always protect the oppressed against the tyranny of the oppressor.

4. I shall not become a member of any other organization and shall not furnish security or tender apology in the course of the nonviolent struggle.

5. I shall always obey every legitimate order of my superior officer.

6. I shall always live up to the principle of nonviolence.

7. I shall serve all humanity equally. The chief object of my life shall be attainment of complete independence for my country and my religion.

8. I shall always observe truth and purity in all actions.

help other oppressed nations to liberate themselves." (Mohammad Yunus, *Frontier Speaks,* p.11.)

9. I shall expect no remuneration for my services.

10. All my services shall be dedicated to God; they shall not be for attaining rank or for show."[6]

A genuine popular movement, the *Khudai Khidmatgar*'s main objectives were to win complete independence for India and drastically reform the social, political, and economic life of the Pashtuns while preserving Hindu-Muslim unity, all strictly within the framework of nonviolent means. Although it was a local resistance movement centered in the Frontier, the *Khudai Khidmatgar* was part of India's civil disobedience struggle and the Indian National Congress (the main nationalist party). The *Khudai Khidmatgar* pledged an informal cooperation with the broader struggle.

The Indian National Congress

In December 1929, during the famous meeting of the Indian National Congress at Lahore, Jawaharlal Nehru (earlier an advocate of a violent war of liberation and later Prime Minister of India) declared the commitment of the Congress to obtain full independence for India. To achieve this objective, a major civil disobedience campaign was proclaimed. Ghaffar Khan, as well as the Vice-President of the Provincial Congress Committee and other notable political leaders from the Frontier, was also present at the conference. Ghaffar Khan approved the Congress plan, and in early 1930 the Peshawar Congress Committee announced that Ghaffar Khan and the *Khudai Khidmatgar* were its partners for the coming disobedience struggle. Ghaffar Khan traveled to key places in the Province and urged the people of the Frontier, together with the *Khudai Khidmatgar,* to take part in the Congress civil disobedience campaign. In August 1931, the relationship became a formal alliance that continued until the day of India's independence: August 15, 1947.

---

[6] Pyarelal [Nair], *A Pilgrimage for Peace: Gandhi and Frontier Gandhi Among N.W.F.P. Pathans,* p. 50.

Training and volunteer work

After being accepted in the *Khudai Khidmatgar* organization and taking the oath, individuals were required to participate in training camps where they received instructions about the goals and programs of the movement. The reform programs of the *Khudai Khidmatgar* movement demanded a considerable change in the cultural model of the Pashtun society. Therefore, an elaborate program of training and instruction was prepared to be carried out in the special training camps. At the beginning, during the early 1930s, these camps were not well organized, but gradually they developed into an efficient system of training for potential resisters. Participants included *Khudai Khidmatgar* members, as well as others from the surrounding areas who wished to take advantage of the general educational courses offered by the camps.

The basic ideas of the reform operation were explained to new volunteers in the first meeting by Ghaffar Khan himself. Benefits of cleaning and sweeping houses and spinning one's own cloth were explained to the people. Cleaning houses of nonmembers of the movement, in which high ranking officials, as well as Ghaffar Khan himself, personally participated, was intended to render services and win the loyalty of the people. Working for and with one another improved unity and cooperation and set the groundwork for the nonviolent action that would take place. It was reasoned that activities such as digging, spinning, and cleaning, and other physically demanding work that was performed in the camps raised social and political awareness, and also taught discipline and hard work. Also, these activities psychologically prepared the volunteers for the nonviolent war with the British. This idea of volunteer work was an integral part of the movement throughout the struggle, and would remain so even at the height of its civil disobedience campaign.

Schools and drills

Opening schools where writing, reading, political awareness, cleaning, and sanitation were taught was one primary task of the *Khudai Khidmatgar.* The schools also communicated to the public that one goal of the *Khudai Khidmatgar* movement was to make the country self-sufficient, and therefore economically independent of the colonial power. In order to strengthen the nation's hand-loom weavers against the imported British cloth, the *Khudai Khidmatgar* distributed the *charkha* (spinning wheels) to the people and taught them to spin thread. In a similar vein, pressing oil seeds for cooking oil and grinding wheat for flour to feed the camp volunteers were considered important tasks for camp residents.

Participants were required to attend late afternoon meetings, and they were often joined by residents from nearby villages. In these meetings, anti-colonial ideas and issues were addressed. Discussions centered on planning for action, the importance of unity among the people, information about prisons and how to survive and endure them, and, most importantly, the importance of adhering to the organization's principle of nonviolent discipline. After one instance of violence, Ghaffar Khan fasted for three days to admonish the perpetrators.[7] Banerjee also reports that the persons who committed violence were removed from the movement—even Ghaffar Khan's son Ghani. Such persons usually asked for pardon but were readmitted to the movement only after at least three years of good behavior.[8]

Also important were poetry and skits to explain various concepts and ideas to the people. There was time for music and amusement.[9]

During meetings, the unity of all Pashtuns was emphasized, and, as a precondition, members were asked to completely resolve all internal differences and feuds before joining the movement. "We are at war against the British for independence, but we have no weapons, our only weapon is patience. If you can fight this war, then wear a red uniform and come and join us,"[10] Ghaffar Khan said.

A large tent was used to conduct general educational courses (as distinct from *Khudai Khidmatgar* training programs), to hold meetings, and as a place to spin thread. The *Khudai Khidmatgar* lived separately from other people under a policy of stringent military regulation. Here they performed their routine drills. An-

---

7 Banerjee, *The Pathan Unarmed*, p. 121.
8 Banerjee, *The Pathan Unarmed*, pp. 121-122.
9 Banerjee, *The Pathan Unarmed*, pp. 75-76.
10 Banerjee, *The Pathan Unarmed*, p. 80.

other large tent was used as a medical clinic, a mosque and a supply depot. The usual routine for the *Khudai Khidmatgar* in the camp included drills, physical exercise, and running to prepare the *Khudai Khidmatgar* for long marches and daylong protests. Also included was practical instruction for proper cleaning and good sanitation in the camp. Additionally, classes were focused on political subjects such as nationalist movements (with special attention to the history and duties of the *Khudai Khidmatgar* movement), spinning the raw cotton into threads on the *charkha* (spinning wheel), and grinding wheat into flour to make bread for the camp.

Nonviolent discipline and military style

Introducing and stressing to the Pashtuns the importance of maintaining nonviolent discipline in the movement was a complicated task. The leadership of the *Khudai Khidmatgar* succeeded by serving others and practicing teamwork, preaching religious and moral principles, and strongly advocating the elimination of internal rivalries. One particular measure to promote adherence to nonviolent discipline in the movement was the administration of the nonviolent *Khudai Khidmatgar* in the form of a military organization. Ranks and titles (captain, lieutenant, colonel, general, etc.) were set among the officers and the units and subunits (company, brigade, etc).[11] Members of the *Khudai Khidmatgar* were obligated to live under strict military discipline and daily routines.

The strategy of organizing the *Khudai Khidmatgar* in the military style was not only desirable for the conduct of successful operations, but also proved that—contrary to the characterization portrayed by the British—the Pashtuns, like all people, had the ability to organize themselves and establish self-government. The drills and long marches that resembled military activities were performed only to instill in the participants the importance of discipline, and not as preparations for future violence, as some have suggested.

---

[11] It is important here to note that leadership in the organization was democratic. Candidates were nominated to their various positions and elections were held.

The futility of military methods

Ghaffar Khan stressed that the Pashtuns were "unable to defeat the British on the battlefield . . . [and instead] we were doing politics and that we had to defeat them politically. . . ."[12] Ghaffar Khan understood that a violent uprising by the Pashtuns could not be sustained due to the superior military capabilities of the British and the lack of resources and ammunition of the Pashtuns in the Frontier. Violence would only succeed in provoking further British atrocities and repression against them. On this he concluded: "Earlier, violence had seemed to me the best way to revolution . . . but experience taught me that it was futile to dig a well after the house was on fire."[13] That is, he was aware that the British had succeeded in firmly entrenching themselves in the Frontier militarily and otherwise, and that violent, military resistance would not be useful.[14] Before marching to demonstrations and picketing, the importance of maintaining nonviolent discipline was stressed and it was openly stated that those who intended to use violence should leave right away.

Red Shirts against the British Empire

The *Khudai Khidmatgar* wore red uniforms, earning the nickname: the "Red Shirts." The name was intentionally introduced and spread by the British to be used as a substitute for the name "*Khudai Khidmatgar,*" which had the connotation of religious piety and godliness. After introducing the Red Shirts name, the government then labeled the *Khudai Khidmatgar* as a Communist or "quasi-fascist" group because not only did they wear red uniforms, but they were the only organization that advocated a policy of service without payment.[15] The Communist charge was denied by the *Khudai Khidmatgar,* stating that this was a very obvious attempt by the British to discredit the movement and raise alarm with anti-Communist forces in both India and London. Furthermore, they asked how they could "give the slogans *Allah-O-Akbar* (God is great) in our demonstration and call our-

---

[12] Banerjee, *The Pathan Unarmed,* p. 81, as reported by Mukarram Khan.
[13] Banerjee, *The Pathan Unarmed,* p. 49.
[14] Banerjee, *The Pathan Unarmed,* p. 49.
[15] Banerjee, *The Pathan Unarmed,* p. 105.

selves *Khudai Khidmatgar* (the Servants of God)" and at the same time be followers of Communism, which was viewed as an atheistic ideology. The *Khudai Khidmatgar* explained their reasoning for using the dark red color for uniforms: fabric of this color was very cheap and readily available in the area.[16] The authorities were not convinced and the police often seized their uniforms and burned them. During 1931, the police confiscated and burned more than 1,200 *Khudai Khidmatgar* uniforms.[17]

"The technique of nonviolent confrontation was the very opposite of guerrilla campaigns," Mukulika Banerjee reports, "and in place of the Pathans' traditional use of stealth and camouflage the *Khudai Khidmatgar* was a determinedly extroverted and highly visible presence."[18]

The cooperation between the Muslim *Khudai Khidmatgar* and the predominantly Hindu Indian National Congress concerned the British, who persistently tried to sever this relationship. The British continually accused the *Khudai Khidmatgar* of being a "paramilitary group" and charged that they were fundamentally opposed to the Congress policy of nonviolent struggle. The British also took advantage of Hindu-Muslim difference by telling the pro-government mullahs (Muslim religious leaders) in the Frontier to name Ghaffar Khan and the *Khudai Khidmatgar* as friends of Hindus. This misinformation campaign was used by the British to turn Pashtun opinion against the *Khudai Khidmatgar* and to label them as *kafir* (unbelievers). The interfaith unity made the colonial power so nervous that from the mid-1930s, they directed a great deal of time and effort to create the Muslim League and undermine the Red Shirt-Congress alliance.[19]

Methods of nonviolent struggle

During the civil disobedience campaigns of 1930-1934, the *Khudai Khidmatgar* used the following methods:

1. Refusal to pay taxes or rent to the government.

2. Picketing of government offices.

---

[16] Banerjee, *The Pathan Unarmed*, pp. 103-107.
[17] Banerjee, *The Pathan Unarmed*, p. 88.
[18] Banerjee, *The Pathan Unarmed*, p. 87.
[19] Banerjee, *The Pathan Unarmed*, p. 111.

3. Boycotting of foreign goods (cloth, etc.), and a full scale boycott of liquor stores in Peshawar.

4. Noncooperation with the government administration and contracted services, such as delivering mail.

5. Refusal to settle criminal and civil cases in government courts, opting instead for village councils.

6. Commemoration of anniversaries of important events; for example, the massacre in the Kissa Khani Bazaar in Peshawar on April 23, 1930, when 200 demonstrators were killed by troops under British command.

7. Encouraging officials in the villages who worked as tax collectors or other state workers to resign. If they did not, they were socially ostracized.[20]

Growth and inclusion

In 1930, the *Khudai Khidmatgar* volunteers numbered around 1,000. By the end of 1931, this number had reached 25,000, and by 1938, membership had reached more than 100,000.[21] During the 1930 civil disobedience campaign, thousands of Pashtuns of the Frontier participated in nonviolent picketing campaigns. The *Khudai Khidmatgar* included among their members Hindus, Sikhs, and women, and preached a policy of inclusion of all people. In Bannu, 400 miles from Peshawar, women were involved in picketing and boycotting the institutions of the British rulers, such as courts, police, army, tax offices, and schools.[22]

It was a common understanding among the *Khudai Khidmatgar* that there was no difference between the rich and poor in the struggle to oust the British from their land. The country belonged to both rich and poor and people joined the movement for different reasons. Some were attracted to the organization for good business opportunities, others for economic improvement, and still others for noneconomic reasons like the call for unity and an eventual end to the British rule that was the root cause of the unjust situation. Despite the diversity of the members' backgrounds, after entering the *Khudai Khidmatgar,* they strictly followed the

20 Banerjee, *The Pathan Unarmed,* pp. 73-102.
21 Banerjee, *The Pathan Unarmed,* p. 60.
22 Banerjee, *The Pathan Unarmed,* p. 93.

movement's policy. The *Khudai Khidmatgar* were enormously popular among the population and with a great number of people who, although outside the *Khudai Khidmatgar* organization, actively participated and supported the struggle.[23]

Opposition to nonviolent struggle

Some of the wealthy, landowning *khans* (tribal leaders) and others who benefited financially from the British were opponents of the *Khudai Khidmatgar* inside the Pashtun society. The religious groups in the Frontier were divided in their support. One group of prestigious mullahs supported the *Khudai Khidmatgar* and had become members. Other groups opposed the British rule, but favored the traditional *jihad*[24] and violence and criticized the nonviolent technique adopted by the *Khudai Khidmatgar*. Although Ghaffar Khan had developed the idea of nonviolent struggle independently from Mohandas Gandhi, "nonviolence" was considered to be a Hindu concept. Another group of mullahs mainly in the rural areas who received monetary compensation from the government preached obedience to the British government and discouraged people from antagonizing the government. Using the people's fear of the military strength of the British, they told people that there was no use hitting their heads against the mountains.[25]

Investigating British policies

On April 23, 1930, one month after Gandhi's well-known Salt March, which defied the British Salt Law, a delegation of Indian National Congress officials was scheduled to arrive in Peshawar from Delhi to investigate complaints from the Frontier Province against government policies that were widely regarded as cruel and unjust. The grievances included, especially, complaints about the Frontier Crimes Regulation, a set of laws that targeted the Pashtuns.

A large gathering with several hundred *Khudai Khidmatgar* was waiting in Peshawar Station to receive the delegation, but

---

[23] Pyarelal [Nair], *A Pilgrimage for Peace*, p. 37.
[24] Muslim struggle, usually interpreted as holy war.
[25] Banerjee, *The Pathan Unarmed*, p. 109.

they were told that the Indian National Congress committee had been detained in Punjab and denied entrance to the Frontier. Outraged by the news, the Provincial Congress leaders staged a general demonstration and threatened the British authorities that they would start picketing liquor stores and foreign goods stores the following day.

Shootings and arrests

During the demonstration, two police cars crashed into each other, causing a fire. The soldiers then began shooting at the resisters and continued without interruption for three hours. An estimated 200 people were killed.[26] According to other sources, the number of dead was in the "hundreds,"[27] with many wounded. The government was determined to arrest Ghaffar Khan and some of his followers and charge them with "sedition and wrongful assembly." Ghaffar Khan was arrested that day and his journal, *Pashtun,* was banned.

The horror of the Kissa Khani Bazaar massacre shocked all of India. The British government appointed a committee to investigate the incident, while at the same time making it very difficult for information about the matter to reach other provinces in India. The refusal of two platoons of the Royal Garhwal Rifles to fire on the peaceful and unarmed civilians further concerned the authorities and put to doubt the loyalty of the military forces. As a consequence, the disobedient soldiers were treated harshly, and each received a jail sentence of 10-14 years.[28]

Investigation and withdrawal

Eventually, the news of the massacre did reach other provinces and regions of India. A new higher-level commission of the Indian National Congress was established to investigate the massacre, but it, too, was prevented from entering the Frontier Province. The commission therefore started its work in Rawilpindi in Pun-

---

[26] Banerjee, *The Pathan Unarmed,* p. 57.

[27] Yunus, *Frontier Speaks,* p. 117.

[28] They served their full prison terms since their release was not included in the negotiated settlement of the Gandhi-Irwin Pact in March 1931. See Mohammad Yunus, *Frontier Speaks,* p. 118; and Gene Sharp, *Gandhi Wields the Weapon of Moral Power,* p. 196.

jab, far from the scene. The Congress report revealed that during the Kissa Khani Bazaar incident, the "Peshawaris demonstrated a high standard of heroism, love for their country, and were consistent with the spirit of nonviolence."[29]

The incident forced the British to withdraw from Peshawar because of the inability of its limited number of forces in the Frontier to control the angry city after the massacre of peaceful, unarmed people.[30] The Provincial Congress essentially took over the city for nine days. At the same time, the activities of the *Khudai Khidmatgar* and the difficulties of travel and communication crippled the government's rule in much of the adjacent rural areas for more than two months.[31]

Soon false news of the British abandoning the entire Province and even leaving India spread throughout the Frontier and the surrounding region.

Repression and violent resistance

On May 3, the British declared the Provincial Congress and the *Khudai Khidmatgar* to be illegal. The following morning the city of Peshawar was surrounded by reinforcement troops and the government control over the city was restored. Congress activists were arrested and a curfew was imposed on all movement for 24 hours.

Although nonviolent discipline was strongly stressed by the *Khudai Khidmatgar* leadership and was strictly observed by its members, violence was not completely eliminated from the struggle. The earlier killings of the nonviolent *Khudai Khidmatgar* in Peshawar provoked the population and tribes against the British, and occasionally they reacted by using violence. Sometimes, violence occurred in the tribal regions by individuals outside the *Khudai Khidmatgar* organization, and also in some rural areas. This violence produced a brutal response from the government.

---

[29] Jawaharlal Nehru compared the British atrocities of this time in the Frontier with the first Indian war of independence in 1857, when the British slaughtered thousands of Indians, and also with the massacre of Jallianwalla Bagh, in Amritsar, Punjab, in 1919, when General Dyer's troops, by official count, killed 379 unarmed people and wounded another 1,137 during a peaceful meeting.

[30] Stephen Alan Rittenberg, *Ethnicity, Nationalism, and the Pashtuns* (Durham, North Carolina: Carolina Academic Press, 1988), p. 84.

[31] Rittenberg, *Ethnicity, Nationalism, and the Pashtuns*, p. 66.

Although the British justified their use of violence in the Frontier Province by a propaganda campaign that sought to portray the Pashtuns as a rebellious group that favored the use of violence, the people of the province proved themselves otherwise during the Kissa Khani Bazaar massacre on April 23, 1930, when for the most part they remained nonviolent in face of the most brutal actions against them.[32]

On May 30, in the village of Takar, in Mardan District, the villagers attempted to prevent the arrest of the *Khudai Khidmatgar* leaders in their area and marched with them as they were led towards the District center.[33] A small group of police intervened to stop their procession. During the confrontation, an English police officer was killed. Three days later, in retaliation, the police attacked the village and killed several individuals. The original objective of the British authorities in arresting the *Khudai Khidmatgar* officials was to provoke a violent response from the villagers and find justification for the government's continued suppression and atrocities.

More opposition violence

Bannu was the second largest area of resistance, after Peshawar. A combination of clergy, tribal chiefs, and politicians from the cities kept the anti-government uprising alive.

On August 24, 1930, a large gathering convened in Spin Tangi, Bannu District, although many people were prevented from assembling by the government. At the meeting, a British soldier fired on a prominent local leader named Qazi Fazil Qadr. Even though there was a strong commitment to nonviolent discipline among the participants, a very small number of people had weapons, and a fight broke out. When the fighting stopped, the government had arrested 300 people, killed 80, and wounded many more. During the fighting, a British captain was killed by swords and axes.

Qazi Fazil Qadr was taken to the police station, where the Deputy Commissioner taunted him to give his anti-British slogan. However, he was too weak and passed away. Consequently, the

---

[32] Banerjee, *The Pathan Unarmed*, p. 58.
[33] The Pashtun tradition of giving sanctuary to someone in trouble in their territory.

British sentenced him to 14 years imprisonment, buried him in Bannu prison, and refused to release his body to his family for the required religious funeral ceremony.[34]

During 1931, the tribes in Peshawar Valley and Waziristan further complicated the government problem. For example, the Afridis—the largest single Pashtun tribe, skilled in warfare—twice violently invaded Peshawar. Starting August 7, they paralyzed the government for 12 days. The violent uprising forced the Viceroy to declare martial law in Peshawar District on August 16. The tribal revolt was an unsolicited response to the government's atrocities against the nonviolent people in Peshawar. The Afridis continued scattered raids until October 1931.

British reactions

In December 1931, while Gandhi was negotiating with the British government in London at the Roundtable Conference, the authorities increased their pressure in the Frontier. The Provincial Congress and the *Khudai Khidmatgar* were banned. Ghaffar Khan, along with other leaders, was jailed, and strict control was placed on the *Khudai Khidmatgar* and its anti-government activities. The police and the army were given unlimited power to crush the *Khudai Khidmatgar,* and they often fired on protesters, killing and injuring many of them.[35]

Gandhi returned from London on December 28, 1931, docking in Bombay. The day of his arrival, Gandhi declared in a public speech:

> Last year we faced *lathis* [steel-shod bamboo rods], but this time we must be prepared to face bullets. I do not wish that the Pathans in the Frontier alone should court bullets. If bullets are to be faced, then Bombay and Gujarat also must take their share.[36]

Gandhi attempted to talk to the Viceroy about the imprisonment of Ghaffar Khan and the crackdown on the *Khudai Khidmatgar,* but was ignored.

---

[34] Banerjee, *The Pathan Unarmed*, p. 195.

[35] In Kohat Valley, 50 demonstrators were killed during protests.

[36] S. W. A. Shah, *Ethnicity, Islam and Nationalism: Muslim Politics in the North West Frontier Province 1937-47*, p. 36 and p. 49, n. 79.

The massacre of Kissa Khani Bazaar and its aftermath shocked the British. The Deputy Commissioner was blamed for failing to accurately perceive the situation in the Frontier before the event. The local government was charged for inaction against the growing danger of the *Khudai Khidmatgar*. In an attempt to repair the damage caused by the massacre and to appease the people, the colonial government increased financing for education, health and agriculture, and veterinary medicine. Later, in 1932, the government also replaced the Chief Commissioner with the power of Governor, bringing the Frontier Province to the same level of administration as other provinces of India. Urban and rural elections slowly followed.

Although the *Khudai Khidmatgar* movement had won some short-term successes, the government had more brutal designs for the Frontier in the form of propaganda, torture, and suppression. Following the Kissa Khani Bazaar tragedy, the government launched its intensified propaganda war against the *Khudai Khidmatgar* and accused them of being a paramilitary group for wearing uniforms, drilling, and organizing themselves as a military establishment, while the *Khudai Khidmatgar* rejected the charge.

Increased suppression

To prevent incidents like that of the Kissa Khani Bazaar, the British were determined to show extreme force in order to terrify the population from uprising against their authority. Various means of harsh repression were inflicted. Houses were burned and stocks of grain were destroyed. According to an American tourist, "gunning the red shirts was a popular sport and pastime of the British forces in the province."[37] Members of the *Khudai Khidmatgar* were unclothed and forced to run in the middle of lines of British soldiers while they were kicked and jabbed with rifle muzzles and bayonets. They were thrown from rooftops into filthy ponds, often in extremely cold temperatures. Torture, often to the point of causing serious physical and psychological damage to the individuals, was prevalent.[38] Banerjee also reports that

---

[37] Yunus, *Frontier Speaks*, p. 118.
[38] Pyarelal [Nair], *A Pilgrimage for Peace*, p. 50.

women's *purdah*[39] was sometimes verbally and physically violated, while men prisoners were sometimes exposed to overnight
extreme cold—and even stripped in front of women—and some
were castrated and sexually abused.[40]

From April 1930 to December 1932, the British jailed 12,000
Khudai Khidmatgar members who allegedly took part in demonstrations and picketing. In Haripur Jail alone, 7,000 *Khudai
Khidmatgar* were imprisoned under extremely harsh conditions,
sleeping on the floor with two worn blankets in severely cold
temperatures. Members of the *Khudai Khidmatgar* were forced to
march in Peshawar city in their bare feet with only pajamas on.[41]

Forced labor was another method of punishment, particularly
when the prisons were full. The prisoners were taken to work
sites where they were forced to perform hard labor. They were ill
fed, they slept on site, and they were eventually sent home without payment. There were also reports, cited by Banerjee, that the
authorities paid agents to poison food in the *Khudai Khidmatgar*
training camps.[42] The villagers of the settled districts who helped
the *Khudai Khidmatgar* were also targeted, and in 1932 some 92
villages were fined a total of 20,000 rupees.

Civil disobedience suspended

Finally, in April 1934, Gandhi suspended the civil disobedience
struggle all over India and the government freed all Congress activists from jails in most of India. However, by this time the civil
disobedience movement had lost its effectiveness. The *Khudai
Khidmatgar* and the Provincial Congress leaders were not included in the amnesty. The activities of these organizations remained prohibited.

When Ghaffar Khan and his brother were released in 1935,
they were not permitted to enter their home province, the Frontier. The authorities almost instantly gave Ghaffar Khan another
laborious two-year sentence for giving "anti-government and seditious speeches" in the Punjab. Eventually, after some six years

---

[39] *Purdah* is the traditional Muslim and Hindu practice of seclusion and veiling of women.
[40] Banerjee, *The Pathan Unarmed*, pp. 118-119.
[41] Banerjee, *The Pathan Unarmed*, p. 111.
[42] Banerjee, *The Pathan Unarmed*, p. 114.

of imprisonment, the leader of *Khudai Khidmatgar* returned to his home in November 1937. At the time, the political environment was relaxed and the government allowed some political reforms.

The civil disobedience struggle of the previous years was replaced by electoral party politics[43] as the relationship between India and the British Empire entered a new phase during the years preceding partition and independence.

---

[43] Banerjee, *The Pathan Unarmed,* p. 71.

Sources

Banerjee, Mukulika, *The Pathan Unarmed,* Oxford and Karachi: Oxford University Press, 2000.

Dupree, Louis, *Afghanistan,* London: Oxford University Press, 1997 (first edition Princeton: Princeton University Press, 1973).

Fraser-Tytler, W. K., *Afghanistan: A Study of Political Development in Central Asia and Southern Asia,* London: Oxford University Press, 1950.

Ghaffar Khan, Khan Abdul, *Zama Zindagio Jiddo Jihad,* Kabul: Pashtu Academy, 1969 (in Pashto).

Habibi, Abdul Hai, *Tarikh Mukhtasari Afghanistan (Afghanistan's Concise History),* Kabul: 1965 (in Farsi).

Jansson, Erland, *India, Pakistan and Pashtunistan: Nationalist Movements in the NWFP, 1939-47,* Stockholm: Almquist and Wiksell International, 1981.

Pyarelal [Nair], *A Pilgrimage for Peace: Gandhi and Frontier Gandhi Among N. W. F. P. Pathans,* Ahmedabad: Navajivan, 1950.

Rittenberg, Stephen Alan, *Ethnicity, Nationalism, and the Pashtuns,* Durham, North Carolina: Carolina Academic Press, 1988.

Shah, S. W. A., *Ethnicity, Islam and Nationalism: Muslim Politics in the North West Frontier Province 1937-47,* Oxford and Karachi: Oxford University Press, 1999.

Sharp, Gene, *Gandhi as a Political Strategist,* Boston: Porter Sargent, 1979.

Sharp, Gene, *Gandhi Wields the Weapon of Moral Power,* Ahmedabad: Navajivan, 1960.

Tendulkar, D. G., *Abdul Ghaffar Khan,* New Delhi: Gandhi Peace Foundation, 1967.

Yunus, Mohammad, *Frontier Speaks,* Bombay: Hind Kitabs, Ltd., 1947.

Research assistance for this chapter was provided by Jamila Raqib.

Chapter Nine

NORWEGIAN TEACHERS FIGHT FASCISM—1942

Nazi invasion and resistance

The Norwegian teachers' resistance in 1942 is but one of several anti-Nazi resistance campaigns during the German occupation of Norway in the Second World War. The Nazis invaded this large country with a small population in the north of Europe on April 9, 1940. Significant military resistance lasted only two months.

Following months of confusion, resistance gradually developed in reaction to the regime's brutality. More and more Norwegians were asking how they could act to express their feelings. On what issue should people resist, and how should they do it? "How do we organize our lives if the occupation goes on for 30 or 40 years? How can we preserve our national ways instead of adopting those of the occupation?" some asked.

A list of sources for this case appears at the end of this chapter.

"Nowhere through all these discussions," Håkon Holmboe, one of the resisting teachers, said, "did the *idea* of nonviolent resistance come in. Instead of an idea, it developed as a way to work—a way to do something."[1]

Many people refused to sign an oath of loyalty to the collaborationist Quisling regime. Others refused to turn in their radios as ordered. Small banned resistance newspapers began to appear. "What really helped us in organizing resistance was the pressure of the Nazis," Mr. Holmboe said.[2]

Small symbolic acts of defiance became important. People wore paper clips in their lapels or as necklaces and bracelets to signal "stick together." Even tiny potatoes were worn on match sticks on lapels, and daily got bigger, to indicate that the resistance was growing. People wore flowers on the birthday of the king, who was in exile in England. Other symbolic protests took place. They were sometimes very dangerous.

Strengthening the fascist dictatorship

In February 1942, the Norwegian fascist "Minister-President," Vidkun Quisling, set out to establish the Corporative State on Mussolini's model, selecting teachers as the first "corporation" of the new dictatorship. This system was designed to bring the entire society and the whole population under fascist domination through control of new dictatorially structured institutions.

There was resistance that month. On February 3, Quisling proclaimed the establishment of a new fascist Youth Front with compulsory membership and service for all Norwegian youth between 10 and 18 years old. This action caused the Bishops of the State Church to protest by resigning their State positions, while maintaining their spiritual responsibilities. Also, 150 university professors protested against the Youth Front.

The old teachers' organization had previously been abolished by the fascists in June 1941. On February 5, 1942, Quisling decreed the creation of a new fascist Norwegian Teachers' Union with compulsory membership, and appointed as its Leader the

---

[1] Sharp, "Tyranny Could Not Quell Them!", p. 7.
[2] Sharp, "Tyranny Could Not Quell Them!", p. 6.

head of the Norwegian storm troopers. Clearly, the fascists aimed to control the teachers, the schools, and the youth.

Resistance by the teachers

A secret small resistance leadership group in the capital, Oslo, had already decided the basic points at which they would ask the teachers to resist. In February, this group called on the teachers to act. A statement, short, simple, and easy to remember, was drafted. Every teacher was asked to write, sign, and mail it to fascist officials. Teachers spread the instructions to other teachers throughout the country.

Between 8,000 and 10,000 of the country's 12,000 teachers wrote these letters to Quisling's Church and Education Department. Each teacher said he or she could neither assist in promoting fascist education of the children nor accept membership in the new teachers' organization. All signed their names and addresses to the wording prescribed by the underground for the letter.

The teachers knew that this action would be dangerous. "'They' have their ways of stopping us, but it is the only way we have to express our opposition and we must do it," Mr. Holmboe later said.[3] "It gave us a feeling of not being alone, a feeling of strength." "It was a matter of conscience."[4]

The fascist government threatened them with dismissal from their jobs and in panic then closed all schools for a month. Teachers held classes in private homes. Despite censorship, news of the teachers' resistance spread. In early March, tens of thousands of letters of protest from parents poured into the government office. The news of the parents' resistance reached almost every home in the country.

Arrests and concentration camps

After the teachers defied the threats, beginning on March 20, about 1,000 male teachers were arrested and sent to jails and concentration camps. Throughout the teachers' incarceration,

---

[3] Sharp, "Tyranny Could Not Quell Them!", p. 8.
[4] Sharp, "Tyranny Could Not Quell Them!", p. 9.

their families received from "somewhere" the equivalent of their former salaries.

Conditions in the concentration camps in southern Norway were grim. The Gestapo imposed an atmosphere of terror intended to induce capitulation. On starvation rations, the teachers were put through "torture gymnastics" in very deep snow, and faced great uncertainties. When only a few gave in, the "treatment" continued.

Meanwhile, the schools reopened, and the teachers still at liberty were pressured to submit and accept the fascist teachers' organization. But many told their pupils they repudiated membership in the new organization and spoke of a duty to conscience. Rumors were spread that if these teachers did not give in, some or all of those arrested would be killed. After difficult inner wrestling, the teachers who had not been arrested almost without exception stood firm, even those who were married to arrested men.

Additional rumours were spread that 10 of the teachers would be shot, or one in 10, or that they were to be sent to the far north to clear land mines between German and Russian lines by walking on them. In retaliation for sabotage, some Norwegians in concentration camps had already been shot, and others were later.

Shipped into the Arctic

Then 499 of the teachers were shipped on cattle car trains through the cold, high mountains to the old capital of Trondheim on their way north. Children gathered and sang at railroad stations as teachers were shipped through in cattle cars. Others were kept in a concentration camp in the south and shipped north later. Despite censorship, the news spread, and the slow mountain trip had a major impact on the whole population of Norway. Farmers attempted unsuccessfully to offer milk to the teachers when the train stopped at stations.

From Trondheim, the prisoners were shipped in terrible conditions in overcrowded steamships on a 13-day dangerous voyage far beyond the Arctic Circle to a camp near Kirkenes close to the Soviet Arctic front. The teachers knew nothing of their intended fate. However, they organized lectures and choirs during the voyage. They arrived April 28, when the weather was still cold and rough. Within three days, the teachers were transferred from the control of the Gestapo to that of the regular German army.

After the imprisoned teachers were told of a statement by Quisling's Church and Education Department that all was settled and that the activities of the new fascist teachers' organization would cease, the teachers telegrammed the Education Department on May 13 that they wished to resume their teaching. There was no reply.

As it turned out, however, the new fascist organization never came into being and its dues were never deducted from the teachers' payrolls.

The teachers' triumph

The teachers were kept at Kirkenes in miserable conditions, doing dangerous work unloading ships. One was killed and three seriously injured. There were no beds, bedding, mattresses, or furniture. A sympathetic German soldier, defying orders, showed the teachers how to take some hay from a nearby haystack for bedding without being detected. There were very few Gestapo men among the soldiers.

The teachers did not feel particularly heroic, and had to occupy themselves with survival. Some might have withdrawn their protests, but were given no opportunity to do so. "In many ways, our victory was organized by the enemy," said Mr. Holmboe.[5]

However, their suffering strengthened morale on the home front and posed problems for the Quisling regime. If they took harsher measures against the teachers, the fascists risked permanent antagonism toward the regime.

On May 22, Quisling raged at the teachers in a school near Oslo, "You teachers have destroyed everything for me!"

"That sentence was a triumph for us," one of the teachers said later. "It became a slogan and was taken up and quoted everywhere afterwards."[6] It meant, he said, that the teachers had blocked Quisling's whole plan of organizing the new Corporate State.

---

[5] Sharp, "Tyranny Could Not Quell Them!", p. 16.
[6] Sharp, "Tyranny Could Not Quell Them!", p. 16.

Victorious return

The spring became summer, and the summer was becoming autumn. The cold winter—when there was no sunshine and only darkness—was coming soon. The Kirkenes harbor would soon freeze, preventing ships from taking the prisoners south. However, the teachers were still kept at Kirkenes, working very slowly and trying to keep warm.

Fearful of alienating Norwegians still further, Quisling finally ordered the teachers' release. First, a group of 150 ill teachers, who signed a concession statement that was never used, were sent south on August 29. Then the other teachers who signed nothing were released. Eight months after the arrests, on November 4, the last 300 or so teachers were shipped from Kirkenes homeward, where they were received with triumphal receptions.

Quisling's new fascist organization for teachers never came into being, and the schools were never used for fascist propaganda. After Quisling encountered further difficulties in imposing the Corporative State, Hitler ordered him to abandon the whole project.

Sources

This account is based primarily on interviews in 1957 with Håkon Holmboe, one of the participating teachers, and also several published Norwegian sources. A longer version of this report by Gene Sharp was published as

"Tyranny Could Not Quell Them!" (pamphlet), London: Peace News, 1958 and later.

Norwegian sources include

Arnundsen, Sverre S. (gen. ed.), *Kirkenes Ferda, 1942,* Oslo: J. W. Cappelens Forlag, 1946.

Jensen, Magnus, "Kampen om Skolen," in Sverre Steen (gen. ed.), *Norges Krig* (Oslo: Gyldendal Norsk Forlag, 1947-50), vol. III, pp. 13-105.

Chapter Ten

SAVING JEWISH HUSBANDS IN BERLIN—1943

Dr. Nathan Stoltzfus

The final roundup of Jews

In pre-dawn darkness, long columns of SS troops in army trucks rolled swiftly into Berlin. It was the SS *Leibstandarte Hitler,* wearing black uniforms with steel helmets, decorated with medals of war valor, and bristling with bayoneted rifles and machine guns. As the most elite SS troop, known for its fighting spirit, the *Leibstandarte* had just returned from the gaping German wound at Stalingrad.

On this Saturday, February 27, 1943, their fury at German defeat was turned against the Jews in a new mandate: to make Berlin *Judenrein* (free of Jews) in a massive arrest action the Gestapo

---

A list of sources for this case appears at the end of this chapter.

called the Final Roundup of Berlin Jews. Storming their way into the factories, they began routing all Jews from their work places. The Jews were herded into five huge makeshift collection centers, which were theaters of heart-rending scenes of brutality and fear. It was the beginning of the end for thousands of Berlin Jews.

The wives demand their husbands

When the Jewish workers in intermarriages, primarily men, did not return home as usual this Saturday afternoon of the mass arrests, their German spouses made frantic calls to the police and the factories. Sooner or later, many found out that their loved ones had been interned at a Jewish community building on a central Berlin street called the Rosenstrasse. The women went there immediately to obtain information about their spouses, and to bring them packages of bread and cheese or razors and toiletries. Arriving women congregated on the street, separated from the building imprisoning their loved ones by five uniformed and armed SS guards. Arriving one-by-one or two-by-two, they found themselves among a small but growing crowd.

A growing protest

Several women boldly approached the SS guards and began to complain. Their words even grew threatening. Who did the SS think they were, keeping them away from their families? What had they done to merit the arrest of their loved ones? After all, as "Aryan" German citizens, they were entitled to rights. "If you don't let us in we will come back and make trouble, we will bring a battering ram and break through the door," one said.[1] Before leaving for the night, several women made a promise among themselves to meet each other at that same spot early the next day, and to demonstrate in an effort to get their husbands back.

Early the next morning, February 28, an eyewitness arriving for the first time already heard cries of a group as she approached Rosenstrasse, "We want our husbands back! Let our husbands go."[2] Small groups stood together or walked up and down in

---

[1] Stoltzfus, *Resistance of the Heart,* p. xix.
[2] Stoltzfus, *Resistance of the Heart,* p. xx.

front of the building, hoping to catch a glimpse of a spouse or child through the window. Again and again, they cried out their chorus in unison: "We want our husbands back."

The participants in the crowd kept changing as people came and went. London radio called it an ongoing demonstration procession. Foreign news sources recorded the presence of 600 demonstrators, while eyewitnesses reported upwards of 1,000 at a time. The headquarters of the "Jewish Office" of the Gestapo was just around the corner on the Burgstrasse (Burg Street), where Gestapo men might have heard the crowds or seen them on their way to work, like anyone else in the area. A law of December 7, 1934, prohibited all public gatherings other than "ancient, traditional processions," and the secret police reported on every incident that looked remotely like a demonstration of non-Nazi German solidarity. The Gestapo checked for organizers of the protest, unsuccessfully.

Monday, March 1 was the second full day of the protest on the Rosenstrasse. All traffic had been diverted, and the nearest elevated train station was closed in an attempt to keep the crowd on the Rosenstrasse from growing. But people willing to defy the orders and death threats of the Gestapo, and disobey the Nazi law forbidding unauthorized public gatherings, would walk the extra mile.

Other Jews shipped to Auschwitz

On Monday afternoon, the ubiquitous army of trucks began streaming into the holding centers. One of these was on the Rossenstrasse to which intermarried Jews were sent.

On the first deportation of Jews arrested in this final roundup—1736 Jews—the SS shoved and beat Jews back on the trucks. From there they headed for a Berlin freight train station—and to the extermination camp at Auschwitz. No one was there to protest for these Jews, and not one of them was saved.

At 10 p.m., the British Airforce struck in a massive bombing Berliners would remember as the "first big English air attack." For an hour, the heavy rain of death and destruction continued unabated. On Tuesday, March 2, the German papers inveighed shrilly against the "terror attack" of the night. The bombing, combined with the weight of Germany's debacle at Stalingrad, deflated confidence of people in Berlin. Wartime morale had never been lower. Goebbels' response was Total War, the application of all people and materials for warfare, and the attempt to conscript the female population between 17 and 45 into forced labor. "We are definitively pushing the Jews out of Berlin," he wrote in his diary.[3] He had apparently not yet heard of the protest at Rosenstrasse.

On March 3, 1943, there was a further deportation to Auschwitz of 1732 Jews who were not intermarried, as the protest continued. The Berlin Gestapo continued house and street arrests of all Jews wearing the Star of David, those in intermarriages and "half-Jews."

A hope for success

On Rosenstrasse, the protest carried on. Having originally arrived to get information, the women were drawn into a feeling of solidarity that expressed itself in public protest. Their rebellious clamor continued, and Gestapo threats came and went without effect. Some of the women actually began to hope that their protest would be successful, resulting in the release of their family members. Anyone calculating whether a protest on the street in Nazi Germany was going to win would have stayed home, remarked one protester. "In my opinion, a decision to put one's life on the line for another can only come from the heart," she said. "One is ready, or not. One does it, or not."[4]

By March 4, the Gestapo had forcibly removed a few women protesters. Also on March 4, the Berlin Gestapo deported 13 Jewish intermarried men to the work camps of Auschwitz. In the Reich Security Main Office, where Adolf Eichmann worked, a schism developed over how to handle the protest. One faction advised brute force, another opposed this.

March 6 was the seventh day of the protest on Rosenstrasse. On this day, the antithesis between the increasingly aggressive actions of the local Berlin Gestapo and the sensitivity to public morale of the highest ranking Nazis reached its height. The Berlin

---

[3] Stoltzfus, *Resistance of the Heart,* p. 226.
[4] Stoltzfus' archive.

Gestapo deported 25 intermarried men, none of whom had children. They were headed to Auschwitz, along with 665 other Jews.

Release of the Jews

On this same day, Goebbels decisively put a stop to the protests by releasing all the intermarried Jews and their half-Jewish children. Hitler gave his approval. For the Propaganda Minister, success, based in mass conformity, lay in making it appear as though dissent did not exist, especially in Berlin. Releasing the intermarried Jews was the best way to dispel the open protest, visible not just to Germans but to foreign diplomats, journalists, and spies in the German capital, Goebbels reasoned. To him, the crowd of women calling out for Jewish family members was a truly "disagreeable scene." "Goebbels released the Jews in order to eliminate the protest," Goebbels' deputy Leopold Gutterer recalled in a postwar interview.[5] "The police could have arrested them and sent them to a concentration camp, but that wasn't handled that way because the people openly made public that they weren't in agreement with what was happening," he said.[6]

The Gestapo released 1,700 to 2,000 Jews imprisoned at Rosenstrasse. The vast majority survived the war without going into hiding, living on official ration cards. In Auschwitz, the intermarried Jews who had been deported during the Final Roundup were released on orders from a "high Reich authority." Subsequently, there were no completed efforts to deport as a group German Jews married to non-Jews. At the end of the Second World War intermarried Jews constituted 98 percent of the surviving German Jewish population that had not been driven into hiding.

---

[5] Stoltzfus, *Resistance of the Heart*, p. 244.
[6] Stoltzfus' archive.

Sources

This account is based on original research and a draft prepared by Nathan Stoltzfus. For fuller details and sources, see

Stoltzfus, Nathan, *Resistance of the Heart: Intermarriage and the Rosenstrasse Protest in Nazi Germany,* New York and London: W. W. Norton, 1996.

Chapter Eleven

OUSTING A GUATEMALAN DICTATOR—1944

Dictatorship and discontent

By 1944, General Jorge Ubico y Castañeda had ruled Guatemala for 13 years. Last in a long line of Liberal Party dictators, General Ubico was known for being "thorough, efficient, intelligent, and heartless." When talk of a rebellion surfaced in 1934, Ubico lashed out with a murderous campaign intended to eliminate all opposition. "I am like Hitler," he commented, "I execute first and give trial afterwards. . . ."[1]

During the Second World War, Guatemala joined the Allies. The war not only aggravated economic instability in the Central American nation, it led to the presence of U.S. troops in the country and daily newspaper reports of the war. All this introduced new ideas that were at odds with the Guatemalan status quo. The ideas of political democracy and U.S. President Franklin Roose-

---

A list of sources for this case appears at the end of this chapter.
[1] Rosenthal, *Guatemala,* p. 201.

velt's "Four Freedoms" began to make inroads among Guatemala's small educated elite. Discontent was growing, but slowly.

Nonviolent contagion

In April and May 1944, unrest in neighboring El Salvador drew the attention of many Guatemalans. Although El Salvador's dictator, General Maximiliano Hernández Martínez, had crushed an attempted military coup with extreme brutality, the widespread nonviolent struggle that arose in the aftermath brought the country to a halt. On May 9, Martínez was forced out of office and into exile.

The Salvadoran experience had a profound effect on popular feelings about the dictatorship in Guatemala. Many students, teachers, and members of the professional classes saw the recent events in El Salvador as a model for bringing an end to their own tyrannical regime. In late May 1944, the first signs of public opposition began. Forty-five prominent lawyers asked for the removal of a biased and corrupt judge who regularly tried political opponents of the regime. General Ubico asked them to specify their charges. They did, publishing a series of articles in a major Guatemala City newspaper. This was the first time anyone had publicly asked Ubico for the removal of a public official.

University unrest

Several weeks later, 200 teachers signed a petition asking the government for a wage increase. Two of those who had drafted the petition were arrested, and shortly thereafter five students were detained for "printing propaganda." On June 19, the Student Law Association met at the National University and called for the resignation of the school's dean and for the reinstatement of a professor fired by Ubico for political reasons. On the following day, they were joined by 1,000 students from various departments of the university, and they broadened their demands to include support for the teachers' petition.

The students met again on June 21. This time, they raised the stakes with an ultimatum to Ubico. They demanded autonomy for the National University, the rehiring of two fired teachers, the release of several imprisoned students, and the opening of new departments and areas of study. The students also demanded the appointment of competent professors, not simply ones hired for their political loyalty to the regime. The petition was delivered to the National Palace the next day. The students threatened to call a strike if their demands were not met within 24 hours.

Petition against martial law

Ubico responded by declaring a state of emergency, and accused the students of exhibiting "nazi-fascist tendencies." As the students and teachers went on strike, an important group of professionals (primarily lawyers and a few doctors) came to their defense. Invigorated by El Salvador's successful nonviolent insurrection the month before, some lawyers had been hoping to eventually launch a similar movement in Guatemala. They would have preferred more time to organize, but the students had taken the initiative and this gave the lawyers the impetus to act. In less than two days, they gathered the signatures of 336 "prominent citizens" for a petition explaining the just actions of the students and teachers, rejecting the government's accusations against them, and calling for the lifting of martial law and the restoration of constitutional guarantees. Since 25 of the signatures were illegible, the document came to be known simply as the *Memorial de los 311.*

On June 24, the *Memorial de los 311* was delivered to the National Palace. A group of students gathered that morning to march peacefully past the National Palace and the U.S. Embassy. All wore black and walked in silence in what they termed a "demonstration of pain." Although the protest was small, it was the first since the university strike began. It was an open repudiation of the state of emergency.

In the evening, another demonstration took place that was significantly larger. It filled the streets with teachers, students, professionals, and some workers. Demonstrators sang *La Marseillaise* and the Guatemalan national anthem, and a lawyer read a copy of the Atlantic Charter. When passing the National Palace, protesters shouted the first public appeals for Ubico's resignation. Both demonstrations were peaceful. Later that night, however, the police sent a group of drunken thugs shouting anti-Ubico slogans into a neighborhood religious festival, in an attempt to discredit the movement. The police then moved in, ignoring the *provocateurs,* while beating and arresting hundreds of others.

Under siege

On Sunday morning, June 25, Guatemala City awoke to a virtual state of siege. The city had been completely militarized, with artillery posted outside every strategic location. Morning demonstrations were broken up by soldiers and cavalry. Meanwhile, lawyers Federico Carbonell and Jorge Serrano—the two men who had delivered the *Memorial de los 311*—were summoned to the National Palace. In a meeting with Ubico's cabinet ministers, Carbonell, Serrano, and a few others were recognized as "representatives of the people" (a title that they insisted did not belong to them). The lawyers did what they could to press their case. Nevertheless, the government was inflexible, and simply demanded that they "calm the people."

In the afternoon, Carbonell and Serrano met with members of the diplomatic corps, and then spoke directly with General Ubico late in the day. During the latter meeting, shots were heard in the distance. A women's march of mourning had been attacked by police. When the cavalry charged the crowds and opened fire, several people were wounded, and schoolteacher María Chincilla Recinos was killed. The movement now had its first martyr.

Talks broke down after the killing of Chincilla, and further negotiations were fruitless. "As long as I am president," declared an unrepentant Ubico, "I will never permit a free press, nor free association, because the people of Guatemala are not ready for a democracy and need a strong hand."[2] Carbonell and Serrano responded by sending a new message to Ubico later that evening, indicating that the only way to restore order was for the General to step down.

Paralysis against dictatorship

On June 26, an economic shutdown went into effect. Although plans for a widespread work stoppage had been in the planning

---

[2] Rosenthal, *Guatemala,* p. 211.

stages for almost a week, the nearly complete participation in the strike was due in large part to public outrage over the killing of María Chincilla.

The streets were emptied. Workers, businessmen, shopkeepers, market vendors, and bus drivers joined the already striking students, teachers, and lawyers. Opposition leaders received word from the chief of police that any further demonstrations would be fired upon, even if the protesters were only women and children. Rather than risk more lives, all efforts were thrown behind the economic shutdown.

For five days, Guatemala City was paralyzed. Students distributed leaflets calling on the public to remain nonviolent and to continue resisting. The government's militarization of transportation sectors and threats of reprisals against striking businesses had little effect on the populace. Scores of letters and petitions flooded the National Palace, asking for Ubico's resignation.

The army and police did not know what to do. Everyone was at home, and there was no target or organized group for them to attack. The dictator's power had crumbled, and the people had lost their fear. As Mario Rosenthal wrote:

> Energetic and cruel, Jorge Ubico could have put down an armed attack. He could have dodged an assassin's bullet and cut the assassin down himself. He could have imposed his will on any group of disgruntled, military or civilian, and stood them up against a wall. But he was helpless against civil acts of repudiation, to which he responded with violence, until these slowly pushed him into the dead-end street where all dictatorships ultimately arrive: kill everybody who is not with you, or get out.[3]

Withdrawal of support and resignation

Jorge Ubico handed in his resignation on July 1, 1944, and turned power over to a triumvirate of generals.

Although the June nonviolent struggle movement had only lasted one month, it produced a victory, both for the people and for their method of struggle. Exiles soon returned, political parties formed, and constitutional guarantees were restored. However, one of the junta members, General Federico Ponce, envisioned himself as a new supreme ruler and fraudulently en-

---

[3] Rosenthal, *Guatemala,* p. 200.

sured his own victory in makeshift elections on October 13. Opposition parties and students responded by initiating limited strikes. On October 20, with the backing of students and workers, a group of reform-minded junior officers led by Jacobo Arbenz and Javier Arana launched a swift coup d'état and wrested power from General Ponce. Fair elections soon followed, and Guatemala entered into its 10-year "springtime of democracy."

Sources

This account was written by Joshua Paulson and is based on research by Dr. Christina Clamp, presented in

The Overthrow of Jorge Ubico: A Case of Nonviolent Action in Guatemala, unpublished manuscript: Friends World College, 1976.

Other sources for this chapter are

Rosenthal, Mario, *Guatemala: The Story of an Emergent Latin-American Democracy* (New York: Twayne Publishers, Inc., 1962), pp. 191-222.

Schneider, Ronald, *Communism in Guatemala: 1944-1954* (New York: Praeger Publishers, 1959), pp. 1-19.

Silvert, K. H., *A Study in Government: Guatemala* (New Orleans: Middle American Research Institute, Tulane University, 1954), pp. 1-7.

Dr. Christina Clamp has reviewed and revised this text.

Chapter Twelve

ENDING BUS SEGREGATION IN MONTGOMERY—1955-1956

Joshua Paulson

Racial segregation

Following the abolition of slavery in the wake of the U.S. Civil War, white citizens throughout the southern United States approved local and state legislation calling for enforced separation of the races. This doctrine of segregation was legally upheld by the U.S. Supreme Court in 1896. In Montgomery, Alabama, as in most cities of the former Confederacy, segregation became a social, political, and economic reality characterized by oppression and injustice.

Segregation in Montgomery extended to the city's public transit system, where each bus had a certain number of seats in the

---

A list of sources for this case appears at the end of this chapter.

front reserved exclusively for white passengers. African-Americans were prohibited from sitting next to a white person anywhere on the bus, and if a bus was full, African-Americans would be required to stand in order to provide additional seating for newly boarded whites. Nevertheless, more than 15,000 African-Americans in Montgomery rode the bus every day, making up more than 70% of the total bus-riding population in the city.

For years, African-Americans expressed their complaints and outrage at ongoing mistreatment on the public buses. In many instances, bus drivers would make rude or insulting remarks to passengers. African-Americans were often told to enter the bus in the front to pay the fare, and then to get off and re-board again in the rear so as not to pass by any white people. One elderly gentleman who refused to reboard from the rear was even shot and killed by police officers. There were also many instances of bus drivers ordering the arrest of passengers who refused to vacate their seats in order to accommodate white passengers.

The Women's Political Council

Such ongoing incidents, as well as the general conditions of oppression suffered by the African-American population under segregation, led to the creation of an African-American women's organization in Montgomery, the Women's Political Council (WPC). The group often met with the city's mayor in order to amicably request solutions to minor problems affecting their community.

In the early 1950s, the Women's Political Council received increasing numbers of complaints regarding the treatment of African-Americans on the buses. When a proposal to raise bus fares was brought before the City Commissioners in 1954, the WPC objected unless the following demands were met:

1. a city law that would make it possible for Negroes to sit from back toward front, and whites from front toward back until all the seats are taken;

2. that Negroes not be asked or forced to pay fare at front end and go to the rear of the bus to enter;

3. that buses stop at every corner in residential sections oc-
    cupied by Negroes as they do in communities where
    whites reside.[1]

These were all practices that were common in many other cities throughout the South at the time. Actual desegregation of the
buses was considered too radical a demand, and was not included
in the petition.

The mayor responded simply by asking bus drivers to be more
courteous to all passengers, and to stop more often in African-
American neighborhoods. Although this seemed to work for a
time, just three months later the complaints had again become
numerous. This prompted the Women's Political Council to notify the mayor that "there has been talk from 25 or more local
organizations of planning a citywide boycott of buses. . . ."[2]

Rosa Parks' refusal and defiance

The opportunity to launch such a boycott came on December
1, 1955, when four African-Americans on a public bus were ordered to give up their seats to newly boarded whites and stand.
Three passengers stood up, but Mrs. Rosa Parks quietly refused
to do so. She was subsequently arrested. Mrs. Parks had not
planned on being the cause of a bus boycott. But when word of
her arrest reached members of the Women's Political Council
later that evening, the group decided the time was ripe. Members
spread the word and printed handbills asking African-American
citizens to stay off the buses for a one-day boycott on Monday,
December 5 to protest Mrs. Parks' detention.

When the day of the boycott arrived, even the participants
were stunned at its near-total effectiveness. Buses drove around
empty all day throughout the African-American neighborhoods.
In the late afternoon, a group of influential religious, business, labor, academic, and civic leaders of the African-American community met to create a new organization intended to unite the
community in an ongoing protest against the unjust and unfair
treatment on the city's buses. Dominated by clergy, the group

---

[1] Jo Ann Gibson Robinson, letter to Mayor W. A. Gayle, May 21, 1954. Facsimile
reprinted in Robinson, *The Montgomery Bus Boycott and the Women Who Started It,*
p. viii.
[2] David J. Garrow (ed.), *The Walking City,* pp. 611-612.

called itself the Montgomery Improvement Association (MIA), and elected young Baptist minister Dr. Martin Luther King, Jr. as its president.

That same evening, a mass meeting was held in a local church and was presided over by representatives of the new Association. Buoyed by the near-perfect participation in the boycott, those present voted unanimously to continue the protest until a series of demands was met.

Similar to the demands presented 18 months earlier by the Women's Political Council, these were moderate in nature and not intended to challenge bus segregation. The protesters resolved not to resume riding the buses until (1) courteous treatment by the bus operators was guaranteed; (2) passengers were seated on a first-come, first-serve basis—Negroes seating from the back of the bus toward the front while whites seated from the front toward the back; and (3) Negro bus operators were employed on predominantly Negro routes.[3]

Extending the bus boycott

As the boycott was to be extended indefinitely until the MIA's demands were met, alternate methods of transportation had to be created to accommodate the 15,000 African-Americans who normally rode the bus to work and back each day. On the first day of the boycott, 18 taxi companies owned by African-Americans agreed to transport people at normal bus-fare rates. But this plan proved unsustainable, after such reduced taxi rates were declared illegal by the city government.

By the second week of the boycott, the MIA had created its own private carpool, with "dispatch" and "pick-up" stations established all over Montgomery. Money was raised, donations poured in from all over the country, and new vehicles for the carpool were purchased. The establishment of the carpool system allowed the bus boycott to continue with remarkable effectiveness. However, many people still preferred to walk in order to visibly express their determination.

---

[3] King, *Stride Toward Freedom*, pp. 63-64.

Principle and technique

From the very beginning of the boycott, the MIA maintained unity and discipline in the African-American community through an appeal to Christian love. Religion played a large part in the lives of African-Americans in Montgomery, and this was reflected in the nature of the mass meetings held by the MIA twice a week for the duration of the boycott. Such meetings were generally led by prominent local ministers, and included prayers and readings of scripture that emphasized love and forgiveness. These meetings were also key in imparting a religiously inspired doctrine of nonviolence to the group. According to MIA president Martin Luther King, Jr., "Night after night the group was admonished to love rather than to hate, and urged to be prepared to suffer violence if necessary but never to inflict it. Every 'pep' speaker was urged to make nonviolence a central part of his theme."[4]

Referring to the thousands who participated in the boycott, Dr. King later remarked "it is probably true that most of them did not believe in nonviolence as a philosophy of life, but because of their confidence in their leaders and because nonviolence was presented to them as a simple expression of Christianity in action, they were willing to use it as a technique."[5]

Negotiations fail

The leaders of the boycott assumed their protest would be relatively short-lived. They felt their demands were not difficult to grant even under the laws of segregation, and that once negotiations took place the city would quickly concede. But after the first round of talks between the MIA, city officials, and the bus company were held on December 8, it became clear that the city was not prepared to yield. A second round of negotiations was held later in the month, at which time the MIA even dropped its demand for the bus company to hire African-American drivers on African-American routes. But the city still did not give in. The MIA met with city leaders on only one other occasion, again without any progress. The boycott continued. Meanwhile, the

---

[4] King, *Stride Toward Freedom*, p. 87.
[5] King, *Stride Toward Freedom*, p. 89.

carpool system continued to improve, soon making use of more than 300 vehicles.

After the city failed to "talk down" the MIA in negotiations, it turned to new tactics to defeat the boycott. On January 24, 1956, Mayor Gayle announced that he, along with all the City Commissioners, had joined the extremist White Citizens Council. Shortly thereafter, the city officials embarked on a "get tough" policy toward the MIA and the boycott. African-American drivers were harassed and arrested by police for minor or nonexistent traffic violations. People who chose to walk to work were told they could be "arrested for vagrancy." City officials attempted to make the African-American community break apart and lose its discipline out of fear.

Bombings

Threats of violence against the boycott leaders increased steadily. The first real test of nonviolent discipline for the movement came on the night of January 30, when Martin Luther King, Jr.'s house was firebombed. When informed of the incident, Dr. King rushed home to find a large, angry crowd of supporters outside, many of them armed and prepared to use retaliatory violence against the white community. Dr. King calmed the crowd and appealed once more to discipline, nonviolence, and Christian love in the face of such attacks. Eventually, everyone went home. When another bomb exploded a few days later at the home of E. D. Nixon, a veteran labor activist and leader of the MIA, the community responded in a disciplined fashion. No longer was there talk of violence.

On February 1, the MIA changed course and radicalized its position. The organization had tried moderation, and had asked for a new seating arrangement on the buses within the confines of the segregation laws. But such efforts had failed. So when the white city officials refused to concede during negotiations, and later fueled a campaign of violence and intimidation against the African-American community, the MIA filed a lawsuit in federal court challenging the constitutional legality of segregation itself. Unfortunately, they would have to wait months for the hearing to begin, and even longer for a verdict. And on the same day that the suit was filed, another bomb exploded in Montgomery.

The bombings failed to break the resolve of the African-American community, and Montgomery officials soon resorted to mass arrests. Rather than issue weak citations for traffic violations, this time the city called together the Montgomery County Grand Jury to investigate the MIA for "conspiracy to destroy a legitimate business." On February 21, the Grand Jury indicted more than 100 people on the conspiracy charge.

The loss of fear

By now, though, most fear had already been cast off. No one tried to evade arrest. In fact, dozens of people rushed to the police station to be arrested. People whose names were on the arrest list expressed pride. Many whose names were not mentioned expressed disappointment.

Dr. King was the first defendant to go on trial for conspiracy, and he was convicted and fined by a judge within four days. The remainder of the cases were postponed pending appeal of the King verdict. Instead of demobilizing the movement, the ruling actually gave new momentum and determination to the struggle. By this time, the bus boycott had drawn a great deal of national and international attention, and the verdict against Dr. King helped to galvanize additional support for the boycott.

Three months later, the federal district court finally ruled on the MIA's anti-segregation suit, announcing that bus segregation was indeed unconstitutional. But the battle was not yet over. The City of Montgomery appealed the decision to the U.S. Supreme Court.

Meanwhile, the boycott continued, but not without difficulties. False rumors were spread of misuse of funds and corruption within the MIA. In September, the MIA was informed that the liability insurance for the vehicles used in the carpool would be abruptly canceled. But the boycott now had international supporters, and a London firm announced it would take the insurance. Then, in late October, the City of Montgomery filed a motion in the county court to outlaw the carpool, alleging it was a "private enterprise operating without a franchise."

Victory

The boycott leaders in the Montgomery Improvement Association were deeply worried about the new lawsuit, since a prohibition of the carpool would have threatened the boycott's feasibility. Then, on November 14, only hours before the local court granted the city an injunction to halt the car pool operations, the U.S. Supreme Court issued its own awaited ruling. It was the victory the African-American community had been waiting for, as the high court declared Alabama's state and local laws requiring segregation on public buses to be unconstitutional.

On the evening of November 14, the MIA decided to officially discontinue the boycott. However, thousands of people attending mass meetings that night agreed not to resume riding the buses until the desegregation order physically arrived from the Supreme Court. Later that night, the Ku Klux Klan organized a drive-by "parade" through Montgomery's African-American neighborhoods. Rather than show fear, the residents were unintimidated. Most continued their activities as if nothing was happening, or watched the 40 carloads of hooded Klan members go by from their porches. Some even waved. Unsure of how to react, the Klan simply drove by and disappeared.

Integration and discipline

While awaiting the arrival of the Supreme Court mandate, the MIA worked to prepare the community for integrated buses. Workshops on nonviolent action were held, training people on how to react if insulted or attacked when they resumed riding the buses. On December 20, federal marshals served the desegregation order on the City of Montgomery. The next day, more than one year after the boycott had begun, African-Americans and whites rode together on integrated public transportation for the first time.

There were no major incidents on the buses for the first few days. Then, in the last week of December, buses were fired on throughout the city. The forces of reaction attempted to create a reign of terror, and they succeeded in forcing the bus company to halt all evening and nighttime operations. Reactionary violence climaxed on January 9, 1957 when six bombs exploded in Montgomery. Two destroyed the homes of Rev. Ralph Abernathy and Rev. Bob Graetz, both leaders of the MIA. The others caused significant damage to four African-American churches. And two weeks later, several more bombs went off and an unsuccessful attempt was made to dynamite Dr. King's home.

Once more, the African-American community seemed prepared to respond with violence. But as in the past, they held themselves together with great discipline and did not retaliate. Shortly thereafter, the violence came to an abrupt halt. Desegregation proceeded at a smooth pace, and the integrated buses resumed normal operations.

Although it occurred in local conditions, the Montgomery bus boycott elevated the American civil rights movement to the national level. It was in Montgomery that the tactics of nonviolent action were first employed on a large scale by the fledgling movement, and it was there that religiously inspired nonviolence emerged as the guiding social doctrine for southern African-Americans for much of the following decade.

Sources

Garrow, David J. (ed.), *The Walking City: The Montgomery Bus Boycott, 1955-1956,* Brooklyn, New York: Carlson Publishing, 1989.

King, Jr., Martin Luther, *Stride Toward Freedom: The Montgomery Story,* New York: Harper and Row, 1958.

Reddick, L. D., *Crusader Without Violence: A Biography of Martin Luther King, Jr.* (New York: Harper & Brothers, 1959), pp. 108-145.

Robinson, Jo Ann Gibson, *The Montgomery Bus Boycott and the Women Who Started It,* Knoxville: The University of Tennessee Press, 1989.

Chapter Thirteen

FRENCH DEFENSE AGAINST AN ARMY COUP—1961

French army coup in Algeria

Early in April 1961, French President Charles de Gaulle announced that he was abandoning the attempt to keep Algeria a French colony. Then, in French-ruled Algeria on the night of April 21-22, the French First Foreign Legion Parachute Regiment initiated a coup d'état in the colony. The regiment captured control of the City of Algiers from the French officials, while other rebel military units seized key points nearby. There was no serious opposition to their actions. At least three French generals in Algeria loyal to the legal government—including the Commander-in-Chief—were arrested by the rebels. This was the culmination of earlier policy conflicts between the French army in Algeria and the civilian French government in Paris.

On April 22, the rebel "Military Command" declared a state of siege in Algeria, announced it was taking over all powers of

A list of sources for this case appears at the end of this chapter.

civil government, and warned that it would break any resistance. Four colonels had organized the conspiracy, but this statement was issued under the names of four recently retired generals (Challe, Jouhaud, Zeller, and Salan). The next day, the coup was backed by General Nicot (acting head of the French Air Staff), General Bigot (commanding the air force in Algiers), and three other generals. The usurpers seized control of newspapers and radio stations, giving them (they thought) a monopoly on communications in French Algeria.

The French government in Paris was in trouble. Half a million French troops were in Algeria, leaving very few operational units in France itself. Two French divisions stationed in Germany were of doubtful reliability. The loyalty of the paramilitary *Gendarmerie Nationale* and the *Compagnies Républicaines de Sécurité* was also in doubt. The success of the coup in Algiers hinged on replacing the legal government in Paris. Therefore, it was feared that a parallel coup might be attempted against the government in Paris or that the air force might transport rebel troops to invade France and oust the de Gaulle government.

French defiance

On Sunday, April 23, the political parties and trade unions in France held mass meetings, calling for a one-hour symbolic general strike the next day to demonstrate that they would oppose the coup in Algeria. That night, President de Gaulle broadcast a speech to the French nation, urging people to defy and disobey the rebels: "In the name of France, I order that all means—I repeat all means—be employed to bar the way everywhere to these men until they are brought down. I forbid every Frenchman, and in the first place every soldier, to carry out any of their orders."

The same night, Prime Minister Debré in his own broadcast warned of preparations for an airborne attack and closed down the Paris airports. While stressing "all means"—which obviously included military action—Debré placed his confidence in popular action to persuade soldiers who might be flying in to resume loyalty to the legal government: "As soon as the sirens sound, go there [to the airports] by foot or by car, to convince the mistaken soldiers of their huge error."

Widespread noncooperation

De Gaulle's broadcast from France was heard in Algeria via transistor radios by the population and members of the military forces, many of them conscript soldiers. Copies of the address were then duplicated and widely distributed. De Gaulle credited his talk with inducing widespread noncooperation and disobedience: "From then on, the revolt met with a passive resistance on the spot which became hourly more explicit."

On April 24, at 5:00 p.m., ten million workers took part in the symbolic general strike. De Gaulle invoked emergency powers accorded to the President by the constitution. Many right-wing sympathizers were arrested. At airfields, people prepared vehicles to be placed on runways to prevent planes from landing. Guards were stationed at public buildings. A financial and shipping blockade was imposed on Algeria. That night, General Crepin announced that French forces in Germany were loyal to the government, and the next morning they were ordered to Paris.

Most French troops in Algeria acted to support the de Gaulle government and to undermine the rebels. By Tuesday, two-thirds of the available transport planes and many fighter planes had been flown out of Algeria, making them unavailable for an invasion of France. Other pilots feigned mechanical failures or blocked airfields. Army soldiers simply stayed in their barracks. There were many cases of deliberate inefficiency: orders from rebel officers were lost, files disappeared, and there were delays in communications and transportation. The conscripts generally recognized the power of their noncooperation in support of the legal government.

The coup undermined

Leaders of the coup had to use many of their available forces to attempt to keep control and maintain order among the French troops in Algeria itself. Many officers temporarily avoided taking sides, waiting to see how the contest would go, preparing to join the winning side.

French civilians in Algeria, including the Algiers police, at first supported the coup. But civil servants and local government officials in the City of Algiers often resisted, hiding documents and personally withdrawing from their offices so as not to be seen as supporting the coup. On Tuesday evening, April 25, the Algiers police resumed support for the de Gaulle government. Internal disagreements developed among the leaders of the revolt, with some advocating violent measures. That night, in another broadcast, de Gaulle ordered loyal troops to fire at the rebels. There was no need, however. The coup had already been fatally undermined.

The leaders resolved to call off the attempted coup. The night of April 25-26, the First Foreign Legion Parachute Regiment withdrew from Algiers and rebels abandoned government buildings. General Challe surrendered and the other three retired generals heading the revolt went into hiding.

There were a few casualties (probably three killed) and several wounded in Algeria and Paris. The attack had been decisively defeated by defiance and dissolution. De Gaulle remained President and Algeria became independent in 1962.

Sources

Roberts, Adam, "Civil Resistance to Military Coups," in *Journal of Peace Research* (Oslo), vol. XII, No. 1 (1975), pp. 19-36.

All quotations are from this source.

Chapter Fourteen

CALIFORNIA GRAPE WORKERS' STRIKE AND BOYCOTT 1965-1970

Hardy Merriman

A history of exploitation

For much of the twentieth century, California farm workers suffered from abject poverty, displacement, homelessness, and extreme economic exploitation. Collectively, these farm workers were among the lowest of the lower classes in the western United States, and the vast majority of them worked without union representation.

By the early 1960s, the prospects for organizing California farm workers continued to look bleak. While other industries in

---

A list of sources for this case appears at the end of this chapter.

the United States had already unionized by that time, organizing efforts among farm workers were consistently defeated through physical brutality and the manipulation of *braceros* (low-paid Mexican workers) to break strikes.[1]

The first walkout

In the summer of 1965, domestic Filipino and Mexican-American grape pickers in Delano, California, were ready to take action. The latest indignity that they had suffered was being paid 20¢ to 30¢ less than the *braceros* toiling beside them. Many of these underpaid workers were affiliated with a farm worker organization, the Agricultural Workers Organizing Committee (AWOC), and when the growers denied them equal pay to the *braceros*, the AWOC helped several hundred farm workers at nine different farms stage a walkout.

For four days, the growers waited out the strike, believing that the farm workers' hunger and poverty would force them back into the fields. On the fifth day, however, the bosses shut off electricity at the workers' camps, barricaded families inside of their shacks, and began to recruit Mexican strikebreakers. This led Filipino leader Larry Itliong, the AWOC organizer for the strike, to ask a young Chicano leader, César Chávez, and his Mexican-based National Farm Workers Association (NFWA) for help.

An alliance forms

Chávez decided to bring the proposal to join the strike before his general membership. On September 16, approximately 1,500 NFWA and AWOC members filled Our Lady of Guadalupe Church in Delano. There, Chávez appealed to his membership to support the AWOC strike, saying that the farm workers were in a "struggle for the freedom and dignity which poverty denies us," but adding that "it must not be a violent struggle, even if violence is used against us."[2] After his speech, the NFWA cast a unani-

---

[1] *Braceros* were Mexican nationals who were contracted to work in the United States for a set wage and a single harvest season. They provided cheap and easy labor and were frequently used as strikebreakers.
[2] Dunne, *Delano*, p. 80.

mous vote in favor of joining the strike. Chávez concluded the night by calling on all workers to pledge to be peaceful.

The vote to join the AWOC meant that 48 farms, covering more than 400 square miles, were now on strike. Although the farm workers could not picket the entire area all at once, pickets were organized to assemble at the entrance gates of several struck farms each morning. There, they greeted workers as they entered the fields and attempted to turn them away. In the afternoons, the pickets formed roving teams and drove to nearby fields to yell at strikebreakers.

These actions persisted over the following two months, but during this time worker participation in the strike never exceeded half of the 2,000 workers at the struck farms. The reasons for this lack of participation were varied. Many workers felt that they could not survive without their wages. Others found work at nearby, unstruck farms. Still others were unwilling to join the strike because they feared the violence unleashed against the pickets by the farm foremen.

Repression and violence challenge the strikers

The farm foremen were furious about the strike and beat the pickets while the police stood by and watched. The foremen also drove trucks at the picket lines or used tractors with plough disks to churn up dust clouds to choke the strikers. Hired security guards joined the campaign of intimidation and fired shotguns over the strikers' heads or tempted them to cross picket lines so that they could arrest them. Strikers were also evicted from their farm camps and were sprayed with harmful fertilizer and pesticides.

Under these circumstances, many picketers were tempted to resort to violence against their antagonists. The strikers were poor and hungry and did not necessarily have a religious conviction in nonviolent action. Isolated acts of violence and property destruction started to occur among the farm workers. Piles of grapes in a packing shed were set ablaze at night. Slingshots were fired at strikebreakers in the field. Strikebreakers also received threats and had their windows broken. Chávez reacted to these circumstances by continually urging people to remain nonviolent.

Attracting outside support

Despite Chávez's insistence on solidarity and nonviolent discipline among the workers, the strike was on the verge of unraveling as it entered its fourth week. Small acts of violence threatened to undermine the movement and new strikebreakers were continually brought in to work the fields. The strike needed a plan to generate more volunteers, more publicity, and more money if it were to remain viable.

Chávez looked for an opportunity to link the strikers' cause to people outside of Delano. He received just such an opportunity on October 16, 1965, when Kern County Sheriff Roy Galyen stated that strikers would be arrested for "disturbing the peace" if they continued to picket in groups larger than five or to shout at workers in the fields. In response, Chávez planned an immediate public challenge of Galyen's directive, knowing that if the strikers were arrested, the farm workers would receive widespread media attention and outside support.

The next day, workers gathered for a rally on the outskirts of Delano. David Havens, a local clergyman, stood before the crowd and started a dramatic reading of Jack London's definition of a strikebreaker as a "two-legged animal with a corkscrew soul, a waterlogged brain and a combination backbone made of jelly and glue. . . ."[3] Havens was immediately arrested while the cameras were rolling, and suddenly the strikers had a protest issue that would resonate throughout the state.

Unwittingly adding to this protest issue, Sheriff Galyen issued another decree two days later outlawing use of the word *huelga* (strike). On October 29, the new decree was challenged by 31 volunteers and 13 workers who took to the fields to yell the forbidden word. The demonstrators were arrested and brought to court while the media captured the entire event.

On the same day as the demonstration, Chávez planned to give a talk in Berkeley, California, to a group of student activists. His talk was very well received based on the "coincidental" news that on that same morning, all of the farm worker demonstrators had been arrested. Chávez collected $2,000 in contributions that afternoon and later visited three other California universities, rais-

---

[3] Ferris and Sandoval, *The Fight in the Fields,* p. 106.

ing a total of $6,700 and attracting national media attention and volunteers to his cause. Chávez later said about the Sheriff's arrests, "[W]e took every case of violence and publicized what they were doing to us. . . . By some strange chemistry, every time the opposition commits an unjust act against our hopes and aspirations, we get tenfold paid back in benefits."[4]

Establishing a new support base

Chávez returned from his speaking tour accompanied by dozens of new volunteers—students, church representatives, civil rights activists, and members of urban labor unions. When these new recruits started showing up in the Delano picket lines, the growers realized the potential power of the farm workers' strike. They were no longer simply fighting an isolated group of agricultural laborers; they were fighting a movement.

The growers responded by forming their own groups, such as "Mothers Against Chávez" and "Citizens for Facts," which counterpicketed and cast the growers as underdogs who were oppressed by the farm workers' movement.[5] Their arguments, however, did not have much impact on public opinion. Instead, the growers primarily fought the strikers by relying on the same method that they had used in the past: recruiting more strikebreakers to work the fields.

At first, it was unclear whether this simple reliance on strikebreakers would work against the 1965 strike. Then the November harvest came, and the growers, despite the farm workers' actions and outside support, harvested a record crop. This startling setback revealed the bottom line to the farm workers—that as long as the growers could import new labor, a simple strike would be insufficient to force them to negotiate. This realization led the farm workers to reassess their future plans in ways that ultimately yielded results.

---

[4] Levy, *Cesar Chávez*, p. 194.
[5] Ferris and Sandoval, *The Fight for the Fields*, p. 97.

A new direction for the strike

Following the November harvest, the farm workers were unsure about what to do next. Many wanted to continue taking action, but they had nowhere left to picket. Chávez experimented with opening up new fronts against the growers and in this spirit he sent two workers and a student to track the final shipment of Delano grapes to the Oakland, California, loading docks to ask the longshoremen not to load it. The longshoremen agreed, and before the authorities could intervene, they left 1,000 10-ton crates of grapes rotting on the piers.[6]

This singular action sparked an entirely new direction for the movement—a boycott. The longshoremen's action was so effective that Chávez assigned a team of workers and students to create a boycott plan. Two targets were chosen, Schenley Industries and DiGiorgio Corporation. Both companies were large, had widely visible name brands, offered diverse product lines, held union contracts in their other industries, and profited only marginally from their grape and vineyard operations. It was believed that these two companies would capitulate easily because a grape boycott would 1) generate negative publicity that would hurt product sales in their more profitable enterprises, and 2) cause them difficulty in their other, already unionized, branches.[7]

The boycott got underway using a two-tiered approach. First, a core of young, full-time volunteers were trained and dispatched to 13 cities nationwide to establish boycott centers. These centers organized local unions, community organizations, and church groups to take action against boycotted products. The volunteers also recruited 10,000 people to join them in leafleting consumers, writing letters, picketing storefronts, and harassing store owners to remove struck items from their shelves.

The second tier of the boycott involved allied union activities, particularly "hot cargo" actions, in which other unions would refuse to handle shipments of strikebreaker grapes. The Teamsters and the International Longshoremen's and Warehousemen's Union refused to ship grapes for a brief time. Near Delano, railway men at the switching yard diverted shipments of grapes for a day or two and left them rotting in the sun. The farm workers also

---

[6] Jenkins, *The Politics of Insurgency*, p. 152.
[7] Jenkins, *The Politics of Insurgency*, p. 152.

developed a network of informants called *submarinos* ("submarines") who kept the farm workers abreast of company shipments and plans so that they could picket whenever grape cargo was loaded or unloaded.

In addition to these efforts, the National Council of Churches, as well as the United Auto Workers and the AFL-CIO, pushed allies on the Senate Subcommittee on Migratory Labor to hold three days of public hearings, which began on March 14, 1966. The hearings brought national attention to arrests and anti-union tactics and it lent legitimacy to the farm workers' cause.

The March to Sacramento

In the aftermath of the Senate hearings, the farm workers embarked on another offensive. On March 17, César Chávez and 70 supporters set off on a 300-mile, 25-day march from Delano to the California State House in Sacramento. The march received widespread support and media attention. Rallies were held by the marchers every night and a theater group was founded, *El Teatro Campesino* ("The Farm Worker Theater"), which performed skits dramatizing the farm workers' struggle.

The march increased in size as time went on, and by the time it reached Stockton, approximately three days from Sacramento, its ranks had swelled to 5,000 people and it received constant press coverage. The farm workers carried signs calling for boycotts of Schenley products, and the media attention badly damaged Schenley's public image. The company responded by contacting Chávez and calling for negotiations.

Chávez met with Schenley's lawyers and negotiations proceeded swiftly. The NFWA soon held a union contract whereby Schenley workers gained a 35¢/hour raise and a new union hiring hall, effective immediately. Chávez publicly announced the contract on April 7, 1966, a few days before reaching Sacramento. It was met with great rejoicing among the farm workers. They had gained their first major victory.

Winning over DiGiorgio

After their victory over Schenley, the farm workers intensified the boycott against DiGiorgio. Volunteers throughout the country redoubled their efforts to distribute leaflets and to lobby grocery stores to remove DiGiorgio products. Furthering these efforts, 60 trade unionists and students in Chicago chose a new protest target—food distribution centers—and blocked grape shipments all over the Midwest.[8]

To complement the boycott, the picket lines also kept the pressure on, but suffered a significant setback on May 20, 1966, when DiGiorgio secured a court injunction limiting the number of pickets that could appear at its Delano farm. Undeterred by this setback, three female farm workers proposed replacing the pickets with mass prayer meetings outside of the farm entrance. Chávez seized on the idea, and for the next three months, hundreds of strikers showed up every day to pray at a wooden altar in the back of a station wagon. Even some strikebreakers left the fields in the morning to pray at the altar.

In addition, the farm workers advocated work slowdowns, or *planes de tortuga* ("turtle plans") among strikebreakers and workers in the field. Chávez encouraged these workers "to work slower, to do less, to do inferior work, anything that was legal and moral, but that would cost the grower money."[9]

In response to the pressure that these actions generated, DiGiorgio capitulated and announced that the State Mediation and Conciliation Service would hold union elections on DiGiorgio's vineyard properties. Soon afterwards, however, DiGiorgio changed the rules and made a surprise public announcement: the elections would be held in four days, and DiGiorgio's accounting firm would oversee the process. In addition, DiGiorgio announced that a competing union, the Teamsters, would be added to the ballot along with the NFWA and the AWOC.[10]

The NFWA and the AWOC were outraged by DiGiorgio's sudden announcement, and claimed that the election was rigged for a Teamster victory. They called for a boycott of the elections

---

[8] Ferris and Sandoval, *The Fight for the Fields,* p. 128.
[9] Levy, *Cesar Chávez,* p. 222.
[10] The Teamsters had an interest in the elections because 20 percent of their membership worked in agriculture-related industries (agricultural trucking, canneries, etc.) and an independent farm workers' union represented a threat to their power. The Teamsters had secretly offered a favorable contract to DiGiorgio if that company pressured its workers to vote for them.

and obtained a court injunction on June 23, 1966, removing their names from the ballots.

The elections went forward two days later, with the Teamsters winning. Chávez, however, managed to counter their victory by cornering California Governor Pat Brown at the Mexican-American Political Association convention and pressuring him to get DiGiorgio to agree to an election investigation. Governor Brown, needing the Mexican-American vote in his upcoming election, acquiesced, and an investigation by the American Arbitration Committee was set up.

The Committee invalidated the previous election and declared that a new, three-way (NFWA, AWOC, Teamsters) runoff would be held. In an attempt to increase their chances of winning the elections, the leadership of the NFWA and the AWOC decided to formally join forces and merge their organizations to become the United Farm Workers Organizing Committee (UFWOC).

On August 30, 1966, after weeks of rallying by the strikers and volunteers, the UFWOC won the election among fieldworkers, 530-331, while the Teamsters won a small, separate election among the packing shed workers. Negotiations between the UFWOC and DiGiorgio proceeded over the next seven months and yielded a contract that provided unprecedented benefits for agricultural workers.

This victory gave the farm workers new energy to pursue their cause further, and over the following year, many of Delano's vineyards became unionized. By the fall of 1967, the UFWOC represented about 5,000 workers, approximately 2 percent of California's total farm worker population. Its remaining challenge was to unionize the other 98 percent.[11]

The Great Grape Boycott

With success over many of Delano's vineyards, the UFWOC changed course and decided to take on a larger opponent—the table grape industry. They chose their first target, the Giumarra Corporation, accordingly. Giumarra was the largest table grape grower in Delano, holding 12,000 acres and employing over

---

[11] Jenkins, *The Politics of Insurgency,* p. 162.

2,000 at peak harvest. It also had a long history of worker grievances against it.[12]

On August 3, 1967, 1,200 workers walked out of Giumarra's fields. The company counterattacked by trucking in countless strikebreakers from Los Angeles and other areas. Giumarra also obtained a court injunction four days later that virtually abolished picketing near its ranches.

This injunction crippled the farm workers' efforts and, as with DiGiorgio, it soon became clear that under these conditions a simple strike would be insufficient for the farm workers to achieve their objectives. The UFWOC needed a new course of action and decided to shift more of its energy towards a nationwide boycott.

Student volunteers, as well as 50 strikers, were trained and sent to a handful of cities nationwide to call for a boycott on six Giumarra labels. Giumarra responded to this by working with other California growers to ship its products under 100 different labels used by other, nonboycotted farms. This mislabeling campaign caused widespread confusion among consumers and volunteers about what products to buy and what products to boycott.

After considerable debate, the UFWOC decided to solve this problem by expanding its boycott to include all California table grapes. This decision enlarged the farm workers' operations considerably and required increased inflows of funding and volunteers, as well as a stronger organization of the campaign.

Undaunted by these challenges, Chávez continued to send strikers and their families to assume leadership positions in boycott centers around the United States. These workers, along with many devoted students, constituted a core of full-time boycott workers, spending long hours organizing and leafleting while receiving room and board and $5/week. In addition, many part-time volunteers—professionals, housewives, civil rights activists—participated by picketing stores and attending rallies. Institutional allies, such as church leaders, political officials, and union representatives, also flocked to the cause and were increasingly involved in organizing meetings, providing contacts, and offering funding and office space.

---

[12] Jenkins, *The Politics of Insurgency,* p. 163.

By early 1968, the boycott had made inroads on several fronts. Three dozen mayors and city councils across the country endorsed the strike, and many municipalities stopped purchasing table grapes. Various unions also joined the effort and mounted job actions in support of the boycott. Some supermarket chains also ceased buying grapes out of fear of secondary boycotts against them.[13]

The temptation of violence and Chávez's fast

Although these gains were significant, they represented only a small fraction of what was needed if the boycott was to be completely effective. Despite the farm workers' successes, progress was slow and many strikers had not anticipated the amount of work that a nationwide boycott would require. Some strikers became frustrated with the slow pace, and this transferred into a temptation to use violence. Strikers began blowing up irrigation pumps, scattering nails on roads to puncture farm vehicle tires, and some even started to bring guns to the picket line.

This property destruction and talk of violence led Chávez to begin a private fast in Delano on February 15, 1968. When he publicly announced his decision four days later, he scolded his workers, saying "No union movement is worth the death of one farm worker or his child or one grower and his child."[14] Chávez said his fast was penitence for the union's consideration of violence and that he would start eating again only after all of the strikers renewed their commitment to nonviolence.

Union officials were devastated at this announcement and unsuccessfully tried to lobby Chávez to abandon his fast. Slowly, however, farm workers rallied by his side and the violence ceased. People gathered around him 24 hours a day and the movement started to become reunified. As one observer noted, "[Chávez's fast] turned out to be the greatest organizing tool in the history of the labor movement. . . ."[15]

On March 10, after 25 days of fasting and after dropping 30 pounds in weight, Chávez ate for the first time at a Catholic Mass

---

[13] Mooney and Majka, *Farmers' and Farm Workers' Movements,* p. 161.
[14] Ferris and Sandoval, *The Fight for the Fields,* p. 144.
[15] Ferris and Sandoval, *The Fight for the Fields,* p. 143.

outside of his cabin. He was surrounded by 6,000 supporters and the national media. Even Senator Robert Kennedy showed up. The farm workers' movement was reunited in its commitment to nonviolent methods and it had been thrust into the national limelight.

Reorganizing the boycott

With his fast broken, Chávez resumed actively organizing the farm workers' struggle. He took to personally training hundreds of farm workers and sent them to boycott offices in 20 major cities in the U.S. and Canada.

For all of 1968, these farm workers organized secondary boycotts against large grocery chains. Picket lines, ranging in size from three to 40, were formed at store entrances to greet customers. The grocery stores responded by obtaining court injunctions against mass picketing in front of their stores. Police also arrested picketers and the ultra right-wing John Birch Society started to organize counter-protests as well.

Nonetheless, the boycotters gradually gained the upper hand and succeeded in getting many supermarkets to stop carrying table grapes. As one boycott organizer said, "We just totally disrupted all of these stores and we were a pain. . . . We made life miserable for the stores and so they finally figured out we were more trouble than the grapes were worth. . . ."[16]

The evidence of this was clear. By early 1969, retail grape sales were down 12 percent nationwide, and $3 million to $4 million in grapes rotted on the vine. Shipments to the 41 top grape-consuming cities in the United States were down 22 percent, and grape prices continued to drop because there was an overabundance of supply. In specific cities, meanwhile, the boycott's effectiveness was extraordinary. For example, when compared to sales in 1966 (a year of comparable yield to 1969), 1969 table grape sales were down 34 percent in New York, 41 percent in Chicago, 42 percent in Boston, and 53 percent in Baltimore.[17]

Meanwhile, supermarket chains fought the UFWOC's actions with several measures. Safeway, the West Coast's largest grocery

---

[16] Ferris and Sandoval, *The Fight for the Fields,* p. 153.
[17] Mooney and Majka, *Farmers' and Farm Workers' Movements,* p.163.

chain, started "Freedom to Work" committees, which argued the case for nonunionization and denounced Chávez as a Marxist and a fraud. Safeway and the California Farm Bureau also launched a $2 million campaign with a conservative public relations firm to promote grape consumption under the idea of "consumer rights." Editorials and advertisements appeared extolling the health benefits of grapes, and bumper stickers were printed that read, "Eat California Grapes, the Forbidden Fruit!"[18]

Political allies also mobilized on the supermarkets' behalf. California Governor Ronald Reagan directed the Board of Agriculture to launch a public relations campaign aimed at discrediting the boycott and ordered state agencies to provide growers with welfare recipients and prisoners to work as strikebreakers, until a court overruled it. While campaigning for president, Richard Nixon called the boycott "illegal" and declared that it must be broken "with the same firmness [with which] we condemn illegal strikes, illegal lockouts, or any other form of lawbreaking."[19] As president, Nixon went on to quadruple table grape shipments to U.S. troops in Vietnam, from 555,000 pounds in 1968 to nearly 2.2 million pounds in 1969.[20]

Despite these actions, by mid-1969 the growers were losing the boycott battle. The market was flooded with grapes and few were buying. Ten percent of the previous season's harvest was in cold storage and fruit dealers started to sell grapes on consignment only. North American shipments fell off by one-third.[21]

In February 1970, 40 growers in Coachella, California, succumbed to the protest and began negotiations with the UFWOC. After two months, a settlement was reached in which the growers rehired UFWOC strikers and granted them a raise and substantial benefits. Once the contract was signed, the Coachella growers discovered that the value of their grapes rose by 25¢ to $1 per box, and consumers started to buy them again.

This new competition from Coachella ratcheted up the pressure on the remaining Delano growers. On July 25, 1970, 26 Delano growers, representing 8,000 jobs and half of the state's crop, followed suit and asked for negotiations. Four days later, all of

[18] Ferris and Sandoval, *The Fight for the Fields*, p. 148.
[19] Mooney and Majka, *Farmers' and Farm Workers' Movements*, p.163.
[20] Mooney and Majka, *Farmers' and Farm Workers' Movements*, p.163.
[21] Jenkins, *The Politics of Insurgency*, p. 171.

the Delano growers signed union recognition contracts. Thousands of farm workers gathered outside the hall while the contracts were signed, singing "*Nosotros venceremos, nosotros venceremos*" ("We shall overcome"). Chávez emerged from the hall and merely spoke one word: "Victory."

The UFWOC boycott had succeeded in winning rights for California farm workers. Using primarily nonviolent action between 1965-1970, the farm workers' struggle had grown from a small, local action into a national union that included 20,000 farm workers under 150 grape contracts with companies that accounted for 85 percent of California's table grape market. As César Chávez said, the UFWOC's victories provided proof that "through nonviolent action in this nation and across the world . . . social justice can be gotten."[22]

---

[22] Levy, *Cesar Chávez*, p. 325.

Sources

del Castillo, Richard Griswold and Garcia, Richard A., *César Chávez: A Triumph of Spirit* (Norman, Oklahoma: The University of Oklahoma Press, 1995), pp. 41-59.

Dunne, John Gregory, *Delano* (revised edition), New York: Farrar, Straus & Giroux, 1971.

Ferris, Susan and Sandoval, Ricardo, *The Fight for the Fields: Cesar Chávez and the Farmworkers Movement* (New York: Harcourt Brace and Co., 1997), pp. 82-157.

Jenkins, J. Craig, *The Politics of Insurgency: The Farm Worker Movement in the 1960s* (New York: Columbia University Press, 1985), pp. 131-174.

Levy, Jacques, *Cesar Chávez: Autobiography of La Causa* (New York: W. W. Norton and Co., 1975), pp. 182-328.

Mooney, Patrick H. and Majka, Theo J., *Farmers' and Farm Workers' Movements: Social Protest in American Agriculture* (New York: Twain Publishers, 1995), pp. 150-183.

UFW webpage [http://www.ufw.org]

Chapter Fifteen

CZECH AND SLOVAK DEFIANCE OF INVASION—1968-1969

Invasion to prevent reform

Czechoslovakia had long been regarded as the most hard-line Communist regime among the Soviet satellites. However, from January through August 1968, the Czechoslovak Communist Party and government were in the process of limited but significant democratization. The basic Leninist conception of the dictatorial role of the Communist Party had been renounced and declarations were issued of the importance of freedom of expression and organization.

Leaders of the Soviet Union, as well as heads of other Communist regimes in Eastern Europe, saw this as a major threat. The Soviet leaders were determined to halt the attempt to create "socialism with a human face." When denunciations proved to be insufficient to reverse the process, a decision was made to invade Czechoslovakia. In addition to at least 300,000 Soviet troops,

A list of sources for this case appears at the end of this chapter.

military units from Poland, East Germany, Hungary, and Bulgaria participated.

There are no indications that either the Czechoslovak Communist Party or the government prepared for defense in case of such a contingency. Some Czechoslovak writers, however, had earlier in the summer made statements such as this: "If the Russians invade, don't shoot at them. Practice passive resistance."

Soviet officials expected that the massive invasion of Czechoslovakia by more than half a million Warsaw Pact troops would overwhelm the much smaller, 175,000-strong Czechoslovak army within days, leaving the country in confusion and defeat. The invasion would make possible a coup d'état to replace the reform-minded regime of Alexander Dubcek with a conservative pro-Moscow clique that would restore Communist discipline.

At 11 p.m. on August 20, Czechoslovakia was invaded by land from the east, north, and south. The invasion continued throughout the night. The country's airports were seized and used heavily by the invading forces to bring troops and light tanks into the country. The Soviet troops had orders to be prepared for battle, but also only to fire if fired upon.

The invasion denounced

The invasion was fully successful militarily. Virtually all important Czechoslovak towns were occupied within two days. There were reports that Soviet officials had expected military resistance and were certain they could crush it within four days, install a subservient regime, and withdraw quickly.

Resistance began in the early hours of the invasion. Almost immediately, the people of Bratislava, in the Slovak section of the country, embarked on nonviolent resistance even before the official announcement of the invasion. The example was taken up throughout the country.

During the night of August 20-21, Czechoslovak military forces were ordered to stay in their barracks and not to offer military resistance. This order seems to have been understood and obeyed.

Shortly after 1:50 a.m. on August 21, a statement from the Czechoslovak Communist Party Presidium was read out on the Prague home service radio. It stated that troops of the five Communist states had invaded the country without knowledge of government or party officials. It appealed to all citizens to remain calm and "not to offer resistance to the troops on the march," and declared that the military forces had not been ordered to defend the country. The invasion was denounced as contrary to principles of relations between socialist states and norms of international law. All leading party and government functionaries remained at their posts. The National Assembly and a plenum of the Communist Party Central Committee were being convened to discuss the situation. The statement was rebroadcast several times.

Occupation meets resistance

While Czechoslovak troops obeyed the order not to engage the invaders, resistance of a different kind began almost immediately. At 4:30 a.m., a Prague Radio announcer said: "Let us be courageous and dignified but calm. . . ."[1] An hour later, another announcer said:

> Wherever you meet members of the occupation forces do not allow open clashes to arise which might be regarded as provocations. Wherever you have contacts with foreign soldiers, explain to them that in this country up to their arrival there was absolute calm, no threat of counterrevolution. . . .[2]

Predominantly, even at the beginning, the resistance took the forms of nonviolent protest, noncooperation, and defiance. But at first, there was occasionally scattered, unorganized violent resistance, primarily from young people.

At 6:35 a.m., Czechoslovak Radio broadcast an appeal to the people to remain calm and meet the occupation with "passive resistance."[3] A proclamation from the National Assembly that afternoon referred to the possibility of a general strike.[4]

Around 8 a.m., the government news agency, CTK, received a proclamation from a group of Czechoslovak government and Communist Party officials who supposedly had requested the Warsaw Pact troops to enter the country. It was supposed to have

---

[1] Windsor and Roberts, *Czechoslovakia 1968,* p. 115.
[2] Windsor and Roberts, *Czechoslovakia 1968,* p. 115.
[3] Littell, ed., *The Czech Black Book,* p. 27.
[4] Littell, ed., *The Czech Black Book,* p. 49.

been broadcast before the foreign troops invaded. The news agency refused to release the proclamation.[5]

Early on the morning of August 21, the streets of Prague were crowded with young people. Many went to the Radio Center. The radio broadcasters urged them to attempt to engage the invading troops in conversation as "our only weapon." As Soviet tanks approached, the demonstrators greeted them with hisses and clenched fists. The youths formed a human blockade and the tanks stopped. Then the blockade was extended to include overturned buses and other vehicles. While the radio broadcast a description of the scene, the radio announcer urged the youths through loudspeakers on the street:

> Keep calm. Let your weapon be passive resistance. Don't be provoked into bloodshed. That's what they're waiting for. Don't be provoked.[6]

Between 6:30 a.m. and 3:00 p.m., villagers living along the river Upa in Eastern Bohemia formed a human chain across a bridge blocking Soviet tanks and other motorized units. Unable to cross the bridge, the Soviet column turned around and left.[7]

That morning in Prague, near the Radio Center, young people tried to argue with the Russian tank crews, telling them in Russian that they should go home. When the tanks opened fire, first above the demonstrators and then into the crowd, some of the youths were wounded or killed. Some demonstrators then threw "Molotov cocktails" (gasoline bombs) at the tanks, a few of which caught fire and killed the tank crews. Similar incidents occurred elsewhere.[8]

Meanwhile, Prague Radio and Radio Czechoslovakia continued to recommend a course of action: "The best solution is the act of passive resistance: not to take any notice of anyone, do nothing, to refuse to do anything at all."[9] As late as 8:30 p.m., Prague Radio was discouraging protest demonstrations. Meanwhile, the Czechoslovak Radio urged self-control, dignified calm,

---

[5] Schwartz, *Prague's 200 Days*, p. 24.
[6] Schwartz, *Prague's 200 Days*, p. 212.
[7] Windsor and Roberts, *Czechoslovakia 1968*, p. 121, n. 31.
[8] Schwartz, *Prague's 200 Days*, pp. 212-213.
[9] Windsor and Roberts, *Czechoslovakia 1968*, p.117.

refusal to build barricades, and refusal to be provoked into the use of violence.[10]

Remain calm but resist!

Despite the apparent lack of advance preparations, a remarkable struggle of noncooperation and defiance developed during the ensuing days.

Thousands of anti-Soviet newspapers and leaflets were distributed.[11] Statements encouraging support for the leadership of Party First Secretary Alexander Dubcek, President Ludvik Svoboda, and the government of Prime Minister Oldrich Cernik were printed in several newspapers on August 21. Some of these papers were delivered by Czechoslovak police cars, using flashing lights and blaring sirens in order to pass Soviet checkpoints.

Early on the morning of August 21, the Presidium of the Czechoslovak Academy of Sciences sent appeal letters to UNESCO in Paris, the Embassy of the Soviet Union in Prague, and scientists throughout the world asking for support against the invasion. Several other organizations issued similar calls for support for the constitutional leadership and appeals to the international community.

Prague Radio reported that morning: "People on Wenceslas Square [Prague] are trying to stop vehicles of the occupation troops with their bodies."[12]

At 7:15 a.m., almost immediately after news of the shots at the Radio Center, Alexander Dubcek, First Secretary of the Communist Party, broadcast an appeal: "I beg you to maintain calm and to bear with dignity the present situation. I appeal to you for calm."[13] This was one of the many appeals broadcast by Czechoslovak Radio from government officials and radio broadcasters.

By 8:00 a.m., many methods of resistance were on display in the Old Town Square in Prague. The statue of the great Bohemian religious reformer and martyr Jan Hus was surrounded by hundreds of citizens, and a Czechoslovak flag was placed atop the statue. An artist engaged in a persistent dialogue with a Soviet

---

[10] Littell, ed., *The Czech Black Book,* pp. 30-33.
[11] Schwartz, *Prague's 200 Days,* p. 213.
[12] Littell, ed., *The Czech Black Book,* p. 31.
[13] Littell, ed., *The Czech Black Book,* p. 31.

captain on the purpose of Soviet occupation. Other citizens discussed the recent issue of the newspaper *Rude Pravo* with several Soviet soldiers. Across the Square, the constant chanting of "Dubcek!" could be heard. In a separate part of the Square, citizens sang the national anthem.

Large groups of young people arrived in Wenceslas Square later that morning. After hearing of the shooting that had been reported outside the Central Committee building, they walked to the building and continued to the hospital at Frantisek carrying blood-stained Czechoslovak flags.

The statue of Saint Wenceslas (king of Bohemia, 1378-1419) was draped with Czechoslovak flags and signs that read "Soldiers, go home! Quickly!" in Russian. Leaflets were scattered that demanded the swift withdrawal of the occupation armies. Thousands of newspapers reporting on and denouncing the occupation circulated throughout the country.

Kidnapping, arrest, and refusal

A few hours after the broadcast of the statement by the Presidium of the Central Committee of the Communist Party on August 21, the Soviet KGB (state police) kidnapped the head of the Communist Party, Alexander Dubcek; the Prime Minister, Oldrich Cernik; the National Assembly President, Josef Smrkovsky; and the National Front Chairman, Frantisek Kriegel. The kidnapped leaders might have been killed once the coup had been successful, as had happened to the Hungarian leader Imre Nagy in 1957.

A puppet regime did not replace the kidnapped leaders.

The Soviet officials also held under house arrest the President of the Republic, Ludvik Svoboda, a soldier-statesman who was popular both in Czechoslovakia and the Soviet Union. However, President Svoboda courageously refused to sign the document presented to him by a conservative pro-Moscow clique that would have given the mantle of legitimacy to a new hard-line regime.

As a result of the mobilization of nonviolent resistance and the refusal of collaboration, the Soviet political objective was initially blocked. There were thus serious logistical and morale problems that began among the invading troops.

Defiance by radio and Party congress

The invasion was not going smoothly. Harry Schwartz of *The New York Times* observed: "Twenty-four hours after the invasion began, the Kremlin knew it had blundered. It had neither a compliant government nor a compliant people in Czechoslovakia."[14]

The secret broadcasting stations that had been established by the military for use in case of a West German invasion had been turned over to the civilian resistance groups. People on the streets of Prague listened on transistor radios to the resistance broadcasts. Telephone contacts to the stations enabled the broadcasters to give very specific instructions to demonstrators in a particular location to keep discipline and avoid provocative violence. It was also possible through the clandestine radio network to convene several official bodies, and these organizations opposed the invasion.

The Extraordinary Fourteenth Party Congress, the National Assembly, and the remaining government ministers all issued statements similar to the emergency statement by the Party Presidium already broadcast that the invasion had begun without the knowledge of party or governmental leaders. There had been no "request" for intervention. Some of the convened bodies selected interim leaders who carried out certain emergency functions.

On the morning of August 22, the Extraordinary Fourteenth Congress of the Communist Party had already convened for a secret emergency one-day meeting at a factory in Prague-Vysocany, with 1,192 of 1,543 previously elected delegates attending. The Congress had intended to convene on September 9. Most of the delegates from Slovakia were blocked from arriving in Prague by Soviet forces, but delegates maintained such complete secrecy that the Soviet officials did not know the location of the Congress.

The Congress declaration denounced the invasion as unjustified, denied it had been requested by party or government officials, and insisted that there had not been any counterrevolution. The Congress demanded "that normal conditions for the functioning of all constitutional and political authority be immediately created and that all detained officials be released forthwith

---

[14] Schwartz, *Prague's 200 Days*, p. 222.

so that they can resume their posts." ". . . Socialist Czechoslovakia will never accept either a military occupation administration or a domestic collaborationist regime dependent on the forces of the occupiers."[15]

The Congress demanded the departure of foreign troops, and called for a one-hour protest strike on August 23 at noon if negotiations on withdrawal had not begun within 24 hours, and if Party leader Dubcek had not made a timely statement on the matter. The declaration stated that the Party would take additional steps. The Congress also sent warm greetings of support to Dubcek, who had already been seized. The Czechoslovak Communist Party had turned into a resistance organization against the Soviet Union.

The National Assembly met and demanded "the release from detention of our constitutional representatives . . . in order that they can carry out their constitutional functions entrusted to them by the Sovereign people of the country." It also demanded "immediate withdrawal of the armies of the five states."[16]

On the morning of August 22, two sets of leaflets were distributed condemning traitors. There was also a petition campaign supporting the release of Alexander Dubcek.

Strikes and other nonviolent resistance

On August 22, Czechoslovak Radio broadcast calls from factory workers for a one-hour or indefinite general strike if interned constitutional and Party leaders were not released by 6 p.m.

All kinds of graffiti were painted and drawn throughout Prague. Nazi swastikas were painted on Soviet tanks. Slogans on walls included "Socialism yes, occupation no." "Ivan, go home. Natasha is in bed with Igor." "Home, dogs." The morale of the occupation troops plummeted.[17]

The clandestine radio network during the first week both created many forms of resistance and shaped others. It had not only convened the Extraordinary Fourteenth Party Congress, but also called one-hour general strikes, requested the rail workers to slow

---

[15] Littell, ed., *The Czech Black Book,* p. 81.
[16] Remington, ed., *Winter in Prague,* p. 382.
[17] Schwartz, *Prague's 200 Days,* p. 213.

the transport of Russian radio tracking and jamming equipment so that it arrived days late, and discouraged collaboration within the State Police. There is no record of any collaboration among the uniformed public police. Indeed, many of them worked actively with the resistance.

Broadcasters on the radio argued the futility of acts of violence and the wisdom of nonviolent resistance. The radio instructed students in the streets to clear out of potentially explosive situations and cautioned against rumors. The radio was the main means through which a politically mature and effective resistance was shaped.

Role of resistance radio

Through the radio, different levels of resistance and various parts of the country were kept in steady communication. With many government agencies put out of operation by Russian occupation of their offices, the radio also took on certain emergency functions (such as obtaining manpower to bring in potato and hop harvests) and provided vital information. This ranged from assuring mothers that their children in summer camps were safe to reporting meager news of the Moscow negotiations.

All the while, citizens ignored the Soviet troops. At noon on August 23, the sirens sounded throughout Prague to "officially" commence the general strike called by the Party Congress, and young people urged everyone to leave the streets.

Negotiations in Moscow

Totally successful militarily, the Soviet Union now faced a strong political struggle. In the face of unified civilian resistance, the absence of a collaborationist government, and the increasing demoralization of their troops, the Soviet leaders agreed on Friday, August 23 that the defiant President Svoboda would fly to Moscow for negotiations. He was allowed to broadcast to the nation before departure. Once in Moscow, Svoboda refused to negotiate until Dubcek, Cernik, and Smrkovsky could join the discussions.

A dilemma faced by the Czechoslovak leadership during negotiations in Russia was whether to offer too little, possibly enraging the Soviets and blocking any hopes of acceptable terms, or to offer too much, and risk being viewed as traitors by their own people. The leaders did not know how long and how effectively the nonviolent struggle could continue. They were apparently doubtful of the disciplined capacity of the populace for sustained resistance in the face of severe repression. There had been no preparations and no strategic planning for such a contingency.

After the negotiations in Moscow, Smrkovsky reported upon his return to Prague that they had had "extremely little or almost no information" about what was happening at home.[18] They could not, therefore, know whether the resistance was still strong or whether it remained disciplined. They did not know what leverage they had in the negotiations. They did know that a violent outbreak or a collapse of resistance could be disastrous.

Resistance continues

On the evening of August 23, Czechoslovak Radio reported that arrests would probably occur throughout the night, and appealed for all citizens to paint over or remove street signs, house plates, name plates, and highway signs. The City of Prague responded with lightning quickness and became practically anonymous. It was claimed that the only sign that remained correct read "Moscow—1500 kilometers."

It should not be understood that the resistance was completely solid. There were several high-level collaborators who sought to do the bidding of the invaders. Also, some people took advantage of what was at times a chaotic situation to loot and riot.

During the day of August 24, Soviet troops intensified their efforts to control the Czech population in Prague. The troops searched automobiles, scoured the city by helicopter for clandestine radio transmitters, and dropped leaflets justifying the need for the presence of occupation troops. A curfew was imposed between 10 p.m. and 5 a.m. Occupation troops tore down posters, which were often replaced within hours by inscriptions and graffiti such as "Dubcek Avenue."

---

18 Schwartz, *Prague's 200 Days*, p. 232.

Denunciations and troop reliability

The invasion produced a major international setback for the Soviet Union. The events included a debate in the United Nations Security Council, denunciation by many usual supporters of the Soviet Union, and the worldwide denunciation by Communist parties and Communist-front organizations, including the World Federation of Trade Unions. International protests occurred throughout August 27, including demonstrations in Italy, a general strike in Austria, a work stoppage in France, and two minutes of national silence in Holland.

On August 25, the Czechoslovak government informed the Soviet Embassy about promises broken by Soviet occupation troops: several detained officials had not been released, the disarming of Czechoslovak army units had continued, and occupation troops had not vacated all towns, villages, and buildings, nor those areas where Czechoslovak Army troops were stationed.

Czechoslovak Radio reported the appearance of visible guilt and sorrow of many of the occupation troops. One tank crew "refused to obey an officer's orders to disperse a crowd of people."[19] Another report said that "some Hungarian troops are reported to have been made to operate without ammunition, because of their unreliability."[20] There were many other reports of extreme morale problems among the invading soldiers.[21] There were even reports of a few suicides of Soviet soldiers or officers on the streets of Prague.[22]

There were reliable reports that large numbers—or even all—of the initial invasion troops had to be rotated out of Czechoslovakia within four days and replaced by fresh troops.

The ten commandments

According to an account in the newspaper *Lidova Demokracie* on August 26:

> This spontaneous expression of resistance on the part of the unarmed Czechoslovaks has morally disrupted the occupation

---

[19] Littell, ed., *The Czech Black Book*, p. 152.
[20] Windsor and Roberts, *Czechoslovakia 1968,* p. 127.
[21] See Littell, ed., *The Czech Black Book,* pp. 212-213 and also, pp. 112, 114, 134, 164, and 190.
[22] For example, see Littell, ed., *The Czech Black Book,* p. 86.

force. No general staff in the whole world could have thought up such a plan. It was born in the heads of fourteen million Czechs and Slovaks, who are rebuffing their uninvited guests and showing by their psychological resistance that it is possible to face down even the mightiest army with calm and common sense. This is something the generals in the Kremlin never expected.[23]

In the countryside, agricultural workers worked extra hours in support of the struggle. On August 26, factory workers at the Foundries received news from the Horka Poricany Agricultural Cooperative that they planned to donate over five tons of potatoes to the citizens of Prague, stipulating that the money gained from the sales would be donated to the Fund of the Republic.

Also on August 26, the newspaper *Vecerni Praha* published "Ten Commandments" of resistance:

1. Don't know
2. Don't care
3. Don't tell
4. Don't have
5. Don't know how to
6. Don't give
7. Can't do
8. Don't sell
9. Don't show
10. Do nothing[24]

A compromise and incremental political controls

After four days of negotiations in Moscow, a compromise settlement was reached. This left most of the Czechoslovak leaders in their positions but called for the Party to exercise more fully its "leading role," and left Soviet troops in the country. The compromise seems also to have included the sacrifice of certain reform-minded leaders and reforms.

---

[23] Littell, ed., *The Czech Black Book*, p. 213.
[24] Littell, ed., *The Czech Black Book*, p. 218.

The compromise, called the Moscow Protocol, created severely mixed feelings among the people. Observers abroad saw it as an unexpected success for the nation and its leaders. An occupied country is not supposed to have bargaining power. But most Czechs and Slovaks saw it as a defeat and for a week would not accept it.

Both the negotiations and the settlement were an admission by the Soviet leadership that their military means had failed to achieve their objectives. They had therefore shifted to political means, backed by military might, and gained a significant degree of success.

The Soviet leaders continued efforts throughout the following months to gain their objectives through incremental political steps. With the assistance of certain Czech and Slovak Communists, an attack was launched on the legitimacy of the Extraordinary Fourteenth Party Congress, claiming it had been summoned unconstitutionally, and its actions therefore were nullified. At the same time, more Dubcek supporters were added to the Central Committee of the Party.

Czechoslovak Communist Party and government bodies took concrete steps to bow to Soviet wishes. The National Assembly on September 13 legalized "temporary" censorship of the press and banned political groups that were outside the Communist-dominated National Front. In October, Soviet Premier Kosygin came to Prague to sign a treaty legalizing the "temporary" stationing of Soviet troops in the country, without stated limits of time or numbers. Under Soviet pressure, two magazines were banned. The directors of Czechoslovak radio and television were fired, but so were some officials who had supported the invasion.

During these months, Dubcek, Cernik, and Husák made speeches preaching "realism" and friendship with the Soviet Union. Thousands of Czechs and Slovaks left the country permanently.

In mid-November, the Communist Party Central Committee, increasingly under Soviet influence, passed a resolution assessing what had happened since January. It asserted that "negative activity in the media" and "confusion of views in the Party and in society" had resulted in sweeping and unjust accusations against the Party and the government. "This destroyed the activity of important organs of political power." The resolution also stated that "The press, radio, and television are first of all the instruments for carrying into life the policies of the Party and the state."[25] Dubcek remained First Secretary of the Party, but his authority was reduced.

Popular resistance and Soviet controls

Despite all this, popular resistance to the occupation troops continued. It sometimes took the form of open demonstrations. The press, radio, and television found ways to express the country's true feelings. This was sometimes done in direct criticisms of Soviet justification of the invasion and sometimes in indirect and symbolic ways. The new censorship was self-censorship, but it operated under the threat that the publication would be banned.

On November 7, there were mass street demonstrations in Prague, Bratislava, Brno and other cities. Later that month, tens of thousands of students conducted four-day sit-ins at high schools and colleges to protest the occupation. Factory workers sent them food.

Such popular pressure helped to bolster Dubcek and his friends. Despite repeated retreats before Soviet pressure, the situation did not return to the earlier times of police terror. "Thus," wrote Harry Schwartz of *The New York Times*, "more than one hundred days after the invasion, something of a stalemate existed in Czechoslovakia." "But Czechoslovakia was still, in early December 1968, the freest of the Soviet satellite states, the only such country in which anti-Soviet sentiments and the desire for freedom were widely articulated." Schwartz added that the outcome of the invasion had proved to be unsatisfactory for both the Soviet Union and Czechoslovakia.[26]

Out of a population of over fourteen million, about 70 people were killed and 1,000 wounded in shootings that resulted from popular resistance to the invasion and the ensuing occupation.

Despite the absence of prior planning or explicit training for civilian resistance, the Dubcek regime managed to remain in power until April 1969, when the government and Party leadership capitulated and was replaced by the Husák regime. The pre-

---

[25] Littell, ed., *The Czech Black Book*, pp. 244-245.
[26] Littell, ed., *The Czech Black Book*, pp. 251-252.

invasion leadership had retained its position about eight months longer than would have been possible with military resistance. The Russians subsequently gained important objectives, including the establishment of a subservient conservative regime. However, the long-term struggle was not finished. In 1989, a new nonviolent struggle began, and the Communist regime collapsed in the face of the "velvet revolution."

Sources

This account is based in part on research prepared by Carl Horne and Christopher A. Miller. It is primarily based on

Littell, Robert (ed.), *The Czech Black Book,* New York: Frederick A. Praeger, 1969

Remington, Robin Alison (ed.), *Winter in Prague,* Cambridge, Massachusetts: M.I.T. Press, 1969.

Schwartz, Harry, *Prague's 200 Days,* New York: Frederick A. Praeger, 1969.

Wechsberg, Joseph, *The Voices,* Garden City, New York: Doubleday, 1969.

Windsor, Philip and Roberts, Adam, *Czechoslovakia 1968,* New York: Columbia University Press, 1969.

Other sources included contemporary accounts from *The New York Times,* the London *Observer,* and the London *Sunday Times.*

Chapter Sixteen

AFRICAN LABORERS STRIKE
NAMIBIA—1971-1972

African strikers cripple the mines

In December 1971, African laborers conducted a successful strike against the oppressive labor control system in Namibia, then called "South-West Africa," and ruled by South Africa with its harsh apartheid system. Quickly spreading throughout the country, the strike soon affected every major mine, and involved 13,000 to 22,000 African workers. The strike crippled the mining industry upon which the country's economy was heavily dependent. As a result, the South African government was forced to negotiate new labor agreements that officially abolished the oppressive contract labor system but did not make major improvements in working and living conditions.

A list of sources for this case appears at the end of this chapter.

South African control of mines and labor

Prior to 1990, South Africa retained control of South-West Africa in defiance of resolutions by the United Nations General Assembly and decisions of the International Court of Justice.

Half of the territory's economy was based upon the mining industry, and most mines and modern developments were found in the "Police Zone," the southern two-thirds of the country. Mining companies produced copper, lead, lithium, tin, vanadium, and diamonds.

In 1971, Namibia had a population of 750,000, of which the largest ethnic group, the Ovambos, a group of related tribes, constituted 45 percent of the population, or 344,000 people. Europeans totaled 90,000. The remaining population was composed of other indigenous tribes.

The various African ethnic groups were largely settled in prescribed tribal areas (Bantustans), or "homelands," as part of South Africa's apartheid policy. Most of the Bantustans were found in the northern one-third of Namibia, where about half the land is desert. The first homeland to be created by the South African regime was Ovamboland, located between Angola and Namibia's "Police Zone," or "white area." Many Ovambos also lived in southern Angola, then a Portuguese colony. The total area where Ovambos resided, including southern Angola, was called Ovambo.

The official Ovambo "homeland" was an undeveloped region with a subsistence agricultural economy. Paying jobs were difficult to find. Ovambos, however, had to earn money to pay the required taxes. Therefore, they were forced to look outside their "homeland" for work.

Ovambos, as all indigenous inhabitants of Namibia, were allowed to work in the "white area" only under the contract labor system, and could only enter there with a pass issued by the employer or officials. They were not allowed to settle there, nor otherwise move about. Ovambos were primarily employed in mines, on farms, or as house servants. At the time, they provided 90 percent of the mine work force, and 70 percent of the labor for the European-controlled industries.

The contract labor system

At the time of the strike, the South-West Africa Native Labour Association operated the contract labor system, and was the only channel to employment. Laborers were placed in "classes" according to physical fitness and age, and distributed to employers for a period of 12 to 18 months. Workers were paid according to class, with minimum monthly wages ranging from R3.75 ($4.95) to R10 ($13.20).[1] Many laborers received somewhat more than minimum wages, however. An employer also supplied housing, food, and some clothing, as well as travel expenses to the work location. In the Police Zone, an employee had no choice of jobs, nor voice concerning wages or working or living conditions. He traveled alone to the place of employment, and lived in a designated African township, or in a compound, where eight men typically roomed together. Families were thus often separated two-thirds of the time for a lifetime.

Despite the circumstances, it was unlawful for an employee to strike or break his contract, although employers sometimes did so. Under these conditions, 40,000 to 50,000 Ovambos worked as contract laborers.

The initial signs of deep unrest among Ovambos emerged after the International Court of Justice ruling in June 1971 against continued South African control of the territory. Several teachers and civil servants were dismissed after they criticized a tribal chief who supported the South African occupiers. To muffle the rising protest, armed police arrested about 800 Africans in June in the Windhoek compound, claiming they were there "illegally." In response, spontaneous labor strikes were launched in Windhoek, the capital, and in the port city of Walvis Bay. These first efforts, however, lacked both plan and strategy, and even organization.

On June 30, leaders of two African Lutheran churches wrote letters in support of the International Court decision, which were read in all churches. Copies were also sent to South African Prime Minister John Vorster. Other tribal chiefs, churchmen, and Africans also gave their approval. Churches, including the Dutch Reformed Church, had long condemned the contract labor system, labeling it a "form of slavery." They argued that, as a result of

---

[1] R refers to Rands, the South African currency.

the system, family life was broken and prostitution and alcoholism had become commonplace.

Between August and December, church leaders met several times with Prime Minister Vorster and Jan de Wet, the Commissioner General for the Northern Native Territories. At one of these meetings, de Wet denied that the contract system was a "form of slavery." He said that if Ovambos were unhappy with the system, they would not let themselves be contracted.

Strike and arrests

On December 10, 1971, a newspaper reported that contract workers in Walvis Bay were planning a strike for December 14. Those workers also wrote letters to friends throughout Namibia urging them to join in the strike, thereby launching a united, coordinated effort against the contract labor system.

On December 12, workers of the Windhoek compound, where about 6,000 Ovambos lived, met and decided to strike the following day. Inhabitants of the compound began a "food boycott" in protest against the rations given to them under terms of the contract. They also complained about overcrowding and unfavorable housing accommodations. Police were sent to the Walvis Bay area to assure maintenance of essential services and to attempt to contain the strike to that area. However, Ovambos elsewhere were prepared to strike.

On Monday morning, December 13, 5,200 residents of the Windhoek compound—trash collectors, porters, hotel and airport employees—refused to go to work. Municipal, construction, and commercial operations were also halted. The food boycott continued as workers not only refused to eat food from compound kitchens, but also destroyed the food. Instead, they bought food at neighborhood stores. Boer police surrounded the compound that day, closed the gate, and refused to allow anyone to leave or enter. There were also reports of police brutality and destructive behavior.

Residents of Windhoek were immediately affected by the strike. Trash was not collected. European students and children, as well as Colored (mixed race) and African workers from South Africa, assisted to keep services in operation.

More policemen were sent to other strike areas on December 13, including Walvis Bay, where 14 strike leaders were arrested. Policemen sympathizing or collaborating with Ovambos were dismissed. G. White, the Chief Bantu Commissioner for South-West Africa, held a meeting in Walvis Bay with strikers and churchmen. The strikers pointed to de Wet's statement that they voluntarily accepted the contract labor system as a reason for their going on strike. No solution was reached.

The following day, White addressed workers of the Windhoek compound, begging them to return to work. They refused, saying they would only return to work if the contract were discontinued. White then announced that Ovambo chiefs and headmen would meet with representatives of the South-West Africa Native Labour Association, with de Wet chairing the meeting. De Wet said the meeting would be held at Grootfontein on February 9 and 10, 1972, to discuss the workers' complaints. Until then, workers chose to return to Ovamboland. Meanwhile, 13 strike leaders were arrested.

The strike spreads

Services in Windhoek were paralyzed as the strike extended to the Klein Aub copper mine on December 15. There, 640 workers walked off the job and production was halted. On the 16th, a "mass exodus" began from Windhoek as the first 1,000 strikers voluntarily boarded trains for Ovamboland and "repatriated" themselves. Later that day, the big mine at Tsumeb was struck by contract workers. Out of a total of 4,090 African workers, 3,700 wished to be repatriated, and production there ceased.

On December 17, more workers struck at Walvis Bay after receiving their paychecks, joining the 10,000 laborers already on strike. Hotel workers at Windhoek also ceased work. Another Tsumeb mine, Kombat, also lost 800 Ovambo workers that evening, halting night shifts and greatly decreasing the resident population. The strike was not restricted to industrial centers, but farms in rural areas were also hit. While the strikers from the Tsumeb mine were being repatriated on December 19, almost all workers at the Berg Aukas lead and vanadium mine also stopped work, halting production. The total number of strikers now reached 12,000.

Government efforts to replace the strikers were almost a total failure. Convicts, European schoolboys, and Kavango workers replaced some of the strikers. De Wet also requested help from the Damaras, an ethnic group whose leaders had rejected the strike. South African authorities, meanwhile, declared that "agitators" were responsible for initiating the strike.

On December 20, 500 workers struck at Grootfontein's municipal compound and hospital. Companies attempted to persuade laborers not to strike. An Ovambo construction crew refused to work at the Uis tin mine, while another 300 workers stopped working inside the mine, bringing production to a standstill. Newspapers reported that "South Africa is heading for a labour calamity;" the strike had taken on "grave proportions," and was "assuming nationwide dimensions." Nevertheless, more than 100 South African policemen flew home for the Christmas holidays. Europeans at the Tsumeb mine, however, had their Christmas leaves cancelled.

On December 29, a strike began at the Rosh Pinah mine, a major supplier to the Iron and Steel Corporation of South Africa. The same day, an emergency meeting was held in Pretoria with Mr. M. C. Botha, South Africa's Minister of Bantu Administration and Development, as well as with mining executives, industrialists, and administrators of South Africa. After the meeting, Botha announced that the Government would strive to revise the contract labor system in the territory.

The strike continued to sweep across the territory in the new year as the Oranjemund diamond mines, the last of the major mines, were struck on January 3. Workers here were soon granted a 10 percent wage increase. Work stoppages also occurred at the Karibib lithium mines, at the Huseb mines, and at a construction firm in Windhoek. An additional 600 Ovambo workers in Ovamboland also deserted their employers. The total number of repatriated strikers reached 13,000 early in January, with reports of the total number of strikers being as high as 20,000 to 22,000.

Organization, repression, and negotiation

The repatriated strikers elected a committee to represent themselves. The committee then drafted a set of demands, distributed the demands in leaflets, and sought negotiations with the government. The demands included the following:

1. freedom of the worker to sell his labor to the highest bidder and choose his own job;

2. freedom to change jobs at any time;

3. freedom to bring families to live at or near work locations; and

4. wages according to the type of work, and not according to skin color. Increased wages so workers would be able to pay their own travel costs to the place of employment, instead of payment by the employer.

The strikers also called for a new pass system, including tribal identity and recognition as citizens of South-West Africa. The leaflet ended by saying that freedom of employment did not mean trouble or unrest.

On January 12, 1972, police reinforcements were flown from South Africa as a "precautionary measure." Additional reinforcements arrived by road. De Wet said that "agitators" were trying to spark an uprising, and police were sent to prevent that from occurring. Furthermore, the Government said that the additional forces had been requested by the Ovamboland government.

On January 17, a decision by the Ovamboland Legislative Council prohibited the repatriated strikers from meeting. All public assemblies were banned, and police were instructed to enforce the new regulation. Just a few days earlier, on January 14, the Council had unanimously condemned the contract labor system, declaring it "an evil and an insult to Ovambo dignity," and had completely endorsed the strikers' demands.

Abolition of the contract labor system

On January 19, the United Nations Council for Namibia met to discuss the labor strike. After hearing three petitioners from prominent African organizations, the Council announced that the contract labor system plainly violated the Universal Declaration of Human Rights. The Council unanimously condemned the contract system and demanded its immediate abolition.

On the afternoon of January 20, after two days of negotiations at Grootfontein, the contract labor system was abolished and replaced by a new labor policy. Labor bureaus were to be established in Ovamboland, where workers could apply for work. The recruiting organization, the South-West Africa Native Labour Association, was discontinued. Specific earnings, working conditions, periods, hours, and benefits would be designated in the contract. Both sides were free to end a contract. Proof that an employer could provide sufficient food and housing was now required. Free medical treatment would also be supplied, and the rankings of laborers by class, based on physical condition and age, were to be abolished. However, provisions to have a worker's family accompany him to the employment location, a major demand of the striking workers, were not included.

M. C. Botha, Minister of Bantu Administration and Development, officially recognized the new accord and said that workers could again be employed under the terms of the new agreement. Following Botha's announcement, Mr. Nangutuula, an associate of the South-West African Peoples Organization, who was serving as the strikers' committee chairman, in a radio broadcast called for the strikers to return to work.

Impact on Angola

The Namibian strike also had repercussions in Portuguese-ruled Angola. As many as 53 percent of Ovambo laborers came from southern Angola, and some 13,000 had returned home. Various sections, totaling 100 miles, of the border fence, which divided Angola from Ovamboland and split the Ukanawanya tribe, were destroyed. Three hundred Portuguese soldiers were mobilized.

During January, the Ovambos attacked Angolan militiamen and pro-government chiefs, demanded European expulsion from Ovamboland, an end to livestock inspection, and burned stock kraals. South African troops intervened. An Ovambo man was reported killed on January 18, and three policemen injured. On January 26, another Ovambo man found cutting the border fence was killed.

Meanwhile, notwithstanding the new agreement, church leaders issued a statement declaring that the basic grievances of the old contract system still remained. Apparently, most strikers had rejected the new agreement.

More repression and violence

On January 26, the South African government announced that it would send defense units to Ovamboland with orders to act "firmly," to help police restore and maintain order. The Ovamboland Legislative Council had reportedly also requested police assistance. The following day, January 27, the South African Government imposed a news blackout in Ovamboland. No unauthorized persons were allowed to enter the tribal area. Officials were not allowed to brief the press. Nevertheless, Botha denied that a state of emergency existed in Ovamboland, saying that the unrest was the work of "agitators."

The strikers continued to meet to discuss the new agreements, although meetings had been declared illegal. Violence apparently erupted as police moved in to break up these meetings.

In Ovamboland between January 28 and February 1, at least 10 more people were killed in clashes with police. Two others were killed by fellow tribesmen. On February 1, it was also reported that Reverend Colin Winter, the Anglican Bishop of Damaraland, had his entry permit to Ovamboland revoked. By February 28, 20 clergymen had been expelled from South-West Africa.

The Government of South Africa released on February 4 a proclamation of the "Regulations for the Administration of the District of Ovamboland"—i.e., emergency regulations for the area. All gatherings of more than five individuals were declared unlawful, except funerals, church meetings, and family affairs. Botha nevertheless still denied that a state of emergency existed there.

In Windhoek, on February 14, the trial of the 12 men arrested during the initial stages of the strike began. The 12 were arraigned on charges of intimidating or inciting other laborers to stop work, or breaking their own contract by striking. All pleaded not guilty to all charges. The accused were identified by numbers throughout the trial. Although the defendants spoke several different tribal languages, the proceedings were held in Afrikaans. Evidence against the accused consisted chiefly of letters or other writings taken from the strikers after their arrest and police interpretation of possibly innocent actions. The charges of breaking contract were dropped.

The Secretary-General of the United Nations, Dr. Kurt Wald-heim, visited Namibia March 7-9. He met with Ovambo leaders in Ovamboland, and examined the compound near Windhoek. He found conditions at the latter "not satisfactory." Evidence was also received by the United Nations Council for Namibia.

Continuing strikes and police brutalities

Strikes continued throughout March in the country. In April, European employers were still short of labor. Apparently, most strikers still refused to accept the new settlement. Other strikers returning south for work had discovered that working and living conditions were unchanged.

In May and June, more reports surfaced concerning the unrest in Ovamboland earlier in the year. The government admitted only that 10 Ovambos had been killed by police during the distur-bances. According to confirmed reports of South-West African People's Organization (SWAPO) officials in London, however, more than 50 persons had been killed. Others were listed as hav-ing disappeared. There were also reports of police torture in Ovamboland.

On June 5, the court finally reached a decision ending the trial of the 12 strikers arrested in December. Eight defendants were found guilty of intimidating workers, and were fined R25 ($33) or sentenced to 25 days in jail. Other charges were dropped, and the remaining defendants were acquitted on all counts. Inquiries during the court proceedings revealed shocking testimonies and dreadful details regarding treatment of contract laborers by em-ployers.

During August, an inquest was held into the shooting deaths of eight of the Ovambo workers killed during January disturbances. The court found that all eight men were killed by police "in the execution of their duties." However, evidence of police brutality and unprovoked shootings had been presented at the hearing.

Continued unrest and a taste of power

Throughout September 1972, "great unrest" was still evident in northern Namibia. The country's economy further suffered from a "chronic labour shortage," and the danger of recurring strikes troubled the territory. The Matchless mine was still out of operation. In Windhoek, emergency steps had to be taken to ease financial burdens that resulted from the strike. Maintenance deficits of the Katutura compound reached R51,181 ($65,000) above estimates for 1971-72, with that figure expected to increase to R81,890 ($104,000) during 1972-73.

The strike by the Ovambo workers is a significant landmark in Namibia's long history of exploitation by Europeans. The contract laborers exhibited a remarkable display of solidarity and unity in their courageous efforts to attain human rights. By the withdrawal of Ovambo labor, the entire vital mining industry was brought to a virtual halt. Many commercial operations were paralyzed, and essential services were crippled in the capital of the territory. The racist South African Government was forced to negotiate new agreements with the African workers or face an economic collapse.

The new settlement included both successes and shortcomings. The hated contract labor system was abolished. However, migratory labor still continued, despite the modified circumstances under which the system was administered.

Nevertheless, by demanding reforms and withdrawing their essential labor, the Ovambos had forced South African officials to the bargaining table. By striking, the African workers revealed a portion of the power that they possessed. That taste of power promised to lead to basic changes.

Eighteen years later, South-West Africa was finally liberated and became the independent nation of Namibia.

Sources

This account is based on a draft prepared by Curt Goering in 1976, based on an unpublished research manuscript by Suzanne Wedel and Curt Goering. This account is based on documents assembled by the American Committee on Africa, and made available by Mr. George Houser, then its Executive Secretary.

These sources include various issues of the following publications in late 1971 and early 1972: *African Affairs; Africa Confidential; African Diary; African Digest; African Studies Review; Africa Today; Anti-Apartheid News; Cape Times; Christian Science Monitor; Financial Mail; Financial Times; Fortune Multinational Report; The Guardian* (London); *Johannesburg Star,Keesings Contemporary Archives; The Times* (London); *New Statesman; New York Times; Observer* (London); *Rand Daily Mail; Republic of South Africa Gazette; SABC-Survey/Current Affairs; Sechaba; United Nations Monthly Chronicle; Virginia Weekly; Wall Street Journal; Washington Post; Windhoek Advertiser;* and *X-Ray.*

Fact sheets and bulletins issued by African Bureau, American Committee on Africa, and the Friends of Namibia Committee, as well as the bulletins "Facts About Namibia," "Guerrilheiro," "Bulletin of the Committee for Freedom in Mozambique, Angola, and Guiné," were also consulted. An unpublished manuscript by George Houser also provided valuable background data.

Other sources included a variety of documents, letters, cables, records of telephoned reports, speeches, statements, written reports, and press releases, from a considerable variety of organizations, individuals, corporations, religious bodies, court records, and government officials.

Chapter Seventeen

MOTHERS OF THE PLAZA DE MAYO, ARGENTINA 1977-1983

Joshua Paulson

"All the necessary people will die"

Between 1976 and 1983, tens of thousands of people "disappeared" in Argentina. After the military conducted a coup d'état in 1976, it implemented a "Process of National Reorganization" with the goal of eradicating all sectors of possible "subversion" from Argentine society.

The strategy was perhaps best defined by General Videla, the coup leader and president of the first military junta: "In order to guarantee the security of the state, all the necessary people will

---

A list of sources for this case appears at the end of this chapter.

die."[1] He went on to define a "subversive" as "anyone who opposes the Argentine way of life."[2] Rather than simply detaining left-wing activists or publicly assassinating them (thus turning them into martyrs), the plan was to kidnap, torture, and then execute them extra-officially, all the while disavowing knowledge of their whereabouts. The victims would simply "disappear."

At the beginning, resistance to military rule was almost non-existent. Indeed, many sectors of the population had actively campaigned for a military takeover due to the corruption and apparent stagnation of the civilian government.

Challenge by the mothers

In 1977, after thousands had already disappeared and the so-called dirty war against left-wing activities was at its height, a small group of women grew desperate. Their children were missing, and there was strong evidence to suggest they had been kidnapped by military or paramilitary death squads. The women had spent months inquiring at government offices, military headquarters, and police stations. They were always told that no one knew anything about the fate of their children. A few of the mothers then decided to take their campaign to the prominent Plaza de Mayo, outside the presidential palace in the center of Buenos Aires.

Their first "meeting" was held at the plaza on April 30, 1977. It was attended by 14 women whose sons or daughters had "disappeared." The mothers could not simply stand together, as this would have been tantamount to holding an illegal demonstration. So they began to walk slowly in a counterclockwise circle around the center of the square. They attracted little attention at first, as there were few people around to observe the protest. Nevertheless, they were emboldened by their action. They decided to speak with other mothers and then plan a weekly walk around the plaza each Thursday afternoon, when the plaza was typically more crowded.

---

1 General Jorge Videla, October 23, 1975, quoted in Simpson and Bennett, *The Disappeared and the Mothers of the Plaza,* p. 75.
2 General Videla to a foreign journalist, quoted in Simpson and Bennett, *The Disappeared and the Mothers of the Plaza,* p. 76.

They usually did not carry signs or placards, but rather wore the names of their missing children embroidered on white head scarves. The head scarves would soon become the mothers' most visible symbol and trademark.

The military was caught off-guard by this most unlikely sector of opposition. The junta's moral authority was based on an avowed defense of the Argentine family and Christian values. Now, after having physically eliminated political opposition groups and thousands of potential "subversives," the military regime was being publicly challenged by a small but growing group of Argentine housewives and mothers.

The mothers themselves came from diverse religious and political backgrounds, and many had nothing in common other than the fact that their children had been kidnapped and probably murdered by the military regime. Most had no previous political involvement, yet they were determined not to let the government take their children with impunity.

Defying arrests and "disappearances"

At the end of 1977, the military finally cracked down. Following a meeting of mothers and supporters, nine women were detained by a paramilitary squad. Three more were taken two days later, and none was ever heard from again. Nevertheless, the protests continued, although in smaller numbers. At the gathering place in the plaza on the following Thursday, only about 40 women showed up, down from the several hundred who had been present in previous weeks.[3] Although they were now clearly risking their lives, the remaining mothers did not give up. Their numbers were small throughout the following year, but they usually managed to maintain a weekly presence in the plaza.

By the end of 1978, the Mothers of the Plaza de Mayo, as they were then known, faced their most difficult period. The plaza was completely sealed off by metal barriers and squadrons of military police. No longer able to march in the plaza, they resorted to "lightning actions," gathering on one side of the square and running across to the other side before being caught by police. Such

---

[3] See Simpson and Bennett, *The Disappeared and the Mothers of the Plaza,* p. 163.

actions continued throughout most of 1979, although the number of participants dwindled due to constant repression.

Defiance increases

At the end of 1979, the Mothers agreed that they needed to go on the offensive again. They decided they would return to the Plaza de Mayo on the first Thursday of 1980, then return every Thursday thereafter until they were either killed or the truth about all the "disappeared" was revealed and those who had tortured and killed them had been punished.[4]

Although many of the women were beaten or arrested, and some were even "disappeared" themselves, the Mothers reclaimed the plaza as their own. As international attention to their campaign increased, they continued to march each Thursday, and on no other occasions did they allow the military to keep them out.

Thousands join the March of Resistance

By this time, the regime itself was showing signs of decay. Throughout the most severe years of the dictatorship, the Mothers were the only open, public sign of resistance to the military regime. Now, however, faced with a devastating economic crisis and an overwhelming failure in the war with Great Britain over the Malvinas/Falkland Islands, workers and the middle class took to the streets as well. On December 10, 1982, the Mothers of the Plaza de Mayo held a 24-hour "March of Resistance" on the avenue leading off the plaza. For the first time, thousands joined the Mothers, emboldened by their example and the persistent weakening of the regime.

Faced with overwhelming levels of public discontent, the military dictators eventually decided to restore civilian rule. New elections for a civilian government were planned for the end of 1983. Although the military government issued a decree prohibiting the mention of human rights violations on television or radio or in the printed press, it could not keep the issue of the "disap-

---

4 See Simpson and Bennett, *The Disappeared and the Mothers of the Plaza*, p. 168 and Fisher, *Mothers of the Disappeared*, p. 108.

peared" out of the upcoming presidential campaign, largely as a result of the persistence of the Mothers.[5]

Victory over terror

After the return to civilian rule, the Mothers continued their campaign on behalf of the "disappeared." They focused first on rejecting the military's declaration of amnesty for itself, and later on challenging President Menem's pardon for military officers that had in fact been imprisoned for human rights violations during military rule.

Although such relatively small actions of a small group of mothers did not directly bring an end to the dictatorship, "it was the willingness of the Mothers to take action that kept the flame of opposition burning in public view during the worst years. . . . They successfully countered the military's calculation that if the terror was absolute enough, no one would dare to complain."[6]

---

[5] Fisher, *Mothers of the Disappeared,* p. 120.
[6] Simpson and Bennett, *The Disappeared and the Mothers of the Plaza,* p. 169.

Sources

Bouvard, Marguerite Guzman, *Revolutionizing Motherhood: The Mothers of the Plaza de Mayo,* Wilmington, Delaware: Scholarly Resources, Inc., 1994.

Fisher, Jo, *Mothers of the Disappeared,* Boston: South End Press, 1989.

Simpson, John and Bennett, Jana, *The Disappeared and the Mothers of the Plaza,* New York: St. Martin's Press, 1985.

Chapter Eighteen

POLAND'S SELF-LIBERATION 1980-1989

Joshua Paulson

Prologue to struggle

The people of Poland had endured a difficult history. For 120 years, the country had been wiped off the map of Europe as it was divided up by its neighbors. Under rule by the Russian Empire, there were several brave but futile violent rebellions. Poland again became independent after the First World War. Before the Second World War, the Polish government itself was not always a model of democracy. At the start of the Second World War, Hitler and Stalin divided up the country between themselves. When Nazi armies invaded in 1939, brave Polish soldiers charged the

---

A list of sources for this case appears at the end of this chapter.

tanks on horseback. During the Nazi occupation, about 10 percent of the population, including most of the Jews, were killed.

Later, the Soviet Army imposed a harsh Communist regime on the country.

Under Communist rule, there were protests and strikes. Labor unrest was widespread in 1956, student demonstrations in 1968, and again strikes, with significant violence, occurred in 1970. In the mid-1970s, the two currents of dissidence (workers and intellectuals) got together when intellectuals such as Adam Michnik formed the Committee for Defense of Workers (KOR) to help defend the workers, and this group was the main force behind the underground press and publishing in that decade.

In June 1979, Pope John Paul II, the "Polish pope," visited his home country and was heard by millions. His visit constituted a challenge to the legitimacy of the regime as it showed that, despite the Communist ideology, masses of Poles remained deeply religious.

Various strikes due to economic conditions occurred in May and July 1980, and were settled through economic concessions by the regime.

Strike for independent unions

In August 1980, Polish workers in the Baltic port city of Gdansk shocked the rest of the Eastern Bloc and the world by rising up peacefully against a "workers' state." The immediate spark for this strike had been the firing of Anna Walentynowicz, a popular employee at the Lenin shipyard at Gdansk. Unlike earlier Polish strikes, which had been settled with simple pay increases, the workers at the Lenin Shipyards had more far-reaching objectives.

Workers in other local industries soon launched their own "solidarity strikes," and an Interfactory Strike Committee (MKS) was formed. The MKS declared that no striking factory or business would return to work until all of them had attained the same goals. Conscious of their geopolitical situation, they carefully drafted a list of 21 demands designed to exclude demands that could provoke a Soviet or Warsaw Pact invasion. Nevertheless, the demand topping the list was one unheard of in Socialist-bloc countries: the right of workers to form independent, self-governing trade unions separate from the structures of the government and the Communist Party.

For two weeks, the tri-city area of Gdansk, Sopot, and Gdynia was shut down. The strikers conducted their affairs in an orderly manner, so as to avoid any provocations that could lead to violence. The strikes were confined to the workplaces themselves ("occupation strikes"), so as not to repeat the street violence that took place during previous work stoppages in 1970. For a short time, the strikers exercised almost complete control of the Gdansk area, even issuing permits for food stores to remain open and allowing certain train and bus routes to continue operating.[1]

Successful negotiations

The Communist government felt obliged to negotiate, and on August 23 sent Deputy Prime Minister Jagielski to begin talks with the MKS, which soon had the representation of more than 500 striking enterprises. Although the authorities had debated military action against the strikers, the military forces themselves overruled any such measures.[2] Jagielski was thus instructed to end the strikes as soon as possible through a negotiated solution, even one that would be tantamount to near capitulation. On August 31, an agreement was signed between the Interfactory Strike Commission and representatives of the government and the Polish United Workers Party, as the Communist Party was officially known, ending the strikes and granting the workers the right to organize their own independent unions.

One month later, 500 representatives of 36 new independent trade unions converged on Gdansk to form a national trade union federation, known as Solidarity. Vast numbers of workers immediately deserted the official Party unions and flocked to Solidarity. By mid-1981, Solidarity enjoyed a membership of around 10 million (in a country of 30 million), while another 3 million farmers had joined its rural sister organization.[3]

The possibility of Soviet military intervention was reduced by problems with the army reservists themselves. The mobilization

---

[1] MacDonald (ed.), *The Polish August: Documents from the Beginnings of the Polish Workers' Rebellion*, p. 10.
[2] Ash, *The Polish Revolution*, p. 62.
[3] Berend, *Central and Eastern Europe, 1944-1993*, p. 258.

of Soviet army reservists in the Carpathian Military District in August-December 1980—possibly for an invasion of Poland—was met with very serious discipline problems. The mobilization was met with confusion, disorder, and wholesale desertions, in such large numbers that punishment of the deserters was impossible.[4]

Martial law and arrests

Throughout 1981, economic conditions in Poland continued to worsen, and nationwide strikes by Solidarity were common. The union was now wielding independent power, and both Warsaw and Moscow felt threatened. Following a deadlock in government-Solidarity negotiations in November 1981, the government of General Wojciech Jaruzelski declared a "State of Near-War" and imposed martial law on December 13. Constitutional guarantees were suspended as thousands of Solidarity members and leaders were arrested or interned. As the Communist Party itself was becoming unreliable and approaching a state of collapse, General Jaruzelski conducted a coup d'état to keep Communist control from dissolving.

Solidarity was totally unprepared for the coup. Initial resistance to the military takeover was valiant but ineffective. Activists who made it through the first night of martial law attempted uncoordinated defensive actions across the country. Most of these were attempts at peaceful occupation strikes, all of which were crushed by military force. Meanwhile, riot police responded violently to demonstrations in Gdansk, Warsaw, Lublin, and Krakow on December 16, wounding several hundred people and killing at least 10.[5] By mid-1982, more than 10,000 people had been interned as a form of "preventive detention," and more than 3,000 arrested for "political crimes."[6]

---

[4] Gene Sharp, *Making Europe Unconquerable* (Cambridge, Massachusetts: Ballinger Publishing Co., 1985), pp. 75-76 and the cited sources.
[5] Ash, *The Polish Revolution*, p. 266.
[6] Malcher, *Poland's Politicized Army*, pp. 218-219.

Constructing an independent society

Martial law officially ended in July 1983, although political prisoners were not released until late 1986 and Solidarity remained outlawed. Solidarity was weakened and divided by the imposition of military rule, but it did not go away. Small, loosely coordinated activist cells developed in order to carry the Solidarity struggle "underground." Although a few Solidarity leaders and underground splinter groups advocated violent guerrilla actions,[7] most firmly rejected the use of violence. "The struggle, they said, was to create a 'parallel society,' not to overthrow the government."[8]

The main thrust of the underground Solidarity movement was therefore the construction of an independent society, "which consisted of removing as large a public domain as possible from the government's control."[9] One of the underground Solidarity leaders, Wiktor Kulerski, had recommended this type of struggle, arguing that it would lead to a situation in which "the authorities control empty shops but not the market, workers' employment but not their livelihood, state-owned mass media but not the circulation of information, printing houses but not publishing, the post and telephone but not communications, the schools but not education." Kulerski projected that this would lead to a situation in which the state would be left with the police and a few hard-core collaborators, and the government would either fall or have to make peace with the independent society.[10]

Underground publications sprang up by the hundreds and issues were distributed by the thousands. Dozens of books were published in defiance of censorship regulations. Illegal radio and television broadcasts sporadically took to the airwaves. Government efforts to form a surrogate trade union to replace Solidarity were met by generalized boycotts. All over Poland, symbolic actions took the place of strikes and street demonstrations, boosting popular morale. In one case, in February 1982, inhabitants of the town of Swidnik demonstrated their opposition to the mass me-

---

[7] Malcher, *Poland's Politicized Army*, pp. 219-221.
[8] Ost, *Solidarity and the Politics of Anti-Politics*, p. 152.
[9] Kaminski, *The Collapse of State Socialism*, p. 215.
[10] Quoted by Peter Ackerman and Christopher Kruegler, *Strategic Nonviolent Conflict* (Westport, Connecticut and London: Praeger, 1994), p. 307.

dia by leaving their homes and taking walks down the main street during the evening television news broadcasts. Soon, the street became so crowded that the "protest walkers" made news themselves.[11]

During this development of self-reliant institutions outside of government and Party control, the political situation was likened to the government and Party bouncing around like a boat on the surface of the sea of society, able to strike into the water and perhaps catch a "fish," but unable to control the society and population.

New strikes and free elections

In 1986, a general amnesty for political prisoners was declared and Solidarity again surfaced as an above-ground organization, though still technically illegal. Two years later, in May 1988, an outbreak of wildcat strikes swept the country in response to new price increases. In August, a second wave of major strikes broke out, this time with just one major demand: the legalization of Solidarity. With a reform-minded regime now in Moscow and a Communist Party in Warsaw looking toward economic liberalization, the strikes put the Jaruzelski regime in an untenable position.

Unwilling to return to martial law, the government suddenly invited Solidarity leaders to hold "round table" talks with the government. Both parties signed an agreement in April 1989 calling for immediate political and economic reforms, including free elections for one-third of the seats in the National Assembly and all the seats in the newly restored symbolic Senate. When the elections were held in June, Solidarity won a landslide victory, obtaining all the "free" seats in the Assembly and 99 of 100 seats in the Senate.

By August 1989, the changes were occurring too fast for the Communist Party to maintain even a semblance of control, and its monolithic power vanished. On August 21, General Jaruzelski agreed to allow a coalition of small parties led by Solidarity to form a new government, and he named a Prime Minister from the ranks of Solidarity. The first non-Communist government in

---

[11] Kaminski, *The Collapse of State Socialism*, pp. 215-216.

Eastern Europe since the Stalin era was born. Solidarity emerged victorious—exactly nine years after the workers' struggle began.

Sources

Ash, Timothy Garton, *The Polish Revolution: Solidarity 1980-1982,* London: Jonathan Cape, 1983.

Berend, Ivan T., *Central and Eastern Europe, 1944-1993* (Cambridge: Cambridge University Press, 1996), pp. 254-266.

Castle, Marjorie, "The Final Crisis of the People's Republic of Poland," pp. 211-241, in Curry and Fajfer (eds.), *Poland's Permanent Revolution.*

Curry, Jane Leftwich, "The Solidarity Crisis, 1980-81: The Near Death of Communism," in Curry and Fajfer (eds.), *Poland's Permanent Revolution,* pp. 167-209.

Curry, Jane Leftwich and Fajfer, Luba (eds.), *Poland's Permanent Revolution,* Washington, DC: The American University Press, 1996.

Curry, Jane Leftwich and Fajfer, Luba, "The Never-Ending Crises," in Curry and Fajfer (eds.), *Poland's Permanent Revolution,* pp. 243-260.

Ekiert, Grzegorz, *The State Against Society: Political Crises and their Aftermath in East Central Europe* (Princeton: Princeton University Press, 1996), pp. 257-304.

Kaufman, Michael, *Mad Dreams, Saving Graces: Poland, a Nation into Conspiracy* (New York: Random House, 1989), pp. 79-100 and 231-267.

Kaminski, Bartlomiej, *The Collapse of State Socialism: The Case of Poland* (Princeton: Princeton University Press, 1991), pp. 138-161 and 213-236.

Kemp-Welch, A., *The Birth of Solidarity* (New York: St. Martin's Press, 1991), pp. 200-224.

MacDonald, Oliver (ed.), *The Polish August: Documents from the Beginnings of the Polish Workers' Rebellion,* Seattle: Left Bank Books, 1981.

Malcher, George C., *Poland's Politicized Army: Communists in Uniform* (New York: Praeger Publishers, 1984), pp. 209-222.

Potel, Jean-Yves, *The Promise of Solidarity: Inside the Polish Workers' Struggle, 1980-1982,* New York: Praeger Publishers, 1982.

Taras, Raymond, *Consolidating Democracy in Poland* (Boulder: Westview Press, 1995), pp. 113-160.

Walesa, Lech, *A Way of Hope,* New York: Henry Holt and Co., 1987.

Ost, David, *Solidarity and the Politics of Anti-Politics,* Philadelphia: Temple University Press, 1990.

We are grateful to Anna Husarska for her review of the manuscript and helpful suggestions.

Chapter Nineteen

SCHOOL BOYCOTTS IN SOUTH AFRICA—1984-1987

Joshua Paulson

Renewed school boycotts

During the many years of European oppression and the racial separation policy of apartheid in South Africa, many methods of protest and resistance were used by Africans and other non-Europeans in attempts to produce change. One of these methods was for students to refuse to attend classes because of grievances against the general system or specific school policies.

Although these school boycotts did not end the oppression by themselves, they mobilized and organized people to resist and helped to build up the forces that finally led to fundamental change.

A list of sources for this case appears at the end of this chapter.

Since the 1940s, school boycotts had become a regular tool of student protest by non-European South Africans against separate and unequal education, and against the racist apartheid system itself.

In the early 1980s, the Congress of South African Students (COSAS)—an organization of high school students loosely allied with the outlawed African National Congress and the United Democratic Front—accumulated significant experience in conducting such boycott campaigns. They led thousands of students in walkouts in 1980 and 1983. Even though their leaders were "banned" from public activities, the Congress of South African Students soon managed to establish more than 40 branches in the country.

In January 1984, a new wave of school boycotts broke out at the secondary school level with the national backing of COSAS. The students' demands were initially focused on limited educational issues, such as the manipulation of test results, excessive corporal punishment, and an age requirement barring older students from registering for classes.[1] As the boycotts grew, these demands were widened to include broader political grievances in opposition to proposed educational reforms and the continuing survival of apartheid education. COSAS also called for the establishment of democratic "Student Representative Councils" in order to channel student issues and demands to school and government officials, and to provide for greater organization and power among the students themselves.[2]

Repression and new demands

The 1984 boycotts spread slowly. For the first three months of the boycott campaign, no more than 25 schools were involved at any one time. Even within the schools targeted, attendance often varied and the boycotts were sometimes only partially honored. Nevertheless, the government's initial response was to threaten permanent closures at many of the affected schools and to take police action against student activists. In the Atteridgeville/Saulsville area in February, one student was killed and 18

---

[1] Hyslop, "School Student Movements and State Education Policy," p. 192.
[2] Bot, *School Boycotts 1984,* p. 10.

others injured by the police. In Cradock, seven schools were closed by the Department of Education in March and a three-month ban on public meetings was imposed.[3]

For months, the school boycott campaign remained a relatively small, regional affair. Later in 1984, however, several larger political issues became focal points for student protests. In September, the government announced rent increases in the areas of the East Rand and the Vaal Triangle. This led to even more walkouts by students, and soon more than 150 schools were being actively boycotted by approximately 160,000 students.[4] Students expanded their demands to include the withdrawal of police and army units from the townships, the release of students arrested or detained during the boycotts, and a reversal of the decision to increase rent in the townships.

By the end of September, more than 250,000 students were on strike, many of them motivated by a police crackdown on students in the Vaal Triangle that had resulted in at least 77 deaths.[5] As a consequence of the spreading boycotts, the Minister of Education and Training, Dr. Gerrit Viljoen, announced a number of apparent concessions and new educational reforms. Among these concessions were the formation of new bodies for student representation, the opening of closed schools, the lifting of age limits for students, and the postponement of final examinations. However, the government's proposals made no mention of the hundreds of detained student activists or the police and army presence in African townships. The ideas for student representation called for by Viljoen also fell far short of the students' demands for Student Representative Councils.[6]

Students rejected the concessions, and the boycotts continued. In October 1984, the student organization sought the support of African trade unions. As a result, a successful one-day solidarity strike was conducted by African workers in the East Rand. In November, more than 400,000 students and an equal number of workers took part in a two-day general strike, temporarily shut-

[3] Bot, *School Boycotts 1984*, pp. 37-39.
[4] Bot, *School Boycotts 1984*, p. 46.
[5] Hyslop, "School Student Movements and State Education Policy," pp. 193-194.
[6] Bot, *School Boycotts 1984*, p. 13.

ting down both schools and industry throughout the Southern Transvaal region.[7]

The school boycotts continued well into 1985, affecting both primary and secondary African schools. The government cracked down in the winter of 1985. It declared a State of Emergency in July and banned COSAS in August. Violent street clashes between students and police became commonplace. By the end of 1985, urban African education was virtually nonexistent, and student demands had become far more political than educational, advocating "liberation now, education later."[8]

Alternative "People's Education"

When it became clear that the boycotts were not producing major political change, large numbers of students, parents, and teachers joined together to form the National Education Crisis Committee (NECC). This committee advocated "a struggle over the nature and direction of the educational system, rather than a withdrawal from it," with a new slogan of "People's Education for People's Power."[9] Under this rubric, the NECC established leadership over the movement and promoted a generalized return to school, but without changing the focus of the struggle to end apartheid in South Africa. In many respects, the NECC established itself as an alternative educational authority, separate from the official Department of Education. In late 1986, the NECC even prepared "People's Education" study materials to be used as part of school curricula in those schools in which students had returned to classes, but in which the authority of the government Department of Education was minimal.[10]

Although school boycotts continued sporadically throughout 1986, students gradually accepted the "alternative education" ideas espoused by the NECC and the boycotts finally came to an end in January 1987.

The boycott campaign had not led to the immediate downfall of the apartheid system in South Africa, as many students had

---

[7] Hyslop, "School Student Movements and State Education Policy," p. 194 and Bot, *School Boycotts 1984,* pp. 1-2.

[8] Hyslop, "School Student Movements and State Education Policy," p. 197.

[9] Hyslop, "School Student Movements and State Education Policy," p. 200.

[10] Hyslop, "School Student Movements and State Education Policy," p. 204.

hoped. Nevertheless, the government failed in its attempts to win the support of students and the population for its plans to implement only minor reforms in African schools, without changing the overall system of separate and unequal education. These struggles contributed to a growing change in power relationships that eventually made possible the end of apartheid and European domination in South Africa.

Sources

Bot, Monica, *School Boycotts 1984: The Crisis in African Education,* Durban: Indicator Project South Africa, 1985.

Hyslop, Jonathan, "School Student Movements and State Education Policy" in William Cobbett and Robin Cohen (eds.), *Popular Struggles in South Africa* (London: Africa World Press, Inc., 1988), pp. 183-209.

Chapter Twenty

PEOPLE POWER AGAINST THE PHILIPPINE DICTATOR—1986

Joshua Paulson

Election fraud

The assassination of Philippine opposition leader Benigno Aquino, Jr. in 1983 led to widespread and increasingly militant protests against the dictatorial regime of Ferdinand Marcos. Faced with shrinking popularity and hints by the U.S. government that he was losing his legitimacy, Marcos called for quick presidential elections to be held on February 7, 1986. Marcos was sure he would be given a new mandate to continue in office, either by winning the elections or simply by having them rigged.

A list of sources for this case appears at the end of this chapter.

Plans for people power protests

The major opposition parties united behind Benigno Aquino's widow, Corazon Aquino, in an unprecedented challenge for the presidency. Following a short campaign marked by vote-buying and the murder of more than 70 opposition workers, thousands of poll watchers observed ballot-stuffing and the falsification of returns on election day. Repulsed by these actions, some of the official vote counters refused to legitimize the vote rigging and walked out while television cameras broadcast their defiance.

Although Marcos claimed he had won, Mrs. Aquino refused to concede, and on February 13 she met with 350 opposition leaders to discuss their next moves. Aquino firmly rejected all suggestions to turn to violence, and proposed instead to launch a lengthy campaign using strictly nonviolent methods and what she termed "people power."

Her plan included a memorial service for the victims of electoral violence to be held on the day of Marcos' scheduled inauguration, a one-day general strike scheduled for the following working day, a boycott of all businesses owned by Marcos and his cronies, the delayed payment of utility bills, and the development of an organizational plan "on the neighborhood and community levels for concerted protest actions which are nonviolent in nature."[1]

But before Aquino's resistance campaign could begin in earnest, a group of reformist Army officers lead by Defense Minister Juan Ponce Enrile prepared to carry out a coup d'état against Marcos. Their plan was discovered, however, and when faced with a government crackdown they took refuge inside two adjacent military camps, Aguinaldo and Crame, on February 22. The rebel officers were soon joined by the Vice Chief of Staff, Fidel Ramos, and about 300 troops.

Thousands protect disobedient soldiers

On the evening of February 22, the rebels held a televised press conference. Without mentioning the aborted coup, Enrile and Ramos announced their resignations from the government, their decision to withdraw all support from President Marcos, and

---

[1] Yap, *The Making of Cory*, p. 127.

their recognition of Corazon Aquino as the legitimate winner of the elections. They called for both popular and military support.

Shortly thereafter, Manila's Roman Catholic Church leader Jaime Cardinal Sin made a nationwide appeal on Radio Veritas for people to go to camps Aguinaldo and Crame in order to protect the rebels and prevent bloodshed. The people responded, and by midnight more than 50,000 people had gathered outside the camps. Within two days, this number would grow to over a million.

Recognizing both their own lack of firepower and the large numbers of people outside willing to protect them, the rebel leaders developed a coordinated defense plan that was intended to make full use of "people power." Initially, this plan had only three major components: to prepare a localized military defense of Camp Crame in the case of assault; to use nonviolent "people power" to effectively create a human barrier around the rebel camps wide enough to prevent artillery from being used at close range; and to work around the clock convincing other military officers to defect.[2] Supporters outside would be sent to block roads, establish barricades, and create diversions.

Tanks blocked by masses of people

Shortly after 2 p.m. on February 23, Marcos sent the first wave of tanks and armored transports against the rebels. The loyalist advance was halted a good distance from the camps by crowds of more than a million people. Protesters included nuns who knelt in front of the tanks in prayer and priests who climbed atop military vehicles to lead the people—and the soldiers—in praying the rosary.

Demonstrators attempted to befriend the soldiers, in some cases successfully, and offered them candy and cigarettes. With no way of reaching their objective without killing or injuring thousands of civilians, loyalist troops turned back.

---

[2] See Aguirre, *A People's Revolution of our Time,* pp. 19-25.

A more powerful weapons system

In the evening, Aquino went on the radio to call on all her supporters to continue protecting the rebels. Marcos, meanwhile, attempted to negotiate with Enrile and Ramos to convince them to surrender. Ramos, however, replied:

> We have no intention of surrendering inasmuch as it is the people's power protecting us. This certainly is a more powerful weapons system at our disposal. These people are unarmed. However, the power that they hold to support us is much more powerful than the hardware at Marcos' command.[3]

On the morning of February 24, the crowds outside the two camps had dwindled to a few thousand again. The rebel forces were now consolidated in Camp Crame, leaving Camp Aguinaldo empty. At dawn, Marcos gave orders for his troops to attempt another assault, and this time they managed to disperse some of the crowds with riot police. They proceeded to take over Camp Aguinaldo, and filled it with mortars, howitzers, machine guns, rocket launchers, and 1,000 rifles, all pointed at Camp Crame.

Marines refuse to fire

In midmorning, the Marine commander of the loyalist troops in Camp Aguinaldo, Colonel Braulio Balbas, was given orders to open fire on the rebels in Camp Crame. He stalled for hours, and finally confessed that:

> . . . it is futile to fire at Crame. There are thousands of civilians between the two camps and inside Crame. There will be lots of casualties on both sides, not only in Crame but also on our side.[4]

Balbas then ordered his troops to return to their base, and the Marines issued a statement later in the day affirming that "the Marines will no longer participate in a subsequent military operation that will unnecessarily result in the injury or death of innocent unarmed civilians."[5]

---

[3] General Fidel Ramos, quoted in Yap, *The Making of Cory,* p. 174.
[4] Colonel Bralio Balbas, quoted in Yap, *The Making of Cory,* p. 180.
[5] Brigadier General Tadiar (Marine commandant), quoted in Aguirre, *A People's Revolution of our Time,* p. 37.

Surrender to civilians

At midday on February 24, Enrile and Ramos announced that 90 percent of the Armed Forces of the Philippines had defected. The rebels sent helicopter gunships to destroy loyalist aircraft on the ground before they could be used to bomb Camp Crame, and sent six warning rockets into the ground around the National Palace. A Navy frigate defected and also turned its guns on the National Palace.

Rebel army troops launched an assault on the government television station, and after 15 minutes of fighting that resulted in the wounding of one loyalist officer, thousands of unarmed civilians arrived at the station and took it over as the Marcos loyalists surrendered to them. Rebel broadcasts then began to be aired on television.

Marcos ordered his remaining troops to attack Camp Crame and to retake the television station, but his officers refused to comply.

Aquino is inaugurated

Late in the afternoon on February 24, a desperate Marcos ordered a "final suicide assault" against the rebels.[6] But by now even the United States Government had decided it was time for Marcos to go. The U.S. Embassy contacted him and convinced him to call off the attack.

Marcos packed his bags, and the next day was on his way out of the country. He left shortly after Corazon Aquino was inaugurated as President of the Philippines. "People power" had prevailed.

---

[6] Yap, *The Making of Cory*, p. 181.

Sources

Aguirre, Col. Alexander P., *A People's Revolution of our Time: Philippines, February 22-25, 1986* (Quezon City: Pan-Service Master Consultants, 1986), pp. 1-40, Appendices.

Johnson, Bryan, *Four Days of Courage: The Untold Story of the Fall of Marcos,* Toronto: McClelland and Stewart, 1987.

Komisar, Lucy, *Corazon Aquino: The Story of a Revolution* (New York: George Braziller, Inc., 1987), pp. 93-123.

Lande, Carl H., "The Political Crisis," in John Bresnan (ed.), *Crisis in the Philippines: The Marcos Era and Beyond* (Princeton: Princeton University Press, 1986), pp. 114-144.

University of Santo Tomas Social Research Center, *The Philippine Revolution and the Involvement of the Church* (Manila: Social Research Center, Univ. of Santo Tomas, 1986), pp. 7-34, 75-83.

Yap, Miguela G., *The Making of Cory* (Quezon City: New Day Publishers, 1987), pp. 96-194.

Chapter Twenty-one

BURMESE DEFY THE MILITARY DICTATORS—1988-1990

Joshua Paulson

Spontaneous student protests

Post-independence Burmese democracy was crushed by a military coup d'état in 1962 and has never recovered. In 1988, what began as a series of spontaneous student protests against police brutality grew into a nationwide campaign to bring down a 26-year-old military dictatorship and restore democracy to the country.

Following the death of a student at the hands of riot police in March 1988, angry demonstrations erupted in Rangoon and were fired upon by police and army units. Hundreds of students were

---

A list of sources for this case appears at the end of this chapter.

killed, and thousands more were arrested. The universities were shut down, and student leaders were expelled.

In June, the students took to the streets again. They demanded the reinstatement of students expelled in March and the punishment of those responsible for the massacres of students. For the first time, many students began to speak out openly against the government's economic policies and against the military dictatorship. On June 21, a student march was brutally attacked by riot police. This time, the assaults prompted violent responses from some of the students. Clashes continued into the evening, killing at least 80 civilians and 20 riot police. In response, the Government banned public gatherings and imposed a curfew.

In July, after the unrest had spread to other cities and towns across Burma, the military government appeared to make concessions to the demands of the students. The police chief of Rangoon resigned, the curfew was lifted, and expelled students were allowed to reapply for classes. The ruling Burmese Socialist Programme Party held an extraordinary congress in which General Ne Win, the ruler of Burma for nearly three decades, announced his resignation as Party chairman and called for a national referendum on the issue of replacing one-party rule with a multi-party democracy. The Party congress, however, refused to accept Ne Win's proposal of a referendum on democracy, and named Sein Lwin—the man widely held responsible for the student massacres in Rangoon—as the new Party chairman.

General strike and killings

On August 8, a general strike began. Hundreds of thousands of people demonstrated across the country, demanding the immediate resignation of the military regime and the installation of an interim government in order to prepare for multi-party elections. Shortly before midnight, troop units appeared when peaceful demonstrators approached city hall in Rangoon. The troops opened fire indiscriminately, killing hundreds. Over the course of the following days, army and police units attacked demonstrators in at least 40 cities and towns across Burma. Demonstrators in Rangoon fought back with any weapons they could get their hands on. Between August 8 and 11, more than 1,000 demonstrators were killed across the country.[1]

Despite long-standing efforts of the Ne Win regime to control the Buddhist monks (the *Sangha*), during this uprising they played major roles in the struggle. They joined other Burmese in demonstrations against the dictatorship. In some places, the monks were so powerful that, for example, in August 1988 they took over the administration of Mandalay and some outlying villages.

Despite the special status of Buddhist monks in Burmese society, they became targets of military repression and some were killed.[2] Although martial law was in effect, the unrest was so widespread that after the Ne Win government fell, two new governments offered by the military could not survive even when they included civilians. On August 12, Sein Lwin unexpectedly presented his resignation and Dr. Maung Maung, a civilian, was named Prime Minister. After a week of relative calm, demonstrations resumed. A new general strike was called on August 22. Two days later, with more than half a million people participating in daily demonstrations in Rangoon, martial law was suddenly lifted. Some political prisoners were released from jail, and it appeared once again that the demonstrators' demands might be met. By August 31, thousands of people had resigned from the ruling Burmese Socialist Programme Party, and the demonstrations were growing without further interference from police or army units.

Government control crumbles

Resistance continued, and early in September the pro-democracy movement became more organized, and government authority was crumbling. Citizens' councils were established to run day-to-day affairs in at least 50 cities and towns that had come under the control of students, Buddhist monks, and other civilians. On September 9, several hundred Air Force troops broke ranks to join the marchers on the streets of Rangoon in

---

[1] Lintner, *Outrage,* p. 196.

[2] Following the collapse of the democratic struggle, the military regime, the SLORC (the State Law and Order Restoration Council), instituted major new controls over the *Sangha* to ensure that the monks would not become a political problem again.

opposition to the regime. On September 10 and 11, both the ruling party and the Parliament called for general elections to be held under a multi-party democratic system.

A new coup d'état

Just as victory for the students and the pro-democracy movement seemed at hand, opposition leaders argued about which of them should head a new democratic government.

At that point, the army carried out a new coup d'état. On September 18, a State Law and Order Restoration Council (SLORC) was established by the military forces. It proceeded to dissolve Parliament, the Council of State, and other government bodies. Martial law was declared. Gatherings of more than five people were banned. A curfew was implemented across the country from 8 p.m. to 4 a.m. Repression returned with a cold, methodical efficiency. Within days, hundreds of protesters were shot dead in the streets, most of them students without any weapons. Thousands more were arrested or "disappeared."

Resistance crumbles and organizes

Under the threat of continued terror, most demonstrations ceased and the general strike collapsed.

After the massacres of 1988, thousands of students fled to the border areas controlled by ethnic rebels, and tried to start a military struggle against the dictatorship.

On September 24, three prominent opposition figures formed the National League for Democracy (NLD) and registered it officially as a political party, taking advantage of the SLORC's promise to allow multi-party elections within two years. Aung San Suu Kyi—the daughter of national independence hero Aung San—was named General Secretary of the NLD. She toured the country, preaching discipline and urging people to remain nonviolent. She attracted crowds of tens of thousands of people in support of the democracy movement and in defiance of the ban on public gatherings.

In mid-1989, the SLORC increased its campaign of harassment and intimidation against the NLD and Aung San Suu Kyi. Opposition continued, however, albeit in a different form than the mass demonstrations of 1988. As one observer noted,

> [A] new movement was taking shape. . . . The large crowds that gathered around Aung San Suu Kyi did not shout slogans or wave banners; they listened attentively to her speeches and afterwards asked intelligent, relevant questions. Perhaps even more importantly, the troops that were sent out to disperse the crowds began to get down from their army lorries—to listen to her message.[3]

Election victory and continued repression

The multi-party elections were held in May 1990, and in spite of the continuing repression, the NLD received more than 80 percent of the vote. The military dictators, however, refused to recognize the results. They have since retained control of the State. In July 1990, the government placed Aung San Suu Kyi under house arrest, and many young NLD activists were killed or imprisoned.

The students who fled to the border areas to wage a military struggle met mostly with failure. Since then even the areas long held by ethnic guerrilla armies have shrunk to tiny zones.

Despite continued imprisonments and other repression, NLD activists and followers of Aung San Suu Kyi have succeeded over the years in gaining international recognition for their struggle and have in limited actions repeatedly challenged the dictators inside Burma.

As of late 2004, the Burmese struggle for democracy is still unresolved. The military dictators remain in control, although under a new name, the State Peace and Development Council. Again under house arrest, the activities of the democratic leader, Aung San Suu Kyi, are restricted, and many National League for Democracy members and leaders are in prison or exile. Some prisoners are occasionally released, but new persons are imprisoned. These prisoner releases usually coincide with the visits of foreign dignitaries or United Nations-related activities—all related to attempts at easing economic sanctions.

Despite continuing imprisonments, torture, and killings, Burmese democrats and ethnic groups have maintained their spirits

---

[3] Lintner, *Outrage,* pp. 172-173.

of opposition to the dictatorship. In the mid-1990s, gradually recognizing military realities, some militant students who had been committed to military struggle since 1988 began instead to promote nonviolent struggle, called "political defiance" in Burma, as the main form of struggle needed to bring about democracy. However, some of those explorations have since been reversed. The efforts to spread the understanding of the power of nonviolent struggle infuriated the military dictators, especially in 1995 and 1996, but a powerful movement has not yet developed.

Very serious problems remain in developing and carrying out a nonviolent struggle strategy for liberation of Burma. The Burmese democrats have as yet been unable to overcome political factionalism, prepare a grand strategy for ending the dictatorship, and create a movement strong enough to restore their long-lost democracy.

Sources

Aung San Suu Kyi, *Freedom from Fear and Other Writings,* New York: Penguin Books, 1991.

Fink, Christina, *Living Silence* (New York: Palgrave Books, 2001), pp. 214-216.

Freedholm, Michael, *Burma: Ethnicity and Insurgency* (Westport, Connecticut: Praeger, 1993), pp. 58-72.

Lintner, Bertil, *Outrage: Burma's Struggle for Democracy,* London: White Lotus, 1990, Second Edition.

We are grateful for the assistance of Robert Helvey.

Chapter Twenty-two

UPRISING AND REPRESSION IN CHINA—1989

Joshua Paulson

Power struggle over reforms

With Deng Xiaoping's emergence as China's "paramount leader" after 1977, the Communist government embarked on a campaign of economic modernization designed to make the country more competitive in the global economy. Intellectuals, "technocrats," and students were allowed greater freedom of expression in exchange for their assistance in implementing such a program.

As the economic modernization progressed in the early 1980s, a power struggle emerged at the top echelons of the regime. Younger Party elites believed that reform should be accelerated in

---

A list of sources for this case appears at the end of this chapter.

the political sphere, in tandem with economic reforms. In contrast, the so-called Gang of Elders—eight Party veterans associated with the founding generation of revolutionaries, many of whom no longer held official posts—were most concerned with ensuring stability and protecting their own positions of authority, even at the expense of reform.

This power struggle became evident in December 1986, when Beijing students demonstrated in support of what they believed to be dominant reformist tendencies within the Communist Party. Although the students thought their actions were patriotic and supportive of the Party, many were arrested and a crackdown against "bourgeois liberalization" ensued. Among the casualties of this campaign was Communist Party General Secretary Hu Yaobang, who was dismissed from his post in January 1987. Hu was a reformer who had been viewed in a positive light by many students and critical intellectuals. After Hu's removal, the power struggle between moderate reformers and hard-line octogenarians continued, with the hard-liners gradually gaining the upper hand.

Mourning coupled with demands

When Hu Yaobang died of a sudden heart attack on April 15, 1989, students leaders took advantage of his death to begin a new campaign in support of accelerated political and economic reforms. Hu had not fallen into total disgrace after his dismissal, and was still a member of the ruling Politburo when he died. The students thus reasoned that their public expressions of mourning, although unauthorized, would not be suppressed.

On April 16, posters appeared at dozens of Beijing campuses, praising Hu and criticizing his political adversaries in the government. On the following day, the first large student demonstrations occurred, as thousands marched to Tiananmen Square to mourn Hu's death.

In the early morning hours of April 18, hundreds of students began a sit-in at the Great Hall of the People and demanded to be received by a ranking member of the Standing Committee of the National People's Congress. They carried a list of demands, which included an official reassessment of Hu's actions that led to his removal from office in 1987, the release of political prisoners, freedom of speech and of the press, more funding for education, an end to corruption, and democratic elections to the National People's Congress. It is important to note that during this early stage of the movement, the students did not call for the abolition of the Communist Party, or even a change in the governing regime. Most saw no contradiction between socialism and democracy. They simply wanted the system to be cleaned up and democratized from within, in order to be more responsive to the people.

Student demonstrations spread

Over the course of the days leading up to the official memorial ceremony for Hu Yaobang on April 22, Tiananmen Square was occupied daily by thousands of students. Although the unofficial demonstrations of support for Hu were mostly tolerated by authorities at this stage, the Beijing Government declared temporary martial law on April 19 after 2,000 students laid siege to Xinhua Gate, one of the main entrances to the Zhongnanhai compound where most of China's top leaders lived and worked. Students there had demanded to speak face-to-face with Premier Li Peng, and a few began shouting slogans against the government and the Communist Party. As Chu-Yuan Cheng put it, the protests outside Zhongnanhai "represented the boldest expressions of dissent since the height of the Cultural Revolution in the late 1960s."[1]

News of the events in Beijing spread rapidly around the country. Large unofficial demonstrations were reported in the cities of Shanghai, Tianjin, Nanjing, Changchun, Changsha, Wuhan, and Xi'an, as well as in the provinces of Hunan and Anhui. In Xi'an, 10,000 students and many workers broke into the provincial government building and demanded dialogue, unsuccessfully, with the governor of Shaanxi province. Their demands went beyond the legacy of Hu Yaobang to encompass issues related to rising inflation, stagnant salaries, and housing problems.

Official editorial condemns student actions

After the official mourning period for Hu Yaobang was over, the student movement did not ease up its pressure on the gov-

---

[1] Chu-yuan Cheng, *Behind the Tiananmen Massacre*, p. 125.

ernment. On April 23, an Autonomous Federation of Students was established with representatives from each of the major Beijing universities. It ratified the student demands given to the National People's Congress on April 18, and called for a university boycott of indefinite duration to begin on April 24. The federation also sent more than 200 students to at least 18 other cities across the country to "network" with the students outside Beijing and draw support for the growing student movement from the ranks of workers and bureaucrats. Until mid-May, the federation loosely coordinated student activities, drafted documents and demands, and was entrusted with representation of the students when dialogue occurred with the authorities.

On April 24, the university boycott began. Students refused to attend classes in Beijing, Shanghai, Nanjing, Tianjin, and Wuhan. Two days later, the Autonomous Federation of Students held its first press conference, and student leaders announced that their immediate aim was the opening of a dialogue on political reform with government officials. They also affirmed that their tactics toward that goal would be nonviolent.

Meanwhile, the Chinese Government—in the absence of reformist Communist Party General Secretary Zhao Ziyang, who was on a state visit to North Korea—issued its first public response to the students. An official editorial, titled "The Necessity for a Clear Stand Against Turmoil" and published in the State journal *The People's Daily*, condemned and insulted the students. It claimed that the student movement was "a well-planned plot . . . to confuse the people and throw the country into turmoil. . . . Its real aim is to reject the Chinese Communist Party and the socialist system at the most fundamental level. . . ."[2]

Massive student marches and demonstrations

The students were not deterred. Most were angered by the government's response to their movement, which they felt was patriotic. On April 27, more than 50,000 university students marched around Beijing for 14 hours in reaction to the *People's Daily* editorial. They sang Communist Party anthems and shouted that they had done nothing wrong. For the first time, thousands

---

2 Zhang Liang (comp.), *The Tiananmen Papers*, p. 76.

of workers and residents who in previous weeks had acted as passive bystanders joined them or cheered them on from the sidelines. Unarmed police were deployed in an attempt to control the marchers, but no violence broke out and discipline among the students remained strong. The size of the demonstration and the popular support it received apparently shocked the authorities, who for the next week oscillated between threatening a crackdown and offering to partially concede some of the student demands.

Outside Beijing, there were reports before the publication of the *People's Daily* editorial that students had grown tired of the demonstrations and that the movement was losing steam. That process reversed itself after students learned of the editorial. Large student demonstrations were held in Changchun, Tianjin, Shanghai, Hefei, Xi'an, Nanjing, Hangzhou, Wuhan, Chengdu, Chongqing, and Changsha. Within days, the protests spread to previously quiet cities such as Shenyang, Dalian, Shijiazhuang, Nanning, Jinan, Shenzhen, Kunming, Yinchuan, and Guilin.

On April 29, Premier Li Peng instructed government officials Yuan Mu and He Dongchang to begin a "dialogue" with the students. The first such meeting, between Yuan, He, and 45 students from Party-sponsored student organizations, was essentially a monologue. Yuan and He defended the April 26 *People's Daily* editorial, insisted there were no serious problems with corruption in the government or the Communist Party, and told the students they were simply being manipulated by sinister forces behind the scenes, and that they should return to classes. The tape of the dialogue was broadcast on national television, resulting in student demonstrations in 23 cities throughout China.

The protests continued into the month of May, leading up to an important symbolic anniversary. May 4, 1989, marked the 70th anniversary of the first major student movement in China's modern history. This was thus chosen by the Autonomous Federation of Students in the Capital as the date of its next major demonstration. On May 3, the government attempted to seal off Tiananmen Square in anticipation of the protest. But on May 4, tens of thousands of students from more than 50 university campuses flowed past barricades of unarmed police and into the Square. Residents along the route generally expressed support for the marchers, as did many journalists incensed at the decision by

Shanghai Party leader Jiang Zemin to close down the *World Economic Herald* newspaper, ostensibly for violations of Party discipline.

During the rally, student leader Wuerkaixi read a "New May Fourth Manifesto," stating that

> this student movement has but one goal, that is, to facilitate the process of modernization by raising high the banners of democracy and science, by liberating people from the constraints of feudal ideology, and by promoting freedom, human rights, and rule of law.[3]

Nearly 100,000 provincial students held simultaneous demonstrations in 51 cities throughout China.

Divisions among the students

After the May 4 demonstrations, the university boycott officially ended—although many students in Beijing continued to press for a prolonged strike—and the student movement entered a new phase characterized by internal division.

The first issue that sparked heated debate was whether or not to continue demonstrating during Soviet leader Mikhail Gorbachev's official state visit to China on May 15. Some students argued that the Sino-Soviet summit would attract so much world press that the government would be forced to respect their movement if it was visible during that time. Others suggested that continued protests during Gorbachev's visit, especially with the eyes of the world on China, would only anger and embarrass the regime, driving it to repressive action. The debate was won by those favoring continued action.

On May 8, the student planning committee in Beijing announced that the boycott of classes would continue unless five conditions were met. These included a government retraction of the statements made in the April 26 *People's Daily* editorial, legalization of the Autonomous Federation of Students, reinstatement of the fired editor of the *World Economic Herald,* concrete measures against government and Party corruption, and reconsideration of Beijing's laws restricting popular protests.

---

3 Han Minzhu (ed.), *Cries for Democracy,* p. 136.

Mass hunger strike

More discussion then ensued among the students to decide which additional actions should be taken during the Gorbachev visit. One group proposed launching a mass hunger strike. This suggestion was initially turned down by the Autonomous Student Federation as "too radical." The federation, however, was losing its ability to coordinate the burgeoning movement. On May 13, about 2,000 students began a hunger strike and a permanent sit-in at Tiananmen Square.

Although the federation gave its belated support to the hunger strikers, the "moral authority" of those prepared to give their lives in the struggle quickly propelled the hunger strikers themselves to the leadership of the movement. The number of hunger strikers soon exceeded 3,000, while more than 25,000 students, workers, and residents camped out in the Square to support and protect them.

The hunger strikers created their own organization, the Hunger Strike Group, which effectively displaced the student federation as coordinator of the movement in the Square. The hunger strikers had only two demands:

> First, we demand that the government promptly carry out with the Beijing Students Dialogue Delegation a substantive and concrete dialogue based on the principle of equality of the parties. Second, we demand that the government set straight the reputation of the student movement, and that it give it a fair and just evaluation, affirming that it is a patriotic student democracy movement.[4]

Early government attempts to open a dialogue with the hunger strikers failed, partly because the government representatives expressed inflexibility and partly because the student movement was so split that the student "representatives" could not guarantee they actually carried representation of the whole movement.

Meanwhile, at high-level government meetings, moderate Communist Party General Secretary Zhao Ziyang expressed sympathy with the students and suggested the student movement be controlled through dialogue and a vocal recognition of the students' motives as patriotic, thus softening the tone of the April 26 editorial. He also suggested conceding to major student demands

---

[4] Han Minzhu (ed.), *Cries for Democracy*, p. 202.

in areas in which those demands also reflected official Party policy, such as by taking strong moves against government corruption. But by this time, unbeknownst to the students, Zhao and his allies had already lost the power struggle in the government. In the coming weeks, the octogenarian Gang of Elders would increasingly take sides with the hard-line members of the Politburo.

Tiananmen Square occupation

While Gorbachev and hordes of foreign media were in China between May 15 and 18, hundreds of thousands of demonstrators packed Tiananmen Square in support of the hunger strikers. Gorbachev's visit was moved to the second tier of newspaper headlines as the world press focused intensely on the students and their rapidly expanding movement. The hunger strike itself attracted high levels of support from the population, outraged at a government that seemed unresponsive to thousands of students who were highly regarded in China and were prepared to die for what seemed to be relatively soft demands. By the evening of May 16, more than 600 hunger strikers had lost consciousness.

With the open participation of workers and residents, and the spread of the demonstrations to more than 80 cities nationwide, the movement grew out of the hands of the student leaders. While still centered in Beijing, it had evolved into a national people's movement. More than one million people demonstrated in Beijing alone on both May 17 and May 18, the largest "unauthorized" demonstrations in China's history. Hundreds of thousands of other protesters marched or demonstrated simultaneously in 28 provinces in support of the hunger strikers.

Demands of the new protesters often deviated significantly from the original goals of the students. Thousands of demonstrators called openly for the retirement of Deng Xiaoping and the resignations of Premier Li Peng and President Yang Shangkun. As the number of protesters grew larger and the demands became more radical, discipline also became more difficult to enforce. Increasingly, students had to create their own task forces to maintain order during marches and demonstrations, and to keep them from turning violent or provocative. On some occasions, they even formed human shields to protect soldiers and police from mob violence.

Zhao Ziyang's fall from power and Li Peng's dialogue

Communist Party General Secretary Zhao Ziyang led a group of Politburo members to meet with hunger strikers in a Beijing hospital before dawn on May 18. Zhao told the students their aims and those of the government were one and the same, that they were patriotic, and that their demands would be addressed if they ended the hunger strike. His tone was urgent, reflecting a knowledge that his own power was coming to an end, and with it, the most important voice in the Politburo supporting a nonrepressive stance toward the students.

Later in the morning, Premier Li Peng opened a televised dialogue with hunger strikers and student leaders. Li refused to discuss any issues raised by the students, or to negotiate resolutions to any of their demands. He simply demanded that the hunger strike "end immediately," and that the Square be cleared. "You have gone too far," he told them.[5] The meeting was short, and the students were outraged. What the students did not know was that Li Peng, Politburo hard-liners, and the Gang of Elders had already decided to launch a crackdown on the student movement and declare martial law in Beijing. By the end of the day, Zhao Ziyang had been effectively removed from office and was bypassed in all major decision-making.

Meanwhile, protests continued to grow in the provinces. On May 19, large demonstrations were held in more than 100 cities. In Shanghai, 70,000 marched and a solidarity hunger strike had already taken a severe toll on more than 200 students. In Changsha, workers joined students in protests, sometimes chanting slogans against the Communist Party leadership. Also in Changsha, 300 students conducted a hunger strike of their own. Violence broke out in Shaoyang, as crowds torched vehicles and stormed the municipal offices of the Communist Party. Riots also reportedly broke out in Taiyuan, and 3,000 students in Fuzhou blockaded railway traffic for six hours.

---

[5] Stefan R. Landsberger, "Chronology of the 1989 Student Demonstrations," in Saich (ed.), *The Chinese People's Movement*, p. 172.

Martial law

On the evening of May 19, Premier Li Peng addressed a meeting of Party, government, and military representatives to announce the imminent implementation of martial law in Beijing in order to "curb the turmoil" generated by student protests whose aim, he said, was to "subvert the leadership of the Chinese Communist Party, to overthrow the People's Government that was legally elected by the National People's Congress, and thoroughly to repudiate the people's democratic dictatorship."[6] Four group armies from the Beijing, Shenyang, and Jinan military regions immediately moved into positions in urban districts of Beijing.

On May 20, protesters in Tiananmen Square were told to evacuate the Square immediately or "face the consequences." The hunger strike had already been called off the previous evening, but some students decided to continue the fast anyway. Others vowed to simply continue the occupation of the Square as a "sit-in." They issued a new document rejecting the declaration of martial law and calling for a general strike, while urging their supporters to "avoid confrontation with the army" and to refrain from "anything that will cause bloodshed."[7]

Defiance of martial law

By midmorning the same day, large crowds of Beijing residents had emerged to prevent the 250,000 People's Liberation Army troops from reaching the center of the city and Tiananmen Square. More than one million people took to the streets, openly defying the declaration of martial law. Most troops were unable to reach their assigned destinations. Five hundred thousand demonstrators in Shanghai and 300,000 in Xi'an also immobilized their respective cities for hours to protest against the army occupation of Beijing and to demand the resignation of Li Peng. Similar demonstrations against martial law broke out in 130 other cities as well.

Such actions continued for more than a week across China. Most notable, however, were the attempts in Beijing to effectively annul martial law through popular action. Every day, hundreds

---

6 Zhang Liang (comp.), *The Tiananmen Papers,* p. 225.
7 Simmie and Nixon, *Tiananmen Square,* p. 136.

of thousands of Beijing residents formed human barricades to ensure that the army could not reach Tiananmen Square. Large numbers of protesters, outnumbering soldiers, frequently surrounded and immobilized army units for hours at a time. They prevented their movement toward the Square while simultaneously offering them water and food, and engaging them in conversation. There were also reports that fuel lines were cut and tires deflated on military vehicles throughout the city.

Many protesters did not believe that the "People's Army" would repress the people. This belief was reinforced by the fact that, after being stopped by nonviolent demonstrators, some tanks, armored personnel carriers, and troop transports turned back toward the outskirts of the city. Other soldiers simply took off their uniforms and blended into the crowd. Shortly after martial law was declared, the commander of the 38th Group Army based outside Beijing was even relieved from command, later to be court-martialed, for refusing a direct order to move his troops into the city.

News of such events boosted the demonstrators' self-confidence. As the stalemate between the population and the army continued, students believed for a time that they were actually winning and that the hard-liners in the government might fall. But by May 26, it was clear that Li Peng remained firmly entrenched in power, that the military was neither moving against the students nor withdrawing to its barracks, and that the National People's Congress was not going to oppose martial law.

Furthermore, most officers and troops did, by and large, follow orders during this time. For the first week of martial law, troops were under strict orders to engage in dialogue with the population and to avoid violent confrontations at all cost. The fact that they had not moved on Tiananmen Square or attacked defiant demonstrators simply meant they had not yet been ordered to do so.

Students: stay or withdraw?

Among the students and the demonstrators in the Square, a debate ensued as to whether they should call off the sit-in and withdraw, or continue to resist in the Square. On May 21, student leaders agreed to an orderly withdrawal and a continuation of the boycott of classes. Later in the day, however, they met again and decided to stay in the Square.

A compromise was reached one week later. The student leaders announced they would remain in the Square until May 30, hold one last major demonstration against martial law and in favor of democratic reforms, and then withdraw. It was assumed that this proposal would be accepted by all, but the next day it was put to a democratic vote of the students remaining in the Square.

To the surprise of the leaders, the proposal was overwhelmingly rejected. They had not counted on the fact that by this time most of the students from Beijing universities had already withdrawn from the Square and gone home. Of the students who remained, the vast majority were from other provinces and had only recently arrived. These students did not feel represented by the Beijing student leadership. Furthermore, they did not wish to leave the Square without feeling like they had accomplished something. On May 29, the remaining students announced they would stay for another three weeks, until the next scheduled meeting of the National People's Congress.

Nationwide protests continue

During the last week of May, demonstrations in the provinces continued throughout the country. Hundreds of thousands marched in over 100 cities, protesting martial law and demanding Li Peng's resignation. Most of the protesters were students and professionals, although workers took part in Xi'an, Jinan, Taiyuan, Chengdu, and Chongqing. Rubber workers announced a strike in Nanjing.

Many other students from across the country continued to leave their hometowns and crowd passenger trains en route to Beijing. Some students near Beijing also blocked the movement of military trains, hoping to interfere with the army's ability to carry out its directives under martial law.

Decision made to use troops

By May 29 and 30 it was clear that the movement was in decline, both nationwide and in Beijing. No demonstrations were reported in Beijing on these days. The number of students in

Tiananmen Square dwindled to fewer than 10,000, with most being from the provinces. Tens of thousands of other provincial students had already left Beijing, exhausted by the constant protests or fed up by the infighting of the student movement. Demonstrations continued in many cities, but they tended to be smaller. Many students returned to class.

On June 1, Li Peng presented the ruling Politburo with a report identifying the remaining students as "terrorists" engaged in a "counterrevolutionary riot" whose aim was an armed seizure of State power. The report called on the Central Military Commission to "take swift and decisive measures immediately to suppress the counterrevolutionary turmoil in Beijing."[8] On the following day, the Politburo and the Elders met and decided to clear Tiananmen Square. Troops received orders to begin advancing on the city center.

Meanwhile, the crowds guarding the students and the Square became increasingly restless. Confrontations, but little actual violence, occurred between residents and soldiers in numerous parts of Beijing on June 2 and 3. Advancing troops, most of whom were still without weapons, were no longer treated amiably by the population. They were often humiliated, insulted, or taunted by the crowds. In several instances, students attempted to protect soldiers and to restrain the crowds when violence erupted.

The soldiers open fire

On the afternoon and evening of June 3, radio and television broadcasts warned residents of Beijing to remain indoors. It was clear that military action was imminent. Nevertheless, many students and residents persisted in their refusal to believe their lives were in danger. This was partly because the events of previous weeks had made the demonstrators believe they were not facing extreme repression, and partly because they believed the soldiers would in fact refuse any order to shoot the people.

The order for the final assault to seize Tiananmen Square by military action was ratified and delivered to the People's Liberation Army and the military police at 9:00 p.m. on June 3. The Square was to be cleared by dawn on June 4, and "all means nec-

---

[8] Zhang Liang (comp.), *The Tiananmen Papers,* p. 338.

essary" were authorized to suppress the "counterrevolutionary riot."

When soldiers fired on the people for the first time, on Fuxingmenwai Boulevard on the road to Tiananmen, the demonstrators could not believe they were using live ammunition. Expecting rubber bullets, the front line of students simply placed padded jackets or pillows in front of their bodies. Only when these students fell and did not get back up did the other protesters realize the army had indeed been authorized to use deadly violence against its own population.

Most of the deaths occurred in the pre-dawn hours of June 4, during the advance toward Tiananmen Square. Once the assault began, while most students remained nonviolent, many protesters fought back violently. Some used iron rods, clubs, batons, or bamboo poles as weapons. Some military vehicles were attacked and burned, often with their occupants inside. But by dawn, the Square had been cleared.

On the following day—some reports indicated for as long as three days—students and residents opposed the troops in several parts of Beijing. Sometimes people attempted to block troop movements by forming human barricades at street intersections, where they were often shot at by soldiers and police. Torching of military vehicles continued. Similar confrontations, at times including the use of violence, flared up in cities across China as police faced angry crowds protesting the brutal events in Beijing.

The number of casualties from the June 3-4 military action will never be known precisely. Educated estimates suggest approximately 2,600 people were killed and more than 7,000 wounded, including both civilians and soldiers.

Some soldiers refused, most fired

During seven weeks of mostly nonviolent demonstrations, students and their supporters across China undertook a formidable challenge to the Chinese regime. They launched one of the largest hunger strikes in history, paralyzed parts of important cities such as Beijing, Shanghai, and Xi'an, and managed to resist the imposition of martial law for nearly three weeks.

Perhaps as many as 1,000 soldiers dropped their weapons and fled rather than following orders to attack civilians. A number of officers were court-martialed and may have been executed for refusing to order the troops under their command to carry out the operation. Nevertheless, such acts of bravado and heroism were not sufficient to prevent the massacre. For the most part, and despite early rumors to the contrary, the army fell into line and followed its orders when asked to kill the students and their supporters.

By June 10, protests against the massacre had subsided across the country, although many students remained at home rather than attending classes. Military action was reduced, and the main focus of the government shifted to restoring its international image as a country open for business.

Meanwhile, security forces hunted all those implicated in "counterrevolutionary" activities. One month after the massacre, more than 2,500 people had been arrested in the crackdown, and public executions of at least 30 "counterrevolutionaries" were held in Beijing, Shanghai, Jinan, Dalian, and Changsha. The "democratic spring" in China had come to an end.

Sources

Byrnes, Michael T., "The Death of a People's Army," in Hicks (ed.), *The Broken Mirror*, pp. 132-151.

Calhoun, Craig, *Neither Gods nor Emperors: Students and the Struggle for Democracy in China,* Berkeley: University of California Press, 1994.

Cheng, Joseph Y. S., "A Chronology of Selected Documents and Statements," in Hicks (ed.), *The Broken Mirror,* pp. 475-496.

Chu-yuan Cheng, *Behind the Tiananmen Massacre: Social, Political and Economic Ferment in China,* Boulder, Colorado: Westview Press, 1990.

Des Forges, Roger V. and others (eds.), *Chinese Democracy and the Crisis of 1989: Chinese and American Reflections,* Albany, New York: State University of New York, 1993.

Han Minzhu (ed.), *Cries for Democracy: Writings and Speeches from the 1989 Chinese Democracy Movement,* Princeton, New Jersey: Princeton University Press, 1990.

Hicks, George (ed.), *The Broken Mirror: China After Tiananmen,* Chicago: St. James Press, 1990.

Khu, Josephine M. T., "Student Organization in the Movement," in Des Forges and others (eds.), *Chinese Democracy and the Crisis of 1989,* pp. 161-175.

Landsberger, Stefan R., "Chronology of the 1989 Student Demonstrations," in Saich (ed.), *The Chinese People's Movement,* pp. 164-189.

Niming, Frank, "Learning How to Protest," in Saich (ed.), *The Chinese People's Movement,* pp. 83-105.

Saich, Tony, "When Worlds Collide: The Beijing People's Movement of 1989," pp. 25-49, in Saich (ed.), *The Chinese People's Movement.*

Saich, Tony (ed.), *The Chinese People's Movement: Perspectives on Spring 1989,* Armonk, New York: M. E. Sharpe, Inc., 1990.

Scobell, Andrew, "Why the People's Army Fired on the People," in Des Forges and others (eds.), *Chinese Democracy and the Crisis of 1989,* pp. 191-221.

Simmie, Scott and Nixon, Bob, *Tiananmen Square,* Vancouver, Canada: Douglas and McIntyre, 1989.

Unger, Jonathan (ed.), *The Pro-Democracy Protests in China: Reports from the Provinces,* Armonk, New York: M. E. Sharpe, Inc., 1991.

Woei Lien Chong, "Petitioners, Popperians, and Hunger Strikers: The Uncoordinated Efforts of the 1989 Chinese Democratic Movement," in Saich (ed.), *The Chinese People's Movement,* pp. 106-125.

Zhang Liang (comp.), *The Tiananmen Papers: The Chinese Leadership's Decision to Use Force Against Their Own People—In Their Own Words,* New York: Public Affairs, 2001.

This chapter also relied on eyewitness accounts from Bruce Jenkins and Gene Sharp as well as declassified U.S. Government documents, available from the National Security Archive on the internet at

http://www.seas.gwu.edu/nsarchive/NSAEBB/NSAEBB16/ documents/index.html

Chapter Twenty-three

THE LIBERATION OF CZECHOSLOVAKIA—1989

Joshua Paulson

Attack on nonviolent students

Nineteen eighty-nine was the year of change in Eastern Europe. Following the summer victory of Solidarity in Poland, the quiet collapse of State socialism in Hungary, and the opening of the Berlin Wall in Germany on November 9, it was now Czechoslovakia's turn.

The dramatic events began on November 17, with a student demonstration in Prague to commemorate the death of Jan Opletal, a Czech student killed by the Nazis 50 years earlier. Fifteen thousand students initially took part, including a large contingent

---

A list of sources for this case appears at the end of this chapter.

of the official Communist Party youth organization that had approved the event.

The speakers took up an increasingly anti-government tone, and eventually the demonstration began to move. As they marched toward Wenceslas Square in Central Prague, their numbers grew to over 30,000. At the entrance to the Square they were met by special anti-terrorist squads and riot police.

The students placed candles on the ground, raised their hands to show they had no weapons, sang songs, and in some cases attempted to hand flowers to the police. Nevertheless, the students were brutally attacked. Hundreds were wounded or arrested, and at least one student was killed.[1]

The students immediately resolved to go on strike. Using computers and mimeograph machines, students published and distributed proclamations, fliers, and anti-government propaganda. On November 18, after occupation strikes were declared at several universities, they were joined by students from the film and drama schools. Actors canceled their performances and turned theaters into meeting places and centers of political discussion. The actors issued a call for a two-hour general strike on November 27.

The birth of Civic Forum

On the evening of November 19, diverse members of pre-existing opposition groups held an emergency meeting in a Prague theater. They had been convened by Václav Havel, Czechoslovakia's best-known playwright, dissident, and founding member of the "Charter 77" human rights organization. The group immediately decided to turn itself into a Civic Forum, "as a spokesman on behalf of that part of the Czechoslovak public which is increasingly critical of the existing Czechoslovak leadership and which in recent days has been profoundly shaken by the brutal massacre of peacefully demonstrating students."[2]

In addition to supporting the call for a general strike, the Civic Forum had four initial demands. They called for the release of all

---

[1] See Ash, *The Magic Lantern,* p. 30 and Berend, *Central and Eastern Europe, 1944-1993,* p. 283.

[2] Quoted in Ash, *The Magic Lantern,* p. 82.

political prisoners, the resignation of certain government and Communist Party officials held responsible for the 1968 Warsaw Pact invasion, the resignation of those responsible for the recent attack on student demonstrators, and the establishment of a special commission to investigate this attack.

Mass demonstrations and rattling keys

The following day, 200,000 people gathered in Prague's Wenceslas Square, demanding the resignations of Party and government officials. The government was unsure how to respond, and this time made no attempt to use violence against the protesters. The demonstrations continued each day after working hours, and the previously puppet Socialist Party allowed the Civic Forum to use its balcony overlooking the Square to speak to the crowds.

Demonstrations in excess of 300,000 people would soon become part of the daily routine in Prague, and popular demands were widened to include free elections and political democracy.

On November 22, the first preliminary talks were held between Prime Minister Adamec and a delegation of the Civic Forum and the "People Against Violence" (PAV), which was coordinating protests in Slovakia.

Two days later, on November 24, Civic Forum leader Václav Havel was joined in Prague by Alexander Dubcek, the legendary reformist leader of 1968. Havel and Dubcek addressed the afternoon demonstration together. Just before the protest ended for the day, 300,000 people took out their keys and shook them. This symbolic rattling of keys was to become a trademark of future demonstrations. The sound of the keys symbolized the end of what has gone before, just as a bell rings at the end of a school day. The ringing sound of the keys in this case symbolized a widespread recognition that the end of the Communist dictatorship had arrived.

Resignations and negotiations

Later in the evening, it was announced that the entire Politburo and Central Committee of the Communist Party had resigned.

Real changes were still lacking, however, and the demonstrations continued. The two-hour general strike on November 27 was an overwhelming success. Even Czech television crews—which were now devoting much of their energies to covering the opposition demonstrations—announced they were "joining" the strike, and spent the two hours broadcasting nothing but scenes of plazas full of demonstrators all over the country.[3]

Direct negotiations between the Civic Forum/PAV and Prime Minister Adamec continued on November 28. Adamec promised to name a new government by December 3 and to release all political prisoners by December 10. He also promised to remove the article dealing with the "leading role" of the Communist Party from the Constitution.

Taking advantage of the government's rapid concessions, the Civic Forum and People Against Violence drew up a new list of demands, including the resignation of President Husák by December 10. They also established a December 31 deadline for Adamec to dissolve the People's Militia, allow basic freedoms of expression, and set a timetable for free elections.[4]

Communist collapse

On December 3, Adamec named his new cabinet, with a large majority of Communist Party members. This was unacceptable to the Civic Forum and PAV, who called for a new wave of demonstrations to begin on December 4 and threatened another general strike for December 11.

As massive popular protests again swept Prague and Bratislava, the Czechoslovakian Government suddenly found itself under extreme external pressure as well. The East German Government had fully collapsed, with Communist Party leaders under house arrest, and the Warsaw Pact had formally renounced and condemned the 1968 invasion of Czechoslovakia (which had propelled President Husák to power). On December 7, following inconclusive negotiations with the Civic Forum/PAV, Prime Minister Adamec resigned.

---

[3] Ash, *The Magic Lantern,* p. 106.
[4] Ash, *The Magic Lantern,* p. 110.

President Husák then invited the Civic Forum/PAV to join "roundtable" talks with the Communist Party and its satellite parties to discuss the composition of a new government. The talks lasted only two days. On December 10, President Husák announced the establishment of a new government composed primarily of non-Party members and participants in the Civic Forum and the People Against Violence. He then submitted his own resignation.

By the end of the month, Alexander Dubcek returned to power as Chairman of the Federal Assembly and playwright Václav Havel was named President. In just 24 days, the population whose hopes had been thwarted by a military invasion 20 years before had risen up without violence and defeated the Communist government. It became known as the "Velvet Revolution."

Sources

Ash, Timothy Garton, *The Magic Lantern* (New York: Random House, 1990), pp. 78-130.

Berend, Ivan T., *Central and Eastern Europe, 1944-1993: Detour From the Periphery to the Periphery* (Cambridge: Cambridge University Press, 1996), pp. 277-284.

For opposition under the Husák government before 1989, see

Havel, Václav, *Disturbing the Peace: A Conversation with Karel Hvizdala,* New York: Alfred A. Knopf, 1990.

Renner, Hans, *A History of Czechoslovakia Since 1945* (New York: Routledge, 1989), pp. 118-161.

Chapter Twenty-four

LATVIANS RESTORE INDEPENDENCE—1991

Soviet occupation and early resistance

The independence movements that swept through the Baltic republics of Latvia, Estonia, and Lithuania in the final years of the Soviet Union's existence were overwhelmingly nonviolent ones. The movements relied on nonviolent protests, noncooperation, and defiance in efforts to prevent renewed Soviet military intervention and political dominance. Latvia's struggle for independence serves as an important case in point.

The Soviet occupation of Latvia after the Second World War era was marked by very strong efforts to eliminate independent civil society and promote the "Russification" and "Sovietization" of Latvian society.[1] Expressions of Latvian culture and language were discouraged at best, and forbidden at worst. Many Latvians

---

A list of sources for this case appears at the end of this chapter.
[1] "Russification" refers to the efforts to turn the people of the country into Russians in culture and language.

fought against the Soviet occupying army with guerrilla tactics in the first years of the occupation. However, by 1952 it was evident that the guerrilla resistance had failed. Limited nonviolent resistance followed for the next 30 years, primarily expressed by young students who refused to join the Communist Youth organizations, and by citizens who refused to vote in Soviet elections or to speak Russian in the streets. Latvian Communists were also known to resist Russification policies through a defense of Latvian culture and interests within official Soviet institutions.

Organization and demonstrations

In 1986, the first open, public resistance to Soviet rule in Latvia took shape with the creation of "Helsinki-86," an independent human rights group formed to "monitor how the economic, cultural, and individual rights of our people are respected."[2] Members wrote signed letters to Soviet authorities and the international community protesting the continuing Russification policies, political oppression, and the linguistic and cultural discrimination suffered by Latvians in their homeland.

Throughout much of 1987, Helsinki-86 openly defied the government by organizing the first large, unofficial demonstrations in Latvia since Second World War, commemorating the dates of key events in Latvia's history. Members of the organization were harassed or arrested at demonstrations, vilified in the press, and slandered in public. Nevertheless, they refused to be silenced.

The activities of Helsinki-86 were contagious. On April 19, 1988, thousands of people took part in a funeral march for Gunars Astra, a prominent Latvian dissident and political prisoner. For the first time since the Second World War, the Latvian national anthem was sung in public during the march, and the original Latvian flag was flown.

Two months later, many Latvian intellectuals and artists publicly spoke out against Soviet policies for the first time. When their actions were condemned by the Latvian Communist Party, some newspapers openly rejected "attempts by some senior Party and Soviet apparatus officials to disguise their economic and ideological errors by an attack on the policy of democrati-

---

[2] Eglitis, *Nonviolent Action in the Liberation of Latvia*, p. 9.

zation. . . ."[3] Instead of fear, the Party's declarations had inspired only defiance.

Two million protesters

The national movement grew at a fast pace. Latvian independence organizations formed, and protest marches with more than
500,000 participants were not uncommon. On August 23, 1989,
less than one year after it was founded, the Popular Front of Latvia joined with the Estonian and Lithuanian independence
movements to form a human chain connecting the capitals of the
three Baltic republics. More than two million people participated,
in an attempt to remind the world of the Hitler-Stalin pact[4] and
its consequences for the Baltic countries.

Moscow was furious, in part because the Popular Front of
Latvia had been viewed by Communist reformers as an organization that could work for changes *within* the Soviet system, and
thus mobilize the Latvian grassroots movement in the direction of
limited reforms advanced by the backers of *glasnost* (openness)
and *perestroika* (restructuring). The Popular Front of Latvia,
however, would prove to be much more than a "loyal opposition."

An independence government elected

When the first democratic elections for the Latvian Supreme
Council (Soviet) were held on March 18, 1990, pro-independence
candidates of the Popular Front and the National Independence
Movement of Latvia won overwhelmingly. Two months later, the
Latvian Supreme Council declared its intent to restore independence, and the country was renamed "The Republic of Latvia"
(replacing "Latvian Soviet Socialist Republic"). From this time
on, the Supreme Council was viewed by most Latvians as the
country's legitimate government. It took over the leadership roles
of the independence movement.

However, due to the earlier Soviet deportation of many Latvians and the Soviet introduction of Russians during the previous

---

[3] Eglitis, *Nonviolent Action in the Liberation of Latvia,* p. 15.
[4] The Hitler-Stalin Pact had divided Eastern Europe into spheres controlled by Nazi
Germany and the Soviet Union.

50 years, nearly half of the Latvian population was not ethnically Latvian. Although many Russians in Latvia supported independence, hard-liners refused to recognize the legitimacy of the Latvian Supreme Council, and were backed up by thousands of Soviet troops stationed in the Baltics. On May 14, 1990, Soviet President Gorbachev declared Latvia's declaration of independence to be null and void.

Terror and organized nonviolent resistance

In the Latvian capital of Riga, terrorist provocations by the Soviet Interior Ministry's infamous "Black Berets" increased as autumn approached. Their actions included attacks against civilians and municipal authorities, as well as a series of bombings. Pro-Soviet hard-liners called for the direct intervention of Moscow to "restore law and order," and a Soviet imposition of a loyal regime seemed imminent.

In this climate, the popular pro-independence organizations began looking toward nonviolent methods as ways to protect the republic in case of a Soviet military attack. Improvised nonviolent resistance would be replaced by organized nonviolent resistance for defense.[5]

---

[5] This option was supported by the receipt by the pro-independence government of page proofs of Gene Sharp's then-new book, *Civilian-Based Defense: A Post-Military Weapons System,* Princeton, New Jersey: Princeton University Press, 1990, prepared with the assistance of Bruce Jenkins. The proofs were initially obtained at a November 1989 conference in Moscow by the Lithuanian philosopher Grazina Miniotaite, who delivered them to Audrius Butkevicius, Director General of Lithuania's Department of National Defense. Butkevicius then sent 50 photocopies of the page proofs to various destinations in the Soviet Union, including the Baltic states of Latvia and Estonia. The Latvian Government asked Olgerts Eglitis to produce a Latvian manuscript translation, which was used in planning Latvia's immediate defense. In Estonia, the English text was used, and in Lithuania, a manuscript translation was also used in their defense planning. Gene Sharp and Bruce Jenkins visited Riga, as well as Vilnius, Lithuania, and Tallin, Estonia, from November 14 to December 7, 1991, and consulted with Latvian Defense Minister Talavs Jundzis and other members of the Supreme Council's Commission on Defense and Home Affairs, as well as members of independence organizations, who affirmed Latvia's intention to employ organized civilian resistance in the event of a large-scale Soviet attack. *Civilian-Based Defense* was later published in Latvian with introductions by Valdis V. Pavlovskis, then Latvia's Defense Minister, and Talavs Jundzis, the previous Defense Minister.

On December 11, 1990, the Popular Front of Latvia issued an "Announcement to All Supporters of Latvia's Independence."[6] Olgerts Eglitis, an important participant in this struggle, writes:

> The Announcement became known as 'The Appeal for the Hour X,' since it set up a program for how to act at the moment when a coup d'état or imposition of presidential rule began. The Popular Front called upon the people to resort to nonviolent means in such a case. This Appeal was in fact the first plan for national defense by nonviolent means, civilian actions. It advised people, for example, to comply only with the laws of the Supreme Council, to ignore the orders of the military and any imposed governors, to not participate in any elections or referenda, to document all the crimes perpetrated by the occupiers, etc.[7]

Instructions for nonviolent struggle

The first test of the Announcement came on January 2, 1991, when Black Berets violently occupied the Press Building in Riga, and the Soviet Government announced that additional paratroopers would be sent to the Baltic states under the pretext of ensuring compliance with military conscription. On January 9, the National Independence Movement of Latvia issued an appeal calling on its followers to "nonviolently resist the actions of the USSR military authorities and their supporters."[8] The Movement urged Latvians to resist conscription, to pretend not to speak Russian when confronted, and to confuse the army by taking down or replacing street signs, signposts, house numbers, and tablets of place names.

On January 11, Soviet paratroopers opened fire on peaceful civilians in neighboring Lithuania, and two days later infantry and tank units killed 14 people and wounded 200 others who were protecting the Television Center in the Lithuanian capital of Vilnius.

---

[6] For the full text, see Eglitis, *Nonviolent Action in the Liberation of Latvia,* pp. 45-47.

[7] Eglitis, *Nonviolent Action in the Liberation of Latvia,* p. 29.

[8] Eglitis, *Nonviolent Action in the Liberation of Latvia,* p. 48. For the full text, see pp. 48-49.

Barricades and appeals to soldiers

Latvian leaders assumed they would be next. On the morning of January 13, the Supreme Council deputy chairman began radio broadcasts calling on the civilian population of Latvia to protect the parliament building, communications centers, and other important strategic locations in Riga. Plans were drawn up to establish human and material barricades throughout the city. By mid-afternoon on January 13, 500,000 people had gathered in Old Riga to protest the repression in Lithuania and express their determination to defend Latvia against a similar attack. They blocked off roads leading into the capital with tractors, buses, and heavy machinery.

However, the awaited attack did not materialize. Boris Yeltsin, chairman of the Russian Supreme Soviet, joined the leaders of Lithuania, Estonia, and Latvia on January 13 in protesting the use of violence and the intrusion into affairs of the Baltic states. Yeltsin also issued an "Appeal to Russian Soldiers," calling on them to refrain from acting "against legally constituted state bodies" in the three republics, including the Supreme Councils. Some Russian officers and troops even began to show signs of rebellion, refusing to follow orders to be restationed to the Baltics, or indicating they would not follow future orders to use violence against civilians.

Nevertheless, tensions remained high for the next eight months as Black Berets continued to use terror to provoke the Latvian population. On January 16, one Latvian died of a bullet wound to the head. On January 20, the Black Berets attacked the Latvian Interior Ministry, killing five people and wounding nine others. However, the citizens refrained from responding with violence of their own, knowing that if the Black Berets themselves were attacked it would provide an excuse for direct military intervention from Moscow.

Nonviolent Defense Center

On June 20, the Latvian Supreme Council approved a proposal for the establishment of a Nonviolent Defense Center, amid new rumors of an imminent coup in Moscow or an army assault against the Baltic states. The Center's "Basic Principles of Nonviolent Defense of the Republic of Latvia" affirmed that the methods used by Latvian defenders in the case of a coup or military attack would be:

> . . . open civil disobedience to the orders, decrees, and laws of the adversary; sabotage of these orders and decrees; hidden disobedience; interfering with the actions of the adversary or precluding them with means that do not threaten anyone's life (barricades, human chains, etc.); various kinds of nonviolent protests, demonstrations, strikes, boycotts; distribution of information (also destroying of or interfering with information important to the adversary); convincing the adversary; individual protests; protest letters, telegrams, demonstrative transgression of laws and decrees, leaving the workplace demonstratively, etc.[9]

The document also laid out instructions for how the population should act at the beginning of a coup d'état, after a coup has taken place, and during prolonged usurpation or occupation by the enemy.

Resist everywhere

On August 19, word came from Moscow that a military coup was in progress. Anticipating large-scale resistance in the Baltics, the Soviet army had occupied Riga in the early morning hours, closing all entrances to the city and blocking major streets. The Nonviolent Defense Center secretly rushed 2,000 copies of its instruction booklets to Latvia's cities and villages. Since Riga was already under army occupation, people were not asked to come to the capital, as they had done in January, but rather "to make every village, town, and home a center of resistance."[10] The Supreme Council called on local governments to refuse collaboration, and issued a declaration to the international community stating the readiness and preparation of Latvian citizens to wage a nonviolent defense of their homeland.

Resistance began in earnest. However, full implementation of the defense plans was not necessary. The putsch was thwarted just two days after it began, unable to withstand widespread

---

[9] Eglitis, *Nonviolent Action in the Liberation of Latvia,* p. 62.
[10] Eglitis, *Nonviolent Action in the Liberation of Latvia,* p. 39. For the full text of the instruction booklet, see pp. 52-65.

nonviolent resistance not only in the Baltics, but in Moscow itself.

Two weeks later, Latvia achieved its full independence.[11]

---

[11] In November 1992, the parliament of independent Latvia adopted the "Law on National Defense," which stated, in part, that one task of Latvia's defense program was to instruct the people of the Republic of Latvia "on how to conduct nonviolent national defense," and in cases in which violent actions are directed against the national constitutional order, "to organize civil disobedience against the illegal power." In January 1993, Gene Sharp and Bruce Jenkins again visited Latvia to confer with Defense Ministry officials concerning development of this component. In April 1994, Bruce Jenkins visited Latvia, as well as Estonia and Lithuania, concerning development of this policy. This is one of the few cases in which additional exploration of the relevance of nonviolent struggle occurred.

Sources

This chapter was drafted by Joshua Paulson on the basis of

Eglitis, Olgerts, *Nonviolent Action in the Liberation of Latvia,* Cambridge, Massachusetts: Albert Einstein Institution, Monograph Series, 1993.

This source was supplemented by an interview with Gene Sharp and a review of the text by Bruce Jenkins. See also the proceedings of the 10-year anniversary conference in Riga held January 19, 2001, and published as

Tälava Jundzazs, ed., Janvära barikädes kä tautas pretestïbas forma totalitärajam rezïmäm un täs mäcïbas, Riga: Latvijas Zinätnu Akadëmija, 2001.

Chapter Twenty-five

BLOCKING THE SOVIET HARD-LINE COUP—1991

Joshua Paulson

Gorbachev and the hard-liners

Throughout 1991, Soviet President Mikhail Gorbachev was warned repeatedly about the possibilities of a hard-line coup d'état against him to reverse his reformist policies of *glasnost* (openness) and *perestroika* (restructuring). Although Gorbachev often tended to dismiss the rumors, the threat was very real. Hard-liners occupied key positions in the military, in the Communist Party, in the KGB, and in Gorbachev's own cabinet, and were thus in a good position to carry out such a coup.

In the summer of 1991, President Gorbachev and the leaders of a number of key Soviet republics finalized the draft of a new Union

---

A list of sources for this case appears at the end of this chapter.

Treaty. The treaty was designed to both preserve the integrity of the Soviet Union and devolve many vital decision-making processes to the individual republics themselves. This was considered by Gorbachev to be an important element of the democratization process.

The hard-liners in Gorbachev's cabinet and in the Communist Party, however, realized that once the Union Treaty was signed it would be too late to turn back the clock. A group of them had been quietly making plans for a coup since late 1990, and they knew this would be their last opportunity. The Treaty would have effectively decentralized political authority throughout the Soviet republics. Not only was this idea anathema to the plotters' fading dreams of empire, but they knew that a coup attempted after such a decentralization of power would likely face much more serious resistance from the provincial republics themselves, unwilling to return to centralized Soviet control. The only hope, they believed, was to declare a State of Emergency before the treaty was signed, centralize authority around a small ruling junta, and roll back the reforms and all threats to the Union—with or without President Gorbachev.

Action against Gorbachev

The Union Treaty was due to be signed on August 20. The plotters, therefore, made their first moves on August 18. Gorbachev and his family were resting on holiday at the family's vacation residence in the Crimean town of Foros, on the Black Sea. He was scheduled to return to Moscow the following day, in order to make the final preparations for the signing of the Treaty. In the late afternoon, Gorbachev found that his telephones were not functioning and that all his communication with the outside world had been severed. He was then visited by a group of government officials, including the head of ground forces of the Soviet Army, a KGB official in charge of Gorbachev's personal security, and even his own Chief of Staff.

The visitors informed the President that they represented a newly formed "State Committee for the State of Emergency." They told Gorbachev he had two options: to go along with the Committee and authorize the State of Emergency, or to resign. He resolutely refused to do either. Unable to extract Gorbachev's cooperation, the putschists left him imprisoned and isolated in his vacation home, while they returned to Moscow.

News of the coup reached the Soviet public on the morning of August 19. The plotters expected little resistance, either inside or outside of the government and its institutions. They had reason to be confident. Gorbachev's domestic popularity had declined steadily throughout the year, as he attempted to maneuver politically between radical reformers and Communist Party hard-liners, losing the support of both in the process. The downside of his reforms—unemployment, increasing poverty, shortages—had become painfully clear to large sectors of the populace. The hard-liners were counting on the economic difficulties and Gorbachev's low popularity rankings to win the support of these sectors.

Furthermore, the State Committee for the State of Emergency itself included almost all of the USSR's top officials, with the exception of Gorbachev himself. These included Gennadii Yanaev, the Vice President; Valentin Pavlov, the Prime Minister; Vladimir Kryuchkov, the Chairman of the KGB; Dmitrii Yazov, the Defense Minister; and Boris Pugo, the Interior Minister. Also collaborating openly were the Chairman of the Supreme Soviet, Anatolii Luk'yanov, and Gorbachev's Chief of Staff, Valerii Boldin.

First reactions to the coup

Initial reaction to the coup was remarkably subdued. Leaders of Soviet republics outside Russia, with the significant exception of the independence-minded Baltic states, did not respond either in favor of the coup or against it. Throughout the Russian Federation, most local authorities either supported the coup or adopted a "wait-and-see" attitude. On the morning of August 19, life continued normally for the vast majority of the population. There were no strikes and no demonstrations. The putschists believed they had successfully carried out a bloodless coup.

But events soon turned against the hard-liners. KGB chief Kryuchkov expedited an "arrest list" at 7:20 a.m. on August 19, with the names of 70 individuals considered threatening to the new regime. The list included a number of notable reformers who had previously been allies of Gorbachev, as well as prominent members of the liberal opposition, recently elected Russian

President Boris Yeltsin, his top advisers, and key Russian legislators. However, Kryuchkov's subordinates failed to act on the warrants. Only five people were actually arrested.

Defiance of orders

Boris Yeltsin himself spent several hours in the early morning of August 19 at his home meeting with other high-ranking Russian Federation—as distinct from Soviet—officials to discuss a response to the coup. An elite KGB unit had the house surrounded for the duration of the meeting, with standing orders given at 5:00 a.m. to arrest Yeltsin and his aides. The KGB officers on the ground, however, argued among themselves and eventually refused to comply with their orders. By the time an armored unit arrived prepared to storm Yeltsin's house and make the arrests, the Russian leaders had already departed.

From Yeltsin's *dacha* (country home), the Russian officials traveled quickly to the "White House," the large building on the Moscow River that housed the Russian Parliament (Supreme Soviet). According to one observer, their plans were to "use the parliament building as a barricade, an oasis and symbol of democratic resistance, [and] communicate with the outside world by whatever means possible. . . ."[1] At 10:00 a.m., Yeltsin and the leader of the Russian Parliament arrived at the White House. Most of the members of the Presidium of the Supreme Soviet were already present. The putschists had sent army ground troops into Moscow by this time, and had placed tanks outside the White House. However, they neither attempted to seize the White House before Yeltsin's arrival nor to cut off the building's communications with the outside world.

Once in the White House, the first action of the provincial government was to ratify an "Appeal to the Citizens of Russia," drafted an hour earlier at Yeltsin's home, and to broadcast it from a makeshift radio station located inside the building. The Appeal denounced the declaration of a State of Emergency, calling it a "right-wing, reactionary and anti-constitutional coup d'état."[2] The Presidium of the Russian Supreme Soviet then

---

[1] Remnick, *Lenin's Tomb*, p. 462.
[2] Remnick, *Lenin's Tomb*, p. 466.

drafted and publicized a new document affirming the absolute il-
legitimacy of the State Committee for the State of Emergency,
warning that "the fulfillment of decisions of the so-called Emergency Committee will be considered as complicity in this crime
against the state with all the consequences that arise from this."[3]

Calls for noncooperation

Through their actions on the morning of August 19, the President, the Vice-President, and legislators of the Russian Federation
worked tirelessly to promote the existence of an alternative authority—an elected, constitutional authority—to that being proclaimed by the Emergency Committee. A group of approximately
100 deputies of the Russian Supreme Soviet spent the day on the
phones with military officers, demanding their support for the
constitutional order and reminding them that any actions undertaken in compliance with the State Committee for the State of
Emergency could be considered treasonous. Other deputies left
the building to "carry out agitation among the soldiers" and to
"depropagandize" them.

At noon, President Yeltsin himself stepped outside the White
House with General Kobets, the Russian defense minister and a
loyal Yeltsin ally. Yeltsin and Kobets proceeded to climb on top
of one of the tanks sent by the putschists, and spoke to the small
crowd of citizens that had begun to assemble in defense of the
White House. Yeltsin proclaimed all decisions and decrees of the
Committee to be illegal, and called on all Russian citizens "to
give an appropriate rebuff to the putschists and demand a return
of the country to normal constitutional development."[4]

On the evening of August 19, in his continuing attempts to di-
vide the armed forces and incite noncooperation with the coup
leaders, Yeltsin issued a new decree to all State employees, bureaucrats, and members of the security forces and military organs
of both the USSR and the Russian Federation. He affirmed that
the Russian Government would give legal and moral support to
all those who refused to comply with unconstitutional orders
from their commanders or bosses. This proclamation elicited a re-

---

[3] Khasbulatov, *The Struggle for Russia,* p. 144.
[4] Remnick, *Lenin's Tomb,* p. 466.

sponse from Air Force chief Yevgeni Shaposhnikov, who not only thanked the Russian Government and announced his refusal to cooperate in the coup, but placed the Soviet Air Force at President Yeltsin's disposal. It was later revealed that throughout the three-day ordeal, Shaposhnikov had several planes readied and placed on high alert. Their orders were to bomb the Kremlin if putschist troops managed to successfully storm the White House.

The tanks turn around

Later in the day, Shaposhnikov's "defection" to the constitutional order was joined by a company of tanks surrounding the White House. Many of the occupants of the tanks, it seems, had not been briefed on their mission. Initially unaware that they were participating in a coup d'état, more than a few had second thoughts when they listened to Yeltsin's noontime speech, spoke with citizens who were constantly haranguing them, and received later proclamations from the Russian Federation Government. They turned their turrets around at 10:40 p.m., and the tanks were cheered by the crowd. But their action was of only symbolic significance: the tanks had no shells.

Shortly thereafter, a more important defection occurred. At 11:00 p.m., a large battalion of paratroopers under the direct command of General Aleksandr Lebed arrived at the White House and promptly announced its "neutrality." While Lebed would not immediately take a stand against the State Committee for the State of Emergency, neither would he attack the White House. The coup leaders withdrew his unit the following morning for being "unreliable."

Journalists' resistance

Journalists also played their part in the resistance on the first day of the coup. One of the first acts of the putschists had been to suspend freedom of the press. Only one television station in Moscow was allowed to operate, and the printed press was told to print exclusively the declarations of the State Committee for the State of Emergency. Nevertheless, Yeltsin's "Appeal to the Citizens of Russia" was printed on page two of a late edition of *Izvestia,* one of the Soviet Union's largest-circulation newspapers.

The appeal had been printed against the direct order of the editor, but the paper's staff insisted they would burn the presses if it were not included.

Other Russian citizens were informed of Yeltsin's defiance by watching the evening news on the "official" television station. One segment, titled "Moscow Today," was designed to demonstrate how calm the capital city was after the change of regime. The program showed that, indeed, most of Moscow was calm and operating normally. But the segment also included footage from the White House and excerpts from Yeltsin's speech on the tank. The response from the coup leaders in the Interior Ministry was immediate. "The story on Moscow was treacherous!" the editors of the program were told. "You have given instructions to the people on where to go and what to do!"[5]

The parliament building surrounded

The footage of Yeltsin on television, and the printing of his appeal in the newspaper, gave hope to those who were opposed to the coup and feared it might have already succeeded. As night descended on August 19, more than 10,000 unarmed civilians gathered outside the White House to defend their government. The civilians joined a defense force of about 1,000 armed soldiers and guards under orders from Russian Federation officials, in addition to the small paratroop units and tanks that had "defected." Twelve makeshift barricades were erected in the streets surrounding the building, and four others were set up inside the White House itself. Rumors were rife of an imminent attack on the White House by army units loyal to the putschists.

An attack was indeed planned for that night, but it never came. Army officials were concerned about the "neutrality" of General Lebed's armed paratroopers around the White House, worried they might actually defend the building if it were attacked. Many officers were willing to go along with a bloodless coup, but they did not want civil war. Others simply tried to stall, inventing excuses about their units being "not quite ready" or "not prepared" for combat. When dawn broke on August 20, the White House

---

5 Remnick, *Lenin's Tomb*, p. 474.

was still intact, and was still surrounded by thousands of loyal citizens.

Limited strikes and opposition

Elsewhere in Russia, resistance to the coup was sporadic. Calls for a general strike were only adhered to in the mining zones of Novokuznetsk and Vorkuta, though sector strikes also occurred in Nizhniy Novgorod, Vladivostok, and Murmansk. In the Urals, meanwhile, the Stalinist local military commander announced his adherence to the Emergency Committee, and ordered his subordinates to "round up any suspicious people." Nevertheless, more than 100,000 people demonstrated openly in the main square of the city of Sverdlovsk. No one was arrested.

In Leningrad, liberal mayor Anatoly Sobchak had managed to convince the city's military chief early on August 19 to withdraw from participation in the coup and to confine the local army units to their barracks. Among the other Soviet republics, moderate to strong opposition to the coup surfaced only in the Baltics, Moldavia, Ukraine, and Kyrgyzstan.

For the most part, the USSR was quiet. Millions of Soviet citizens, including Russians, thought the coup might put food in the stores and lead to a reduction of prices. Millions more simply did not care. Few felt sorry for Gorbachev. In Moscow, no more than 50,000 people demonstrated against the coup at the height of popular resistance. As one analyst noted, "it was an extraordinarily committed minority—and not the 'Russian masses'—that came to the aid of their beleaguered government."[6]

Yeltsin's appeal to military forces

On the afternoon of August 20, the stalemate outside the White House continued. The "friendly" troops who had previously surrounded the parliament building were replaced by troops from Central Asia who spoke Russian poorly, and had been ordered to avoid any contact with the population. Eager to create more splits within the military, Boris Yeltsin issued a new appeal to the military forces. He stated that because the Commander in

---

[6] Dunlop, *The Rise of Russia and the Fall of the Soviet Empire*, p. 229.

Chief had been forcibly deposed and the Vice President and the Defense Minister were engaged in unconstitutional actions, they could not "carry out the duty of running the Armed Forces of the USSR or of the defense of the territorial integrity and sovereignty of the Republics of the USSR as a whole."[7] Therefore, President Yeltsin decreed that he had assumed full command over the Soviet Armed Forces located within the territory of the Russian Republic until such time as Soviet President Gorbachev returned to carry out his duties. In his new capacity, Yeltsin countermanded all orders and commands issued by Defense Minister Yazov and KGB chief Kryuchkov after August 18, and decreed that all military units and KGB troops in Russia were to return to their barracks.

Yeltsin's decree succeeded in creating new divisions within the armed forces, as it clearly forced commanding officers to choose between the de facto authority of the putschists and the legal authority of President Yeltsin. Most of those who openly announced their support for Yeltsin at this point, however, were in distant regions and far removed from the events in Moscow. Most of the military forces remained with the putschists. And when night fell on August 20, Yeltsin received word that an army and/or KGB assault was imminent.

Attack and defiance

Shortly after midnight, the feared attack began against the White House. KGB units, tanks, and armored personnel carriers closed in on the vicinity of the building. At 12:30 a.m., a column of armored personnel carriers broke through a weak outer barricade manned by civilians. They then came up against a blockade of trolley buses. Three civilians were killed as the military vehicles attempted to break through. Horrified at the deaths of their comrades, civilians at the barricade threw Molotov cocktails (bottles with gasoline) at the armored personnel carriers. A number of vehicles were burned, and others were evacuated. Later in the morning, many soldiers of this unit defected and joined the defenders of the White House.

---

[7] Khasbulatov, *The Struggle for Russia*, p. 156.

After the failure of this first assault, the putschists ordered several more attacks throughout the pre-dawn hours of August 21. Not a single attack materialized, however. Generals Grachev and Lebed, in command of most of the Soviet Union's paratroop battalions, refused to order their troops to open fire on the White House. Secretly, General Grachev—who had already defected—prepared eight heavy transport planes with paratroopers to defend the White House, if necessary.

Two crack KGB units, Alpha and Beta, also failed to complete their missions to assault the White House. During a planning meeting of the Alpha Group, one of the officers told his colleagues that the putschists "want to smear us in blood. Each of you is free to act according to his conscience. I for one will not storm the White House."[8] A massive KGB attack from the land and the air was nevertheless planned for 2:00 a.m. on August 21. The officers in charge of the ground offensive, however, announced to their superiors that they would not move in until the helicopter strike force arrived to drop troops onto the roof of the White House. But a downpour of rain began shortly before the planned assault, and the helicopter pilots refused to fly in "stormy weather."

Tank attack blocked

In a last-ditch effort to take the White House, the putschists ordered loyal paratroop divisions with tanks and armored personnel carriers into Moscow shortly before dawn. All of these advances were stopped on the ground either by barricades erected by the Russian defenders, or by large groups of civilians who had placed their bodies in the path of the vehicles. The troops were unwilling to repeat the events that had led to bloodshed earlier in the evening. The attack was aborted.

When the sun rose on the morning of August 21, the coup had virtually collapsed. The failure to seize the White House and its occupants for the second consecutive night created an overwhelming feeling among all but a few coup participants that the cost of success—a massacre, perhaps followed by civil war—was unacceptable.

---

[8] Remnick, *Lenin's Tomb,* p. 483.

Military defections to the side of the Russian Government continued. At 8:00 a.m., the Ministry of Defense held an urgent meeting, and decided to withdraw all military forces from Moscow that afternoon.

The coup collapses in a changed country

A delegation of the Russian Federation Government was sent to the Gorbachev vacation home in the Crimea, without interference from the putschists. The Soviet leader's isolation was ended calmly, and the most important coup participants were promptly arrested. The putsch was over.

It has been remarked that when President Gorbachev returned to Moscow early in the morning of August 22, he arrived home in a different country. Six years of *glasnost* (openness) had produced important effects on the populace and on the state bureaucracy itself. Many of these changes were not apparent until the coup forced people to take sides. When faced with that choice, significant members of the press did not want to return to the years of publishing only official, bland, and censured news. Middle- and lower-level KGB officers did not want to dedicate their lives to domestic repression again. The military forces did not want to shed the blood of their fellow citizens in order to safeguard the political ambitions of the putschists.

Thus, when ordered to enforce the mandates of the Emergency Committee for the State of Emergency, many members of the security apparatuses (Army, Air Force, KGB) at all levels hesitated, stalled, or refused outright to comply with their orders. Their position of insubordination was aided substantially by the efforts of the elected government of the Russian Federation to create an alternate legal authority to which government officials, soldiers, officers, and police could swear allegiance. Although most of the populace remained indifferent, the thousands of civilians who blockaded the streets forced officers to choose between bloodshed and refusal to cooperate with the putschists. Eventually, the coup plotters lost the support of key elements of the military forces, the KGB, and the press. Such events ultimately proved to be decisive in determining the fate of the August coup.

Sources

Brown, Archie, *The Gorbachev Factor* (New York: Oxford University Press, 1996), pp. 252-305.

Dunlop, John B., *The Rise of Russia and the Fall of the Soviet Empire* (Princeton: Princeton University Press, 1993), pp. 186-255.

Gorbachev, Mikhail, *The August Coup: The Truth and the Lessons,* New York: Harper Collins, 1991.

Kagarlitsky, Boris, *The Disintegration of the Monolith* (New York: Verso, 1992), pp. 133-138.

Khasbulatov, Ruslan, *The Struggle for Russia: Power and Change in the Democratic Revolution* (New York: Routledge,1993), pp. 139-169.

Palazchenko, Pavel, *My Years with Gorbachev and Shevardnadze: The Memoir of a Soviet Interpreter* (University Park, Pennsylvania: Pennsylvania State University Press, 1997), pp. 299-342.

Remnick, David, *Lenin's Tomb: The Last Days of the Soviet Empire* (New York: Random House, 1993), pp. 433-490.

Chapter Twenty-six

DEFENDING DEMOCRACY IN THAILAND—1992

Christopher A. Miller

Another military coup

By 1991, Thailand had already suffered 16 military coups d'état since the end of the absolute monarchy in 1932. On February 23, 1991, a military clique, identifying itself as the National Peace Keeping Council (NPKC), staged another coup, ousting the parliamentary government headed by Chatichai Choonavan. The NPKC was composed of graduates of Chulalongkorn Military Academy, including, most prominently, Army Commander-in-Chief General Suchinda Kraprayoon and Air Force Commander-in-Chief Air Chief Marshal Kaset Rojananil.

A list of sources for this case appears at the end of this chapter.

The NPKC justified the coup as necessary to reform the evident corruption among certain politicians and to end what they felt was a "parliamentary dictatorship." They claimed to have already received thousands of letters urging them to oust Chatichai. Initially, this coup seemed to mimic the pattern of previous ones in Thailand, as drafting of a new constitution soon followed and a general election was scheduled for March 1992.

Establishing political control

The objectives of the new military regime became evident soon after the coup. The NPKC first aimed to establish its control of Parliament by mid-June by forming a new political party, the Samakkhi Tham Party. It gained the most seats in Parliament by recruiting members from already well-established parties in the current Parliament. Political alliances were ensured with other party leaders in case a coalition was later needed.

The second goal of the military regime was accomplished when Mr. Sawasdi Chotepanich was appointed President of the Supreme Court through pressure exerted by the NPKC.

A restructured constitution was the third objective. The NPKC handpicked a committee to rewrite the constitution, with the aim of perpetuating the military's political power. Throughout 1991, several NPKC leaders promised not to assume the position of Prime Minister, the last piece of the government unclaimed by the junta. Yet the military faction displayed an extremely effective ability to seize firm control over the Parliament and many of its members, the courts, and the constitution.

Growing nongovernmental organizations

Nongovernmental organizations (NGOs) had been an emerging factor in Thai politics since the 1970s. Initially, these organizations focused their efforts on rural development projects in response to what they saw as failures on the part of government-sponsored development programs. Limited success in influencing development projects made many NGOs realize that a wider base of support and a more coordinated effort were needed to increase effectiveness.

As more NGOs were established throughout Thailand, their efforts expanded, focusing increasingly on recommendations for, and the formulation of, local, regional, and, at times, national development policy. This expansion of political agendas for many NGOs led them to become a formidable source of opposition against the military government.

While the February coup generated criticism from many organizations, groups, and labor unions, the most explicit responses came from the Campaign for Popular Democracy and the Students' Federation of Thailand. One student leader's reasoning clearly explained the basis of the students' opposition: "no coup has ever been carried out on behalf of the workers or on behalf of the majority of the people."[1]

Organized opposition

On April 19, 1991, the Students' Federation of Thailand rejuvenated the Campaign for Popular Democracy. The Campaign was a decade-old organization of middle-class democratic intellectuals and professionals, as well as representatives from 19 organizations, including labor, academic, poverty, women, teachers, and human rights groups. The Campaign decided to launch activities to increase public awareness of the Thai constitution, encourage democratic practices, and assist in coordinating activities among other NGOs with these aims.

Rival draft constitutions

The Campaign for Popular Democracy quickly became a vehicle for opposition to the military-dominated government. It contested the constitution drafting committee established by the new military junta by writing protest letters and issuing press releases. Many NGO leaders experienced difficulty in relating the abstraction of the constitution to the daily lives of the less educated population. The Campaign then decided that the people should draft their own constitution. Several councils were established by the Campaign throughout the provinces to draft what would be their respective sections of the "people's constitution." These

---

[1] Callahan, *Imagining Democracy*, p.113.

completed sections were then submitted to the Campaign for editing and review. The final People's Congress Constitution was presented to the National Assembly on June 24, 1991.

The junta's constitutional drafting committee published its own draft constitution several weeks later, with basically no recognition of the "people's constitution." Three clauses in the draft constitution of the junta's committee generated substantial controversy. The Prime Minister was not to be an elected member of Parliament. The Senate, which would consist predominantly of appointees chosen by the National Peace Keeping Council, would be granted extensive powers. Additionally, future amendments to the new constitution would be extremely difficult.

Increasing opposition

As opposition mounted against the military government's draft constitution, the Campaign and the Students' Federation organized a conference, attended by over 50 NGOs and four political parties, on how to proceed in a campaign to make drastic amendments to the NPKC's draft constitution. It was decided that the Campaign would hold a demonstration on November 19 if proposed revisions were not incorporated.

On November 18, General Suchinda repeated his promise not to accept the position of Prime Minister and announced limited concessions to the appeals for revisions to the draft constitution. These concessions did little to appease the opposition.

The Campaign held to their decision to hold a demonstration the next day. Between 50,000 and 70,000 people attended the rally at Sanam Luang, a large open park in the center of Bangkok, on November 19. Speakers at the rally promoted the outright rejection of the military government's draft constitution.

Nonetheless, the new constitution was promulgated by Parliament on December 7, possibly under pressure from the Royal Palace. The general election was then set for March 22, 1992.

Military successes

The Campaign for Popular Democracy assumed a powerful role among the opposition in organizing two critical programs in early January. One of these, the Poll Watch, aimed to curb vote-buying (which was common) and other subversive election tactics with assistance from approximately 25,000 volunteers. The second program was the Forum for Democracy, a televised program where citizens discussed issues with politicians directly. Both programs were instrumental in expanding the political consciousness of many Thais nationwide.

The March 22 general election was extremely disappointing for the opposition parties, as the military's new party, Samakkhi Tham, gained a majority in Parliament. Samakkhi Tham announced on April 7 that General Suchinda, despite his previous promises, would be the new Prime Minister, even though he was not a member of Parliament. He was formally appointed by the King later that day.

Challenge by hunger strike

On the morning of April 8, outside the Parliament Building in Bangkok, Captain Chalard Vorachat, a lesser-known politician, began a hunger strike and pledged to remain on it unto death unless General Suchinda resigned. The military-backed government labeled Chalard a "professional hunger-striker," and he was sent a coffin to mock his efforts. Yet these government denunciations only boosted sympathy and support for Chalard. The democratic forces gained momentum, as new anti-Suchinda groups were forming daily.

As Chalard's health worsened, the Students' Federation tried to maintain the momentum of the growing opposition against the junta. Although admittedly unprepared, the students staged a demonstration on April 20 at the Royal Plaza, which was attended by between 50,000 and 100,000 people. The festival-like atmosphere intensified as vendors sold food and drinks, speeches blared through megaphones, thousands of leaflets promoting nonviolent resistance were distributed, and more than 30 people joined Chalard in his hunger strike.

Nonviolent struggle against coups

The key points on resisting coups by nonviolent struggle had been taken from a lengthy article by Gene Sharp in *Poochakarn,* a prominent daily newspaper, which the paper had reprinted from the Thai political science journal. The Campaign stated that "our principle was to struggle in a nonviolent way against General Suchinda's appointment using symbolic and direct action."[2]

General Suchinda labeled the demonstrators as simply a small minority of individuals soured by their poor showing in the March election. Air Chief Marshal Kaset issued the first warning on April 20 that peace and order would be maintained through whatever means necessary. Undaunted, the Students' Federation announced that another demonstration would be held on May 4 at Sanam Luang.

As crowds gathered at Sanam Luang on May 4, Major-General Chamlong Srimuang, leader of one of the opposition political parties, announced his own hunger strike, in addition to that of Chalard, that would not end until General Suchinda resigned. This news caused the opposition to splinter. Some supported Chamlong and some did not. Some opposition parties saw Chamlong's actions simply as ones intended to promote his own party.

Massive demonstrations

Despite this factionalism, 60,000 people gathered in front of Parliament the same day. In the evening, Chamlong asked supporters to return two days later, on May 6, when General Suchinda would announce the new government's policies.

Over 100,000 people answered Chamlong's call to return to Parliament on May 6. As General Suchinda presented the government's policy statement, opposition party members walked out in protest. They returned only to vehemently criticize Suchinda's legitimacy as Prime Minister and the limited constitutional concessions granted by General Suchinda a few days earlier.

The crowds remained in front of the Parliament and swelled through the next day. With nearly 150,000 people in front of Parliament on May 7, Chamlong consulted with specific individuals on moving the crowds and decided to move the massive crowd to Sanam Luang. Many spent the night there fearing for Chamlong's safety. The following night he unilaterally assumed control and moved the crowd again down Ratchadamnoen Avenue. By 9 p.m.,

---

2 Callahan, *Imagining Democracy,* p. 120.

Chamlong tried to lead the crowd to the Royal Plaza, but police and troops blocked the demonstrators' passage over the Phan Fa Bridge. The situation was extremely tense, yet demonstrators responded to Chamlong's appeals not to provoke the armed barricade.

Continuing contest

On the morning of May 9, Chamlong, visibly too weak to continue, ended his fast. That afternoon, House Speaker Arthit Urairat announced that the Government and the opposition parties had agreed on four amendments to the constitution, including certain limitations on the Senate's power and the guarantee that the Prime Minister would be an elected official.

Chamlong reverted to consulting with other opposition leaders. It was decided that demonstrations would be halted for one week to let the government fulfill its commitment to amend the constitution.

Official government responses to the demonstrations of the previous four days were limited, but General Suchinda suggested that leftists were recreating a guerrilla insurgence. Air Chief Marshal Kaset refused to rule out a declaration of martial law, and speculation rose about the possibility that the military clique was preparing to stage another coup to regain control.

Rival communications with the public

The military government held a tight grip on Thailand's television and radio stations throughout the first half of 1992. The stark contrast between the state-run media and independent newspapers, which gave widespread coverage of the demonstrations, intensified people's interest in the political situation.

Because of Thailand's high illiteracy rates among its rural population, informal reading groups were formed with one person reading aloud articles on current political issues. The use of fax machines, mobile telephones, and electronic mail was also highly important in disseminating information outside the control of the State.

On May 13, government officials stated that House Speaker Arthit misspoke on May 9, and that no agreements had in fact been reached on amendments to the new constitution. Hours later, in anticipation of further protests, General Suchinda stationed roadblocks on the main roads into Bangkok. Meanwhile, the new Interior Minister ordered provincial governors to forbid anti-Suchinda rallies throughout their provinces.

Increased opposition coordination and conflicts

Many opposition leaders agreed that the previous demonstrations lacked coordination. In response, 26 organizations convened at the Royal Plaza on May 14 and selected representatives to form the Confederation for Democracy. The new umbrella organization was headed by a seven-member executive, who quickly announced their demands of amendments to the new constitution and called for Suchinda's resignation. Their first concrete responsibility was to organize the demonstrations scheduled for May 17.

The Confederation for Democracy members felt that General Suchinda should be forced to resign, as this would be the crucial factor in ensuring democratic practice. The Campaign for Popular Democracy, however, felt that ousting Suchinda would not solve the problems Thailand was facing, and that broader and more extensive efforts were needed to ensure a more democratic Thailand. This led to the absence of the Campaign within the Confederation for Democracy. Several opposition political parties withdrew their support as well and did not participate in the demonstration.

Competing rallies

To regain some degree of popular support, the military government organized and funded pro-government rallies throughout the provinces on May 15. These pro-Suchinda rallies were extremely unsuccessful, and some even backfired. People herded to sites in two provinces were misinformed of the purpose of the rallies, and these quickly turned against the Government. Later that day, General Suchinda stated that he could not guarantee that violence would not erupt during the demonstration scheduled to resume the next day.

The Confederation for Democracy and the demonstrators were aware that violence might be used against them when they returned to the large Sanam Luang public park on May 17. The pro-military government had already deployed troops and assigned police to the areas surrounding Sanam Luang. Yet, in open defiance, the number of demonstrators at Sanam Luang increased throughout that day.

The demonstrations turned into social events with a more festive tone than the previous protest in April. Men, women, and children from all social classes were present. Many held Thai flags and called for democracy. Areas were blocked off where donated food and water were distributed.

Focus on nonviolent resistance

Leaflets were distributed with "198 Methods of Nonviolent Action," which was referred to in Thai as "198 Ways to Fight the Demons." Thousands of different leaflets were distributed on nonviolent resistance and on how to defend against coups d'état. Speakers used these ideas in speeches, some of which were printed in independent Thai newspapers. One man was seen trying to engage in discussion with one of the soldiers:

> Are you really going to shoot us? We are both Thais you know. We came in peace. We're no troublemakers. We've got no weapons. Why do you want to hurt us? Please go back to your barracks.[3]

The soldier ignored him.

Huge crowds

The Campaign for Popular Democracy played an important, although independent, role during the Sanam Luang demonstration in providing security. Approximately 400 marshals, carrying no weapons, settled minor disputes in the crowd and checked for roadblocks and troop movement in the surrounding area. The Campaign also formed an intelligence unit of 20 men. Their equipment was simple: motorbikes, mobile phones, radios, and newspapers. All intelligence information was fed to a central command that constantly moved as a unit around Bangkok over the next few days.

---

[3] Sridaradhanya, ed., *Catalyst for Change*, p. 7.

The estimated size of the crowd at Sanam Luang varied widely, from 200,000 to 500,000. It was predetermined that if the group became too large, several members of the Confederation for Democracy executive would lead large groups to the Government House. By 9 p.m., the demonstrators split into two groups, and Chamlong led the first towards Government House. They approached Phan Fa Bridge and were stopped by police backed by troops erecting barbed wire behind a row of fire engines. Chamlong was no longer at the front of the crowd, and his pleas and those of other Confederation for Democracy leaders for demonstrators to remain nonviolent went unheard or were ignored.

Blockade and violence

At 10 p.m., when the demonstrators reached the blockade, they tried to break through the barbed wire, and police fired water cannons to stop the progress. People responded by throwing debris and attempted to overtake the fire engines. Police retaliated without hesitation and beat people climbing on the fire engines. The sight of police beating unarmed people created utter outrage. One person shouted:

> You are slaves. Who ordered you to kill these people? Do we have to pay taxes for your salaries for you to come kill us? You have to think, and you must not follow orders that betray the people.[4]

As midnight neared, the violence continued, as people tossed Molotov cocktails (bottles filled with gasoline) and torched police vehicles. Nanglerng Police Station was set aflame, yet police made no attempts to intervene. Speculation surrounded this event, since the first reported signs of vandalism involved police themselves damaging vehicles. One Special Branch Officer and one policeman who were later interviewed indicated that those who torched the police station were most likely hired as *agents provocateurs* to create a pretext for the government to use violence.

---

[4] Sridaradhanya, ed., *Catalyst for Change,* p. 12.

Repression leads to disaffection

Although the government attempted diversionary tactics, such as extending a Buddhist festival and holding free concerts away from Sanam Luang, their primary efforts relied on military means. Not all government and military officials, soldiers, and police agreed that such harsh methods of "defense" were reasonable. This was evidenced early on, when navy troops allowed citizens to pass across Pin Klao Bridge. Also, an anonymous group known as Ai Laem, whom many thought could only be experienced police officers, continually jammed police radio communications over several weeks throughout May 1992.

More demonstrations and a state of emergency

Although most demonstrations were held in Bangkok, large demonstrations were also held on May 17 in Chiang Mai and Nakhon Si Thammarat, and smaller ones in seven other cities. The government did not suppress the demonstrations in the provinces, but kept surveillance over them. The Campaign for Popular Democracy linked Bangkok and the provinces by using telephones to transmit speeches given in Bangkok that were amplified through loudspeakers in the city of Chiang Mai in northern Thailand.

At midnight, May 18, as the clash continued near Phan Fa Bridge, General Suchinda declared a state of emergency and forbade gatherings of more than 10 people in public. He also announced a three-day holiday in Bangkok, and urged citizens to stay inside, as it would now be necessary to use violence to control the situation. It was later determined that the crackdown, Operation Paireepinart/33 ("Destroy the Enemy") had actually been approved on May 6. The Capital Security Command deployed 4,800 police and 13,000 troops in the operation. The seesaw battle raged on, with troops firing shots seemingly at will into the crowd.

Troops fire on demonstrators

Many people spent the night on the streets near Phan Fa Bridge, and early the next morning (May 18) Chamlong tried to establish some degree of control and attention over the still sizable crowds. Chamlong asked them to remain seated or to lie on the ground if troops started to fire. The volume of the national anthem escalated as people began to sing and clap their hands to show they were unarmed. Troops surrounded the motionless citizens, sending many home in fear for their lives.

At 3 p.m., troops moved into the crowd and arrested Chamlong and many others who were still sitting on the ground. The troops fired their weapons continuously into the air to disperse the remaining demonstrators. Many people were forced to lie face down on the ground, while others scattered, only to quickly regroup in a different area. About 10,000 people moved by this regrouping method onto Ratchadamnoen Avenue in front of the Public Relations Building. The crowd remained there, and the numbers grew to about 50,000 by 6 p.m. They jeered and dared the troops to fire at them.

As anxiety rose, people started smashing nearby parked cars, and back near Phan Fa Bridge, buses were pushed towards the barbed wire. Around 11 p.m., the Public Relations Building was set on fire (some claimed by pro-military provocateurs). Troops then opened fire on the demonstrators in both areas.

About 30 doctors and nurses converted the lobby of the nearby Royal Hotel into a makeshift field hospital. Over 150 people received emergency care in the Royal Hotel on May 18 alone.

During the night and into the morning of May 19, motorcycle gangs took to the streets of Bangkok. Vandalism, looting, and gun fighting ravaged the city. The government formed undercover police, "headhunter groups," to eliminate these vandals by any means believed necessary.

More brutalities and defiance

At 5:00 a.m., troops stormed into the Royal Hotel and ordered people who were seeking shelter from the nightlong violence to take off their shirts and crawl on their hands and knees outside to await transport to a suburban prison. Troops walked on the backs of the hovered people while abusing and harassing doctors, nurses, and reporters for supporting the insurgence.

As the conflict continued, many shops throughout Bangkok did not open. Major companies and banks were ordered closed by the military government. The motorcycle gangs ran rampant most of the day. Later, a large crowd of nonviolent protesters gathered at Ramkhanheang University. Almost 50,000 people willingly defied the ban on large gatherings and barricaded themselves inside the university campus, where they held an all-night vigil on May 19.

Scattered pockets of resistance sprang up throughout Bangkok on May 20. Troops quickly dispersed any crowds, forming mostly near Ratchadamnoen Avenue, and the area was successfully sealed by five that afternoon. At 7:30 p.m., the Interior Minister announced a curfew effective from 9:00 p.m. to 4:00 a.m. Protesters at Ramkhanheang University continued to defy the government orders, and the campus soon resembled a small, autonomous town outside the junta's control.

Continued anti-military resistance

The international community responded harshly to the events. A number of calls were made by humanitarian groups to their respective governments to review international aid programs to Thailand. Thai Airways, chaired by Air Chief Marshal Kaset, faced passenger boycotts in Japan, Europe, and the United States. The economic difficulties of the airline were complicated by the staff's demands for Air Chief Marshal Kaset and other military figures to resign from the Board of Directors.

At midnight on May 21, King Bhumiphol brought Chamlong and General Suchinda before him. Their meeting was aired as an emergency television broadcast. The King asked that they resolve their differences through mutual conciliation, then left them to do so. Thereby, Thailand could return to its "former status."

Without Suchinda's resignation, the protesters remained at Ramkhanheang University and said:

> If we continue to rally peacefully and some people still burn things, we will petition His Majesty the King that the persons who destroy public property are the military.[5]

Despite the king's appeal, protests continued against the military generally. People withdrew money from the Thai Military Bank. Taxi drivers refused to carry known military soldiers. Military-sponsored concerts were boycotted.

---

[5] Sridaradhanya, ed., *Catalyst for Change,* p. 28.

Amnesty, resignation, and constitutional change

On May 23, the Suchinda Government issued a royal decree granting a general amnesty to all those involved in the crackdown, perpetrators and victims alike. Although the decree was subsequently rejected by the House of Representatives, its legality was upheld by the Constitutional Tribunal established by the National Peace Keeping Council the previous year. Suchinda also agreed that the Prime Minister must be an elected member of Parliament. He resigned the next day.

On May 25, representatives of the Confederation for Democracy, students, workers, and businesses went to Parliament to continue pushing for amendments to the constitution. As international aid was being withdrawn, the business community took a more active role in demanding a dissolution of Parliament.

The draft amendments to the constitution breezed through two readings that day, and were promulgated on June 10, although this was done by the NPKC-dominated Parliament. The amendments stated, notably, that the Prime Minister must be a member of the House of Representatives and that the Senate could not censure the government. Anand Panyarachun was appointed Interim Prime Minister by House Speaker Arthit Urairat on June 10. The Parliament was dissolved on June 30, and a new election was scheduled for September of the same year.

Casualties

Six investigations later reported on the May events. The number of civilian deaths varied, but minimally stood at 52, most due to gunshot. Statistics of injured civilians varied as well, but over 300 cases were documented, the majority of which resulted from gunshot wounds from behind to the head, neck, or lungs. There were no reported troop or police casualties.

Eight centers were established over the following months to account for those missing, which stood at approximately 250 in September 1992.

Preventive actions

By early August, Interim Prime Minister Anand had enforced several executive actions to ensure that another incident similar to the events of May would not occur. The Internal Peacekeeping Law and the Capital Security Command were dissolved, and the three top commanders, General Suchinda, Marshal Kaset, and General Issarapong, were transferred to positions of considerably less power.

There was no possibility of a new military coalition to contest the September election, and the political parties were thus left to take their chances at the polls. Poll Watch was active again in the September election, this time with over 60,000 volunteers. As a result of that election, Anand Panyarachun became the Prime Minister.

Despite the outbreaks of violence among the predominantly nonviolent crowds and the identifiable split among the opposition, it is significant that to date (February 2004) another military coup has not been attempted in Thailand since these 1992 demonstrations. The constitution adopted in 1997 contains a clause that grants citizens the right to employ nonviolent resistance against future coups d'état.

Sources

Callahan, William A., *Imagining Democracy: Reading "The Events of May" in Thailand,* Singapore & London: ISEAS, 1998.

Iacopino, Vincent, *"Bloody May": Excessive Use of Lethal Force in Bangkok: The Events of May 17-20, 1992,* New York: Physicians for Human Rights and Human Rights Watch, 1992.

McCargo, Duncan, *Chamlong Srimuang and the New Thai Politics,* New York: St. Martin's Press, 1997.

Paisal Sridaradhanya, ed., *Catalyst for Change: Uprising in May,* Bangkok: Post Publishing, 1992.

Suthy Prasartset, "The Rise of NGOs as Critical Social Movement in Thailand," in *Thai NGOs: The Continuing Struggle for Democracy,* Bangkok: Edison Press Products Co., Ltd., 1995.

We are grateful to Professor Kasian Tejapira of the Political Science Department of Thammasat University for reviewing this account and for making recommendations for improvements.

Chapter Twenty-seven

REMOVING THE DICTATOR IN SERBIA—1996-2000

Joshua Paulson

Early dissent

By the year 2000, President Slobodan Milosevic had ruled what remained of the Yugoslav Federation—Serbia and its sister republic, Montenegro—for 13 years. His tenure was marked by the breakup of Yugoslavia, Serbia's participation in four wars that resulted in more than 210,000 deaths, the creation of nearly three million refugees, and isolation from the international community. After fomenting genocidal "ethnic cleansing" in the former Yugoslav states of Croatia and Bosnia-Herzegovina, as well as in the province of Kosovo, Milosevic was indicted on war crimes charges by the International War Crimes Tribunal at The Hague.

A list of sources for this case appears at the end of this chapter.

Demonstrations against Milosevic's near-dictatorial rule occurred frequently during the 1990s, and were often met with repression. Opposition leaders were arrested, tanks were sometimes called into the streets, and crowds were occasionally fired on by police or army units. Although large anti-government demonstrations swept through the capital, Belgrade, in 1991, Milosevic and his Socialist Party of Serbia managed to hold on to power, largely by promoting popular nationalist policies and the expansionist dream of a "Greater Serbia."

By the second half of the decade, much of the population was dissatisfied with international isolation, the stigma of lost wars, thousands of dead, a ruined economy, average salaries under $70 per month, staggering inflation, and high unemployment. Many blamed Milosevic directly for their problems, but the "established" democratic opposition had difficulties uniting around an anti-Milosevic platform. The divided opposition allowed Milosevic to maintain a stranglehold on local and state government even as he and his party lost popularity.

Municipal elections and student protests

On November 17, 1996, watershed elections were held at the municipal level across Serbia. A loose opposition coalition made up of five small parties known as Zajedno ("Together") won for the first time in 40 cities, including Belgrade, Nis, and Cacak. Milosevic, however, had packed local election committees with members of his own party, and they refused to certify opposition victories in 40 cities.

The Zajedno coalition called for marches and street protests to demand recognition of their electoral victories, and within two weeks the daily demonstrations in Belgrade grew from under 2,000 participants to more than 100,000. Workers were notably absent in the demonstrations, unlike the protests that swept the rest of Central and Eastern Europe seven years earlier.

Serbian students, meanwhile, called for parallel protests of their own. They demanded recognition of the Zajedno victories, as well as the resignations of top University of Belgrade officials. The removal of Slobodan Milosevic did not yet figure among the student demands.

At first, Milosevic responded by ignoring the protesters altogether. When this did not seem to work, the government took action against the independent media and the opposition press, shutting down Radio B-92 on December 3 and jamming the signal of Radio Index. Some arrests were made. Still, the daily demonstrations continued well into 1997.

On day 55 of the protests, following an all-night standoff between student protesters and police in the frozen Belgrade streets, a delegation of students met with government representatives. The government then announced it had agreed to respect "the will of the citizens" and to reinstate the stolen opposition victories. Zajedno protests came to an end as opposition politicians took office in Belgrade and 39 other municipalities. Student protests continued for another 51 days until the rector and the dean of the University finally submitted their resignations.

Otpor

In 1997, Slobodan Milosevic's term in office as President of Serbia ended and he was constitutionally ineligible to serve another term. To remain in power, he had himself elected President of Yugoslavia and eventually rewrote the constitution to allow himself to be re-elected two more times to the new post. A few students, however, were committed to making sure his new term in office would be his last.

On October 10, 1998, a handful of student veterans of the 1996-1997 protests gathered in Belgrade to form a new organization known as Otpor ("Resistance"). Although their earliest organizing focused on opposing a new University Law, they soon realized that they could "do nothing by opposing only part of the Milosevic system."[1] Their primary objective then shifted toward ridding themselves of Slobodan Milosevic. To that end, they had three key demands: free and fair elections in Serbia; a free university; and guarantees for independent media.

Otpor, like much of the population, had little faith in the established political opposition, which was composed largely of bickering political parties with power-hungry and protagonistic leaders. Many opposition politicians had ties either to the govern-

---

[1] Steve York, notes from an interview with Vukasin Petrovic.

ing regime or to the former Communist state, and few were considered honest or trustworthy. The students therefore decided to shape Otpor into a new type of political organization. It had a horizontal leadership structure, completely decentralized, without any "heads" to be beheaded or co-opted by the regime. Each regional office was virtually autonomous, while being supported in its actions by all the other Otpor chapters. "The idea was, cut off one Otpor head, and another 15 heads would instantly appear," said one member of the group.[2] Its aim was to spread resistance through the countryside, where Milosevic's support had always been strong.

These students had no confidence in violence because they saw that guerrilla warfare tactics would only play into Milosevic's hands.[3] At the founding of Otpor, its members firmly committed the organization to the use of only nonviolent forms of resistance. Otpor strove to use creative yet courageous methods of nonviolent action, rather than violence, in order to achieve its goals. The symbol that the group chose as its trademark was a stylized black-and-white raised fist, consciously drawing on 1930s-era Communist imagery.

On December 17, 1998, Otpor carried out its first nationwide action, a march from Belgrade to Novi Sad. Conscious of the fact that the level of opposition would have to rise dramatically in the provinces for Milosevic to be defeated, the students took back roads along the route, passing through as many small rural communities as possible. Belgrade, where the main Otpor office was based, was already an opposition stronghold, so most of Otpor's organizing was concentrated in other university towns and small communities.

Otpor's campaigns were generally of a symbolic nature, using nonviolent methods of protest and persuasion. They worked first and foremost to eliminate the climate of fear among the population, knowing that "when fear disappears the regime loses a central pillar of its power."[4] One of Otpor's first targets was a new Information Law restricting freedom of expression. They printed and distributed leaflets, held marches and sit-ins, painted anti-

---

[2] Roger Cohen, "The Hidden Revolution: Who Really Brought Down Milosevic?" *The New York Times Magazine*, November 26, 2000, p. 45.
[3] Cohen, "The Hidden Revolution," p. 45.
[4] Cohen, "The Hidden Revolution," p. 44.

Milosevic slogans on walls, and engaged in witty street theater and other creative acts of defiance often intended to ridicule the regime. To a significant degree, as many activists noted, Otpor existed more as a "state of mind" than as an organized group. Srdja Popovic, one of Otpor's founders, put it simply: "Our ambition is to change the political consciousness of the Serbian populace."[5]

Otpor organizers developed the movement's tactics based on a continual analysis of the regime's sources of power. The goal was to alter the balance of power between the Milosevic government, the democratic opposition, and the "third sector" of nongovernmental organizations and "uncommitted" elements of civil society. Otpor identified Milosevic's authority[6] as his most important source of power, and also his most vulnerable. Otpor's actions were thus consciously designed simultaneously to bolster the students' moral authority among the population at large and to weaken the authority of the regime. This effect was accentuated when large-scale arrests and repression began several months after the group's founding congress.

During the first half of 1999, Otpor was relatively inactive due to the 78-day NATO bombing war against Yugoslavia. During the bombing, almost all anti-Milosevic activities generally came to a halt.[7] In the summer, with the war over, Otpor reorganized with a new intensity aimed at increasing its presence in the Milosevic heartland of rural Serbia. By December, Otpor had established 50 regional branches in smaller towns across the country. The number grew to 80 by the time Otpor held its founding Congress on February 17, 2000. One thousand representatives from 70 cities across Serbia attended the Congress. The resolutions adopted by the Congress asked Otpor members to "cooperate with other local democratic forces and with all individuals, independent media, unions and NGOs who are aware of the situation" in Serbia. The group also demanded that "the authorities stop immediately the language of hatred, repression and threats, violence and State terrorism," since "no government is worth even one drop of Serbian blood." Finally, Otpor called on "all

---

[5] http://www.otpor.net
[6] "Authority" here refers to legitimacy, or the right to direct, guide, or be obeyed voluntarily. Authority is a main source of power.
[7] Gene Sharp, various discussions in Belgrade, May 2001.

citizens of Serbia, sons and daughters as well as their parents, to fight poverty, fear, oppression and desperation and by doing so become a part of the widest front of Otpor and support the idea of free Serbia."[8]

After its founding Congress, Otpor grew rapidly. Believing that the easiest and quickest way to remove Milosevic would be to pressure him to call early elections, then win those elections and defend the popular will, the group developed a broad plan of action with three phases. The first phase was to "establish a strong nonviolent movement whose goal is to run a campaign against Milosevic." This was to be carried out primarily through small, often symbolic actions that would be likely to produce positive results. The campaign would be considered successful when Milosevic agreed to new elections. The second phase would be to win those elections, by creating "a big campaign machine, whose only goal is to generate a massive turnout." The idea for this second phase, according to Srdja Popovic, was "to get the maximum number of people involved in political life. This we saw as the route to a better future, *beyond* the removal of Slobodan Milosevic." The third, and most ambitious, stage would then be to take advantage of the new political climate to "change the system," educate a new political generation with new values, and to turn Serbia, then the "Pariah of the Balkans," into a normal European nation.[9]

Assistance

Otpor, like other opposition organizations, received technical and financial assistance from external sources during this period. Both the U.S.-based National Democratic Institute and the International Republican Institute had for some time been sponsoring pro-democratic activities in Yugoslavia. The National Democratic Institute had focused primarily on support for building opposition political parties and means of improving contacts in the media.

In September 1999, the Center for Civic Initiatives, a Serbian nongovernmental organization, translated and published Gene

---

[8] http://www.otpor.net
[9] Steve York, notes from an interview with Srdja Popovic.

Sharp's *From Dictatorship to Democracy*. According to the Center, in all about 5,500 copies were distributed. Members of Otpor and the Democratic Party, one of the country's largest opposition parties, were among those who obtained copies.

Between March 31 and April 2, 2000, the International Republican Institute sponsored a workshop on the technique of nonviolent struggle in Budapest, Hungary, for 30 Otpor activists. The workshop primarily focused on the "theory of power, its sources, how those sources of power are expressed in organizations and institutions (pillars of support), how to analyze them to identify strengths and weaknesses, then how to think strategically to neutralize or destroy them."[10] Otpor coordinators believed this workshop, given by Albert Einstein Institution consultant Robert Helvey, a retired U.S. Army colonel, provided them with "invaluable practical training" in helping them to improve their use of nonviolent methods, to which they were already committed.[11] The major influence in Otpor's strategic planning for nonviolent struggle is credited by Srdja Popovic to the power analysis in Gene Sharp's *The Politics of Nonviolent Action,* supplied by Robert Helvey during the Budapest workshop.[12]

Training manuals

Otpor drafted a training manual for the group's members, titled "Resistance in Your Neighborhood: How to Resolve the Serbian Crisis Peacefully." The manual included adapted and condensed elements of *The Politics of Nonviolent Action*.[13] The manual emphasized the need to analyze the regime's six sources of power. Attention was then called to the groups and institutions supplying those sources, known as "pillars of support." Once identified, it was necessary to systematically undermine and remove those pillars supporting the regime by use of nonviolent struggle methods.

---

[10] Robert Helvey, correspondence, February 22, 2001.
[11] Srdja Popovic, "The Theory and Practice of Strategic Nonviolence: An Analytical Overview of the Application of Gene Sharp's Theory of Nonviolent Action in Milosevic's Serbia." Unpublished draft, cited with permission.
[12] Srdja Popovic, conversations with Christopher A. Miller and Gene Sharp, Belgrade, May 2001.
[13] Gene Sharp, *The Politics of Nonviolent Action,* Boston: Porter Sargent, 1973 and later printings.

The manual offered a comparative analysis of the strengths and weaknesses both of the regime and of Otpor. It then presented the characteristics of nonviolent struggle and its mechanisms of change. The manual also identified factors in the choice and application of a winning technique, the inevitability of repression, and the need for offering the population low-risk resistance methods. Specific suggestions were made for acts of resistance. The importance of planning was emphasized, and the basics of organization were also presented. On these bases, a mass Otpor campaign would develop.

According to Srdja Popovic, "Through two years of our nonviolent struggle, Otpor's human resources team developed six different training programs based on the technique of nonviolent struggle. More than 400 activists of Otpor were trained in nonviolent methods, through Otpor's 'user manual' for working with activists, based on various 'working with volunteers' manuals, and especially Gene Sharp's *Politics of Nonviolent Struggle* [*sic*]. More than 1,000 activists were basically trained in methods of nonviolent action in 42 cities of Serbia."[14] These activists, meanwhile, used the Otpor manual to train thousands of other members across Serbia in the year 2000.

Otpor encouraged acts of individual resistance for new activists, such as individual conversations at the workplace or in social situations, the placing of Otpor stickers in prominent places, telephone calls to repressive institutions (such as to the police to complain about a particular arrest or a repressive measure), cheerful distribution of Otpor printed material to neighbors, and the ignoring of government representatives in the local vicinity.

Once individual actions succeeded in creating a handful of committed activists in a particular neighborhood, group actions could then be performed. While again mostly symbolic in nature, such actions tended to be creative and witty, and sometimes provocative, virtually taunting the regime to take repressive action against the participants. Actions included the promotion of banned music and the publication and distribution of anti-Milosevic materials, conducting street theater productions designed to ridicule the government, and the organization of

---

14 E-mail from Srdja Popovic to Rosalyn Abraham in the office of Peter Ackerman.

marches and concerts against the regime and in defense of independent media.

Repression and response

When repression against the movement began in earnest shortly after the Otpor founding congress, it was welcomed by the group, as they found there was a direct correlation between arrests of Otpor members and membership spurts. "In one case," said an Otpor activist, "we got 500 new members in one day." Another Otpor member added, "We fed on the repression of the regime, and in all towns and cities where they arrested our people, the movement accelerated its growth. Immediately afterwards we were approached by new people, sometimes even pensioners, prepared to continue with resistance."[15]

Repression usually took the form of censorship, arrests, or beatings. The repression exposed the nature of the regime, which became more "dictatorial" with each passing day as it shut down independent media and arrested Otpor activists. Due to the raised stakes, each visible Otpor action also had a pronounced effect in helping the populace at large cast off its fear of the regime. After Otpor members were jailed, crowds of demonstrators repeatedly rallied in front of the police stations to demand their release. "We showed them that we could be arrested and then come back to fight again and again," said one activist.[16]

By May of 2000, Otpor was present in over 100 towns across Serbia, and had nearly 20,000 members. Only about 60 percent were students. Approximately 300 Otpor activists had been arrested by this time, although most spent a maximum of just a few days in jail. Within two months, more than 1,000 other Otpor members would be detained as the government stepped up its repressive campaign against the resistance movement.

On May 16, the government accused Otpor of planting bombs at the offices of Milosevic's Socialist Party of Serbia and of the Yugoslav Left, the political party run by Milosevic's wife. Otpor was also accused of attempting to murder a prominent Milosevic ally, and of assassinating Bosko Perosevic, the Socialist Party gov-

---

[15] From a *Vreme* article, republished on the Otpor Web site, http://www.otpor.net
[16] Steve York, notes from an interview with Vukasin Petrovic.

ernor of the Vojvodina province. On May 17, the government seized control of Studio B, Belgrade's independent television and radio station, and shut down independent Radio B-92 and Radio Index. Over the following two days, police in Belgrade violently dispersed Otpor and student protests, arresting and beating dozens.

Meanwhile, posters appeared around Belgrade accusing Otpor activists of being "Madeleine Youth" (in a reference to U.S. Secretary of State Madeleine Albright, the original sponsor of the 1999 NATO bombing war against Yugoslavia). These posters were designed to resemble the Nazi occupation posters of the Hitler Youth organization. Some posters depicted the Otpor trademark fist stuffed with U.S. dollar bills. At the end of the month, authorities closed Belgrade University and banned student gatherings on the campus. Government authorities labeled Otpor an illegal and violent terrorist organization.

During this time, discipline among the opposition activists became increasingly important. Otpor leaders concede that they were "almost forced to go underground." Communication between organizers often was carried out only through coded messages. Otpor training sessions during this time focused on disarming the repressive machine through fear control and by helping activists prepare for arrest. The group also intentionally made its symbolic actions even more "silly and benign," in order to make the "inevitable arrests of activists all the more senseless."[17]

In the late spring and early summer, Otpor continued to grow, and arrests and beatings were on the rise. The group campaigned to unite the various opposition political parties around a single platform focused on winning the local and legislative elections scheduled for later in the year. The 1996 Zajedno coalition had long since collapsed, but several key opposition parties had tentatively signed a unity agreement in January with the goal of free elections. In the spring, however, they continued to bicker over personal and political differences, and it was unclear whether they would manage to enter the fall elections as a unified block.

---

[17] Srdja Popovic, "The Theory and Practice of Strategic Nonviolence: An Analytical Overview of the Application of Gene Sharp's Theory of Nonviolent Action in Milosevic's Serbia." Cited with permission.

Otpor, which at this point was larger and more popular than any single political party, insisted on opposition unification in nearly all of its public statements.

Milosevic calls early elections

Increasingly concerned about the possibilities of a unified opposition, Slobodan Milosevic announced on July 27 that he was calling an early presidential election, to be held at the same time as the local and legislative elections on September 24. His term as Yugoslav president was not set to expire until July 2001, but since he had recently changed the constitution allowing himself to be re-elected to two additional four-year terms, he was now banking on the hope that the opposition parties would fail to unite before September. He was wrong.

Otpor managed essentially to shame 18 opposition parties into forming a coalition known as the Democratic Opposition of Serbia (DOS), and promised them they would deliver at least 500,000 votes if the coalition launched a common candidate for federal president. The candidate who emerged, Vojislav Kostunica, was a constitutional lawyer known as "the nonviolent nationalist." He had been a cofounder of the Democratic Party in 1992 before splitting off to form the Democratic Party of Serbia. He was noncharismatic, but was considered honest and shared Otpor's underlying interest in turning Yugoslavia into a "normal" European nation.

Otpor, meanwhile, had a head start on the election campaign. The group's contacts in the government had leaked Milosevic's decision to call early elections nearly two weeks beforehand, such that when the president made the announcement, Otpor already had more than 60 tons of anti-Milosevic electoral propaganda printed and awaiting distribution. By this time, Otpor had acquired extensive experience in mass-marketing techniques and had begun to focus its energies on two campaigns to win the elections for the opposition coalition and Kostunica. The first, *Gotov Je!* ("He's Finished!") was designed to break the Serbian mindset that Milsosevic was invincible. The campaign was also intended to change a common voting tendency of casting ballots for whoever was already in power. Hundreds of thousands of posters went up across the country with images of Milosevic under the

"He's Finished" slogan, effectively declaring that the dictator had already lost. T-shirts were printed and television spots were taken out with the same message.

The second campaign, *Vreme Je!* ("It's Time!"), was a simple get-out-the-vote campaign that was nonpartisan in nature. Otpor figured that the key to defeating Milosevic at the polls was high turnout, and that if at least four million voters cast ballots, Milosevic would be history, even if he attempted to use fraud (which Otpor assumed he would do).

Meanwhile, Otpor's humorous street theater continued to provoke the wrath of the regime. Four Otpor activists and two of their mothers were arrested in Belgrade for distributing badges to passers-by labeled "I'm a national hero," in mocking reference to Milosevic's attempts to have himself officially designated a national hero. On September 3 and 4, the offices of Otpor in Belgrade, Novi Sad, and Mladenovac were raided by police. More than 10 tons of computers, printed campaign material, posters, T-shirts, and other items were seized in what seemed to be a final attempt at intimidation against Otpor before the elections. In the same week, more than 250 Otpor activists had been arrested nationwide.

Otpor, however, had the last laugh: after its offices were raided, the group publicly announced the time and place for delivery of what it said would be replacement materials. On that date, large trucks arrived at the Otpor office. When the police arrived to confiscate the "subversive" material, they were caught on camera seizing what turned out to be completely empty boxes.

Elections

The Yugoslav general elections were held on September 24. Turnout was the highest ever, about 80 percent, thanks in part to the Otpor campaign. This was the key to the election victory. Early returns released by the opposition late on the night of September 24 suggested that the DOS coalition's presidential candidate, Vojislav Kostunica, had won 55 percent of the vote, compared to just 34 percent for Milosevic.[18] The opposition also swept local elections in Belgrade and other important cities.

Over 20,000 people gathered in Belgrade the following evening for an opposition victory rally and concert in support of Kostunica. Milosevic, however, had yet to concede his defeat. On September 26, the government-controlled Federal Election Commission accepted Milosevic's second-place showing, but denied that Kostunica had achieved the necessary votes to win outright in the first round. The Commission reported Kostunica won only 48.22 per cent, compared with 40.23 per cent for Milosevic, and called for a runoff election to be held between the two on October 8.

Opposition members of the Federal Election Commission denounced fraud and said they had been excluded from the official certification proceedings. Based on returns from 98 percent of the constituencies, the leaders of the opposition coalition continued to insist that Kostunica had won over 50 percent of the vote in the first round, and that a runoff was out of the question.

"This is an offer that must be rejected," said Kostunica. "The victory is obvious, and we will defend it by all nonviolent means."[19] Thousands of people in Cacak and Novi Sad protested the official results, and the DOS leaders called for mass demonstrations in Belgrade and other major cities on September 27. The leader of the Serbian Orthodox Church, Patriarch Pavle, even met with Milosevic and urged him to concede. The Patriarch further called on "everyone, including the army and the police, to defend the interests of the people and the state rather than individuals."[20]

On Wednesday, September 27, over 200,000 Kostunica supporters gathered in Republic Square in Belgrade. It was the largest opposition demonstration ever recorded in Serbia. Meanwhile, 35,000 people demonstrated in Novi Sad, 25,000 in Nis, and 15,000 in Kragujevac. During the Belgrade rally, Kostunica

---

[18] Later in the week, the opposition downgraded these figures to 51.34% for Kostunica and 36.22% for Milosevic, still within the bounds of a first-round victory. Final official results released after the revolution, on October 7, gave Kostunica 50.24% of the vote, to 37.15% for Milosevic.

[19] *The New York Times,* September 27, 2000, p. A1.

[20] Serbian Orthodox Church statement, cited in *The New York Times,* September 27, 2000, p. A10.

reached out to the army and police forces: "Our message to the army and the police is that we are one. The army and the police are part of the people; they exist to protect the people, not one man and his family."[21] Thousands of people shouted *Gotov Je!* ("He's finished!"), a key Otpor slogan, and shook baby rattles, apparently in reference to an expression suggesting that Milosevic was "broken like an old baby's rattle."

Opposition leaders were worried that a boycott of the runoff election might allow Milosevic to claim a default victory by running unopposed. Realizing that they had only until October 8 to force Milosevic to accept defeat and step down, the leaders of the 18 opposition parties in the coalition met twice on September 28, and emerged with a three-part campaign scheduled to last 10 days. First, they would challenge the official results from the first round of balloting in the courts. Second, they would employ popular pressure on the regime through the use of demonstrations, selective strikes, and civil disobedience. Finally, they would encourage Milosevic's political and military allies to desert him and join the opposition.

Focus on the provinces

Some sectors of the opposition, including Otpor, did their best to prepare for a post-electoral contingency against fraud. They were sure Milosevic would both lose the election and then try to steal it. The Democratic Opposition of Serbia therefore called for a massive rally in Belgrade on Friday, September 29. Opposition leaders planned to ask the Serbian people to "perform any act of civil disobedience they have at their disposal" or simply to remain in the square until Milosevic accepted defeat. However, so few people turned out that the demonstration was suspended until the evening. One of the protesters, a 17-year old student, said, "We'll stay to protest, but I don't think he'll go that easily. We need total civil disobedience, not this kind of thing today, which is ridiculous. Everyone needs to come out on the street and block the system."[22]

---

21 *The New York Times,* September 28, 2000, p. A14.
22 *The New York Times,* September 30, 2000.

In the provinces, where Otpor had put so much effort into promoting creative resistance, that is exactly what happened. While Belgrade politicians worried about the low turnout for demonstrations in the capital, major national highways were blocked across the country. Much larger demonstrations took place in Cacak, Nis, Novi Sad, Valjevo, and Kraljevo. The once-monolithic State media began to crack, as State television workers in Kragujevac temporarily halted regularly scheduled programming to protest the bias of "official" news. At the Novi Sad television station, 150 workers signed a petition asking for the resignation of the chief editor. Six other editors at the station were fired when they refused to broadcast the State news program and promised equal coverage of opposition activities.

A few strikes also broke out, mainly in opposition strongholds such as Cacak. Students walked out of classes, artists and actors went on strike, and some public and private offices closed. Quietly, 7,500 workers at the Kolubara coal mines 40 miles south of Belgrade walked off the job, insisting they would not return to work until Kostunica's electoral victory was recognized. The Kolubara mines produced coal for the Obrenovac power station, which in turn produced nearly half of Serbia's electricity. A prolonged strike at the mines would seriously jeopardize the ability of the country to function normally.

Meanwhile, opposition leaders arrived at a consensus that Monday, October 2 must be "D-Day," the time to step up the pressure on Milosevic using rolling strikes, demonstrations, road blockades, and school boycotts. In many parts of the country, limited blockades and strikes began a day early. One thousand workers at the Kostolac coal mine in eastern Serbia joined their Kolubara comrades and walked off the job.

In Belgrade, newly elected opposition mayor Milan Protic called for a citywide general strike. He said he believed the pressure would have to be systematically increased throughout the coming week, with an escalation of opposition actions and strikes "until Milosevic realizes he is no longer president."[23] Protic's call was echoed by Velimir Ilic, the charismatic and popular opposition mayor of Cacak, who called for a total blockade of his own town. "Our victory is as pure as a diamond. Kostunica is the

---

[23] *The Boston Globe,* October 2, 2000, p. A8.

elected president, and we must persist in our resistance," he told a crowd of 10,000 that had gathered for the seventh consecutive night of demonstrations in Cacak.[24]

At the Kolubara mines, general manager Slobodan Jankovic resigned in support of the striking workers. Later in the day, hundreds of special police entered the mine in an attempt to keep it in operation. They failed, largely because the workers had already removed key parts of important equipment and machinery, precisely in case of a police takeover. "It would take us three days to get working again," said one worker, "but it would take them 15 days."[25]

Meanwhile, cracks grew wider in the state media. More than 60 reporters at *Vecernje Novosti,* a popular tabloid paper that was put under State control earlier in the year, signed a petition demanding that the paper produce balanced news coverage within 24 hours and recognize Kostunica's electoral victory. Eight local Belgrade radio stations said they would stop broadcasting state news. And at Studio B, a television station formerly controlled by the opposition before it was taken over by state authorities in May, workers threatened a strike unless news coverage became balanced.

General strike

On Monday, October 2, the general strike began. It was the first attempt at a nationwide general strike in Serbia since the Second World War. The objective was to shut down roads and highways throughout the country, fortify the strikes at Kolubara and other key industries, and close schools and businesses. The aim was "to try and show to Mr. Milosevic that he can no longer command the country."[26]

Although garbage piled up in Belgrade, and students took to the streets, the capital city was relatively unaffected on the first day of the strike. Once again it was in the provinces, formerly the most important base of Milosevic's support, where resistance was strongest. Novi Sad, Cacak, Pancevo, Uzice, and Nis were shut

---

24 *The Boston Globe,* October 2, 2000, p. A8.
25 *The New York Times,* October 4, 2000, p. A10.
26 *The New York Times,* October 4, 2000, p. A3.

down completely. Highways and railroads were blocked across the country by cars, trucks, and throngs of people. Most schools and businesses were closed.

State-run television stations were stormed by demonstrators in the towns of Prokuplje and Novi Sad. Government workers in Novi Sad joined the strike as well. Industrial workers and railway employees in Ucize also went on strike, and the main highway there was blockaded by hundreds of protesters. Even the Serbian Society of Composers and the Alliance of Composers' Organizations of Yugoslavia asked their respective memberships to stop composing music until Milosevic conceded the election. The government weather bureau said there would be no more forecasts until Milosevic left office.

At the Kolubara mines, striking workers received a visit from Vojislav Kostunica, who told them, "Thank you for what you've started, just hold on and we will finish this struggle together."[27] Opposition leaders announced the strikes would continue through the week, culminating in a mass rally in Belgrade on Thursday, October 5, attended by hundreds of thousands of people from across the country.

Milosevic responded with an appearance on nationwide television to denounce the actions of what he called the "traitorous opposition." He accused the opposition leadership of working for foreign governments and NATO. He added: "The leadership of the democratic opposition, with the money that they have received from abroad, is buying, blackmailing, and scaring citizens . . . and is organizing strikes and violence in order to stop production, work and any activity—to stop life in Serbia."[28]

On the following day, October 3, the Milosevic government threatened a harsh crackdown against the opposition, promising that "special measures" would be taken against strike leaders and organizers. Strikes and highway blockades were declared illegal, and opposition media was banned. In the early morning, the police arrested Dragoljub Stosic, the head of the Belgrade public transport union, and forcibly removed a human blockade of the bus garage. Arrest warrants were issued for 11 leaders of the Kolubara strike, as well as for two opposition politicians who

---

[27] *The New York Times,* October 3, 2000, p. A1.
[28] *The New York Times,* October 3, 2000, p. A8.

had assisted the Kolubara strikers, on "accusations of sabotage." During these days, the regime drew up a list of 40 opponents targeted for assassination. Otpor's Srdja Popovic was number eight.[29] The government also initiated rolling blackouts in opposition-controlled districts, blaming the Kolubara strikers and the opposition for the lack of coal needed to power the electricity generators.

Despite such repression, the resistance continued to spread. In Belgrade, 50,000 students marched from the city center toward Dedinje, the suburban home of President Milosevic, chanting "the police are with us!" Thirty thousand people demonstrated in Novi Sad, 10,000 in Nis, and 40,000 in Kragujevac, where Kostunica made a morale-boosting visit to his supporters. The city of Cacak remained on strike and almost fully barricaded from within. In Majdanpek, workers at the copper mine there used their dump trucks and other equipment to block all entryways to the mine with rocks and dirt, then promptly declared themselves to be on strike.

For the first time since the elections, reports surfaced of divisions within the security forces. Press reports spoke of entire special police units who did nothing but stand by and watch as protesters blocked roads. One special police battalion in Belgrade was reported to have turned in its riot equipment, and in at least one instance, local police flatly refused orders to remove roadblocks established by the opposition.

The ongoing strike at the Kolubara mines, meanwhile, had become the focal point of resistance to the regime. The workers themselves were aware of the mines' strategic importance, even though most opposition leaders were slow to come to this realization. As one Kolubara worker put it, "This is the only industry that really works in this country. This is the heart of Serbia, and we have to keep our grip on it."[30] One of the major differences between the opposition demonstrations of 1996 and those of October 2000 was that the former included few, if any, workers. The fact that miners had gone out on strike against the Socialist regime of President Milosevic had an important symbolic effect

---

[29] Srdja Popovic, from a personal conversation with Christopher A. Miller and Gene Sharp, Belgrade, May 27, 2001.
[30] *The New York Times,* October 4, 2000, p. A10.

similar to that produced by the workers of Poland's Solidarity movement when they struck against a workers' State in 1980.

The government was perhaps faster than the opposition in recognizing the threat posed by the Kolubara strike, and General Nebojsa Pavkovic, Yugoslavia's top military commander and Milosevic's Chief of Staff, was sent to the mines to try to coerce the workers to end the strike. He left empty-handed several hours later. Later, one of the Kolubara workers explained the strikers' determination in simple but stark terms: "We can either stay here four more days or four more years. It's really a very simple choice."[31]

Victory at Kolubara

On Wednesday morning, October 4, hundreds of special police armed and outfitted in full riot gear were sent into the Kolubara mines to occupy the facilities, arrest the strike leaders, and beat back demonstrators. The workers refused to leave, and used cellular phones to call for help. In nearby Lazarevac, the independent radio announced the police takeover. Within hours, more than 20,000 people from surrounding towns, and some from as far away as Cacak and Belgrade, arrived at the mines to confront the police.

By early afternoon, more than 1,000 civilian demonstrators were backed up on a bridge near the mine entrance, blocked by a police barricade. The police themselves were uneasy about their assigned task, and showed no hurry to disperse the demonstrators. Then, slowly, a bulldozer driven by three elderly men approached the police barricade and "almost gently" plowed right through it. The police did not dare intervene as thousands of people surged forward into the mine complex, some of them shouting "Otpor!" One police commander was reported to have commented, "I'm fed up with this. After this, I'm throwing my hat away and going home. The police in Serbia are more democratic than you think."[32]

---

[31] *The New York Times,* October 4, 2000, p. A10.
[32] *The New York Times,* October 5, 2000, p. A1.

In the evening, president-elect Kostunica visited the victorious miners and their supporters. By the following morning, the police sent by Milosevic to end the strike had disappeared.

The provinces come to Belgrade

On the night of October 4, the opposition was presented with a new piece of outrageous news. The Milosevic-dominated constitutional court had heard the appeal by the opposition coalition of the election certification, and theoretically ruled in its favor. But rather than declare Kostunica the winner of the presidential election, the court simply said there had been fraud on September 24, and that the whole presidential election would therefore have to be run over again on a future date to be decided by the Federal Parliament, itself controlled by Milosevic supporters. For the opposition, the decision was considered worse than the idea of holding a second round of voting on October 8, as it implied that Milosevic would be allowed to stay in power until his legal term expired in July. If the opposition coalition needed a spark to make people angry and give the resistance additional momentum on the eve of its planned mass concentration in Belgrade, this was it.

Thursday, October 5 was the day selected by the opposition for the provinces to come to Belgrade and hold a massive rally against Milosevic. The Democratic Opposition of Serbia had set a deadline of 3:00 p.m. for Milosevic to concede defeat, cancel the arrest warrants issued on October 3, and fire the top management of Radio Television Serbia. According to opposition coalition leader Zoran Djindjic, "Our idea was to assemble a large crowd to sit down in front of the federal parliament and stay there until the election commission turned up with real results."[33] Several massive motorcades of vehicles, sometimes covering all four lanes of superhighways, poured into Belgrade. They often peacefully talked drivers blockading their movement into moving aside, and blocking trucks were pushed to the side of the road. By noon, nearly half a million people from the countryside had swarmed into Belgrade. But to Djindjic's surprise, few shared his idea of sitting and waiting.

---

[33] Johanna McGeary, "The End of Milosevic," *TIME,* October 16, 2000, p. 63.

Of those who made their way into Belgrade on October 5, a large contingent hailed from the opposition stronghold of Cacak. The mayor, Velimir Ilic, had his own idea of how the day's events should proceed. Ilic personally led a 12-mile-long column of cars and trucks with more than 10,000 people from Cacak to Belgrade on the morning of October 5. They brought along bulldozers—dubbed "people's tanks"—which helped them break through a half dozen police barricades on the outskirts of the city. Prior to the journey, Ilic had coordinated his plans with two special police officers from Cacak, and two from Belgrade, who in turn encouraged other crucial police elements in the capital to defect. Their plan was to fill Belgrade with demonstrators and seize two key pillars of the Milosevic regime: the federal parliament building and the broadcasting studios of Radio Television Serbia. "We wanted to get rid of Milosevic once and for all," said Ilic, "and we knew we could only achieve that by liberating the parliament and television."[34]

Ilic was not the only opposition leader negotiating defections out of the security forces. Otpor and other opposition leaders had been deepening their contacts with elements of the police, anti-terrorist units, and the army well before the September elections. During the first few days of October, Otpor sent polite letters to army commanders and the police general headquarters, letting them know in advance that "Serbia was coming to Belgrade." The group also sent individual "care packages" of food and newspapers to soldiers and policemen.

The mayor of the southern city of Nis and an important Otpor ally, Zoran Zivkovic, later reported that "we had secret talks with the army and police, the units we knew would be drafted to intervene. And the deal was that they would not disobey, but neither would they execute. If they had said no, other units would have been brought in. So they said yes when Milosevic asked for action—and they did nothing."[35]

By early afternoon, the Cacak delegation had joined hundreds of thousands of other demonstrators outside the federal parliament building, which was protected by special police forces.

---

[34] McGeary, "The End of Milosevic," p. 63.
[35] Roger Cohen, "The Hidden Revolution: Who Really Brought Down Milosevic?" *The New York Times Magazine,* November 26, 2000, p. 118.

Many of these police, however, were now secretly working for the opposition. As crowds pressed against the barricades, the Cacak bulldozer pulled up and parked on the steps of the Federal Parliament. When the police line broke, many of the police either refused their orders to attack the protesters or, in some cases, attacked or restrained those police who had not yet switched sides. Nevertheless, hundreds of rounds of tear gas were quickly fired against the demonstrators, provoking outrage among the impassioned crowds. Thousands of people, some armed with sticks and metal bars, surged forward into the Parliament building. After a short clash, the remaining police surrendered and a few rooms in the building were set afire.

One block away, another group of protesters attacked the offices of Radio Television Serbia. The building was under heavier guard than the Federal Parliament building, and police there fired live ammunition at the crowd, wounding four people. One woman was killed when she was run over by an opposition bulldozer nearby. The street battle outside the television station lasted about an hour. When it was over, the police retreated and protesters burned the building. A police station in Belgrade was also set afire. The downtown police station was stormed, looted, and trashed, but was not burned. Radio Television Serbia broadcasts went off the air, to be replaced in the evening by a slide reading "This is the new Radio Television Serbia broadcasting. . . ."

Later in the afternoon, confronted with thousands of demonstrators outside ready to storm the building, the central police station in Belgrade surrendered to the opposition. The official Tanjug news agency suddenly defected as well, and released a bulletin calling Vojislav Kostunica the "elected president of Yugoslavia." Demonstrators also took back independent radio station B-92 and Studio B Television for the opposition, and both quickly resumed broadcasting. With the State media and many of the security forces now on the side of the opposition, and the army confined to its barracks, Milosevic's strongest pillars of support had crumbled beneath him. In the evening, more than 100,000 people gathered outside the still-smoldering Federal Parliament and Belgrade city hall, chanting the Otpor campaign slogan: *Gotov Je! Gotov Je!* ("He's Finished!").

The dictator falls

On the following morning, October 6, Russian Foreign Minister Igor S. Ivanov met with both Milosevic and Kostunica. Russia had been the only important nation supporting Milosevic's attempts to hold onto power by not recognizing an outright Kostunica victory in the first round of elections. But after the uprising of the previous day, even Russia had now switched sides. Ivanov told Milosevic that if he "gave up power now, the world would not press for his extradition to face war crimes charges in The Hague."[36] After that, events moved rapidly.

The Constitutional Court suddenly and inexplicably reversed its earlier ruling, saying it had approved Kostunica's appeal of the September 24 election results. Rather than invalidate the election, it now ruled Kostunica the winner of the first round with just over 50 percent of the vote. In the evening, Kostunica announced that he had met during the day with Milosevic and Army Chief of Staff Pavkovic, and that both men had congratulated him on his election as president.

Shortly before midnight on October 6, Slobodan Milosevic addressed the nation on television and announced his immediate resignation as President of Yugoslavia. Attempting to maintain an air of legality around all his actions the past week, he said: "I've just received official information that Vojislav Kostunica won the elections. The decision was made by the body that was authorized to do so under the Constitution, and I consider that it has to be respected."[37]

We'll be watching you . . .

On Saturday, October 7, Vojislav Kostunica was sworn in as Yugoslavia's president before the newly elected Yugoslav Parliament. Due to the Federal Parliament building having been partly damaged by fire, the ceremony was held in a Belgrade convention center.

Early the following week, key Milosevic allies in government, including the Yugoslav Prime Minister and Interior Minister, ten-

---

[36] *The New York Times,* October 7, 2000, p. A1. Six months later, however, Milosevic was extradited to The Hague.
[37] *The New York Times,* October 7, 2000, p. A6.

dered their resignations. The European Union lifted major economic sanctions against Yugoslavia, and pledged $2 billion for national reconstruction efforts. Early elections were called for the powerful Serbian Parliament in December, which were won by the Democratic Opposition of Serbia coalition with a two-thirds majority.

Meanwhile, Otpor, the student organization whose creativity and courage laid the groundwork for Milosevic's electoral defeat and subsequent collapse, placed at least 80 large, looming billboards around the country, aimed at the new government. Featuring a large bulldozer in Otpor's trademark black-and-white imagery, the message read, "Be careful. . . . We're watching you."

Otpor's short-term goal of removing the dictator had succeeded. Now, with the opposition in power, the more formidable goal of changing the system and turning Serbia into a "normal" European nation was just beginning.

Sources

Sources included newspaper and magazine articles from

The New York Times (September 24-October 17, 2000)

The Boston Globe (September 28-October 19, 2000)

TIME (October 16, 2000)

Newsweek (October 16, 2000)

The New York Times Magazine (November 26, 2000)

ABCnews.com

numerous documents and reprinted news articles online at http://www.otpor.net

correspondence with Srdja Popovic and Robert Helvey

various Otpor documents and notes from interviews provided by Steven York

These were supplemented by interviews in Belgrade by Christopher A. Miller and Gene Sharp in May 2001.

We are grateful for corrections and comments by Velimir Curgus Kazimir of the Fund for an Open Society Yugoslavia.

Chapter Twenty-eight

ASSESSING THESE DIVERSE CASES

Selected diverse cases

These 23 cases are among the significant applications of non-violent struggle in the twentieth century. However, there have been many other cases in which nonviolent struggle was the main means by which conflicts were waged, and many more examples of uses of the methods of this technique. Many additional cases have occurred in Latin America and Africa, for example, as well as in the Middle East and in Muslim countries. Also, the widespread use of labor strikes and economic boycotts is not adequately represented in this selection. General strikes and other large-scale strikes are included here only as parts of a broader struggle.[1]

---

[1] See the important study by Wilfred H. Crook, *The General Strike: A Study of Labor's Tragic Weapon in Theory and Practice*, Chapel Hill, North Carolina: University of North Carolina Press, 1931.

The cases presented have wide geographic and cultural diversity. They include one from Eurasia (Russian Empire 1905), 10 from Europe (Germany 1920, Norway 1942, Berlin 1943, France 1961, Czechoslovakia 1968, Poland 1980-1989, Czechoslovakia 1989, Latvia 1991, Soviet Union 1991, and Serbia 2000), six from Asia (India 1930-1931, the North-West Frontier Province of British India 1930-1934, the Philippines 1986, Burma 1988-1990, China 1989, and Thailand 1992), two from North America (Montgomery, Alabama, 1955-1956 and the grape strikes and boycotts of 1965-1970), two from Latin America (Guatemala 1944 and Argentina 1977-1983), and two from Africa (Namibia 1971-1972 and South Africa 1984-1987). The diversity of these cases is sufficient evidence to deflate any earlier claims that nonviolent action is primarily of Eastern or Asian origin or that it is a Western or a European-American import.

The diversity of these cases also demonstrates that this technique of nonviolent struggle has relevance for possible application in a wide range of conflicts in place of both passivity and violence. Such future cases may range from very small local conflicts, such as the boycott of a store that has especially high prices and poor service, to major conflicts in which the population attempts to bring down an extreme dictatorship.

However, the cases presented here cannot be used to reach statistically sound conclusions about this technique because we do not have enough knowledge of all the cases in the twentieth century in which the methods of nonviolent struggle have been applied. We have, however, attempted to make the cases included here somewhat representative. There is some geographical dispersion of the cases, some historical spread in years, some diversity in the types of issues at stake, some difference in the numbers of resisters involved, some variation in the scale of the action (ranging from a single city to an empire), and some differences in the type of opponents confronted, as well as their reputations for cruelty and violence. Therefore, even granting the limitations of these cases, they are sufficient to challenge many of the widespread misconceptions about nonviolent struggle.

Applications and issues

The achievements of these applications of nonviolent struggle are significant, although not all of them were successful. Among the cases included here, a powerful empire (Russia 1905) was paralyzed, and another (British in India 1930-1931 and the North-West Frontier Province 1930-1934) seriously challenged, but neither struggle by itself successfully defeated the empire. Three attempted coups d'état (Germany 1920, France 1961, and the USSR 1991) were defeated. Eight dictatorships (Guatemala 1944, Argentina 1977-1985, Poland 1980-1989, the Philippines 1986, Czechoslovakia 1989, Burma 1988, China 1989, and Serbia 2000) were resisted, but not all successfully. Some (Guatemala 1944, the Philippines 1986, Czechoslovakia 1989 and Serbia 2000) were significant successes, while two other cases (Burma 1988 and China 1989) ended with massacres. Two foreign-occupation regimes (Norway 1942 and Latvia 1991) were successfully resisted. One new invasion and occupation (Czechoslovakia 1968) was strongly resisted, but unsuccessfully. Three cases of serious internal social oppression (Montgomery, Alabama, 1955-1956, Namibia 1971, and South Africa 1984-1987) were strongly challenged. One system of economic exploitation of agricultural workers (U.S. grape strikes and boycotts of 1965-1970) was challenged and successfully overcome. One limited case of resistance to genocide (Berlin 1943) was successful. A new threat to constitutional rule was defeated (Thailand 1992).

These cases, in addition to illustrating the broad applications of nonviolent struggle in a variety of circumstances, also show the diversity of issues around which nonviolent action can center. While some struggles focused on toppling a dictatorship, fighting an invasion, or defending a democracy, the objectives in other struggles varied from trying to secure rights for an oppressed population (Montgomery, Alabama, 1955-1956 and South Africa 1984-1987), to correcting economic injustices and exploitation (Namibia 1971-1972 and U.S. grape boycotts of 1965-1970), to finding arrested or "disappeared" loved ones (Berlin 1943 and Argentina 1977-1983), to advancing political reform (Czechoslovakia 1989 and China 1989), to organizing workers under totalitarian controls (Poland 1980-1989).

Complexity and violence

All of these cases are complex. A myriad of factors was involved in each one, and while no two are identical they are all examples of different applications of the technique of nonviolent struggle. These differences strongly suggest that future applications of nonviolent struggle also may be widely diverse in their purposes, dynamics, situations, and other important elements.

Significant violence occurred alongside nonviolent methods during several of these struggles. These cases include Russia 1905, India 1930-1931, the North-West Frontier Province 1930-1934, Burma 1988, China 1989, and Thailand 1992. However, the violence never obscured the overwhelmingly nonviolent character of the resistance. Violence clearly was not helpful, however. For example, in Russia, although the general nonviolent character of the struggle remained clear, the violence in Moscow doomed the revolution to defeat.

Number of participants

The number of people participating in these cases varies widely. Only a handful of Argentine mothers of "disappeared" children began their action in the Plaza de Mayo. Their numbers grew or shrank in the course of the conflict, at times involving thousands of protesters. Similarly, the numbers in some other cases were often relatively small, at least in the beginning.

The women of Berlin began by ones and twos coming for information. Eventually they became a protest that grew to hundreds and finally to around 6,000. The other cases involved minimally hundreds or thousands, and the larger cases involved hundreds of thousands and perhaps even millions, as in the cases of the Russian Empire 1905 and China 1989.

All of these struggles were conducted largely by people who had no moral or religious prohibitions against the use of violence, although believers in ethical or religious nonviolence occasionally were active in the conflicts. The masses of participants in the struggle either had approved of earlier violence (or even participated in it), or might well have chosen to do so in a different conflict situation. Although by the 1920s and 1930s Gandhi was a believer in principled nonviolence, he was also heavily political in his choice of nonviolent struggle and his guidance on how it should be conducted.[2] Certainly, other prominent Indian nationalists who participated in the nonviolent struggles, such as Jawaharlal Nehru (later Prime Minister), had been advocates of violent revolution.

In some conflicts, religious issues and terminology were totally absent. In a few cases, such as the U.S. civil rights movement, appeals to nonviolent discipline on religious grounds were supported by people who would never have called themselves "pacifists." In one case, that of the Pashtun[3] resistance movement against British rule in the North-West Frontier Province, the predominantly Muslim political resistance invoked religious language and pleas.

Resisting population groups and leadership

Various population groups participated in these nonviolent struggles. Often, students and other young people were extremely important in the early stages, such as in Guatemala 1944, China 1989, Czechoslovakia 1968, South Africa 1984-1987, Burma 1988-1990, Thailand 1992, and Serbia 2000. But struggles conducted predominantly by students are sometimes weaker than is required for success if they do not gain support from other important sectors of the population. That support is necessary for application of the potentially coercive methods of mass noncooperation. The mobilization of workers, the middle class, peasants and farmers, communications and transportation operators, higher economic groups, and government functionaries can give the movement considerably greater power.

Wide participation, however, does not guarantee success. If the support from other sectors of the society is only relatively weak, the struggle will remain weak. The strong participation by significant population groups in political and economic noncooperation at times can seriously weaken and even immobilize the opponents. Nevertheless, the ability to mobilize large numbers of participants does not reduce the need for careful strategic planning in

---

[2] See Gene Sharp, *Gandhi as a Political Strategist,* Boston, Massachusetts: Porter Sargent, 1979.
[3] Also called Pushtun, Pathan, or Pashtoon.

order to focus nonviolent struggle against the opponents' vulnerable and crucial points to produce greatest effectiveness.

In some cases, leaders were clearly present. At times, they played a major role, as in India 1930-1931, Montgomery, Alabama, 1955-1956, and the U.S. grape boycotts of 1965-1970. However, in retrospect, some individuals may be given greater recognition than their actual role at the time might suggest. In other cases, it was difficult or impossible to find any leaders, except perhaps temporarily or in very small parts of a vast struggle movement. Examples of this include the Russian Empire 1905, Burma 1988, and China 1989.

Objectives and provocations

A significant factor in the start of nonviolent struggle has sometimes been an immediate provocation or a sudden attack. Such cases also have tended in the past to be more spontaneous than others. For example, the cases of Germany 1920, France 1961, and the Soviet Union 1991 all occurred in response to attempted coups d'état. A new invasion of Czechoslovakia provoked the 1968-1969 struggle. New political and governmental initiatives provoked resistance in Norway 1942, Berlin 1943, and Thailand 1992.

In some cases, nonviolent struggles have occurred in which long-established political conditions were attacked by nonviolent protests and resistance that were not necessarily triggered by any major sudden provocation. This was the case in the Russian Empire 1905, India 1930-1931, Guatemala 1944, Burma 1988, China 1989, Czechoslovakia 1989, and Latvia 1991. Long-established social and economic conditions and oppression were also important in the struggles in Montgomery, Alabama, 1955-1956, the U.S. grape boycotts of 1965-1970, Namibia 1971-1972, South Africa 1984-1987, and Poland 1980-1989.

The Pashtun Muslim nonviolent resistance movement in the North-West Frontier Province of British India 1930-1934 is unique among these cases, as the nonviolent struggle was a component of an existing movement of basic educational, social, economic, and political reforms.

In many cases, also, there were individuals or groups among participants—and even among leaders—who were convinced that violence was necessary for victory or who simply thought that they needed to apply it for their own integrity, regardless of the effect. There were, for example, many Indians who were convinced that a violent war of liberation was needed to oust the British.

Sometimes during a specific conflict, diverse objectives were sought by different groups acting in approximately the same time period and at the same general location. One example of this is in Germany 1920. Not only was a right-wing putsch attempted, against which large-scale noncooperation was successfully waged, but several different political groups aimed instead for a social revolution. They waged not only strikes, but also violent struggle that continued after the putsch had been defeated.

Diversity of methods

Many of the specific methods of action sketched in Chapter Four were used in these cases. The impact of the individual methods naturally varied considerably from case to case. The impact seems to have been influenced not only by the skill, numbers, and competency with which the methods were applied, but also by the actions of the opponents and by factors in the broader conflict situation.

Some of the cases, such as Norway and Guatemala, seem to have been relatively simple, although this outward appearance sometimes disguises a more complex reality. Other cases, such as Russia 1905 and Thailand 1992, were clearly extremely complex.

In some cases, such as Norway 1942, Berlin 1943, Montgomery, Alabama, 1955-1956, Namibia 1971-1972, and Argentina 1977-1983, very few individual methods were used. These included the following: civil disobedience of government orders, the sending of organized letters of protest, persistent gathering and refusal to disperse, transportation boycotts, labor strikes, resignation from government employment, and departure from the political jurisdiction.

In the larger cases, such as the Russian Empire 1905-1906, India 1930-1931, Poland 1980-1989, and China 1989, many specific methods were used, including symbolic activities, labor strikes, creating new institutions, and occupying streets and significant places with masses of people. Even in the relatively small and brief case of Guatemala 1944, group petitions, student strikes, professional strikes, marches, and an economic shutdown were all used.

However, in only a few of these cases were the specific methods of nonviolent action used because earlier it had been carefully calculated that they would be instrumental in applying a developed strategy to achieve the group's objectives. In the conflict of farm workers and grape growers, the methods given greatest weight by the union changed from farm workers' strikes, to longshoremen, truckers, and railwaymen refusing to ship grapes, to consumers' boycotts. These shifts occurred, as experience showed that greater and additional leverage was required and available.

Often, some of the methods used, such as strikes, disobedience, and boycotts, were apparently selected simply because they expressed rejection of the policies or objectives of the opponents, even though it had not been assessed whether those methods would help to achieve the resisters' objectives.

The start of open conflict

Whether aggrieved people passively submit, resort to violence, or apply nonviolent struggle depends on many factors.

It is difficult to determine whether, and to what degree, the initiators of a specific struggle patterned their coming action on the basis of a known previous case. This clearly occurred in the Guatemalan struggle of 1944, where participants knew a lot about the struggle in nearby El Salvador a few weeks earlier. Russians before 1905 had considerable experience in the use of strikes in conflicts with employers. Some Chinese resisters in 1989 knew generally—but without much detail—about the U.S. civil rights movement, the 1986 Philippines ouster of Ferdinand Marcos, and Indian resistance movements involving M. K. Gandhi. High government officials in Estonia, Latvia, and Lithuania in 1991 were familiar with analyses of the use of nonviolent struggle against foreign invasions and coups d'état.

In several of these cases, the resisters clearly understood that their noncooperation would make an impact on the situation. For example, strikers on the railroads in the Russian Empire understood that their strikes could paralyze transportation in the Empire. Norwegian teachers fully recognized that without their cooperation, the imposed fascist teachers' organization could not really function.

The start of some of the cases was deliberately planned, especially in the smaller conflicts such as Montgomery, Alabama, though without plans for development of action as the struggle progressed. However, the degree of planning in these 23 cases, and certainly its adequacy, varied widely. In some cases, planners had considered only a very limited or temporary action. In other cases, however, the momentum of events led to the unforeseen involvement of many thousands of participants in the struggle. This seems to have been the case in China 1989 and even Poland 1980-1989. Sometimes, the beginnings of a conflict were initiated by relatively mild methods of peaceful action, such as a march, as that to the tsar's Winter Palace in January 1905, which was met by extreme brutalities. These brutalities then provoked vast numbers of people to join the struggle using stronger nonviolent methods, such as strikes and defiance of regulations.

In a very few cases, the broad outlines of how the struggle should begin, and how it should grow and expand with many more methods and large numbers of resisters, were planned in advance. For example, the Indian National Congress had placed Gandhi in charge of planning the 1930-1931 struggle, and he clearly did develop and lead a struggle based on a general strategic conception.

Widespread absence of strategic planning

Almost always in the 23 cases there was, however, little or no prior consideration of strategy, advance planning, preparations or training, or even review of the range of available methods and selection of the most suitable ones for that particular conflict. The people using nonviolent struggle usually had little real understanding of the nature of the technique that they sought to wield, and were largely ignorant of its history and its requirements for effectiveness.

In none of the cases had the participants conducted a strategic estimate (as will be discussed in Chapter Thirty-six[4]) of the strengths and weaknesses of each side prior to an open clash. If

---

[4] For a fuller discussion of the strategic estimate, see Appendix A.

such an analysis had been prepared, it certainly would have assisted the planners of the nonviolent struggles. It might then have been possible to make a much more effective use of the strengths of the resisters and to undermine the identified weaknesses of the opponents. This could in turn have made success for the nonviolent resisters more likely, and perhaps limited some of the later unfortunate developments.

These limitations do not mean that past resisters or leaders were at fault. Often, there was no group present with specialized knowledge of nonviolent struggle to help in decision-making and to provide guidance as the struggle developed. There were no handbooks on how to plan the struggle. There were no studies of strategy and tactics for anyone to consult, or to use in organizing the resistance, conducting the conflict, and maintaining discipline. Under such conditions, it is not surprising that there were often defeats, or only partial victories, or that violence sometimes erupted—which helped to bring defeat. With such handicaps, it is amazing that the practice of the technique has been as widespread, successful, and orderly as it has been.

In some of these cases, the usual absence of a clear strategic plan to guide the overall struggle appeared not to have been a serious problem. In other cases, however, this absence contributed to uncertainty and unfortunate actions by the resisters. The absence of a strategy made it easier for the movement to take unwise actions that contributed to its own weakening or collapse (China 1989, Russia 1905, Burma 1988). In some cases, special groups attempted to use the nonviolent struggle movement to advance their own very different political agendas. These agendas sometimes included serving the opponents or manipulating the situation so that a special group could become the new dictators.

Sometimes the absence of a strategy meant simply that courage and sacrifices expended did not contribute to achieving the objectives of the struggle, and thus were wasted. Sometimes a resistance group did achieve its objectives, but the nonviolent struggle was later forgotten or belittled and a different explanation was accepted for what caused the changes that had actually been achieved by the nonviolent struggle. In these instances, our knowledge of the past, and therefore awareness of future options, has thereby been weakened.

None of these cases included advance plans to consolidate the gains once won and to block possible future attempts to impose new oppression. The impact of this was most pronounced and most serious in Burma 1988.

The opponents

None of the opponents in these 23 cases could be described as "soft" or as "pushovers" for the nonviolent resistance group. Many of these opponents had clearly demonstrated their willingness to beat, imprison, and often kill persons who defied them.

Simplistic assertions that nonviolent struggle will usually succeed despite serious odds, or that this technique has no chance if used against ruthless regimes, do a disservice to a reasoned assessment of the potential of this technique. The conflict situations are always more complex than that, and the nature of the opponents and their conditions, objectives, and resources are important factors in determining how the conflict develops.

The condition of the opponent group or regime is very important. Some opponent regimes have been approximately self-reliant, while others at times are highly influenced by, or dependent on, a foreign military power. For example, the Communist regimes in Poland in the 1980s benefited from the presence of an occupying Soviet army.

Wise strategic analysts and planners will therefore examine carefully the status and condition of weaknesses and conflicts within the opponents. Poorly chosen resistance actions, especially violent ones, are likely to strengthen the opponents. Wise resistance strategists may instead focus actions to aggravate the opponents' weaknesses in efforts to win the resisters' objectives.

Opponent regimes that have been strongly supported by an external military and political power may be particularly vulnerable when that foreign regime is no longer able or willing to support unpopular governments. This perspective has been applied to analysis of the status of Communist regimes in the late 1980s and early 1990s that had been long backed by the Soviet Union, such as Latvia in 1991. Detailed analyses of this factor in particular cases can be instructive.

Successes and failure

Measured by the high standard of winning their objectives or failing to win those objectives, there are several clear victories: Germany 1920, Norway 1942, Berlin 1943, Guatemala 1944, the Philippines 1986, Czechoslovakia 1989, Latvia 1991, Thailand 1992, the Soviet Union 1991, and Serbia 2000. In South Africa and Argentina, the actions of the struggle group contributed to major change, although they were by no means the sole, or even major, factors in achieving the downfall of their respective regimes. In Poland, there were shifts back and forth from success to defeat to success again. The Montgomery, Alabama, bus boycott was a success, although the intervention of the U.S. Supreme Court greatly facilitated the ending of segregation on the buses. In some cases, as in the Russian Empire 1905, violence fatally undermined the revolution at the point of near victory and the tsarist regime survived for 12 more years. There were also partial successes. In Namibia 1971-1972, for example, where more was won than might have been expected, but not all of the strikers' objectives were achieved.

Clear defeats also occurred, as in China 1989 and Russia 1905. India in 1930-1931 has been called a qualified success by some, noting that the British were forced to negotiate with the Indians. Others viewed the final agreement as a defeat, pointing to unfavorable terms that, in light of the mass mobilization, Gandhi arguably did not need to accept. This issue requires a critical assessment of the then-current and anticipated future resistance capacity of the Indians.

However, some cases that were a failure in achieving their objective nevertheless appear to have contributed to the success of a later campaign, such as Czech and Slovak resistance to the Warsaw Pact invasion in 1968 and the collapse of Communist rule in 1989. This phenomenon merits careful examination.

Casualties

In Montgomery, Alabama, 1955-1956, the homes of three leaders were bombed, but in that specific struggle no one was killed. During the grape strikes and boycotts initiated by the United Farm Workers in California, there was harsh repression but no deaths. However, in several of the other cases some resisters died as a result of repression against nonviolent struggle activities or other conflicts during the unrest. In Burma in 1988 well over 1,000 were killed, perhaps many more. In the Chinese case of 1989, it was clearly thousands.

Sometimes the numbers of wounded and dead were significant but stunningly small considering the issues at stake for the opponents and the nature of the opponent regimes. Compared to cases of violent struggle over similar issues against comparable opponents, the casualties seem small indeed. At other times, thousands were shot down in the streets. In some cases, the movement collapsed soon after this occurred, as in China in 1989. In other instances, the resistance responded by quickly growing into a massive revolutionary movement that threatened to collapse the regime, as in the Russian Empire in 1905.

Sometimes the severity of repression appeared to be so extreme that it may have been intended to provoke retaliation with violence by or in the name of resisters. Resistance violence would then allow the regime to justify a violent crackdown on the resisters. In some other cases, including labor strikes, *agents provocateurs* employed by the opponents have been used to provoke violence. Such attempts do not appear to have occurred in most of these cases, according to the available sources, but these attempts did take place in Guatemala 1944.

Impact on the opponents' troops

In most of these cases, nonviolent resisters had to face down police or soldiers capable of employing extreme violence. In some cases, the troops ordered to repress the nonviolent resisters carried out their orders efficiently.

In other cases, police or soldiers were deliberately less then efficient, and in a few instances their actions even favored the resisters. Indians under British command at Dharasana in the India 1930-1931 case beat the nonviolent raiders brutally, but when their officers were not observing, they let up on the beatings. Russian imperial soldiers in late 1905 were on the verge of mutinying when the violence of the Moscow Rising renewed their willingness to obey. Czechoslovak police in 1968 transported resistance newspapers in police cars to other parts of Prague. An estimated

1,000 Chinese troops refused to shoot students in Tiananmen Square in 1989. However, most soldiers obeyed orders despite earlier widespread efforts of Chinese demonstrators and the population to befriend troops in Beijing. In the Philippines in 1986, military units ordered to attack mutinying soldiers instead defected to join the resisters also. During the hard-line coup in the Soviet Union in 1991, some KGB troops and Soviet soldiers refused to attack nonviolent resisters. In Serbia in 2000, the Otpor (Resistance) group had made important contacts with police, soldiers, and officers prior to the October elections, with a view that when the time came for major nonviolent struggle to oust the Milosevic regime, these agents of repression would not be available to support the government. Many of these policemen and soldiers, in fact, later provided information and support to the resistance.

Learning from these cases

Much can be positively learned from these experiences. First of all, they show that resistance is possible in a wide variety of situations and conflicts, even extremely difficult and repressive ones. These struggles also shed light on many of the possibilities of using this general technique of action in acute conflicts, as well as identifying problems that need attention.

Some of the particular actions in these conflicts may reveal ideas for future action, while other events may signal serious warnings of actions to be avoided. These cases have been offered here in part to show the reality of nonviolent struggle in a world of much violence and oppression, as people have struggled to shape their own futures by their own efforts. These cases should not, however, be treated as models that should simply be imitated. They are all far from perfect.

The hope is that these chapters, and other accounts and lists of cases of the past century and earlier, will contribute to recognition among scholars of the need for major research to fill the present severe gaps in our knowledge of struggles of past decades and centuries.

Also, a comparative review of these cases can provide important insights into the operation of nonviolent struggle. While not the last word, these insights may be sufficient to give plausibility to important interpretations of how nonviolent struggle operates and to refute some claims about its requirements (for example, that a charismatic leader or religious base is required) and limitations (that it cannot succeed in face of harsh repression) that appear to be very questionable in light of these experiences.

The development of the technique of nonviolent struggle will be greatly assisted by more understanding of applications of this technique in the twentieth century. We need to give attention to how those past applications were practiced and to what their weaknesses and strengths were. What lessons may they have for future struggles?

Important among the factors that will influence how nonviolent struggle develops and is applied in the future is whether the population can learn how to apply this alternative effectively. The possibility of this will be greatly enhanced if people understand more about how this technique actually operates in open conflicts.

Increasing effectiveness?

As we gain more knowledge about this type of conflict, a new possibility emerges. By learning more about the factors that have helped it to be effective, when it has been, we can ask whether, and if so how, we can increase the effectiveness of future nonviolent struggles.

We are now trying to learn more about the nature of this technique, its requirements, its strategic principles, and its potentialities. How can its weaknesses be avoided or counteracted? How can its strengths and capacities be increased and applied? How can nonviolent action be refined, made more effective, and applied in place of violence to meet complex and difficult problems? How can this technique be used in those types of conflicts for which it has often been assumed only violence could be adequate?

The development of nonviolent struggle will be greatly assisted by more understanding of the applications of this technique in the twentieth century. It appears that in the very few cases in which some strategic planning occurred, such as in India and Serbia, that the planning contributed to increased effectiveness. It is reasonable, therefore, to project that increased strategic planning could produce a significantly greater chance of future successes.

Due to advances in the practice of nonviolent struggle in recent decades, scholarly studies, and the continuing strategic development of the technique, it is now possible to increase the effectiveness of nonviolent struggle beyond past practice.

This greater power will come not only from courageous and disciplined action, but also from careful planning based on deep understanding of the dynamics and requirements of nonviolent struggle, and, very importantly, from that rare quality of wise strategic planning.

Before further exploration of strategy, however, it is first important to understand the dynamics of nonviolent action: how it works. This is the topic of the next Part of this book.

PART THREE

THE DYNAMICS OF NONVIOLENT STRUGGLE

INTRODUCTION TO THE
DYNAMICS

Part Three offers a relatively brief summary of the workings, or dynamics, of nonviolent struggle in conflicts. Anyone seeking to understand or use nonviolent struggle needs to have a good grasp of these dynamics. The application of this technique produces a fluid, changing, interactive process that is never static. The workings of this technique are also very complicated.

Persons and groups seriously interested in the operation of this technique are encouraged to examine the more detailed study in Gene Sharp, *The Politics of Nonviolent Action,* Part Three, *The Dynamics of Nonviolent Action* (Boston: Porter Sargent, 1973 and later printings). That text and this summarized discussion are based on twentieth century cases and analyses. They make only minor reference to the importance and application of strategy. The chapters in Part Four of this book focus exclusively on the impact that strategic planning can play in increasing the future effectiveness of this technique as it is developed and practiced in the twenty-first century. However, before proceeding to a discussion

---

The chapters of Part Three are heavily based on the extreme condensation of *The Politics of Nonviolent Action,* prepared by Jaime Gonzales Bernal and published in Spanish in Mexico as *La Lucha Política Noviolenta: Critérios y Técnicas* (private printings, 1987); Santiago, Chile: Ediciones ChileAmérica CESOC, 1988. Revised, expanded edition with a new translation, Miami: Hermanos al Rescate. 1998. Part Three, however, is a newly revised English text.

of strategy, we must first examine the dynamics of this technique in greater depth. How does it work in conflicts?

Chapter Twenty-nine

LAYING THE GROUNDWORK
FOR NONVIOLENT ACTION

Confronting the power of the opponents

Nonviolent resisters use their power against the power of their opponents. The technique of nonviolent action controls and wields power by using psychological, social, economic, and political methods.

Frequently, the opponents are either a government or a group that has the support of the State's courts, police, prisons, and military forces. Groups using nonviolent struggle wisely refuse to confront their opponents with violent weapons, with which their opponents have overwhelming advantage. Instead, in strategic terms, the nonviolent struggle group counters the opponents' violent power *indirectly* in ways that operate to the resisters' advantage. An asymmetrical conflict ensues, with the two sides fighting by contrasting means.

Nonviolent struggle operates to weaken the opponents by alienating the institutions and groups that supply the sources of the opponents' power, frustrating the effective utilization of the

361

opponents' forces, and at times weakening their will to use their available capacities. The reduction or removal of the sources of the opponents' power is an attempt to reduce or destroy their capacity to continue the struggle.

Social sources of power changes

The power of both the nonviolent struggle group and the opponents is variable. The variations in the respective power of the contending groups in this type of conflict situation are likely to be more extreme, to occur more quickly, and to have more diverse consequences than do the power variations in a conflict when both sides are using violence. Furthermore, the nonviolent struggle group may, by its actions and behavior, help to increase or decrease the relative power of the *opponent group.*

The first source of the variations in the power of each side is that the strength of the leaders of both the resistance and the opponents depends on the degree and quality of the support and participation the leaders receive from their own group or from the bureaucracy and agencies of repression that they control. Bureaucrats and agents of repression of the opponent group are more likely to reduce their efficiency and to increase their noncooperation with their own officials when the resisters use nonviolent means instead of violent action.

The second source of variations in the power of the two groups is the degree to which the general population gives sympathy and support to the nonviolent resisters or instead to the opponents and their policies and actions. Increased support for the resisters is more probable if the movement is nonviolent than if it is violent.

The third source of these variations in the power of the two sides is the opinion and practical support of the national and international communities. Public opinion and external support can help to strengthen or weaken either group, but this impact very clearly cannot be relied upon as the major force for achieving change.

Risks and variations in nonviolent action

As with all types of conflict, nonviolent struggle involves risks. One is the risk of defeat. Use of this technique is no guarantee of success. Other risks include insecurity and danger for the resisters. Repression is a likely response when the resistance seriously challenges the established order. In nonviolent struggles resisters can be injured, suffer economic losses, be imprisoned, and even be killed. Historically, however, these risks are significantly reduced in nonviolent struggles, as compared with struggles in which both sides use violence. In explosive situations, there is also a risk of the eruption of violence by frustrated people, which could seriously damage the nonviolent struggle movement. Furthermore, extreme dictatorships may deliberately act harshly against innocent people in order to frighten others into compulsive submission. The Chinese saying is "Kill the chicken in order to frighten the monkey." However, to do nothing in a situation of oppression is to invite not only continued violence by the opponents, but also by the dominated group.

The variety of the characteristics of nonviolent struggle movements is enormous, as the previous cases illustrate. No two cases are alike. To facilitate the analysis of the dynamics of nonviolent action in this and later chapters, however, certain assumptions are made here:

- That methods from all three classes of protest and persuasion, noncooperation, and intervention are used, but especially noncooperation.
- That large numbers of people are participating, mostly acting under nonviolent discipline for the duration of the struggle.
- That the opponent group is either the existing regime or has the backing of the State.
- That some civil liberties are present, although they may be sharply reduced during the conflict.

Leadership in nonviolent struggle

We also assume here the existence of a leadership group of the resisters that directs the action. This is not always the case. Even when such a leadership group is present, it will not necessarily be well informed about this technique. These leaders need to become experts on nonviolent struggle. Knowledge about nonviolent struggle also needs to be spread widely. Greater knowledge and understanding of the nonviolent technique throughout the population will increase the difficulty for the opponents to "behead" the movement by imprisoning or killing the leaders. Leaders serve as spokespeople and offer, organize, and can implement solutions to problems. Leadership can be by group, committee, individual, or a combination of these. In some cases, it has been difficult to identify leadership in such movements.

Casting off fear

A prerequisite of nonviolent struggle is to cast off or to control fear of acting independently and of the potential sufferings. This is for several reasons:

- Cowardice and nonviolent struggle do not mix. The coward seeks to avoid the conflict and flees from danger, while the nonviolent resister faces the conflict and risks the dangers involved.

- Fear arises from the assumption of one's weakness. Nonviolent resisters, however, ought to have confidence in their cause, principles, and their means of action.

- Casting off fear, or controlling it, depends on gaining confidence in one's power to act effectively to produce changes. Fear can be removed in stages. Participation in struggle helps.

- Proposed resistance action should be proportionate to the bravery of the participants, not more dangerous than they can bear. Frightened activists can only engage in weak actions.

- To end brutalities more rapidly, it is helpful to demonstrate that the severe repression is not achieving the opponents' objective of halting resistance.

- In short, bravery in this technique of struggle is not only moral valor, but a practical requirement.

Preparations for nonviolent struggle

In all campaigns, careful planning and preparations are essential. When possible, the following types of preparations should be considered in order to maximize the possibility of success.

Investigation

Advance investigation will include several elements. First, determine the causes of the conflict, list the grievances, formulate desired changes, give widest possible publicity to causes, facts, and goals, and generate "cause-consciousness"—awareness of the grievances and justification for the coming conflict.

Second, investigate the opponents, including their objectives, beliefs, background, strengths, weaknesses, supporting institutions, sources of power, decision-making processes, allies, and vulnerabilities. Other elements are discussed in Chapter Thirty-six.

Plan the strategy for a possible struggle

Assuming negotiations are initiated (as discussed below), extremely careful strategic planning for the possible future conflict should be completed before such talks begin. Without wise strategic planning and other types of preparations, it is premature to engage in serious negotiations with the opponents. Strength to back claims and demands are required for the opponents to take the resisters seriously.

In many ways, the political principles of nonviolent struggle are very simple. However, the actual workings of this technique are far more complex than the simple operation of the specific methods used. The highest degree of success is not likely to be achieved by chance or simple tenacity. In many conflicts, the operation of nonviolent struggle can be more complex than that of conventional military warfare. If this complexity is understood by the nonviolent resisters and their leaders, they have the opportunity to increase the effectiveness of their struggle beyond what it would be if they only understood the most basic characteristics of this technique.

In general, if one wishes to accomplish something, the chances of achieving that goal will be greatest if one uses one's available resources and leverage to maximum effectiveness. In nonviolent struggle that means having a strategic plan that is designed to move from the present—in which the goal is not achieved—to the future—in which it is achieved.

We will discuss the importance of strategic planning further in Chapter Thirty-five and discuss elements of strategic planning in Chapters Thirty-six and Thirty-seven. With a greater understanding of the dynamics of nonviolent action and examination of the conflict situation, it will be more possible to develop a competent strategy for a particular conflict. The identification of steps to use in the preparation of wise strategies is a new phenomenon, which is discussed in detail in Part Four.

Sharpen the focus for attack

The success of the campaign depends on finding the correct point of attack. It is not wise to try to achieve several major objectives at the same time. The nonviolent leadership will be wise to concentrate action on the weakest points in the opponents' case, policy, or system. The issues must be precise and capable of being clearly understood and recognized as justified. The struggle in a major conflict will usually benefit from formulation of concrete stages in the resistance. Success may depend on phasing the long-term strategy to score a series of minor gains that will eventually lead to a single major victory.

Concentrated strength on a clearly justified specific aspect of the general problem increases the resisters' ability to achieve their larger objectives. One should seek to control the link that guarantees the possession of the whole chain. Repression against nonviolent resisters concentrating on such a point of attack may operate to strengthen the resisters' cause.

Generate "cause-consciousness"

At an early stage, it is important to publicize the facts, issues, and arguments advanced by the nonviolent struggle group through pamphlets, leaflets, books, articles, papers, radio, television, public meetings, songs, slogans, audio- and videocassettes, and in other ways, as may be possible. Quality in these efforts is important. Hatred or intolerance should not be aroused. It is also important not to antagonize potential allies.

Arousing "cause-consciousness" may be divided into several phases. These include activities intended to

- Develop understanding of the issues in the conflict.

- Inform the population of the contemplated action, the requirements for its success, and the importance of engaging or not engaging in particular acts.

- Justify resort to direct action.

- Warn of the hardship and suffering that will be incurred during the struggle.

- Arouse confidence that the likely repression will be worth incurring because nonviolent struggle is more likely than any other type of action to correct the grievances.

- Bolster confidence that in the long run the combination of a just cause and use of this technique will ensure victory.

Quantity and quality in nonviolent action

Careful consideration must constantly be given to the relationship between the number of persons participating in the conflict and the quality of their participation. The best balance between numbers and quality will vary with the situation. Certainly, when employing a technique of action that greatly depends for its effectiveness on the withdrawal of consent, cooperation, and obedience, the number of participants is important in determining the impact of the action.

In general, however, quality is more important than quantity. Lowered standards to obtain large numbers can be counterproductive and can lead to a weaker movement. High standards of nonviolent behavior are required for a movement strong in both quality and quantity. The genuineness of the strength of the resistance is related to such factors as fearlessness, discipline, and tenacity despite repression, and also to wisdom in the choice of strategy, tactics, and methods of action.

Organize the movement

Sometimes an existing organization—or several organizations—may conduct the nonviolent struggle. At other times, creation of a new organization may be required. The organization should be efficient, honest, able to operate with voluntary discipline, and have effective internal communication. It should also have planned in advance how to communicate with its own supporters, in case the opponents break or block lines of communication.

The organizational efforts should focus on

- **The public:** publicizing the facts and grievances; promoting sympathy; disseminating solid information about the nature and requirements of nonviolent struggle.

- **The volunteers:** recruiting; training and incorporating participants into the movement; promoting commitment.

- **The leadership:** preparing replacements for arrested leaders of the movement; setting the procedures for further selection of leadership; supplying information to the leaders.

- **The movement in general:** supporting morale and discipline; preparing participants to act without leaders in times of severe repression; maintaining communications.

Openness and secrecy in nonviolent struggle

Secrecy, deception, and underground conspiracy pose difficult problems for a movement using nonviolent struggle. If operating under a political dictatorship, secrecy will be required at times. Elsewhere, secrecy can pose a serious danger.

Arguments are often made in favor of secrecy in nonviolent struggles in order to surprise the opponents and to catch them unprepared to counter the resistance actions. This is of dubious validity. First, there is a long and successful use of spies and informers within resistance organizations. Also, modern communications technology makes secrecy very difficult to maintain. Second, advance knowledge by the opponents of planned demonstrations, for example, will give the opponents time to consider how to respond. This may reduce the chances of massive brutalities and killings by police and troops who have not received specific instructions on how to act. Third, and most importantly, it is not surprise but the use by a movement of nonviolent struggle that contributes to the opponents' difficulties in handling this type of resistance, as compared to the use of violent resistance.

The effectiveness of nonviolent struggle depends on the very nature of this technique, the choice of strategies of resistance, and the skill of the resisters, as well as their courage and discipline.

An additional danger of practicing secrecy is the reason for its use. Secrecy is often used out of fear, and therefore contributes to fear—which must be abandoned or controlled for nonviolent struggle to operate effectively.

The following discussion assumes that the struggle is occurring within a political system that permits significant civil liberties. Where this is not the case, careful attention is required to determine what knowledge and activities should be secret or revealed.

Nonviolent struggle is based on bravery and discipline. Openness—that is, being truthful with the opponents and the public concerning intentions and plans—may be a corollary of the requirements of fearlessness and nonviolent discipline. Openness leads to liberation from the fear of arrest, disclosure of secrets, break up of resistance organizations, and imprisonment. A mass movement needs to be open. Masses of people cannot participate in a secret resistance movement because secrecy demands that knowledge of plans be held by only a trusted few. Additionally, nonviolent discipline is best achieved in the light of day rather than clandestinely. Secrecy contributes to a smaller movement and can lead to a resort to violence within the resistance movement in order to silence persons suspected of revealing secrets to the opponents.

Secrecy also contributes to paranoia within the movement, a paranoia that tends to increase over time. It often leads to disastrous consequences when internal differences surface under the guise of alleged violations of secrecy. Perhaps one faction may accuse the leader of another faction of being a spy. A paranoid movement cannot function effectively as a resistance movement.

In the struggle to attain freedom, it is necessary to behave like free people. Speaking about psychological liberation when one acts openly and without secrets, on the basis of his experience in the Indian struggles for independence, Jawaharlal Nehru (later

Prime Minister, and earlier an advocate of violent rebellion)
wrote:

> Above all, we had a sense of freedom and a pride in that free-
> dom. The old feeling of oppression and frustration was com-
> pletely gone. There was no more whispering, no round-about
> legal phraseology to avoid getting into trouble with the authori-
> ties. We said what we felt and shouted it out from the house
> tops. What did we care for the consequences? Prison? We
> looked forward to it; that would help our cause still further. The
> innumerable spies and secret-service men who used to surround
> us and follow us about became rather pitiable individuals as
> there was nothing secret for them to discover. All our cards
> were always on the table.[1]

Effects of the openness on the opponents

Openness will facilitate (but not ensure) the opponents' understanding of the nonviolent struggle group's motives, aims, intentions and plans. Direct contact with the opponents may be
repeatedly sought in order to avoid or to correct distortions in
perception that would seriously affect the course of the conflict.
In some situations, advance notice to the opponents' officials
about demonstrations, for example, may not only help to reduce
brutalities by surprised police and troops, but may be interpreted
as "clean fighting" and chivalry.

Revealing material ordinarily kept secret may be interpreted by
the opponents in contrasting ways: the opponents may think that
something more important remains secret, or they may become
more respectful of the sincerity of the group. The opponents may
see admission of the resisters' plans as a weakness and ineptness,
or, to the contrary, as a sign of an exceptionally powerful movement capable of success without secrecy.

Negotiation

Where political conditions permit, the nonviolent struggle
group should pursue, and be seen to pursue, every effort at a settlement before launching direct action. This greatly increases the
group's moral position. Negotiations may help to put the oppo-

---

[1] Jawaharlal Nehru, *An Autobiography* (London: The Bodley Head, 1953), p. 69.

nents in the wrong in the eyes of many persons and groups and to bring sympathy and support to the nonviolent struggle group.

Negotiations will require careful advance consideration by the resisters of what the most important objectives are on which they must remain firm and on what points the negotiators can be flexible or make concessions. Once the demands are set, generally they should not be changed.

It should be remembered that words and moral appeals usually have much less influence on determining the outcome of negotiations than does the strength of the nonviolent resisters. The opponents must consider what the resisters can do if they do not achieve a satisfactory resolution of the conflict short of open struggle. In order to have the greatest effectiveness in both negotiations and in open struggle, the potential resisters need to be well organized and relatively strong—the more organized and stronger the better. However, this is not the occasion for political bragging or bluffing.

It is unlikely that the conflict will be resolved at this stage. Continued preparations for nonviolent struggle during the negotiations are important and realistic. Negotiations are not a substitute for open struggle. A prerequisite for effective negotiations in this situation is a determination and an ability to struggle. The nonviolent army, said Gandhi, should be so well-prepared as to make nonviolent war unnecessary. One ought to demand of the opponents not only promises, but that they should offer some advance deeds as assurances that their promises will be fulfilled.

However, one should not expect miracles. Serious issues cannot be resolved simply by negotiations and dialogue. Fundamental shifts in power relations are often required to correct serious grievances. Effective nonviolent struggle capacity can often give powerful weight to one's words in negotiations. If those strengthened words remain insufficient to induce the opponents to accept the changes sought, then actual struggle will be necessary.

The basic strategy for the struggle having already been determined, if negotiations with the opponents do not show signs of producing satisfactory results, the organizational preparations for the coming conflict will need to be completed.

Sometimes an ultimatum

In some nonviolent struggles, but not all, the next stage will be the issuance of an ultimatum to the opponents. An ultimatum states the minimum demands and the intent to resist. The nonviolent struggle group offers to cancel plans for resistance if the opponents grant those demands (or a major part of them) by a given day and hour. A failure to achieve a mutually agreed upon change will mean that a nonviolent struggle will be launched. The nonviolent struggle group must be capable of carrying out the predicted action.

An ultimatum is issued to influence the opponents, inform the general public, and bolster the morale of the grievance group and increase the willingness of its members to act. Such an ultimatum was common in struggles led or inspired by Mohandas Gandhi, and has frequently been used in labor strikes.

The ultimatum may also be intended to demonstrate that the nonviolent struggle group has made a final effort at a peaceful resolution. This can give the struggle an aura of defensiveness, even as the group prepares for waging strong nonviolent struggle.

In most cases, however, there may be no ultimatum. The nonviolent resisters should not expect that such an ultimatum or declaration will lead to capitulation by the opponents. The opponents are likely to see such a communication as an unjustified challenge to their authority and highly improper behavior for people of a subordinate position. The opponents may therefore become angry, break off any negotiations in progress, or declare that the communication should have been directed to some subordinate official. The opponents may coldly acknowledge receipt of the ultimatum, or ignore it altogether.

If so, the time has come for action.

Chapter Thirty

CHALLENGE BRINGS REPRESSION

A time of thunder

The time for action is also the time for self-reliance and continued internal strengthening. The resisters need to organize themselves, act, and mobilize others. Nonviolent action tends to mobilize power among the population affected by the grievance and enables them to exert control over their lives and society. It helps them gain confidence and increase their strength. "Rely on yourselves" may well be the cry of the resisters. Submission and passivity must be cast off for nonviolent struggle to be effective.

In order to maximize the effectiveness of the coming struggle, a sound strategy appropriate to the specific conflict needs to be adopted. The strategy chosen for the struggle, and the specific methods selected to be used in the conflict, will differ widely from one conflict to another. The process of planning strategy is discussed in Part Four.

With the launching of nonviolent struggle, basic—often latent—conflicts between the opponents and the grievance group are brought to the surface. Through the ensuing "creative conflict and tension,"[1] it becomes possible to address the issues in those underlying conflicts and make changes that may be required to resolve them.

Exponents of nonviolent struggle agree with Frederick Douglass, the eloquent nineteenth century African-American opponent of slavery:

> Those who profess to favor freedom and yet deprecate agitation, are men who want crops without plowing up the ground. They want rain without thunder and lightning. They want the ocean without the awful roar of its many waters. The struggle may be a moral one; or it may be a physical one; it may be both moral and physical. But it must be a struggle. Power concedes nothing without demand. It never did and it never will.[2]

The struggle will bring changes to the grievance group—the general population whose grievances are issues in the conflict. Some changes will be psychological—a shattering of conformity, hopelessness, inertia, impotence, and passivity, increased self-respect, confidence, and awareness of their power. Other changes will be more directly social and political: learning how to act together to achieve objectives.

The withdrawal of consent, cooperation, and submission will challenge the system because these actions can weaken the supply of the opponents' sources of power. How seriously the withdrawal does so will vary with the quality of the action, the number of resisters, and their persistence in face of repression. The social and political milieu is also important. This includes the degree of nonconformity the system can tolerate, attitudes towards the regime, and the prospects for the resistance spreading.

The final outcome of the challenge will be determined by the balance between the seriousness of the challenge and the degree to which the social and political milieu favors each side. The opponents' efforts are clearly important but, by themselves, are not decisive. Take repression, for example. To be effective, repression must produce submission. But it only produces submission if the potential resisters grow fearful and choose to submit. At times,

---

[1] As termed by the important African-American civil rights activist James Farmer.
[2] Quoted by James Farmer, *Freedom—When?* (New York: Random House, 1965), p. 7.

repression may even increase resistance, as discussed in the following chapter.

Initial polarization followed by shifting power

The launching of nonviolent struggle will almost always sharpen the conflict. It will likely cause the conflicting groups to become more sharply delineated and stimulate previously uncommitted people to take sides. Those persons and groups initially inclined toward the opponents will tend to move closer to their position and support for them. On the other side, persons and groups initially inclined toward the nonviolent group will tend to move toward it. This instability and uncertainty in the strength of the contenders seem to be present at the beginning of all forms of open conflict.

The initial polarization period may vary in length. During this period, the nonviolent resisters need to be most careful in their behavior, because it will influence how much support they and their opponents receive. At first, the grievance group may be worse off than previously if it must now cope with repression in addition to the original problem.

If handled properly, this will likely be a temporary situation. Successful nonviolent campaigns produce a strengthened solidarity among the nonviolent resisters, a growth of wider support for correction of the grievance, and a weakening, or even disintegration, of support for the opponents. The nonviolent resisters should attempt continually to increase their strength (numerical and otherwise), not only among their usual supporters and third parties, but even among the opponents.

During the campaign the respective strengths of the two contending groups are therefore subject to constant change, both absolutely and relatively. Such changes can be large and sudden.

This highly dynamic and changeable situation means that specific acts within a nonviolent struggle may have wide and significant repercussions on the power of each side. Each proposed particular resistance action, even a limited one, therefore needs to be selected and evaluated based on its potential wider influences on the overall conflict. The nonviolent resisters' behavior may not only influence their own strength, but may also affect the strength of their opponents. The behavior of the nonviolent group will also help to influence whether third parties support either group during the conflict.

Short-term "successes" at the cost of weakening the resistance in general and strengthening the opponents are most unwise. On the other hand, improvements in the relative strength of the resisters after the initial polarization will be highly important in determining the later course of the struggle and the final result.

The opponents' initial problem

The opponents' initial problem arises because the nonviolent action is disrupting the status quo in ways that require them to respond to the challenge. The type, extent, and severity of the nonviolent disruption will vary. The opponents' tolerance and reactions (both psychologically and in countermeasures) may range widely and may change during the course of the conflict. The degree of dissent the opponents can tolerate will be influenced by the degree to which the society is democratic or nondemocratic. There is likely to be more tolerance in a democratic society and less in a nondemocratic society, although this is not always the case. Nonviolent action also tends to produce and aggravate conflicts within the opponents' camp about what countermeasures should be taken in response to the nonviolent challenge.

The nonviolent resisters need to prevent and correct misperceptions of their intentions and activities. Such misperceptions may cause responses from the opponents that will harm both sides.

Sometimes, when confronted with nonviolent action, the opponents and their officials may become confused, especially if they are surprised by, or unfamiliar with, nonviolent action. Confusion can also occur when the resistance violates the opponents' perception of the world. That perception may be based on accepted assumptions about political reality or an official ideology or doctrine. For example, the opponents may have believed that the State and violence are the most powerful political forces. There may be other sources of the opponents' confusion, including excessive optimism and a favorable self-perception. The opponents' confusion is not necessarily beneficial to the nonviolent group and its objectives.

Frequently, opponents may react to the nonviolent challenge emotionally, seeing it as an affront, an indignity, offensive behavior, and a repudiation of their authority and position. The opponents may regard these aspects of the challenge as more important than the actual issues at stake. The opponents may then either try to obtain verbal acknowledgment of their authority and position, or demand a cancellation of the nonviolent campaign, or both, before they will consent to new negotiations.

In other instances, the opponents may be less concerned with challenges to their dignity or authority and more with the immediate issues at stake. Recognition of the power of nonviolent action will sometimes lead the opponents to make limited concessions with the hope of ending the challenge. At other times, the opponents will make major concessions only after a considerable period of struggle. The opponents may do so only after they have experienced and recognized the real power of the movement.

Occasionally, opponents may genuinely believe that concessions, compromise, or surrender by them would be an unthinkable violation of their mission or duty. Even more serious can be the opponents' fear that giving way on limited specific issues will later lead to complete capitulation. This will make achieving the goal of the resisters even more difficult.

The opponents may attempt to use psychological influences, rather than repression, to induce the nonviolent resisters to be submissive again and withdraw from the struggle. The opponents may send messages such as ". . . not only can you not win, but you are already losing strength." False rumors may also be spread about the movement, its intentions, and its leadership. Attempts may be made to split groups supporting the movement, or to turn resistance leaders against each other. Or a counterattack on the issues themselves may be mounted, with the opponents trying to justify existing policies and to show that there is no justification for the demands of the nonviolent group. Such efforts are aimed at reducing the support that the nonviolent group can mobilize and retain.

Repression

When the opponents are the State, or have its support, the punishments are likely to involve repression through the use of the police, the prison system, and the military forces.

Nonviolent resistance is commonly met with repression when the opponents are unwilling or unable to grant the resisters' demands. Repression is not a sign that the resisters are weak or will be defeated. *Repression is an acknowledgment by the opponents of the seriousness of the challenge posed by the resistance.*

Sometimes the severity of the repression will be in proportion to the seriousness of the nonviolent challenge, but this is not a standard pattern.

The opponents' need to end the defiance may in certain situations be largely symbolic. But in other situations of widespread and growing nonviolent struggle, the pressures on the opponents to halt the resistance will be overwhelming, especially in a system that cannot withstand major dissent.

The impact of the initiation of nonviolent struggle on the opponents will to a large degree depend on the resisters' strategy and the specific methods launched. The other major factor will be the competency and scale with which the strategy and methods are applied. If the strategy is of poor quality or even absent, if weak methods are selected, or if only a few resisters come forward to apply stronger methods when many resisters are needed, or if many persons join the action but do so in undisciplined and incompetent ways, the action will be weak and will pose little challenge to the opponents.

For example, an economic boycott supported by only 10 percent of the population, a strike in which a small minority of the workers participate, or a campaign of political noncooperation backed by the actions of only a small doctrinal group will not seriously threaten the opponents' policies and control. The chances of harsh and massive repression will therefore be lower. However, harsh repression is still possible because the opponents may wish to instill fear of future repression.

On the other hand, if there is an economic boycott backed by 90 percent of the population, or a labor strike in which 98 percent of the essential workers walk out, the action will be strong. Similarly, in a political defiance struggle in which most of the general population disobeys the regime's orders and many of the civil servants, police, and even troops refuse to follow orders, the action will be an extremely strong threat to the opponents. Harsh repression can be confidently expected in such situations.

Repression is intended to end the protest, noncooperation, and defiance. It is the power of competently applied nonviolent struggle that triggers repression from the powers that be in an attempt to maintain their positions and control and to block the nonviolent struggle group from achieving its objectives.

Types of repression

Nonviolent resisters familiar with the technique will not be surprised at the repression inflicted by the opponents. Freedom is not free. There is a price to be paid.

It must be recognized very clearly that harsh repression can be applied against nonviolent resisters. However, it must also be recognized that generally much harsher repression is inflicted on violent resistance movements, resulting in far greater casualties and destruction. This is not because violent resistance is a greater threat to the opponents but because harsh repression against violent resistance is likely to produce fewer negative reactions than harsh repression against disciplined nonviolent resisters. Not even passive submission guarantees safety under totalitarian and other extreme dictatorships. They aim to instill fear by the example of brutal repression whether it is focused on resisters or on people who have done nothing. This fear is intended to induce compulsive submission.

Once the opponents have decided to use repression, the questions are as follows:

- What means of repression will they use?
- Will the repression help the opponents to achieve their objectives?
- What will be the response by the nonviolent group and others to the repression?

Some of the harsh measures that the opponents may use will be official. In other cases, repression may be unofficially encouraged, through the creation of extralegal paramilitary forces or assassination squads, for example. Sometimes there will be threats. Other times the repression will simply be inflicted directly against the resisters without advance warning. Some repression involves police or military action. Other reactions to the nonviolent challenge may include more indirect means of control and manipulation—and occasionally even counter nonviolent sanctions.

The sanctions, or punishments, the nonviolent resisters can expect will vary in form, intensity, and objective. These are the following:

- **Control of communications and information,** as by censorship, false reports, or interruption of contacts.

- **Psychological pressures,** as by verbal abuse, ostracism, encouragement of defections, threats, or retaliation against resisters' families.

- **Confiscation,** including seizure of property, funds, literature, records, correspondence, offices, or equipment.

- **Economic sanctions,** monetary fines, economic boycotts, dismissal from jobs, blacklisting, cutting off of utilities, and similar measures.

- **Bans and prohibitions** of certain activities or organizations, bans of public meetings or assemblies, curfews, court injunctions, and similar measures.

- **Arrests and imprisonment** on serious or minor charges, legal harassment on unrelated or fabricated charges, arrests of negotiators, delegations, or leaders, or varying prison sentences.

- **Exceptional restrictions,** including new laws or decrees, suspension of *habeas corpus* and other rights, declaration of martial law or states of emergency, or mobilization of special military or police forces. Prosecutions may be also initiated on more serious charges such as conspiracy, incitement, rebellion, or treason. Nonviolent resisters may be conscripted into military forces or court-martialed. Mass deportations may be imposed, while individuals may be exiled, detained without trial, or placed in concentration camps.

- **Direct physical violence,** varying in form and severity, planned or improvised. It will tend to grow if the nonviolent struggle movement gains strength or if earlier repression has not resulted in submission. Other countermeasures may be used by the opponents, including "disappearances," assassinations, official executions, or massacres.

Making the repression ineffective

In the face of direct physical violence, the key to success by the resisters depends on their refusal to submit and their maintenance of discipline.

Generally, the opponents' means of repression are more suited to deal with violent opposition than nonviolent struggle. Against nonviolent resisters not intimidated by fear of repression, the repression can tend to lose its power to produce submission. When imprisonment is not feared, it has lost its effectiveness in deterring certain behavior. The resisters may therefore openly defy laws and seek imprisonment, and may even dare the opponents to do their worst. If the number of defiant people becomes large enough, effective enforcement is rendered impossible and repression becomes ineffective. How large that threshold of participation is will vary widely depending on the particular situation.

Persistence

Faced with repression, nonviolent resisters have only one acceptable response: to overcome, they must persist in their actions and refuse to submit or retreat. *If the resisters show in any way that the repression weakens the movement, they will signal to the opponents that if they make the repression severe enough it will produce submission.*

Fearlessness, or deliberate control of fear, is especially important at this stage of the struggle. Firmness in the face of repression will make it possible for mass noncooperation to produce its coercive effects. Also, persistence may contribute to sympathy for the defiant nonviolent resisters. It is essential that the leadership of the nonviolent struggle be, and be perceived to be, courageous and unbowed in the face of repression and of threatened future punishments.

Sometimes, specific methods of nonviolent struggle will by their nature be both more difficult for the opponents to deal with by repression and less likely to provoke the most extreme brutalities. For example, it may be better not to march down the street in face of potential rifle fire, but instead for everyone to stay at home for 24 hours and thereby paralyze the city.

No change of tactics and methods, however, must be permitted to alter the basic nonviolent counteraction to repression: brave, relentless, and disciplined struggle.

Facing repression

Facing repression with persistence and courage means that the nonviolent resisters must be prepared to endure the opponents' punishments without flinching.

Not all suffering is the same, nor does it have the same effects. The results of the suffering of courageous resisters are likely to differ radically from that of submissive people.

Those planning to initiate nonviolent struggle will need to consider the degree of suffering the volunteers are willing to endure and how firmly they will be able to defy their opponents' repression. A bold action likely to draw a repressive response that the nonviolent resisters are not prepared to endure usually should not be taken. It is generally better to chose methods of action that do not set up resisters as clear targets when more effective and less provocative methods are available. The selected methods of action should be in accord with the degree of repression the resisters are prepared to suffer for such action. Very importantly, it should be understood, only methods should be selected that clearly help to implement the selected strategy for the struggle. This point will be discussed further in Chapter Thirty-six.

The resisters' persistence will have several effects. Two are:

- The numerical and quantitative effect of many defiant subjects refusing to obey despite repression will significantly limit the opponents' ability to control the situation and to maintain their policies.

- The nonviolent persistence despite repression may produce psychological or qualitative effects on the opponents, their supporters, third parties, and others.

In some cases of nonviolent struggle, the repression will be relatively mild or moderate. In other cases there will be brutalities. The nonviolent group should be prepared for either scenario.

Facing brutalities

Brutalities may arise because (1) the regime commonly uses terror; (2) a nontyrannical regime decides that only drastic action can crush the resisters; or (3) without orders from the regime, local officers or individuals in the army, police, or even the general public independently commit brutalities.

It is important to remember that beatings, killings, and massacres against nonviolent resisters do occur. The more dictatorial the regime and system generally, the more probable will be extreme brutalities against the nonviolent resisters. However, when challenged nonviolently, all regimes that depend to any degree on violence are likely to resort to violence. Resisters must determine how to respond according to the requirements for effectiveness of the nonviolent technique.

Informed resisters in crisis situations are not surprised by brutalities against the nonviolent group. For them, either to halt the action or to resort to violence would have serious, harmful consequences for the struggle. To be effective, the resisters must persist through the brutalities and suffering and maintain their fearlessness, nonviolent discipline, and firmness. Some time and considerable suffering may be required to demonstrate to the opponents that brutalities will not crush the movement. The price may be severe but, at times, required if fundamental goals are to be achieved.

However, the leadership in a nonviolent struggle will not, on the basis of any criteria, be wise to demand that the resisters undergo suffering or knowingly attract brutalities beyond their ability to bear them. All actions should serve a strategic purpose. If an unwise course of action has been started, it should not be continued out of dogmatism or stubbornness. Yet, when a firm stand or still more daring action is required, there should be no retreat—despite brutalities.

At times, a planned daring and risky action by a smaller group of resisters may be used to produce intense repression from the opponents. By demonstrating the resisters' initiative, courage, and persistence in face of great danger, the risky action may help to improve the resisters' morale and lessen their fear of repression. When this occurs, the harsh repression is usually inflicted on the volunteers themselves, not on the general population, as has occurred in some cases of guerrilla warfare.

The operation of one or more of the mechanisms of change may in time lead to a reduction or a cessation of brutalities, as will be discussed in Chapter Thirty-two. Brutalities may also be reduced when it is clear to the opponents that their repression is rebounding against their own position by alienating their own supporters and provoking increased resistance. When this occurs, the opponents may realize that the extreme repression and brutalities are counterproductive and need to be restricted. It is possible that the worst repression may occur shortly before capitulation by the opponents. At other times, the worst repression from certain extremist members of the opponent group may even occur shortly after their leaders have conceded the claims of the resisters.

Defiance of the opponents' repression, of course, is not deliberately intended to incur suffering from the brutalities of repression. The point is to continue the resistance, and especially the noncooperation, that has the potential to sever the sources of the opponents' power, as discussed in Chapter Two, by using the methods of nonviolent struggle, enumerated in Chapter Four. If a political noncooperation campaign, or a massive strike, collapses as soon as there are arrests, beatings, or deaths, there is no time for the resistance to have an effect. All sacrifices will have been in vain.

If, however, the opponents' use of repression fails and the resisters are willing to persist, widespread noncooperation has the potential of gaining the objectives of the struggle and even of disintegrating the oppressive system.

Supporters of military warfare are well aware that a struggle often requires a cost to be paid. One of the major differences between military conflicts and nonviolent struggles is that, almost without exception, in nonviolent conflicts the cost—in lives, injuries, and destruction—is not paid by nonparticipants but by those who are waging the struggle. Also, the casualties and the destruction suffered by the resisters are almost always far lower in nonviolent struggles than in comparable violent conflicts.

It can be argued that generally nonviolent struggles, as compared to violent ones, produce greater chances of success and less extreme repression, and also that persons not participating in the struggle are usually not seriously affected. This is in contrast to the situation that tends to prevail in guerrilla wars, conventional wars, and other applications of violence in conflicts. In violent conflicts, nonparticipating civilians will usually pay in lives and suffering as a consequence of the violent combat initiated and conducted by others.

The fact remains, however, that serious nonviolent struggle will very likely be met by repression, but the resistance must nevertheless persist.

Chapter Thirty-one

SOLIDARITY AND DISCIPLINE
TO FIGHT REPRESSION

The need for solidarity

Faced with repression, the nonviolent resisters will need to stand together, to maintain their nonviolent discipline, internal solidarity, and morale, and to continue the struggle.

During the initial stages of the struggle, the resisters are likely to identify with the whole population affected by the grievance (the "grievance group"). It is rarely possible to achieve unanimous participation in nonviolent struggle from the grievance group. How many of them will directly participate or support the resisters will vary from one conflict to another. However, it is essential that all who participate in the struggle develop and maintain solidarity with each other, and deliberate efforts may help to achieve that. This solidarity will strengthen their morale and ability to act effectively.

Maintaining morale in nonviolent struggles is extremely important. There appear to be four basic ways of doing this:

A. Maintaining rapport and solidarity

The participants need to feel constantly part of a much larger movement that gives them, personally, support and strength to continue their resistance. They need to feel that others continue in solidarity with them. This is helped by regular contacts and demonstrations of "togetherness." These may include mass meetings, marches, songs, parades, or symbols of unity. A common philosophy, if present, and open lines of communication among activists, leaders and support groups may also help.

B. Generating incentives to carry on the struggle

Efforts may be needed to support the determination to continue the struggle. The participants must believe their action is justified, the gained objectives will be worthwhile, and the means of action have been wisely chosen. Their morale is likely to increase if the resisters understand the technique well and if the goals and means of struggle are, or can be, related to the general population's accepted values.

C. Reducing grounds for capitulation

Because the participants may become discouraged and fatigued, measures should be developed at the beginning of the conflict to prevent or minimize those feelings. At least the original participants should continue their support for the struggle. Specific supports for their morale may be helpful. Special entertainment may be marginally useful. Where the nonviolent resisters and their families lack food, housing, money, and the like—because of participation in the struggle—a major effort to supply these may be needed.

The sufferings incurred in the course of nonviolent struggle are sometimes interpreted by the leaders in ways that make them seem more bearable: "Our people suffer every day, and it is all wasted," said a South African resistance leader, who invited people instead to suffer for the cause of justice.[1]

---

[1] Leo Kuper, *Passive Resistance in South Africa* (New Haven, Connecticut: Yale University Press, 1957), pp. 112-113.

D. Restraints or sanctions

These pressures to continue support for the nonviolent struggle differ radically from the punishments for indiscipline applied in wars, which usually consist of imprisonment or execution. Sometimes in nonviolent struggles, verbal persuasion is sufficient to bolster participation. When persuasion is not adequate, other methods may be used. These include vigils, public prayers, picketing, fines, publication of names of defectors, suspension of membership, social boycotts, economic boycotts, fasting, and nonviolent interjection. Intimidation and threats of physical harm must not be used.

If the resisters' morale and determination remain high, the opponents' repression will have failed. To achieve this, however, the resisters must maintain their nonviolent discipline.

Inhibiting repression

The opponents' difficulties in controlling the movement arise in part because the means of repression generally applicable against nonviolent struggle tend to be more limited than those against violent resistance. Brutalities and other severe repression are more difficult to justify against nonviolent resisters and may actually weaken the opponents' position, as will be discussed in the next chapter.

The degree to which a regime will feel able to defy world—or internal—opinion will, of course, vary, depending on such factors as the kind of regime it is; whether it expects that certain events can be kept secret; the degree to which it is threatened by the events; how dependent it is on the outside world; and whether opinion against the regime will be translated into assistance for the nonviolent struggle group and actions against the opponents.

There is suggestive evidence that nonviolent discipline in the face of repression tends significantly to restrict future repression and to cause especially difficult problems for the opponents.

The opponents prefer violence

The opponents may seek to reduce the special difficulties of repressing a nonviolent resistance movement by falsely attributing violence to the nonviolent resisters or publicizing and exaggerating any violence that occurs. The opponents may even try to provoke violence and break the resisters' nonviolent discipline. Resistance violence is often seen to "legitimize" violent repression. The opponents may provoke violence by severe repression, or they may employ spies and agents provocateurs. If publicly revealed, the news of such acts could disastrously undermine the opponents' usual support and power position. Disciplined nonviolent resistance will help to expose any such agents.

The need for nonviolent behavior

The requirement that volunteers maintain nonviolent discipline is rooted in the dynamics of the technique of nonviolent action. Nonviolent discipline is not an alien emphasis introduced by moralists or pacifists. Nonviolent behavior is a requirement for the successful operation of this technique.

Nonviolent behavior is likely to contribute to achieving a variety of positive accomplishments, including (1) winning sympathy and support, (2) reducing casualties, (3) inducing disaffection and even mutiny of the opponents' troops, and (4) attracting maximum participation in the nonviolent struggle.

How violence weakens the movement

The introduction of violence by resisters will weaken a nonviolent struggle movement by disrupting nonviolent discipline, contributing to a possible shift to violence by resisters. It may lead to a collapse of the movement. Resistance violence shifts attention to the violence itself, away from the issues, the courage of the resisters and the opponents' usually much greater violence. The use of violence by the resisters or members of the broader grievance group tends to unleash disproportionately severe repression and to reverse any sympathy that may be developing inside the opponent group for the resisters. Success in nonviolent struggle requires that only nonviolent "weapons" be used.

Sabotage and nonviolent action

Sabotage—defined for this discussion as "acts of demolition and destruction of property"—is *not* compatible with nonviolent struggle. The dynamics and mechanisms of sabotage are different from those of nonviolent struggle. Sabotage

- risks unintentional physical injury or death to persons serving the opponents or to innocent bystanders;

- requires a willingness to use physical violence against persons who discover the plans and are willing and able either to reveal or to block them;

- requires secrecy in planning and conducting missions;

- requires only a few persons to implement plans and hence reduces the number of effective resisters;[2]

- demonstrates a lack of confidence in the potential of nonviolent struggle, thereby potentially weakening the resisters' tenacity in the use of this technique;

- is a physical-material action, not a human-social action, indicating a basic conceptual shift in how the conflict is best waged;

- attempts to undermine the opponents by destroying their property, not by withdrawal of consent by the population, thereby potentially weakening a fundamental approach of nonviolent struggle;

- creates an environment in which consequent physical injury or death commonly results in a relative loss of sympathy and support for the nonviolent struggle group and the resisters' movement in general; and

- often results in highly disproportionate repression. This repression that has been provoked by sabotage is not likely to weaken the opponents' relative power position, nor to bring support for the resisters.

---

[2] Some of the methods of nonviolent intervention also require only a few persons to apply them. However, their use predominantly occurs in the context of a wider struggle in which many other resisters are applying the methods of noncooperation and protest. Acts of sabotage, however, are not generally applied in combination with mass popular resistance, and may contribute to a reduction of such resistance as confidence is placed in the acts of demolition and destruction. This shift in confidence may lead to a deliberate increase in such acts, which can increase the risk of a general shift to violent conflict of some type.

Other ways to slip into violence

One of the ways the nonviolent struggle may slip into violence occurs when resisters prepare to use it in a possible future situation. Such preparations constitute a great temptation for the resisters or members of the grievance group to use violence, especially in a crisis when limited violence against the opponents has already occurred.

The necessity of discipline

Discipline is crucial, especially when there is danger of violent outbreaks and when participants lack experience and deep understanding of the nonviolent technique.

Under this discipline, resisters must adhere to certain minimum standards of behavior, depending on the particular situation. The absence of discipline will impede or block effective use of this technique.

Continued participation in the struggle and refusal to submit to fear are the most critical aims of discipline, followed closely by adherence to nonviolent behavior. Discipline also includes compliance with plans and instructions. Discipline will help people face severe repression and will minimize the impact of the repression. It also fosters respect for the movement by third parties, the population in general, and, at times, even the opponents.

Promoting nonviolent discipline

Nonviolent action almost always occurs in a conflictual and tense situation. Nevertheless, it is possible to prevent violence and maintain discipline. Tension and aggression can be released in disciplined, nonviolent ways.

In some cases, participants in nonviolent action may intuitively, or by common accord, adhere to nonviolent discipline without formal efforts to promote it. Discipline in nonviolent action is primarily self-discipline. However, in dangerous or risky situations, stronger efforts are needed to promote nonviolent discipline. If a violent attack is to be confronted directly, both discipline and nonviolent behavior are required. Various means of encouraging discipline will be effective only to the degree that they strengthen the will or conscience of individual resisters. Instructions, appeals, and pledges, as well as discipline leaflets, marshals, and other means, may be used to encourage discipline.

In violent situations, resistance leaders have sometimes postponed or called off a nonviolent campaign. At other times, more vigorous nonviolent struggle has been launched to provide nonviolent ways to express hostility and frustration. In the face of a hostile attack, strong discipline may be required to prevent both a violent response and a rout. If leaders wish to avoid a physical encounter, it may be better to move the nonviolent group, to disperse, or to shift to simpler, less provocative methods of action. Sometimes, certain forms of nonviolent action, such as a publicly visible demonstration, may allow for the venting of emotions, while avoiding violence.

High morale is important in achieving and preserving nonviolent discipline. The resisters' morale will often increase if they feel that some significant source of strength not available to their opponents is supporting them. Possible sources might include their chosen technique of action, the justice of their cause, the inevitability of their victory, or the support of powerful friends. But additional means are often still needed to ensure nonviolent discipline. Resisters and the general grievance group need to understand *why* the campaign needs to remain strictly nonviolent.

Wise leadership and carefully selected strategies, tactics, and specific methods, implemented with intelligently formulated plans, will contribute significantly to achieving and maintaining nonviolent discipline. Another contributing element is the training of both the general participants and special personnel. This has at times been done through study groups, workshops, seminars, sociodramas and other means. Speeches, messages, and on-the-spot appeals are also often used to prevent violence and to promote discipline.

Effective organization and communication within the nonviolent group will also contribute to nonviolent discipline. Clear lines of command and communication can produce both general and specific instruction on behavior. "Marshals," for example, can be used to help keep a demonstration nonviolent and disciplined. Pledges of nonviolent discipline have also been used.

Whether or not the arrest of leaders is expected, other persons capable of stepping into leadership positions and able to help maintain discipline should be selected in advance. If known leaders are arrested, this arrangement can lead to the diffusion of leadership. In rare cases of extremely large nonviolent struggle forces that are aiming to gain independence or to destroy a dictatorship, the resistance activities and organizations may grow so strong that they take on characteristics of a parallel government, which in turn helps to maintain nonviolent discipline. If serious violence appears possible, more active nonviolent intervention may be required to prevent the violence.

The inefficacy of repression

If the nonviolent resisters remain fearless, disciplined, and persistent, then the opponents' attempt to force them to submit will likely be thwarted.

Arresting leaders and banning their organizations are insufficient to end the resistance and are likely to stifle the movement only when it is weak and people are fearful. Such repression will likely fail to crush a movement under the following conditions:

- A widespread and intensive education program on nonviolent struggle has been conducted.

- People have considerable experience in using the technique.

- Advance training has taken place and a widely distributed manual is available on how to resist nonviolently.

- Successive layers of leadership have been selected in advance.

- The first leaders set the example of fearless action, risking arrest or other serious repression.

The result of such advanced developments may be the decentralization of leadership, increased self-reliance among the resisters, and adherence to nonviolent discipline.

Repressive measures may even become new points of resistance, without increasing the resistance group's original demands. Various measures of repression may be utilized as new points to practice civil disobedience and political noncooperation to continue the group's struggle to gain its original goals.

In this situation, even an intensification of repression may fail, and may instead aggravate the opponents' problems and further erode their own power. If the methods of noncooperation used have been appropriate for the conflict, and applied widely, strongly, and persistently, the opponents' control of the situation—and even their ability to maintain their position—may become seriously weakened. Instead of repression helping the opponents to restore control, the repression may even trigger the additional force of political ju-jitsu against the opponents.

Chapter Thirty-two

NONCOOPERATION AND
POLITICAL JU-JITSU

An asymmetrical conflict situation

The opponents' difficulties in dealing with nonviolent struggle are primarily associated with the special dynamics of this technique, as we have explored in the chapters of this Part. The main impact of the use of the methods of protest, noncooperation, and nonviolent intervention is due to the leverages they produce as a result of the nature of those methods themselves, as we will discuss shortly.

In addition, under certain conditions, the impact of a disciplined nonviolent struggle that has been met with harsh repression may in some cases be supplemented by a process called political ju-jitsu. This process requires special attention, and we will discuss it in detail after we examine the processes operating in the majority of nonviolent struggles in which political ju-jitsu may be absent.

The "weapons" of nonviolent struggle[1]

To be effective, the nonviolent resisters must apply only *their own* weapons system. These "weapons," or specific methods of opposition and pressure, are capable of changing selected social, economic, or political relationships of power. There are a multitude of such methods. We shall now review these three classes, which were listed in Chapter Four, with primary attention devoted to the potential impact of noncooperation.

Nonviolent protest and persuasion

The class of nonviolent protest and persuasion consists of mainly symbolic acts of peaceful opposition or attempted persuasion, extending beyond verbal expressions but stopping short of noncooperation or nonviolent intervention. Among these methods are parades, vigils, picketing, posters, teach-ins, mourning, and protest meetings.

Their use may simply show that the resisters are *against* something. For example, picketing may express opposition to a law that restricts dissemination of particular literature. The methods of this class may also be applied to express support *for* something. For example, group lobbying may support a clean-air bill pending in the legislature. Nonviolent protest and persuasion also may express deep personal feelings or moral condemnation on a social or political issue. For example, a vigil on Hiroshima Day may express penance for the American atomic bombing of that Japanese city on August 6, 1945. The point of concern for the nonviolent protestors may be a particular deed, law, policy, general condition, or a whole regime or system.

The act of protest may be intended primarily to influence the *opponents*—by arousing attention and publicity for an issue, with a hope to convince them to accept a proposed change. Or, the protest may be intended to warn the opponents of the depth or extent of feeling on an issue, which may lead to more severe action if a change the protesters want is not made. Or, the action may be intended primarily to influence the *grievance group*—the

---

[1] The following discussion of the methods of nonviolent action—and of noncooperation in particular—is heavily based upon Sharp, *The Politics of Nonviolent Action*, pp. 109-445.

persons directly affected by the issue—to induce them to take action themselves, such as participating in a strike or an economic boycott. Sometimes, a method of nonviolent protest and persuasion, such as a pilgrimage, may also be associated with another activity, such as collection of money for famine victims. Or, fraternization within the context of resistance may be intended to help induce a later mutiny by occupation soldiers.

Unless combined with other methods, the methods of nonviolent protest and persuasion usually remain expressions of a point of view, or an attempt in action to influence others to accept a point of view or to take a specific action. This attempt is distinguished from the social, economic, or political pressures imposed by noncooperation or nonviolent intervention.

There are political circumstances in which some of the forms of nonviolent protest, such as marches, are illegal. Under such circumstances, these methods would merge with civil disobedience and possibly other forms of noncooperation.

The impact of the methods of nonviolent protest and persuasion will vary considerably. Also, where a particular method is common, its impact may possibly be less than where that method has hitherto been rare or unknown. The political conditions in which the method is applied are likely to influence its impact. Dictatorial conditions make an act of nonviolent protest and persuasion less possible, more dangerous, and rarer. Hence, a forbidden or less frequent act may be more dramatic and may gain greater attention than it would in conditions in which the act is common or acceptable. Demonstrations of protest and persuasion may precede or accompany acts of noncooperation or nonviolent intervention, or may be practiced in their absence.

The methods of noncooperation

Noncooperation is the second and largest class of the methods of nonviolent action. Overwhelmingly, the methods of nonviolent action involve noncooperation with the opponents.

The many methods of noncooperation are acts of deliberate restriction, discontinuance, or withholding of social, economic, or political cooperation with the person, activity, policy, institution, or regime with which the resisters have become engaged in conflict. The resisters may reduce or cease existing cooperation, or they may withhold new forms of assistance, or both. The noncooperation may be spontaneous or planned, and it may be legal or illegal.

With some forms of noncooperation, people may totally ignore members of the opponent group, looking through them as though they do not exist. With other forms, they may refuse to buy certain products, or they may stop working. The resisters may disobey laws they regard as immoral, refuse to disperse a street demonstration, or refuse to pay taxes.

By applying methods of this class, the resisters often can use their usual roles in the society as means of resistance. For example, consumers refuse to purchase, laborers refuse to work, citizens disobey orders or practice civil disobedience, civil servants stall or ignore illegitimate policies and orders, police and judges refuse to enforce illegitimate edicts, and on and on for a multitude of roles and usual activities.

Noncooperation on a large scale or at crucial points produces a slowing or halting of normal operations of the relevant unit, institution, government, or society. In very extreme applications of widespread determined noncooperation, even a highly oppressive regime can simply fall to pieces. This impact of noncooperation can be produced by extensively and persistently restricting or withholding the sources of political power that were identified in Chapter Two.

The degree of noncooperation practiced and its precise forms vary widely. Noncooperation includes three subclasses: social noncooperation, economic noncooperation (economic boycotts and strikes), and political noncooperation.

Social noncooperation

These methods involve a refusal to continue normal social relations, either particular or general ones, with persons or groups regarded as having perpetrated some wrong or injustice. They may also involve a refusal to comply with certain behavior patterns or social practices. These methods include ostracism of persons, noncooperation with social events, customs and institutions, or withdrawal from the social system as means of expressing opposition. The impact of these methods depends on the previous importance of the affected social relationships.

Economic noncooperation

Economic forms of noncooperation are much more numerous than the forms of social noncooperation. Economic noncooperation consists of a suspension of economic relationships. The first subclass within economic noncooperation is *economic boycotts*— the refusal to continue or to undertake certain economic relationships, especially the buying, selling, or handling of goods and services.

Economic boycotts may be spontaneous, or may be deliberately initiated by a particular group. In either case, they usually become organized efforts to withdraw, and to induce others to withdraw, economic cooperation by restricting the buying from or selling to an individual, group, or country.

Economic boycotts have been conducted by consumers, workers and producers, middlemen, owners and management, holders of financial resources, and governments. The issues in an economic boycott are normally economic, but they are not necessarily so. They can be political, for example. Motivations and objectives of economic boycotts have varied from economic and political to social and cultural.

The second subclass of economic noncooperation consists of various forms of *the strike,* which is the restriction or suspension of labor. The strike involves a refusal to continue economic cooperation through work. It is a collective, deliberate—and normally temporary—suspension of labor designed to exert pressure on others within the same economic, political, and, sometimes, social or cultural unit. A strike aims to produce some change in the relationships of the conflicting groups, usually the granting of certain demands made by the strikers as a precondition for their resumption of work.

The collective nature of the strike gives this type of noncooperation its characteristics and power. Strikes are largely associated with modern industrial organizations. They also occur, however, within agricultural societies and under various other circumstances. Strikes are possible wherever people work for someone else.

Strikes are almost always specific, in the sense of being for or against an issue that is important to the strikers. Theoretically, any number of workers might act together to hold a strike, but in practice the number of strikers must be sufficiently large to disrupt seriously, or to halt completely, continued operations of at least a specific economic unit. As with violence and alternative powerful forms of nonviolent action, the threat of a serious strike may be sufficient to induce concessions from the opponent group. Strikes may be either spontaneous or planned.

Strikes have taken the forms of symbolic strikes, agricultural strikes, strikes by special groups, ordinary industrial strikes, restricted strikes, multi-industry strikes, and combinations of strikes and economic closures. Strikes may paralyze a single factory or the economy of a whole country.

Political noncooperation

The methods of political noncooperation involve refusals to continue the usual forms of political participation under existing conditions. Sometimes they are called political boycotts. Individuals and small groups may practice methods of this class. Normally, however, political noncooperation involves large numbers of people in corporate, concerted, usually temporary, suspensions of normal political obedience, cooperation, and behavior. Political noncooperation may also be undertaken by government personnel—or even by governments themselves.

The purpose of political noncooperation may simply be to protest, or it may be personal dissociation from an issue seen as morally or politically objectionable, without much consideration of consequences. More frequently, however, an act of political noncooperation is designed to exert specific pressure on the government, or an illegitimate group attempting to seize control of the governmental apparatus. The aim of political noncooperation may be to achieve a particular limited objective or a change in broader government policies. Or, the aim may be to change the nature or composition of that government, or even to disintegrate it. Where political noncooperation is practiced against internal usurpers, as in a coup d'état, its aim will be to defend and to restore the legitimate government.

The political significance of these methods increases in proportion both to the numbers participating and to their needed cooperation for the operation of the political system. In actual struggles, this class of methods is frequently combined with other forms of nonviolent action.

Political noncooperation may take an almost infinite number of expressions, depending on the particular situation. Basically, all of the expressions stem from a desire not to assist the opponents through performance or cessation of certain types of political behavior.

Political noncooperation includes the methods of rejection of authority, citizen noncooperation with government, citizen alternatives to obedience, action by government personnel, domestic governmental action, and international governmental action.

Nonviolent intervention

The methods of nonviolent intervention are characterized by the nonviolent resisters taking the initiative to a greater degree than with the methods of nonviolent protest and persuasion and the methods of noncooperation. Methods of nonviolent intervention may be used both defensively—to thwart an attack by opponents by maintaining independent initiative, behavior patterns, institutions, or the like—and offensively—to carry the struggle for the resisters' objectives into the opponents' own camp, even without any immediate provocation. In general, the methods of nonviolent intervention are more risky for the participants than the methods of nonviolent protest and persuasion or noncooperation. Also, by their nature, most of the methods of nonviolent intervention can only be practiced by a limited number of people for a limited period of time. This is, in part, because of the form of action initiated and in part because the participants must exercise more courage and discipline in the face of severe repression than would usually be required, for example, from strike participants.

Nonviolent intervention has taken the forms of psychological, physical, social, economic, and political intervention. The impact of these may differ from their form. Psychological intervention (such as a fast) may have a political impact. A physical intervention (such as sitting down on the streets or in an office) may also make a political point. Social intervention (for example, establishing new relationships that violate separation of racial or ethnic groups) may have psychological or political consequences.

These methods may disrupt, and even destroy, established behavior patterns, policies, relationships, or institutions that are seen as objectionable. Or, they may establish new behavior patterns, policies, relationships, or institutions that are preferred.

Compared with the methods of the classes of protest and persuasion and of noncooperation, some methods of nonviolent intervention pose a more direct and immediate challenge to the status quo. For example, intervention by a sit-in at a lunch counter disrupts the established pattern of service more immediately and completely than would, say, picketing or a consumers' boycott, even through the objective of both types of action may be to end racial discrimination. Although the challenge by intervention is more direct, success is not necessarily more rapid, partly because more severe repression may be a first result—which, of course, does not necessarily mean defeat. Persistence in the intervention is likely to be both required and more costly to the resisters. If they are unwilling to pay that cost, the action may quickly end. However, with persistence and perhaps increased numbers, a victory may sometimes (but not always) come more quickly by the use of the methods of this class than with the use of methods of protest and noncooperation, because the disruptive effects of the intervention are harder for the opponents to tolerate or withstand for a considerable period.

In most cases, use of the methods of nonviolent intervention may induce change through the mechanisms of accommodation or nonviolent coercion, without the opponents' being convinced that they ought to change their policy on the question. However, certain of these methods (especially those classified as psychological intervention, such as the fast) may contribute to the opponents' conversion, or at least to the opponents becoming less certain of the validity of their previous views and policies. These mechanisms of conversion, accommodation, nonviolent coercion, and disintegration will be discussed in the next chapter.

The predominant impact of noncooperation

From this review of the classes of methods of nonviolent struggle, it should be clear that the respective pressures exerted by each class operate whether or not political ju-jitsu is a significant factor in that particular conflict.

Also, determined and strong opponents may more easily withstand the persuasive and moral pressures of the methods of nonviolent protest and persuasion and the more provocative actions of nonviolent intervention than the steady impact of powerful economic and political applications of noncooperation.

The ways noncooperation wields its power will vary with the particular conflict situation, the resisters' chosen strategy, and the forms of pressure they have chosen to apply. However, the opponents will have an extremely serious problem if

- the previous social, economic, or political patterns and institutions no longer function as they previously did;

- the people, groups, and institutions that are required to operate the system, to implement the opponents' policies and programs, and to enforce obedience refuse to do so;

- new programs, policies, and structures of the opponents remain stillborn;

- the supply of the sources of the opponents' power are seriously weakened or severed; and

- these conditions persist despite retaliatory repression.

The resisters are then in a strong position of power. As long as the noncooperation can persist and the resisters remain strong and able to withstand the retaliation for their defiance, there is an excellent chance that they will attain their objectives.

Political ju-jitsu

Nonviolent action operates as though it were especially designed to be waged against opponents able and willing to use violent repression. Nonviolent struggle against violent repression creates a special, asymmetrical, conflict situation. In this situation, repression will not necessarily succeed in stifling the resistance.

In some nonviolent conflicts, but not all, the nonviolent resisters can use this asymmetry on a political level similar to the Japanese martial art of personal combat, ju-jitsu. In traditional ju-jitsu, the attacker's violent thrust is not met with physical blockage or a counter thrust. Instead, the attacked person pulls the opponent forward in the same direction the attacker has already started to strike. This causes the opponent to lose balance and fall forward as a result of the acceleration of the force of the attacker's own forward thrust.

In a comparable sense, in political ju-jitsu the opponents' violent attack is not met with counter-violence, but instead with nonviolent defiance. This can cause their violent repression to rebound against their own position, to weaken their power, and also to strengthen the resisters. It can also turn third parties against the opponents, create internal opposition among the opponents' usual supporters, and even lead them to support the resisters.

There are no guarantees here. The outcome of the struggle depends on various important factors, just as the outcome of a military war does. However, the potential consequences of the operation of political ju-jitsu are so important that a solid understanding of the process is highly merited. In an actual conflict, it may be wise to try to facilitate the process.

For the above changes to occur, the nonviolent resisters must refuse to use violence, because that is where their opponents are stronger. The use of violence predictably makes these shifts of power much more difficult. Instead of using violence, the resisters must continue using nonviolent weapons only, with which they are stronger. This persistence can increase the resisters' power.

Using the opponents' power to weaken them

When brutal repression is inflicted on strictly nonviolent resisters, this can cause the opponents to be exposed in the worst possible light. This exposure, in turn, may lead to shifts in opinion, then in actions, and finally to shifts in power relationships favorable to the nonviolent struggle group. These shifts occur as the result of withdrawal of supports for the opponents, while the supports for the nonviolent group become stronger. The resisters' maintenance of nonviolent discipline helps the opponents' repression to rebound and to throw the opponents off balance politically.

Political ju-jitsu operates in only some cases where major brutalities are inflicted on clearly nonviolent and courageous resisters. At times, political ju-jitsu does not operate at all, or does so in only one or two of the three possible ways. Even then, political ju-jitsu may operate only partially, and not as a dominant factor in determining the outcome of the conflict.

Political ju-jitsu operates among three broad groups:

- The general grievance group and the usually smaller group of nonviolent resisters

- The opponents' usual supporters, on various levels, including among the general population, the opponents' functionaries, administrators, and enforcement agents, and at times even the top echelons of officials

- Uncommitted third parties, whether on the local or the world level

Increasing support and participation from the grievance group

Harsh repression often has an intimidating effect on nonviolent resisters. For example, although various dispersed acts of popular defiance in Beijing followed the massacre in Tiananmen Square the night of June 4-5, 1989, such as attempts to block intersections, these efforts were too limited to develop into a wider struggle employing widespread and tenacious forms of noncooperation. However, such limited reactions to harsh repression are not the universal response in all nonviolent struggles. In another case, a similar massacre on January 9, 1905, in St. Petersburg led to a large-scale revolution that would earlier have been impossible.[2] A careful investigation is merited into the conditions under which these differing responses occur.

Sometimes, the harsh repression against courageous nonviolent resisters will motivate a larger number of people from the general grievance group to join in active resistance. There have been examples of this increase in the number of resisters from various nonviolent struggles, including the Norwegian resistance to Nazi occupation, the U.S. civil rights struggles, the 1944 struggle against the dictatorship in El Salvador, and the Indian struggles for independence from the British Empire.

---

[2] See the quotations and references in Gene Sharp, *The Politics of Nonviolent Action* (Boston, Massachusetts: Porter Sargent, 1973), pp. 679-680.

Repression can legitimize the resistance movement because it "deepens the injustice" and "reveals the true nature of the opponents." The consequences of this may strengthen the resistance in two ways. The determination of the existing nonviolent resisters may intensify, and they may become willing to take more extreme and dangerous actions. Also, the points at which resistance is conducted may be expanded. Additionally, members of the wider grievance group may decide at such times that they should no longer observe from the sidelines, but instead directly participate in the resistance. This process will increase the number of resisters.

Whether or not repression produces these effects varies from case to case. However, the behavior that is most likely to produce the effects of political ju-jitsu is the same type of behavior that is wise if the resisters aim to win. That is, the resisters must withstand the repression, maintain their resistance and nonviolent discipline, and adhere to the strategic plan for the conflict. The resisters at times may wisely change the specific methods they are using, but the resistance must not collapse and they must not resort to violence.

Arousing dissent and opposition in the opponents' own group

Extreme repression against violent resisters is unlikely to provoke protests and opposition from persons and groups within the opponents' own group, who may see the severity of the repression to be necessary or justified. In contrast, extreme repression against nonviolent resisters *is* more likely to create opposition from within the opponents' own group. Harsh repression against nonviolent resisters may be perceived as unreasonable, distasteful, inhumane, or harmful to the opponents' own society.

When the resisters are nonviolent, it is much easier for members of the opponent group to advise caution in dealing with the situation, or to recommend responses other than current measures of repression, or even to dissent from the policy at issue. Severe repression may be seen as too high a price to pay for continued denial of the claims of the nonviolent group.

It has often been argued that the impact of the nonviolent struggles in India in the 1920s, 1930s, and 1940s was greater because the British were "gentlemen." Therefore some people in Britain would protest against beatings and killings of Indian non-violent resisters. This argument is incorrect. The British populace mostly did not protest against harsh repression of the Mau Mau violent resisters in Kenya during British rule in the 1950s or against the saturation bombings of German residential districts during the Second World War. The Indian choice to use nonvio-lent struggle instead of violence greatly facilitated protests in Brit-ain against harsh repression. Crowds of textile mill workers in Lancashire even welcomed Gandhi when he visited them while in England in 1931, even though their work had been hard hit by the Indian boycott of British and other foreign cloth.

The impact of repression against nonviolent resisters on mem-bers of the opponent group may take several positive forms.

A. Questioning both repression and the cause

In the asymmetrical conflict situation—violent repression ver-sus nonviolent struggle—some members of the opponents' popu-lation and their usual supporters may begin to question the violent repression against the nonviolent resisters and also reex-amine the issues at stake in the conflict. Members of the oppo-nent group may have these reactions:

- feelings that the repression and the possible brutalities are excessive and that concessions are preferable to continua-tion of the repression

- an altered view of the nature of the opponents' regime, possibly resulting in a new or intensified conviction that important internal changes are required

- active sympathy for the nonviolent group and its cause

- various types of positive assistance to the cause of the grievance group and aid to the nonviolent resisters

B. Defections in the opponents' group

Revulsion at the brutality of repression against courageous nonviolent resisters at times has caused individuals serving in the opponents' government, police, or military forces to question both the opponents' cause and the means being used to control the resisters. This may result in unease, dissidence, and even defection and disobedience among these members of the opponents' group.[3]

C. Mutiny

Defections sometimes extend to police and troops who are charged with inflicting repression. They may become deliberately inefficient in carrying out orders or may even mutiny. Sometimes only individuals disobey and desert, but there are historical cases where whole military units have deserted or defected to the cause of the nonviolent resisters.

D. Splits in the opponents' regime

Brutalities against the nonviolent resisters at times may also lead the opponents' regime to split into factions with different views concerning policies, means of control, and personnel issues. Individuals or groups with long-simmering personal rivalries may then express those rivalries through legitimate policy differences.

Winning over uncommitted third parties

Repression against nonviolent resisters may at times attract wide public and even international attention to the struggle and may elicit strong sympathy for the suffering nonviolent group. This widespread attention obliges the leaders of the opponents to explain and to justify their policies.

However, "public opinion" favorable to the resisters alone will not lead to their triumph. The nonviolent group should not expect such shifts in opinion and support to occur, much less that the opponent group will concede solely because of such shifts. For example, despite worldwide outrage following the slaughter in

---

[3] Aware that brutal repression may cause the opponent group grave problems, some nonviolent resisters may deliberately take provocative actions with the expectation that brutal repression will provoke defectors from the opponents' forces. Also, the nonviolent group may directly appeal for support from members of the opponent group. Sometimes, new splits are created, and other times pre-existing ones are aggravated. In contrast, violence by resisters generally tends to unite the opponent group. It is a sound strategic principle not to unite your opponents against you. It is wise to act so as to aggravate internal problems and divisions among your opponents, and potentially to achieve some tolerance—or even support—of your position.

Tiananmen Square in June 1989, the Chinese officials for many years refused to admit any error in their actions.

Frequently, determined opponents can ignore hostile opinion until or unless it leads to, or threatens, shifts in power relationships. However, when international indignation is turned into concrete actions, such as withdrawal of credit, severance of supplies, or the imposition of economic and diplomatic sanctions, it becomes more powerful against the opponents and the indignation becomes much more difficult for them to ignore.

Public opinion favoring the nonviolent resisters can be a powerful supporting force, but it is no substitute for the mobilized capacity for nonviolent struggle by the nonviolent resisters and the wider grievance group.

Factors determining the impact of third party opinion

Four groups of factors will determine whether or not the opponents are affected by changes in the opinion of third parties:

(1) **Are the third parties internal or international?** The impact of changes in opinion and the consequent actions of internal, as opposed to international, third parties will differ considerably. Generally, one can expect that internal dissention and opposition to repression are likely to pose a more immediate and serious problem than international opposition. The latter may take considerable time to have an impact, which the opponents may anticipate, leaving time for the resistance to be crushed and the international opposition to fade away. Individual analysis on a case-by-case basis is required, however.

(2) **The nature of the opponents and the conflict situation.** Opponents confronted by nonviolent struggle are not all alike. Some are far more sensitive to public opinion than others. The following questions should be considered: Is the regime democratic or autocratic? What is its ideology and who are the resisters and the grievance group? What is the regime's attitude towards the resistance? How important to the regime are the issues? How do the opponents perceive the role of repression? In what kind of social system are the events taking place? Are the opponents sensitive to the opinion of third parties, or dependent on them in any way?

(3) **Actions that result from changed opinions.** Once the change of opinion of third parties has been achieved, who takes action against the opponent regime, and what type of action is taken?

Third party actions may include protests, public declarations, demonstrations, diplomatic actions, economic sanctions, and the like. They ought to be seen as supplementary and complementary to the internal resistance, but never as the main actions of the struggle. The proportion of successes among past cases of international nonviolent action, especially by third parties, is extremely small. Third party actions have generally been symbolic, and therefore weak. More substantial types of supporting actions, especially among international third parties, have generally been limited to economic sanctions, while technical assistance to support the internal resistance to an oppressive regime has almost always been nonexistent, although that could change.

International action is not a substitute for internal action by the grievance group itself. It is in the nature of the nonviolent technique that the main brunt of the struggle must be borne by the grievance group immediately affected by the opponents' policies.

(4) **Shifts in third party opinion to support the cause of the nonviolent group.** These shifts may aid the resisters by boosting their morale and encouraging them to persist until they win. Such shifts may also help to undermine the morale of the opponent group.

The future of third party support

Third party and international support has generally had limited use and effectiveness. Perhaps, in the future, new forms of support could be launched, such as a supply of literature and handbooks about nonviolent struggle, offering generic advice on how to conduct strategic planning for nonviolent action, providing printing facilities or services, making available radio broadcasting facilities and equipment, and providing bases and centers for study and training in this type of struggle.

Less severe repression and counter-nonviolent action?

By choosing to fight with a technique that makes political ju-jitsu possible, the nonviolent resisters unleash forces that may be more difficult than violence for the opponents to combat.

In the light of the opponents' risks when using harsh repression, they may experiment with less severe control measures and even seek to minimize their own violence. Sometimes they may even use counter-nonviolent action. Such cases of counter-nonviolent action that have already occurred may be the first tentative attempts to move toward a new type of conflict situation in which *both* sides rely on nonviolent action as their ultimate sanction.

Summary: altering power relations

The power of each contender in a conflict in which nonviolent action is used is continually variable. Sometimes this is a result of political ju-jitsu, as well as other forces unleashed by this technique. The shifts induced by political ju-jitsu may become obvious only after they have occurred.

The restriction or the withholding of support from the opponents and the nonviolent resisters will affect the sources of power available to each side. These shifts in power capacity can be extreme.

Whether this potential is realized depends on the circumstances and behavior of the participants. The factors related to the nonviolent resisters include the degree to which they assist the operation of political ju-jitsu by their nonviolent discipline, persistence, and choice of strategy and tactics.

Political ju-jitsu does not operate in all nonviolent struggles, as noted earlier. However, there are other means by which power relationships may be changed by nonviolent struggle. Even in the absence of extreme repression or political ju-jitsu, the methods of nonviolent protest and persuasion, noncooperation, and nonviolent intervention can wield very significant power if competently applied.

Chapter Thirty-three

FOUR WAYS SUCCESS
MAY BE ACHIEVED

Four routes to success

Nonviolent struggle can be successful only when the necessary conditions exist or have been created. More often than is usually recognized, it is within the capacity of the resisters to create many of these conditions through deliberate acts.

It is possible to distinguish four broad processes, or mechanisms, that can bring success: conversion, accommodation, nonviolent coercion, and disintegration.

Conversion

"By conversion we mean that the opponent, as the result of the actions of the nonviolent struggle group or person, comes around to a new point of view which embraces the ends of the nonviolent actor," wrote George Lakey.[1] This mechanism may be influenced by reason, argumentation, emotions, beliefs, attitudes, and morals.

Conversion in nonviolent struggle thus aims not simply to free the subordinate group, but also to free the opponents who are thought to be imprisoned by their own system and policies. Advocates of this mechanism often say that the nonviolent struggle group in its own attitudes and actions seeks to separate the "evil" from the "evildoer," to remove the "evil" while salvaging the "evildoer."

Self-suffering is often considered important in triggering conversion. Some users of nonviolent struggle believe that self-suffering is not only required to neutralize or to immobilize the opponents' repression, but also that it can be the main means to convert the opponents. Suffering, some contend, attacks rationalizations and overcomes indifference. Suffering then is no longer only a risk, it also becomes a weapon.

The greater the "social distance"—the degree of separation of "fellow feeling," mutual understanding, and empathy—between the contending groups, the less the possibility of conversion. The lesser the social distance, the easier will be the possibility of conversion. Some nonviolent resisters seeking conversion of their opponents may take steps to reduce or to remove the social distance between the contending groups in order to facilitate this mechanism.

Conversion may result because of rational and/or emotional changes in the opponents' thinking and views. Precisely what these changes are will differ, depending on the individuals, the events, and how long the process has been in operation. Conversion may result in various changes in the opponents' behavior, beliefs, feelings, or worldviews. Individuals differ widely in their susceptibility to conversion.

The factors influencing conversion include the degree of conflict of interest and the social distance between the contending groups, the personalities of the opponents, shared or contrasting beliefs and norms between the groups, and the role of third parties.

---

[1] George Lakey, "The Sociological Mechanisms of Nonviolent Struggle" (*Peace Research Reviews*, vol. II, no. 6 [December 1968]), p. 12.

If the nonviolent struggle group deliberately seeks to achieve change through conversion of its opponents, it can facilitate this mechanism by refraining from violence and hostility, attempting to gain the opponents' trust by truthfulness, remaining open concerning intentions, exhibiting chivalry, maintaining a pleasant personal appearance and habits, refraining from humiliating the opponents, making visible sacrifices, carrying on constructive work, maintaining personal contact with the opponents, demonstrating trust of the opponents, or developing empathy.

For a variety of reasons, including unsatisfactory fulfillment of the above influential factors, conversion efforts may only partially succeed or may fail completely. Some persons and groups may be especially resistant to conversion. Many practitioners of nonviolent struggle even reject conversion, believing it to be impossible or impractical. If conversion fails, or is not attempted, nonviolent struggle offers three other mechanisms by which change can be achieved.

Accommodation

In accommodation, the opponents are neither converted nor nonviolently coerced. The opponents, without having changed their minds fundamentally about the issues involved, resolve to grant at least some of the demands of the nonviolent resisters. The opponents decide to yield on an issue rather than risk a still more unsatisfactory result. Influences that might otherwise have led to conversion or to nonviolent coercion may be involved. Accommodation occurs while the opponents still have a choice. However, the social situation has been so significantly changed by the conflict that the opponents must accept some changes. Among the factors leading to accommodation are these:

- Violent repression is seen as no longer appropriate.

- The opponents believe they are eliminating a nuisance by accommodating themselves to some or all of the resisters' demands.

- The opponents are adjusting to opposition within their own group, and acting to prevent the growth of that opposition.

- The opponents are acting to minimize economic losses that are expected to grow.

- The opponents are bowing gracefully to the inevitable, avoiding the humiliation of defeat and possibly salvaging something more than would be possible later. At times, the opponents may act to prevent people from learning how much power the populace really can wield.

Nonviolent coercion and disintegration

In nonviolent coercion, the opponents are not converted, nor do they decide to accommodate to the demands. Rather, shifts of social forces and power relationships produce the changes sought by the resisters against the will of the opponents, while the opponents still remain in their existing positions. (This assumes that the changes sought do not include the removal of government officials or the disintegration of the regime.)

Roughly speaking, nonviolent coercion may take place in any of three ways:

- The defiance becomes too widespread and massive to be controlled by the opponents' repression and other means of control.

- The noncooperation and the defiance make it impossible for the social, economic, and political system to operate unless the resisters' demands are achieved.

- Even the opponents' ability to apply repression is undermined or dissolved because their own forces for applying repression (police or military) become unreliable or disintegrate.

In any of these cases, despite their resolution not to grant the resisters' demands, the opponents may discover that it is impossible for them to defend or impose their objectionable policies or system.

Coercion is not limited to the effects or the threat of use of physical violence. The key factors in coercion are

- whether the opponents' will is blocked despite their continued efforts to impose it; and

- whether the opponents have the capacity to implement their will.

Coercion is the use of either physical or nonphysical force to compel or restrict action.

Nonviolent coercion resulting from widespread noncooperation can at times be so effective that it temporarily paralyzes the opponents' power. The concept of disintegration takes the process one step further.

Disintegration results from the more severe application of the same forces that produce nonviolent coercion. However, those forces operate more extremely in disintegration, so that the opponents' regime or group falls completely apart. No coherent body remains capable even of accepting defeat. The opponents' power has been dissolved.

The power of coercion and disintegration is possible because of the capacity of nonviolent struggle to cut off the opponents' sources of power, which were discussed in Chapter Two. This technique becomes coercive or disintegrative when the people applying it decisively withhold or withdraw the necessary sources of the opponents' power in the following areas:

(1) **Authority:** The mere application of nonviolent struggle may both show how much authority the opponents have already lost and also may help to undermine their authority still further. The opponents' authority may weaken or even dissolve. In addition, the people who have repudiated the opponents' authority may then, under extreme circumstances, transfer their loyalty to a rival claimant in the form of a parallel government.

(2) **Human resources:** Nonviolent noncooperation and disobedience may sever the human resources required for the opponents' power. These may include the general population, and the grievance group, as well as the nonviolent resisters. The result may greatly increase the opponents' enforcement problems while weakening their power capacity. Widespread tenacious noncooperation may paralyze the system.

(3) **Skills and knowledge:** A withdrawal of cooperation by key personnel, technicians, officers, administrators, etc., may have an impact on the opponents' power quite disproportionate to the numbers actually noncooperating. A challenge by nonvio-

lent struggle seems especially likely to aggravate conflicts within the opponents' regime, thereby reducing the available skills, knowledge, insight, energy, and the like needed to deal with the challenge.

(4) **Intangible factors:** Nonviolent struggle can threaten habits of obedience, and bring political beliefs and official dogmas into question. The resistance and disobedience may reflect prior changes in attitudes and beliefs, and may also help to erode further the habit of unquestioning obedience and to develop conscious choice of whether or not to obey.

(5) **Material resources:** Nonviolent resistance may regulate the amount of material resources available to the opponents. These resources include transportation, communication, economic and financial resources, raw materials, and the like. Of the 198 methods of nonviolent struggle, 61 are directly economic in form: boycotts, strikes, and several methods of intervention. Other methods may have indirect economic consequences.

(6) **Sanctions:** Even the opponents' ability to apply sanctions against the resistance may be reduced or removed by nonviolent struggle. Those who help to provide the sanctions—the police and the military forces—may carry out orders inefficiently, or in extreme cases ignore them or disobey them completely. Such laxity or disobedience is more likely against nonviolent resistance than violent resistance. The reduced reliability of sanctions, or even their severance as a result of mutinies, will have a serious impact on the opponents' power position.

The factors that produce nonviolent coercion and disintegration occur in different combinations and proportions. The contribution of each factor depends upon the degree to which it regulates one or more of the opponents' necessary sources of power. Nonviolent coercion or disintegration is more likely where

- The number of nonviolent resisters is very large.

- The opponents depend on the resisters for the sources of the opponents' power.

- The group or groups refusing assistance to the opponents are significant in terms of the assistance normally provided.

- The nonviolent struggle group is skilled in applying the technique of nonviolent struggle.

- The defiance and noncooperation can be maintained for significant time.

- For certain services or supplies, the opponents depend on third parties that are supportive of the nonviolent struggle group.

- The opponents' means of control and repression prove to be insufficient or ineffective in the face of massive defiance.

- There is opposition within the opponent group to the policies at issue or to the repression. This includes attention to the number of dissidents, the intensity of their disagreement, and the types of action they use, such as strikes and mutinies.

Skillfully applied nonviolent struggle may offer greater chances of success than political violence in the same circumstances. However, victory cannot be guaranteed. Changes will occur, for better or worse. Frequently, as in all conflicts, the results are mixtures of defeat and success in varying proportions.

Chapter Thirty-four

THE REDISTRIBUTION OF POWER

What consequences of success?

Sometimes one hears extremely different claims about the consequences of successful nonviolent struggle. Some hostile critics have casually claimed that chaos—not a more free or just society—will result. Other critics have said that the result will be a new dictatorship following the breakdown of the previous ordered system. Neither of these possibilities is likely to result when a disciplined nonviolent struggle has occurred, and especially not when it has been at least moderately successful.

Disciplined nonviolent resistance is not chaotic or disorderly. Effective nonviolent action involves both self-discipline and group discipline, as well as order. In fact, the more discipline is evident in nonviolent action, the more effective the struggle is likely to be, and also the less chance of later disorder and chaos.

It is true that several cases of nonviolent struggle have been followed by the establishment of a new dictatorship. Sometimes, for any of several possible motives, an authoritarian or dictatorial group may seek to exploit the unstable transition period by seizing control of the State, as we have already noted. Wise nonviolent struggle strategists and leaders should anticipate this danger and prepare and publicize plans for massive noncooperation to deter and defeat such attempted usurpations.

Both chaos and dictatorship are contrary to major trends in the long-term consequences of nonviolent struggle. Assuming that at least a moderately competent application of nonviolent struggle has occurred, the nonviolent technique of struggle has important lasting effects both on the nonviolent struggle group itself and on the distribution of power between the contenders in the conflict and within the wider system.

Effects on the nonviolent struggle group

The technique of nonviolent action produces changes in the participants. The strength of the nonviolent resisters is likely to grow as the struggle proceeds. Consequently, power becomes more widely diffused in the society, rather than concentrated in the hands of any oppressive elite.

Participation in nonviolent action both requires and produces an end to passive submission to the opponents' will. This participation also helps to correct a lack of self-confidence, negative self-images, a sense of helplessness and inferiority, a dislike of responsibility, or a desire to be dominated, which are often present in subservient populations. During the course of successful nonviolent struggles, these feelings tend to be replaced by their opposites.

Even more important than the changes produced by the nonviolent struggle on the opponents is the strengthening of the former subordinates who have learned to use this technique. This experience teaches them that they can act together with others with the same grievance and can make a major impact on improving their situation. Participation in struggle teaches them that people who were once weak can become strong.

Experience in using nonviolent action has also shown that participation tends to increase the degree of fearlessness among the resisters. Initially, the nonviolent resisters may need consciously to control both their fear and anger. Later, the fear may subside. By learning that they can remain firm in the face of repression, they often gain a sense of liberation from fear. With the reduction or loss of fear, nonviolent resisters diminish, or can even eliminate, one of the major sources of the opponents' power: fear of punishment. This will not only weaken the current opponents but enhance the ability of the grievance group over the long term to remain free of oppression from any future opponents as well.

Jawaharlal Nehru, who was never a believer in ethical nonviolence, reported that participation in noncooperation gave the Indian masses "a tremendous feeling of release. . . . a throwing-off of a great burden, a new sense of freedom. The fear that had crushed them retired into the background, and they straightened their backs and raised their heads."[1] Similar reports have come from very different struggles in other parts of the world.

Hierarchical systems exist in part because the subordinates submit as a result of seeing themselves as inferiors. Therefore, two steps to challenge and to end the hierarchical system are first, to get the members of the subordinate group to see themselves as full human beings who are not inferior to anyone; and, second, to get them to behave in ways consistent with that enhanced view of themselves. Members of the previously subordinated group learn they are capable of resistance and of wielding significant power to correct the problems they face.

Despite the hardships of struggle, the nonviolent resisters may find the experience satisfying. This has been reported from diverse conflicts, including the pro-Jewish strike in Amsterdam, under Nazi occupation in February 1941:

> To those who had participated, the strike provided a sense of relief since it represented an active repudiation of the German regime. . . . In the strike the working population had discovered its own identity in defiance of the occupying power.[2]

Participation may bring a new spirit, sense of self-worth, and hope for the future.

The effectiveness of nonviolent action increases when the resisters and the general grievance group possess a high degree of internal unity. Violence usually excludes some people from participation because of age, sex, physical condition, beliefs, or distaste. However, nonviolent action seems to contribute to internal

---

[1] Jawharlal Nehru, *An Autobiography* (New edition: London: The Bodley Head, 1953), p. 69.
[2] Werner Warmbrunn, *The Dutch Under German Occupation, 1940-1945* (Palo Alto, California: Stanford University Press, 1963), p. 111.

unity, and attracts wider and more heterogeneous groups to take part. This growth has been seen in the labor movement, as E. T. Hiller reported: Conflict "solidifies the group." "Under attack, strikers perceive the identity of their interests."[3]

The withdrawal of cooperation from the opponents and their system need not lead to confusion and disorganization. Instead, such withdrawal tends to produce greater cooperation within the general grievance group and among the resisters particularly. The movement against the opponents requires organization, cooperation, and mutual support within the grievance group in order to meet social needs and maintain social order. The boycott of certain institutions requires the strengthening of other institutions or the creation of new ones. For example, economic boycotts require alternative sources for meeting economic needs. Massive political noncooperation requires development of alternative social and political institutions, in extreme cases potentially leading to parallel government. This was an explicit part of the mid-nineteenth century Hungarian resistance to Austrian rule.[4]

When nonviolent action is used with at least moderate effectiveness, the technique will tend to spread. The same people may use it later under other circumstances, and other people may follow the example in dealing with their own problems. Although violence may also be contagious, the consequences are very different. There were repeated instances during the Russian 1905 Revolution in which strikes and other methods of struggle spread by imitation. Small successes from strikes earlier in the year 1905 led to expansion of trade union organizations and more strikes. Similarly, limited political successes have sometimes prodded nonviolent resisters to press on for larger objectives.[5]

Although the effects of nonviolent struggle on the opponents are very important, in the long run the effects on the nonviolent resisters themselves are far reaching and potentially more important. If people are strong and learn to resist effectively, it becomes difficult or impossible for anyone to oppress them in the first

---

[3] E.T. Hiller, *The Strike* (Chicago: University of Chicago Press, 1928), pp. 30 and 90.
[4] Arthur Griffith, *The Resurrection of Hungary: A Parallel for Ireland* (Third edition. Dublin: Wheland & Son, 1918), p. 170.
[5] See Sidney Harcave, *First Blood: The Russian Revolution of 1905* (New York: Macmillan, 1964), pp. 77, 79-81, 134, 143-144, 154, 171, 176-177, and 215.

place. This strengthening of the grievance group will ultimately alter power relationships in lasting ways.

Diffused power and the nonviolent technique

A free society needs strong social groups and institutions capable of independent action and able to wield power in their own right in order to control an established government or a regime of domestic or foreign usurpers. If such groups and institutions are weak, they need to be strengthened. If they are absent, they need to be created in order to control rulers who do not wish to be controlled.

Here, questions of social organization and political technique converge. There may be a causal connection between the relative concentration or diffusion of power in the society and the technique of struggle—political violence or nonviolent action—relied upon to maintain or to change the social system. Therefore, the choice between political violence or the technique of nonviolent struggle as the society's ultimate sanction may help determine the future capacity of that society to exercise popular control over any ruler or would-be ruler.

It has been widely recognized that violent revolutions and wars have been accompanied and followed by a tendency toward an increase in both the absolute power of the State and the relative centralization of power in its hands. Technological changes in military weaponry and transportation and the breakdown of the distinction of targeting and casualties between civilians and the military forces have accentuated this tendency. As was discussed in Chapter Two, centralized control by a self-selected clique directing the institutions of war can be later turned against the previous government and the population in order to seize and maintain political control. Because political violence often contributes to the destruction of a society's independent institutions, the population of a society that has used major violence may be less capable of resisting internal or foreign oppressors than a society that has used nonviolent methods of struggle and still has strong, independent institutions.

Nonviolent struggle, therefore, appears to have different long-term effects on the distribution of power within the society than does violent struggle. The nonviolent technique does not have the centralizing effects of political violence. Instead, it seems that major application of organized nonviolent struggle increases the potential for greater popular control because this type of struggle contributes to increased diffusion of effective power throughout the society. People learn how to organize themselves and how to conduct resistance against identified opponents. Therefore, people are likely to develop greater freedom of action and, consequently, less dictatorship and greater democracy.

Widespread use of nonviolent action in place of political violence tends to diffuse power among the populace. The people using this technique become more self-reliant by developing their leadership capacities and improving their capacity to apply an effective means of struggle. Also, the power of the post-struggle governments is likely to be more limited, and the population is likely to have developed a reservoir capacity for nonviolent struggle for possible use against future dangers.

The leadership necessary in nonviolent struggle tends to be more democratic, does not rely on violence to maintain group cohesion, and depends upon the acceptance of its moral authority, political and strategic judgment, and popular support. Furthermore, although at times very important, the leadership of nonviolent struggles is changeable and can be temporary. Among the reasons for this are two: the leaders are often arrested or killed and the resistance itself consequently requires greater self-reliance among the participants. Under extreme conditions with severe repression, efficiency requires that the resisters be able to act without reliance on a central leadership group. This situation may affect the kind of leadership that develops and is accepted in nonviolent struggles, as compared to violent conflicts. Leaders of successful nonviolent struggles are less likely than those of successful violent struggles to become tyrants because the nonviolent technique tends to produce greater self-reliance among the population and to strengthen civil society.

The leaders of violent struggles can establish central control for two reasons. First, they are able to regulate and distribute the supply of military weapons and ammunition to the combatants and population. Second, they are able to command the application of violence, even against the population. In contrast, the leaders of nonviolent struggles cannot do this because the weapons of nonviolent action are not material ones.

Following a successful violent struggle, the State with its repressive capacity is likely to be larger than before the struggle. However, in the case of nonviolent struggles this is unlikely, and the population's capacity for popular struggle is likely to have increased. The society's independent institutions are also likely to have been strengthened through their roles in resistance. Consequently, they will be more able to function effectively in the future, both in peaceful times and in crises.

Nonviolent struggle can help citizens become free, organized, disciplined, courageous, and capable of instituting a democracy and of defending it when needed. These people are more likely to be confident in their capacity to act effectively in the future.

People who know they have successful experience in applying an independent capacity for struggle are likely to be treated with greater care by their rulers because the populace is able to resist in order to secure and to defend their claimed rights.

However, it is unrealistic to expect that a successful nonviolent struggle for particular objectives will not only gain those goals but also will solve other problems that were not even in contention during the conflict. A single nonviolent campaign certainly will not eliminate future use of violence by that society or political system. Instead, replacement of violence with nonviolent action is likely to become possible by a series of specific substitutions for particular purposes, if and when those substitutions are seen to be desirable and effective.

The capacities developed to succeed in a nonviolent struggle can be used to defend the attained objectives from future threats, if the population chooses to use these capacities. Gains made by nonviolent struggle can therefore be relatively durable and do not require violence for their preservation.

This is, of course, a tendency, and not a guaranteed process. Following a successful nonviolent struggle, power may become more diffused among the population, giving the people greater control capacity than they previously had over their political future. However, under some circumstances this may not happen. The experience in popular power may be diminished, even in people's memory, and largely lost as people fall back into their previous views and patterns of submission. Which of these occurs, and to what degree, depends on the course of the nonviolent struggle, and on later choices and events. However, experience in the effective use of nonviolent action arms the populace with knowledge of how to wield the nonviolent weapons if they so choose.

All of these indications are suggestive that nonviolent action and political violence may contribute to quite different types of societies. This possibility merits careful examination.

However, these characteristics alone do not ensure that no other forms of perceived social, economic, or political injustice will remain or will be practiced following a successful nonviolent struggle. Nor, in other cases, do these characteristics alone guarantee a vibrant, durable democracy after nonviolent struggle has defeated an oppressive government.

In several cases aiming at major political change, a dictatorial group has seized control of the State as a nonviolent struggle group approached success, as in Burma in 1988, or as the transition of power from the old regime was in process, as in the Russian Empire in 1917.

It is therefore important to plan how the new relationships will be implemented after success and, in cases in which major political change is the objective, to plan carefully the new democratic structure. It is necessary to strengthen the independent institutions of the society. It is also crucial to strengthen the population's capacity to resist new would-be oppressors or dictators. This means to spread among the population both a general understanding of nonviolent struggle and also specific strategies to defend newly won relationships and freedoms.

The future uses and effectiveness of nonviolent struggle depend in part upon gaining increased knowledge of its nature, deepening one's skills in applying this technique in crises, gaining greater strategic insight, and spreading this knowledge throughout society. In developing these capacities, there are roles for the contributions of many people.

PART FOUR

SHAPING THE FUTURE

INTRODUCTION TO
STRATEGIC PLANNING

Knowledge of the past practice of nonviolent struggle and understanding of the processes that have operated in those cases are highly important. They help us to understand what has happened in the past and to think about what may well happen in the future.

However, this knowledge and understanding do not tell us what, if anything, we might do if we wish to make this type of struggle more effective in the future than it has been in the past. Considering the gravity of present conflicts in various parts of the world, and also projection about possible future forms of oppression, domination, and exploitation, it is highly desirable that people who choose to oppose these systems have at their disposal new information about how they can apply this technique still more effectively than it has been applied in the past.

One of the most important skills that will greatly contribute to making this technique more effective in the future is the ability to plan strategies for waging this technique of struggle in a variety of conflict situations.

Of course, the types of conflict situations and the nature of grievances will vary widely. Agricultural exploitation, foreign military occupation, an attempted coup d'état, ethnic conflicts, racial segregation, religious discrimination, and an established internal extreme dictatorship are all different types of conflicts. Furthermore, even within any one of these categories, the individual conflicts will never be identical.

However, the one capacity that could greatly increase the effectiveness of future attempts to apply this technique is the capacity to plan strategies to guide the conduct of the struggle and to apply these new strategies skillfully.

In Chapter Thirty-five, we shall argue that this technique can be made more effective in the future than it has been in the past. This chapter gives an introduction to strategic planning and identifies some factors influencing the success of nonviolent struggle.

In Chapter Thirty-six, we shall introduce the importance of accurately assessing the conflict situation, then offer some tools on how to do so. We introduce the main categories of strategic thinking, ranging from grand strategy to individual methods. The chapter concludes with an examination of the development of a strategic plan before the struggle begins.

Chapter Thirty-seven offers some guidance on how to face various issues that are likely to arise during the course of a struggle, including determination of the objectives, the strengthening of the resisters, the role of leadership, undermining the sources of the opponents' power, and methods of conducting the struggle as the conflict unfolds, such as persistence in the face of repression.

Chapter Thirty-eight focuses on key elements during the struggle, among them preparations of the population for struggle, maintaining the momentum, monitoring the conflict, and bringing the conflict to an end.

The final chapter, Thirty-nine, introduces the potential application of this technique in place of violence in several acute problem areas. These include the dismantling of dictatorships, providing national defense, lifting oppression of rejected groups, the lifting of social and economic injustices, extending democratic practices and human rights, preventing dictatorships, and blocking genocide. These discussions are necessarily only introductory, but are topics on which much further attention is required as we enter a new phase in the historical development and practice of this alternative to both passivity and violence.

Chapter Thirty-five

MAKING NONVIOLENT STRUGGLE MORE EFFECTIVE

Success and defeat in nonviolent struggle

Conflicts conducted by nonviolent struggle have been far more effective in the past than is generally recognized. This is demonstrated by various cases that were described in previous chapters, which are only a sampling of the applications of this technique in the past century.

Nonviolent struggle is not magic. It sometimes succeeds in achieving the objectives for which it is waged and it sometimes fails to do so. Defeat in immediate political terms is always possible, just as it is in war or other violence. "Defeat" here means a failure to achieve the objectives of the struggle. "Success" means that the objectives of the struggle have been achieved. Sometimes, the results of a conflict may be mixtures of success and failure, with the objectives partially achieved and partially not achieved. This is also true of struggles conducted with violence.

The degree of effectiveness of nonviolent struggle must, of course, be compared to the degree of effectiveness of violent

struggle *in achieving the avowed objectives for which it is applied,* not simply in physically crushing the other group. Too often in discussions of effectiveness, it is assumed axiomatically that
violence is the most powerful and effective force available to
achieve the intended objectives. This is not true. If one measures
the degree to which the original objectives of the conflict are actually achieved, the effectiveness of violent struggle is often quite
limited and the effectiveness of nonviolent struggle is often
greater than usually recognized. This is despite the fact that past
cases of nonviolent struggle were usually improvised or had only
minimal planning and preparations.

Dismissing simplistic explanations

In considering how to make nonviolent struggle more effective,
it is essential to dismiss simplistic explanations and apologies for
failure. These sometimes include the assertion that the avowed
goal is not nearly as important as the resisters feeling good about
their actions, that simple abstention from violence is sufficient, or
that willingness of the resisters to die is most important. Feeling
good, not engaging in violence, or being willing to die, when you
have not achieved the goals of your struggle, does not change the
fact that you have failed.

Many of the popular conceptions of what is required to make
nonviolent action succeed are also not valid. Such misconceptions
include the belief that success requires democratic, or even nonviolent, opponents. Some people have argued that success requires world support, the aid of the media, a much longer time
span to succeed than does violence, or a "climate of nonviolence." All of these views are inaccurate.

The opinion has been expressed that if a group is using nonviolent action, the opponents should be expected to respond nonviolently also. If the response is instead violent repression there is
something wrong, it is thought. This view is also incorrect. The
opponent group or regime often depends on violence to maintain
itself and its practices. When the opponents are challenged nonviolently, subsequent violent repression is usually a sign that the
nonviolent movement is threatening the status quo. Nonviolent
action is a technique for combating violent opponents.

Conditions for struggle

Elements of the situation that may be helpful to the application of nonviolent struggle should not be confused with elements that are required, without which the struggle will surely fail. There are favorable and unfavorable internal and external conditions for the practice of nonviolent struggle. However, favorable conditions are not absolute requirements. Some nonviolent struggles have succeeded in very poor circumstances because the struggle group compensated for specific unfavorable conditions by developing their strengths and their skills in how to act under such conditions.

Nevertheless, there is no substitute for genuine strength in nonviolent struggle. If the participants in a nonviolent struggle do not as yet possess sufficient strength, determination, and ability to act skillfully against their opponents, then the simple verbal acceptance of nonviolent struggle will not save them. Deliberate efforts are required to develop that strength, skill, and capacity to act wisely.

If these characteristics are beyond the immediate reach of the potential nonviolent struggle group, then the group should not yet move beyond limited, low-risk campaigns for relatively easy, short-term objectives. Most of its attention should be dedicated to building up its own capacities internally. Only when the group is strong, determined, and skilled should it attempt strategic escalation in the struggle for its long-term objectives.

Factors influencing the outcome

There are many factors that determine the outcome of a nonviolent struggle.[1] Some of these factors lie within the "social situation," some relate to the opponent group, some to third parties, and many others to the nonviolent struggle group. The nonviolent struggle group can influence many, but not all, of these factors.

(1) **Factors in the social situation.** These include the degree of conflict of interest between the two groups, the social distance between them, the degree to which beliefs and norms are shared

---

[1] These factors are taken from Gene Sharp, *The Politics of Nonviolent Action*, pp. 815-817.

by the two groups, and the degree to which the population that is resisting includes significant social groups and institutions.

(2) **Factors associated with the opponent group or regime.** These include the degree to which the opponents are dependent for their sources of power on those who are noncooperating, and the degree of noncompliance that the opponents can tolerate. These factors also include the degree to which the opponents and their supporters are convinced of their views and policies and of the rightness and justification of repression or other sanctions against the nonviolent resisters.

Other factors in this group include the means of control and repression that the opponents may use; the degree to which the agents of repression obey the leadership of the opponent group; the degree of solidarity within the opponent group; the degree of loyalty within its bureaucracy and its police and military forces; the degree to which the opponents' general population supports their group's policy and repression; and the opponents' estimate of the future course of the struggle movement and its consequences.

(3) **Factors associated with third parties.** These include the degree to which third parties become sympathetic to either the opponents or to the nonviolent struggle group, and the degree to which the opinions and good will of third parties are important to both groups. These factors also include the degree to which third parties move to active support for, or noncooperation with, either of the contending groups.

(4) **Factors associated with the nonviolent struggle group.** This category includes the most important group of relevant factors, as they are the ones over which the nonviolent struggle group can exert the most influence. They include the ability to organize or to act spontaneously in accordance with the requirements of nonviolent struggle; the degree to which the resisters and the grievance group are convinced of the rightness of their cause; and the degree of confidence in nonviolent struggle among these groups. Also important are the types of nonviolent methods selected for use by the nonviolent struggle group and whether or not that group is capable of applying these methods; the soundness of the strategy and the tactics chosen or accepted by the nonviolent struggle group; and whether or not the demands made

by the nonviolent struggle group on its own members are within the capacity of these people to meet.

Additionally, the relative ability of the resisters to practice the nonviolent technique is important, as is the degree to which that group can act with discipline to implement plans. The number of participants in the actions will be important for some cases, such as those relying heavily on the use of noncooperation, provided that the numbers are compatible with maintaining both the needed quality of the activities and the requirements for use of the selected mechanism of change.

Whether the general grievance group supports the nonviolent struggle group or hinders its actions will be very important. The severity of repression, and possibly terror, imposed by the opponent group can be important as it balances with the ability of the members of the struggle group to persist in resistance. How long the resisters are able and willing to continue the struggle, their ability to keep the struggle nonviolent, and, in normal circumstances, the ability of the resisters to maintain nonsecretiveness in their actions can also be important.

The presence of effective leadership, or the ability of the group to act with discipline in accordance with a wise strategy without a significant distinguishable leadership group, is an additional factor. So also is the extent to which the resisters can arouse sympathy and support among members of the opponent group. Finally, the degree to which the nonviolent struggle group controls its own sources of power is important.

Increasing the chances of success

Except for some of the factors in the social situation, most of the factors operating in the conflict are subject to change, often considerable change, during the course of the nonviolent struggle. Such changes will result in increased or decreased power for the opponent group and also for the nonviolent struggle group. If these shifts increase the power of the opponent group significantly while the power of the nonviolent struggle group diminishes, it is very likely that the opponents will win. However, if the power of the opponents instead is undermined by restricting their sources of power while the power of the nonviolent struggle group grows, the chances of the nonviolent struggle group being successful are greatly increased.

These changes may be directly or indirectly influenced by actions of the nonviolent struggle group. This is why great care needs to be exercised in planning and conducting these actions. Skill, strength, discipline, wise strategy, numbers, and persistence are among the essential qualities.

Of the factors listed above that are potentially under the control of the nonviolent struggle group, five stand out as especially important: (1) a willingness to act; (2) the strength of the struggle group (including persistence, numbers, and organization); (3) knowledge of nonviolent struggle; (4) adoption of wise strategic plans; and (5) skillful, disciplined implementation of the adopted strategic plans.

A population that wishes to increase its ability to gain important objectives will do well to make strong efforts to increase its capacities in these five areas. However, if only the first three are present, without wise strategic plans, the chances of success are not great. Even with willingness to act by a strong group, the action is unlikely to make much impact without knowledge of what to do and how to do it.

However, knowledge of nonviolent struggle, without the ability to determine how to apply it effectively, is not sufficient either. The development and the application of wise strategies to increase effectiveness in the use of this technique are extremely important.

Failure to plan for success

Some attempts to apply nonviolent struggle have been much more successful than others. As we have seen, various factors contribute to determining whether a specific attempt will succeed or fail.

Success should not be left to chance. Resisters can take deliberate steps to increase the likelihood of achieving their objectives. One of the most important factors in that effort is the use of available resources and actions in ways that increase their effectiveness in the conflict. This requires strategic planning.

Unfortunately, such planning in nonviolent struggles has seldom been given the attention it deserves. Only rarely do people facing the prospect of such conflicts fully recognize the extreme importance of preparing a comprehensive plan before they act.

Some people naïvely think that if they simply assert their goal strongly and firmly, for a long enough period, they will somehow achieve their goal. Others assume that if they remain true to their principles and ideals, and witness to them in the face of adversity, then they are doing all they can to achieve their objectives. Some believe that if they act courageously and sacrificially, there is nothing more that they need to do. Still others simply repeat the type of action they have used in the past, or which they believe is required by their political doctrine, and have faith that they will eventually succeed.

Assertion of desirable goals, remaining loyal to ideals, and persistence are all admirable, but are in themselves grossly inadequate to achieve significant goals. Mere repetition of actions that have failed in the past often makes success unachievable. The technique of nonviolent action has special characteristics, and there are important factors that contribute to its effectiveness, as we discussed earlier.

People in conflict situations often allow themselves to be distracted from their main goal by focusing on trivial issues, repeatedly responding to the opponents' initiatives, and aiming only at short-term activities. Sometimes, too, people do not even attempt to develop a plan to achieve their goal, because deep down they do not really believe that they can succeed. These people—despite the impression they may offer—see themselves as weak, as helpless victims of overpowering forces. Therefore, they believe, the best they can do is to assert and witness, or even just die, in the faith that they are right. Consequently, they do not even attempt to think and to plan strategically about how to accomplish their objective.

This creates a self-fulfilling prophecy. If you do not believe you will succeed, and therefore do not take deliberate steps to increase your chances of doing so, you usually will fail.

Consequences of a lack of planning

In the past, most nonviolent struggles were improvised without advance planning. Some of these conflicts escalated in their scope and impact far beyond anyone's original estimate, leaving the participants unprepared for what was to follow. Such was the case in the Russian Revolution of 1905 and in the Chinese pro-democracy struggle in 1989, for example. In many other past conflicts the groups involved recognized that they needed to plan how to act, but they did so only on a very limited, short-term, or tactical basis. In most cases, these groups did not attempt to formulate a broader, longer-term, or strategic plan of action.

While spontaneity and improvisation have some positive qualities, they also have serious disadvantages. For example, if resisters make gains, they will often not know what they should do next. If resisters in certain conflicts do not adequately anticipate the brutality of their opponents, they may suffer grave setbacks leading to the collapse of their movement. When crucial decisions are left to chance due to a lack of adequate planning, consequences can be equally disastrous.

The result of such failures to plan is that the chances of success in the conflict are drastically reduced, and at times eliminated. Without the formulation of a careful strategic plan of action

- One's energy may be deflected to minor issues and applied ineffectively.

- Methods of action may be attempted that are beyond the capacity of the resisters to apply effectively.

- Strengths of the nonviolent group may remain unutilized.

- The opponents' initiatives will determine the course of events.

- Uncertainty about what to do can spread confusion among the resisters.

- The weaknesses of one's own side will grow and lead to demoralization, and have detrimental effects on the attempt to achieve the goal.

In short, the group's strengths are dissipated or their impact is minimized. Sacrifices are wasted and one's cause is not well served.

Hodgepodge activities do not move the struggle forward, but instead result in scattered and unfocused actions or, worse, in the weakening of the movement. In contrast, directed action in accordance with a plan enables one to concentrate one's strengths to move in a determined direction toward the desired goal.

Long-term planning is also important for another reason. Even after the initial goal of a movement has been achieved, such as in the overthrow of a dictatorship or an otherwise oppressive regime, lack of planning on how to handle the transition to a better system can contribute to the emergence of new oppression.

Strategic planning

The short-term, or tactical, planning that has occurred in some past conflicts in which nonviolent methods have been used has often been useful and has contributed to the accomplishments of these struggles. However, longer-term strategic planning of the overall conflict has distinct additional advantages, enabling the nonviolent struggle group to calculate the most effective ways to bring down oppression, to assess when the political situation and popular mood are ripe for action, and to choose how to start the nonviolent campaign and how to develop it as it proceeds, while contending with the opponents' repression and other countermeasures.

Strategic planning also enables the nonviolent struggle group to become stronger because it knows where it intends to go and because it is aware of possible problems, events, and reactions that the resisters will likely encounter.

The more important the goal, or the graver the consequences of failure, the more important planning becomes. Strategic planning increases the possibility that available resources will be employed most effectively. This is especially important for a movement that has a noble objective but limited material resources and in which its supporters will face danger during the conflict. In contrast, one's opponents usually will have access to major material resources, organizational strength, and the ability to perpetrate brutalities.

The use of strategy is best known in military conflict. For centuries, military officers have engaged in strategic planning for military campaigns. Important thinkers such as Sun Tzu, Carl von Clausewitz, and Sir Basil Liddell Hart have analyzed and refined conventional military strategy. Mao Zedong and Ernesto "Che" Guevara, among others, have attempted to do the same for guerrilla warfare. In both conventional military warfare and in guerrilla warfare, the use of sophisticated strategy is a basic requirement for success.

Just as effective military struggle requires wise strategies, planning, and implementation, nonviolent action will be most effective when it also operates on the basis of sound strategic planning. However, the formulation and the application of strategy in large-scale nonviolent struggles are more complex than in military conflicts. This is because the factors contributing to success and failure in nonviolent struggles are more numerous than in military struggles. In major nonviolent struggles, potentially the whole population and many institutions of the society, not simply the military forces, become combatants. To make the efforts of all these people and institutions most effective requires competent strategies.

The absolute and relative strengths of the opponents and the nonviolent struggle group can vary widely and change quickly during the course of the conflict. The actions and the behavior of the nonviolent struggle group may have unexpected effects far beyond the particular time and place in which they occur. These changes in the strengths of the contending groups can be more extreme in nonviolent struggles than in violent conflicts. Therefore, great care must be taken in the choice of even limited actions and in the resisters' behavior during the conflict.

Levels of strategy

In developing a strategic plan, one needs to understand that there are four levels of strategy.[2] Grand strategy and strategy were very briefly introduced earlier. However, it is necessary to explore them in more depth here. At the most fundamental level is *grand strategy*. Then there is *strategy* itself, followed by *tactics* and *methods*.

Grand strategy can be called the master concept for the conduct of the conflict. It is the broadest conception that serves to coordinate and direct all the resources of the struggle group toward the attainment of the objectives of the conflict.

---

2 These definitions were drafted by Robert Helvey, Bruce Jenkins, and Gene Sharp. Unpublished memorandum, Albert Einstein Institution.

Strategy is very similar, but applies to more limited phases of the overall struggle, such as campaigns for specific objectives. Strategy includes the development of an advantageous situation, the decision of when to fight, and the broad schema for utilizing smaller engagements within the adopted strategy.

Tactics refers to plans for conducting still more limited engagements within the selected strategy—limited in scale, number of participants, time, or particular issue. Tactics refer to how a group will apply its chosen methods and act in a specific encounter with the opponents.

Methods in nonviolent action are the many individual forms of action, such as picketing, social boycotts, consumers' boycotts, general strikes, civil disobedience, sit-ins, and parallel government, which were surveyed in Chapter Four. Among the factors to be considered in the selection of the methods are the mechanism by which change is sought (conversion, accommodation, nonviolent coercion, or disintegration), the degree of control by the resisters of the opponents' sources of power, and the status, strengths, weaknesses, and sources of power of the resisters.

If any of the four levels of strategy is inadequately conceived or developed, or even absent, the overall nonviolent struggle will be seriously weakened. Without knowledge of the broad picture, one may neglect to prepare, or be unable to take, effective steps to achieve the objectives.

The choice of the grand strategy, the implementing strategies, the tactics, and the methods to be used should determine the general direction and the conduct of the conflict throughout its course. These four levels of strategy will be discussed much more fully in the following chapter.

In implementing a strategy, careful support activities are needed. These will require planning and preparations. Such activities are tasks for logistical work. *Logistics* include a range of detailed supportive activities for the conduct of a conflict, such as the arrangement of finances, transportation, communications, and supplies.

Gains from wise strategies

The formulation and the implementation of wise strategies to guide the resisters' actions makes it possible to concentrate their strengths and actions toward the desired goal, aggravate the opponents' weaknesses, strengthen the resisters, reduce casualties and other costs, and help the sacrifices to serve the main goal.

In order to increase the chances for success, nonviolent struggle strategists will need not only to formulate a grand strategy and strategies for individual campaigns, but also to develop a comprehensive strategic plan of action to apply the strategies in concrete terms. The strategic plan will need to be capable of strengthening the population, weakening and then destroying the oppression, and building an improved society. To develop such a plan of action requires a careful assessment of the situation and of the options for effective action.

The strategic plan lays out in broad strokes the anticipated concrete steps that the resisters will need to take to implement the grand strategy and the individual strategies in order to achieve their chosen objectives. It is the operational guide for action. The plan identifies the tasks that need to be carried out on the four levels of strategy and who is to be responsible for conducting them. Factors in the preparation and selection of a grand strategy, strategies, tactics, and choice of methods will be discussed at length in Chapters Thirty-six and Thirty-seven.

The importance of strategic planning cannot be overemphasized. It is the key to making social and political movements utilizing nonviolent struggle more effective.

Chapter Thirty-six

FIRST STEPS IN
STRATEGIC PLANNING

An important but difficult task

The development of sound strategies is one of the most important requirements of an effective campaign. When the grand
strategy, strategies, tactics, and methods have been selected in advance, these should shape the general direction and conduct of
the conflict throughout its course.

A good strategy will aim at achieving the objectives of the
overall struggle, as well as of individual campaigns, through effective mobilization of the strengths of the populace against the opponents. In most major conflicts, wise strategies will also need to
include ways to undermine the opponents' sources of power.

The overall strategic conception—for both the grand strategy
and the strategies for individual campaigns—will make the objec-
tive(s) clear, sketch how the struggle will begin, determine what
kinds of pressures and methods are to be applied to gain the long-
term objectives, and direct the actions aimed to achieve possible
intermediate objectives. The strategies for individual campaigns

should also guide how the struggle can expand and advance despite repression, mobilizing and applying the resisters' resources in effective ways.

"To plan a strategy" means to calculate a course of action that is intended to make it more likely to get from the present to a desired future situation. A plan to achieve that objective will usually consist of a phased series of campaigns and other organized activities designed to strengthen the aggrieved population and society and to weaken the opponents.

Strategists should avoid both overly ambitious plans and excessively timid ones. Wise strategic development will help to ensure the effective interaction of tactics and specific methods to implement the strategy and improve the chances of victory. Clear strategic insight is required if changes from one phase of the conflict to another, and one method to another, are to take place with good purpose and effect. The strategies will also project the intended way in which the struggle will become successful and how the struggle will be concluded.

The development of strategic plans for the conduct of a major struggle is a difficult and complex task. This chapter and the two that follow are intended only to introduce a basic understanding of that task, and to provide limited guidance to those who recognize the need for responsible preparations.

We shall now focus on two important early components of strategic planning. The first is the preparation of a strategic estimate to reveal in greater depth what is the situation within which the conflict is to be waged. The second is to examine the levels of strategy as they may be with advantage developed in the conflict.

PREPARING A STRATEGIC ESTIMATE[1]

Strategy can be developed only in the context of a particular conflict and its background and circumstances. Therefore, all strategic planning requires that the strategists have a profound understanding of the entire conflict situation. This requires attention to the broad context of the conflict, including physical, geographic, climatic, historical, governmental, military, cultural,

---

1 This section draws very heavily on the thinking and analysis of Robert Helvey.

social, political, psychological, economic, and international factors. The identification and analysis of such factors prior to developing strategy is known as a "strategic estimate."[2]

At its most basic level, a strategic estimate is a calculation and comparison of the strengths and the weaknesses of the nonviolent struggle group and that group's opponents, as seen within the broad social, historical, political, and economic context of the society in which the conflict occurs. The strategic estimate should, at a minimum, include attention to the following subject areas: the general conflict situation, the issues at stake, the objectives of both parties to the conflict, the opponent group, the nonviolent struggle group, third parties to the conflict, and dependency balances between the contending groups.

Examining the issues and objectives

Of primary importance, strategic planners will need to examine the issues at stake from the perspectives of both the potential resisters and the opponents. What are the broad issues as seen by each side, and how important are they to the impending conflict?

Not all issues are equal. Some may be seen by one or both sides to be fundamental. Other issues may be viewed as of lesser importance. It is important to determine whether or not the issues are seen by either side to be ones of "no compromise," that is, issues—rightly or wrongly—believed to be fundamental to a group's adherents. Such issues often include strongly held beliefs about the nature of their society, their religion, their basic political convictions, or what they see as the requirements for their people to survive.

The nature of the issues at stake and their perceived importance to each side will have a fundamental impact on the development of strategies for the impending resistance. Therefore, strategists will need to develop clear and accurate statements of the issues at stake in the conflict from the perspectives of both the opponent group and the prospective nonviolent struggle group.

It is important to recognize the distinction between the broad issues of the conflict and the specific objectives of an individual campaign. Issues are more general. For example, in a labor con-

---

[2] See Appendix A for a plan for calculating a strategic estimate.

flict the issues might be seen as wages, working conditions, and respect. However, in a particular strike, the objectives would be more specific, such as a demand for a certain wage increase, implementation of certain safety measures, a demand for medical insurance, or proposals for job security.

Both parties to a conflict may have not only immediate objectives, but also long-term ones that may not be avowed at the time. Strategic planners should accurately assess what each side's objectives are, and to what degree the competing objectives may be compatible or incompatible.

The general conflict situation

Every strategic estimate needs to include a detailed survey of the general conflict situation in which the nonviolent struggle will be conducted. All factors that could have a conceivable impact either on the opponent group or on the nonviolent struggle group should be carefully examined. These include terrain and geography; transportation infrastructure; communications networks; climate and weather; the political, judicial, and economic systems in the country or region where the conflict occurs; population demographics; and types and degrees of social and economic stratification. These also, very importantly, include availability and control of economic and life-support resources; and the status of independent civil society.

It is also important to examine the immediate general political situation in which the struggle must operate. Are special controls, such as martial law or other means of serious repression, in effect? What are the current political and economic trends?

Condition and capabilities of the contending parties

Full and detailed knowledge about all parties to the pending conflict is extremely important. Such knowledge should focus on real capabilities, rather than on each group's statements of intent or simple assumptions about their respective conditions. The strategic estimate is an internal planning document, not a propaganda tool. Inaccurate or exaggerated views of the strengths, weaknesses, and capacities of the contending parties will produce unwise strategies and might even result in defeat.

It is very important to study the demographics of each side's adherents and sympathizers. This examination should include age, gender, literacy rates and educational standards, population growth rates, geographic distribution, socioeconomic class, and other such factors. Are there geographic, cultural, ethnic, or economic boundaries separating the two sides?

Similarly, it is important to know something about the political, social, cultural, and economic "systems" in which each side operates. What are the supports of these systems, and to what degree are they independent of, or dependent on, the other side? Are the supports of these systems independent of the State structure? Is the State structure itself controlled or utilized by the opponents, or are both sides independent of the State?

Attention must also be paid to identifying the opponents' sources of power, and the institutions that serve as "pillars of support"[3] for the opponents by providing these sources of power. Pillars of support are the institutions and sectors of society that supply a regime (or any other group that exercises power) with the needed sources of power to maintain and expand its power capacity. Examples include moral and religious leaders supplying authority or legitimacy; labor, business, and investment groups supplying economic and material resources; civil servants, administrators, bureaucrats, and technicians providing human resources and special skills; and police, prisons, and military forces providing the ability to apply sanctions (including repression) against the population.

A similar review is required of the nonviolent struggle group and the broader "grievance group" (defined as the wider population that suffers from policies and actions of the opponent group and on whose behalf the conflict may be waged). What are the sources of power of those groups, and the institutions that serve as their "pillars of support"?

Part of the process of strategic planning will be to determine, on the basis of this information, how best to strengthen (or create) the pillars of support for the nonviolent struggle group while undermining those of the opponents.

It is also necessary to assess the relative "struggle power" of each side, and to compare them. For the opponents, this means it

---

[3] The term "pillars of support" was introduced by Robert Helvey.

will be important to know the extent and reliability of their administration, military capacity, police and intelligence forces, as well as the degree of support they have from their own population and institutions. Also essential is the identification of weaknesses and vulnerabilities within the opponent group. How unified is the group? Are there power struggles or rivalries among the leadership? Are there any organizations or institutions that normally support the opponent group but might be targeted for transfer of loyalties or for organizational destruction?

For the resisters, it is important to know their capacity to wage nonviolent struggle. This includes their knowledge of this technique, their experience with this type of action, and the adequacy and nature of their preparations. What is the present and the potential degree of support the resisters receive from the general grievance group? What support do the potential resisters receive from other groups, institutions, and contact networks within the population? Which of these can really help? Are there significant internal conflicts, such as rivalries, power struggles, or ideological disputes, within or between sectors of either the general grievance group or the nonviolent struggle group?

Other questions are also important. How much support do the opponents receive from internal and external allies? How well do the prospective opponents understand nonviolent struggle? Is there actual or potential sympathy and support for the opponents within the general resisting population? What are the roles of social, class, racial, and religious factors?

What is the resistance group's access to information? Who are their internal and external allies? To what extent do they enjoy internal social solidarity and support? What are their economic resources? What is the depth of their strategic skill? What is the degree of competency of the group's strategists and leaders? Is strategic competence concentrated in a leadership group, or is such expertise instead diffused among the general population of potential resisters? (The latter would be very rare.) Are there threats to the organizational strength of the resisters?

Third parties

It will also be important to assess what may be the roles of third parties on behalf of each of the sides during a conflict.

These potential roles may include assisting with public relations, providing diplomatic assistance or pressure, providing financial support, applying economic pressures, and providing educational and technical assistance to either side. Third parties may also supply police and military assistance (usually not to the nonviolent struggle group), provide safe areas, and help disseminate knowledge of nonviolent struggle. It will be very useful for the resistance strategists to have accurate information and reasonable projections about who the potential third parties are and what their possible activities might be during the course of the coming conflict.

Dependency balances

A proper strategic estimate should also examine the "dependency balances" that exist between the contending parties. To what degree does or can the opponent group control the economic resources and life-support resources—fuel, water, food, etc.—of the potential resistance group? Similarly, to what degree does or can the nonviolent struggle group control the economic resources and life-support resources of the opponent group? This will reveal the degree of actual or potential dependence of each group on the other group for meeting identified needs. This can be very important in nonviolent struggles, and also can often help determine which methods might be most effective when planning the struggle.

When to launch a struggle

The specific factors presented above are only a sampling of the kinds of factors that will need to be identified in a strategic estimate prior to planning strategy. Once completed, the strategic estimate of the conflict situation and of the capacities of the contending parties serves as the background for the formulation of a grand strategy for the nonviolent struggle group and for the formulation of specific strategies for individual campaigns.

If the strategic estimate reveals that the nonviolent struggle group is weaker than required for a major struggle with the prospective opponents, then the group should not at that time launch a struggle that requires great strength. There is no substitute for, or shortcut to, strength in a movement of nonviolent struggle. If the group is weaker than desired, either the action should initially take only limited forms that can be effective without great strength (which will be discussed later), or more ambitious action should be postponed until the group is stronger. Clearly, major efforts should be put into the strengthening of the population that is primarily affected by the grievances and into developing its capacity to wage effective struggle.

The strategic estimate is what makes this, as well as other decisions faced during the struggle, more clear. While extremely important, however, the strategic estimate is not the only issue to consider when planning strategy. Thorough and in-depth knowledge of this technique of nonviolent struggle is of prime importance. Other relevant factors also require attention throughout the planning process in order to make the nonviolent struggle as effective as possible. Many of these strategic guidelines will be addressed in Chapter Thirty-seven.

LEVELS OF STRATEGY

With the knowledge gleaned from the strategic estimate and the objectives of the nonviolent struggle group in mind, what is the broad conception of how the struggle is to be waged and how the objectives are to be achieved? Making this determination requires, among other things, identification of the intended mechanism of change in nonviolent struggle that is to be relied upon and determination of whether more than one campaign will be required. This is the domain of strategic thinking.

A strategy is the conception of how best to act in order to achieve objectives in a conflict. Strategy is concerned with whether, when, or how to fight, and how to achieve maximum effectiveness in order to gain certain ends. Strategy is the plan for the practical distribution, adaptation, and application of the available means to attain the desired objectives.

As was previously discussed, there are four levels of strategy: grand strategy, strategy, tactics, and specific methods.[4] The most

---

4 These definitions were drafted by Robert Helvey, Bruce Jenkins, and Gene Sharp. Unpublished memorandum, Albert Einstein Institution.

fundamental is grand strategy. Then there is strategy itself for more limited campaigns, followed by tactics and methods that are used to implement the campaign strategies. An understanding of these four elements, and the differences between them, is essential if one is to attempt to develop strategies for a specific conflict.

It should be remembered, of course, that there is no single strategy applicable to the use of nonviolent struggle on all occasions. No single blueprint exists or can be developed to serve all conflicts. Each situation is somewhat different, often radically so. However, general guidelines can be developed for planning strategies, keeping in mind the factors we discussed previously. Planners of a grand strategy for a specific conflict will require a profound understanding, not only of the conflict situation, but also of the technique of nonviolent struggle, and of general strategic principles. Some of these will be discussed in Chapter Thirty-seven.

Grand strategy

Grand strategy is the master concept for the conduct of the conflict. A grand strategy is the conception that serves to coordinate and direct all appropriate and available resources (economic, human, moral, etc.) of the population or group to attain its objectives in a conflict. It is an overall plan for conducting the struggle that makes it possible to anticipate how the struggle as a whole should proceed. How can the struggle be won? How is the desired change to be achieved?

Grand strategy includes consideration of the rightness of the cause of the struggle group, evaluation and utilization of other pressures and influences apart from the technique of struggle, and the decision on the conditions under which resort to open struggle will be had.

Grand strategy very importantly includes the selection of the technique of conflict, or the ultimate sanction, which will be used as reserve leverage in actual or implied threats during negotiations, and later used in an open confrontation of forces if that occurs. In this case, the technique is nonviolent struggle. The selected grand strategy also sets the basic framework for the development of strategies for waging the conflict in more limited campaigns directed toward particular objectives.

Additionally, nonviolent struggle can sometimes be combined in a grand strategy with the use of other means of action that are not violent, and therefore do not threaten the operation of the technique. Fact-finding, publicity, public education, appeals to the opponents, and sometimes negotiations, as well as electoral campaigns in some cases, could in many situations be beneficially used in connection with nonviolent struggle. These means are often used in tandem with economic boycotts and labor strikes, for example. Lawsuits or other legal action have at times also been used to support nonviolent action, as in the case of the Montgomery, Alabama, bus boycott.

Grand strategy also includes consideration of how the struggle itself relates to the achievement of the objectives for which the conflict is waged. The projection of the likely long-term consequences of the conflict also falls within grand strategy.

A grand strategy for a nonviolent struggle should preferably include not only bringing an end to that which is rejected, but also the establishment of something new to replace it. For example, a grand strategy that limits its objective to merely destroying an incumbent dictatorship runs a great risk of producing another dictatorship. A better purpose might be to change the system of domination and to institute a superior political system of greater freedom and democratic controls.

The grand strategy needs to sketch in broad strokes how the nonviolent struggle group should conduct the conflict. This would broadly stretch from the present to a future situation in which its objectives have been achieved. Which general means of pressure and action might be applied in that effort? What is to be the main thrust of the nonviolent struggle against the opponents? Is the pressure to be applied through economic losses? By undermining the opponents' legitimacy? Through political paralysis? What about international pressures? Will other pressures be utilized?

Very importantly, is the nonviolent struggle group able to weaken or remove most or all of the sources of power of the opponent group? These sources include authority (or legitimacy), human resources, skills and knowledge, intangible factors, material resources, and sanctions. Weakening or severing these sources of power by attacking their pillars of support is crucial in struggles against highly repressive regimes, and can cause the power of these regimes to crumble.

If the resisters are strong enough, have sufficient numbers, and focus their noncooperation on these sources, even an extremely ruthless regime can potentially be weakened or disintegrated. The Serbian struggle in October 2000 is an example.

At the beginning of the conflict, however, efforts to fully neutralize or remove the opponents' sources of power are unlikely to be within the capacity of the struggle group. The results of the strategic estimate should help to determine whether the group is capable of applying the required pressures with sufficient force to succeed in a single campaign, or whether it should plan for a series of more limited campaigns. This calculation is a necessary part of the grand strategy, and is discussed more fully in Chapter Thirty-seven.

Strategy

Individual strategies for campaigns with more limited objectives are very important. Strategies for campaigns guide how particular conflicts are to be waged within the scope of the broader struggle and the grand strategy. These limited strategies sketch how specific campaigns shall develop, and how their separate components shall be fitted together so as best to achieve their objectives. Strategy also includes the allocation of tasks to particular groups and the distribution of resources to them for use in the conflict. Sound campaign strategies help guide the struggle by taking the skeletal framework of the chosen grand strategy and filling it out into a comprehensive conception to direct specific aspects of the struggle.

Although related, development of a grand strategy and formulation of campaign strategies are two separate processes. Only after the grand strategy has been determined can the specific campaign strategies be fully developed. Campaign strategies will need to be designed to achieve and reinforce the grand strategic objectives. Factors in the formulation of campaign strategies include the development of an advantageous situation, the decision of when to wage a campaign, and the broad schema for utilizing more limited engagements within the strategy to bring success.

Often, the targets of campaign strategies should reflect the broad issues or grievances outlined in the grand strategy. If the conflict is largely of an economic nature, and a grand strategy has been adopted that prescribes the predominant use of economic pressures, then the strategies for selective campaigns will most likely focus on specific economic targets and will apply pressures such as labor strikes and economic boycotts. If, however, the grand strategy is focused on gaining political freedom, opposing dictatorial rule, or upholding freedom of expression, then the strategies for individual campaigns may focus on specific expressions of those issues, employing relevant methods such as distribution of prohibited literature, exercise of banned free speech, or other methods that may dramatize the extreme nature of the autocratic rule or the violations of human rights and civil liberties.

This is not to say that only economic pressures can be used in struggles over economic issues, or that only political pressures should be applied in predominantly political struggles. Economic noncooperation can be effective in forcing political policy changes—and even regime change—in some cases. Nevertheless, it is often beneficial when planning campaign strategies to select specific issues and targets that are easily recognizable as representative of the broad grievance identified in the grand strategy.

Tactics

The strategy for a campaign for a limited objective will determine what smaller, "tactical," plans and specific methods of action should be used in pursuit of the main goal. A good strategy remains impotent unless it is put into action with sound tactics. However, skillful selection and implementation of tactics will not make up for a bad overall strategy. The choice of tactics to implement a strategy may involve consideration of different fronts, groups, time periods, and methods.

A tactic is a limited plan of action, based on a conception of how best in a restricted phase of a conflict to utilize the available means of fighting to achieve a limited objective as part of the wider campaign strategy. To be most effective, the tactics and methods must be chosen and applied so that they really assist the application of the strategy and contribute to achieving the requirements for its success.

Tactics prescribe how particular methods of action are applied, or how particular groups of resisters shall act in a specific situation. For example, in a labor struggle in which factory workers are striking for union recognition, increased wages, or improved working conditions, tactics include selection of the timing of the strike, of how workers are persuaded to participate in the strike, of what action is to be taken to discourage strike breakers, of how strikers can be supported economically while not working, of what efforts are to be made to encourage public sympathy and support, and of what contacts are to be made with the factory owners.

Tactics are thus the plans for conducting more limited engagements within the selected strategy—limited in scale, participants, time, or specific issue. They specify how a group will act in a specific encounter with the opponents.

A tactic fits within the campaign strategy, just as campaign strategies fit within the grand strategy. Tactics are always concerned with struggle, although strategy also includes wider considerations, in addition to how to fight. A particular tactic can only be understood in relationship to the methods it employs and as part of the broader strategy of a campaign.

Methods

In order to achieve the best results and the most effective implementation of the developed strategies, the choice of nonviolent "weapons," or specific methods, will need to be made carefully and wisely. Many past conflicts have started with the choice of the specific methods of action to be used, rather than development of long-term plans for conducting the conflict. This is not recommended. Instead, the wiser sequence is the development of the grand strategy first, then development of a strategy for an individual campaign. Only then can the planners select the tactics and specific methods of action that are most appropriate. Available methods were listed in Chapter Four.[5] There are others.

The characteristics of the three general classes of methods need to be reviewed.

- **Protest and persuasion:** These methods include vigils, parades, petitions, picketing, and walk-outs. They are largely symbolic in their effect and produce an awareness of the existence of dissent.

- **Noncooperation:** These methods include social boycotts, economic boycotts, labor strikes, and many forms of political noncooperation, including boycotts of government positions, civil disobedience, and mutiny. The methods of noncooperation, widely applied, are likely to cause difficulties in maintaining the normal operation and efficiency of the opponents' political or economic system. In extreme situations, these methods may threaten the existence of a regime.

- **Intervention:** These methods include hunger strikes, sit-ins, nonviolent obstruction, creation or strengthening of alternative institutions, and parallel government. They possess some of the qualities of both previous groups, but may additionally constitute a more direct challenge to the opponents' regime. By disruption of various types, they make possible—but do not guarantee—a greater impact with smaller numbers, provided that courage and discipline are maintained despite repression.

In most serious conflicts, the methods of noncooperation are especially important because they may threaten the capacity of the system to operate. They will require skill in their selection and their application. The advantage of these methods of noncooperation is that, adequately applied for sufficient time, they can be coercive and can even disintegrate the opponents' regime.

The methods of noncooperation often require much time and the participation of many people to achieve their impact. Many of the methods of nonviolent intervention, on the other hand, can be applied by small numbers of people. However, these methods usually require considerable discipline or preparation in order to

---

[5] For full definitions of the methods with historical examples, see Sharp, *The Politics of Nonviolent Action*, Part Two, *The Methods of Nonviolent Action*. There are, of course, many additional methods that exist or can be developed.

be successfully applied, and some can be applied only for limited periods of time. Some of these methods of nonviolent intervention may also be met with especially severe repression. Some methods of nonviolent intervention, such as parallel government, require massive support.

Frequently, methods that apply differing pressures and use different mechanisms may be combined effectively within the same campaign. Fast rules are not possible, but effective combinations of methods require wise strategic planning.

In most struggles, more than one method will be used. In such cases, the order in which the methods are applied, the ways in which they are combined, how they influence the application of other methods, and how they contribute to the struggle as a whole all become very important.

· Sometimes, the combination of methods is relatively simple, especially in a local or limited type of action. Economic boycotts have been used, for example, in support of sit-ins against racial discrimination, and picketing is commonly used in support of strikes. When a general strike is used to support or oppose the mutiny of government troops, however, the situation becomes more complicated, with larger numbers of methods likely to be used.

Whoever plans the nonviolent struggle should be familiar with the full range of nonviolent methods of action available for possible application. The impact of the various methods differs considerably, even assuming that they are competently applied. For example, a protest fast by a highly respected person will have a very different effect than would bureaucratic obstruction by civil servants. The effect of a fast or bureaucratic obstruction, in turn, would differ significantly from a widespread general strike or refusal by police to locate and arrest political resisters. Different methods need to be chosen for different situations, objectives, and strategies.

Choosing methods

Each individual strategy requires a careful selection of the specific methods of nonviolent struggle to be used, followed by their skilled application. The most important specific methods to be used need to have a clear relationship to the objectives of the

462   SHAPING THE FUTURE

campaign or the struggle as a whole, and should contribute instrumentally to achieving those objectives.

The number of methods applied in any single conflict will vary from only one to dozens. The chosen methods need to be matched to the issues at stake, the intended mechanism of change, the capabilities of the population that is to apply them, and the selected campaign strategy. Other factors that need to be considered in choosing specific methods include the situation, the objectives of both the nonviolent struggle group and the opponents, characteristics of the resistance group and the opponents, the expected repression, and the anticipated development of the struggle.

Here some questions should be asked. Very importantly, do the methods being considered contribute to implementing the selected grand strategy and the individual campaign strategy? Do the methods in question apply the kind of pressures against the opponents that have been identified as necessary if the struggle is to be successful? For example, if the strategy identifies economic pressures as the most important, then economic methods such as labor strikes and economic boycotts will likely be required. If, instead, the strategic objective is to undermine the ability of the opponents to rule, then particular methods of political noncooperation are likely to be needed to weaken or sever the supply of the regime's sources of power by attacking its pillars of support.

If the methods being considered do not directly implement the campaign strategies and do not apply the identified needed pressures directly, do they at least facilitate the application of the methods that will apply those pressures, such as by increasing resistance morale or undermining the opponents' morale? For example, if a labor strike is the primary method being employed under the strategic plan, secondary methods such as picketing or an economic boycott may be used to support the strike.

The methods to be used also need to be chosen with consideration of whether they are likely to help produce the change through the chosen mechanism of nonviolent struggle: conversion, accommodation, nonviolent coercion, or disintegration, as we discussed in Chapters Thirty-two and Thirty-three. For example, an extended fast may affect people's feelings and may gain publicity. However, a general strike, a walk-out by civil servants, or an army mutiny may paralyze the regime, producing nonviolent coercion. The methods and the mechanisms need to be matched.

Another important factor in the choice of methods is the type of repression and other countermeasures that are expected. How much repression are the general population, the resisters, and the leaders prepared to suffer while continuing their resistance and defiance?

Also, the number of available resisters is very relevant in the choice of methods and mechanisms. It is obviously unwise to call a general strike if one has only 20 persons committed to participate. With a different method, however, such as a hunger strike, 20 people, depending on who they are, can call significant attention to the grievance and exert significant psychological or moral pressure that can lead to stronger action. Such a small action, however, needs to be conducted with extra high standards of behavior for the participants.

The effects particular methods will produce on the development of the movement are also important. Will they contribute to the progressive development of the struggle, to changed attitudes and altered power relationships, to shifts in the support for each side, and to the later application and impacts of stronger nonviolent methods?

In choosing the methods, one should remember that it may be easier to get people to refrain from doing something that has been ordered than to get them to do something that they do not usually do. This is especially true if the action is very risky or is prohibited.

During the struggle

Specific methods will need to be selected for initiating the conflict. These may be symbolic, or they may be more ambitious, such as the launching of a strike. At the very beginning of a campaign, nonviolent struggle strategists may deliberately use relatively weak methods in order to test, by the population's response, whether the population will be willing to attempt stronger methods and able to withstand more severe repression as the price of success.

Once the struggle is underway, it will be necessary to review the strategy previously selected for the conflict to determine if additional or different methods should also be scheduled for application. Is the use of only a small number of methods dangerous to the success of the struggle, or is such a restriction necessary to concentrate the pressures on the opponents? Can the resisters survive the opponents' pressures and repression as they concentrate their action against these selected few points? Is a shift of methods needed to maintain flexibility in the developing struggle?

More questions will also need to be answered. Will the methods help to gain or keep the initiative in the conflict? If the methods are intended to be applied more widely, are they in fact likely to spread? If the methods require special training or preparations—and hence are suited for select small groups—are such preparations available? If the methods are to be applied by masses of people, can their use be replicated widely without special training or preparations?

Moving from one level of action to another—as from symbolic protests to noncooperation, and from noncooperation to intervention—can involve a progressive increase in the degree of repression that is risked. In reverse, the choice of noncooperation instead of intervention may at times help to produce a relatively less explosive and dangerous conflict situation with relatively less severe repression. These relationships between the classes of methods and the severity of repression are not applicable in all situations and against all opponents, however. Quite mild methods may at times be met with brutal repression, especially if the opponents are a regime that cannot tolerate public expressions of dissent and opposition.

In a long struggle, phasing is often very important. The selection of objectives and the choice and sequence of methods may be the most important factors in that phasing. Often, certain milder actions must precede others, so that it may be possible later to use stronger methods. The decision of when to proceed to a new phase of the struggle must be carefully weighed. Such shifts of methods can help to avoid a static condition and to maintain the initiative.

The strategic plan

The strategic plan is the concrete blueprint for the implementation of a strategy. The plan should answer the questions of who, what, when, where, and how for the strategic components of each campaign.

In small or extremely limited struggles, this strategic plan might exist realistically only on the tactical level. For example, in a limited labor struggle where the grand objective and campaign objective are the same (a contract that includes improved benefits and wages), and with only one or two methods and one campaign involved (a conventional strike following the breakdown of contract negotiations), the strategic plan will lay out the details of when the strike is to begin, who is to participate and what their roles will be, where the picket lines will be, and what logistics will be necessary for provision of food, money, and other material necessities to the families of the striking workers. In such a case, the preparation of the strategic plan will not necessarily be a separate step from the planning involved in selecting tactics and methods for the implementation of the campaign strategy.

In a broader and more complex struggle, however, the strategic plan may exist on multiple levels. In rare struggles in which it is possible to plan concretely for multiple campaigns to operate simultaneously or in short sequence, the strategic plan should specify the order of those campaigns and the timing when each is to begin, based on the strategic relationship between them. It will also identify any subdivisions within the campaigns themselves.

For example, in a broad labor struggle directed against a particular company or industry in which the labor group possesses uncommon strength and popular sympathy, the struggle might include, in addition to strike action, a campaign to boycott all products produced by that company or industry. The campaign strategy may then identify a need to promote and enforce the boycott through varied actions ranging from primary and secondary boycotts and picket lines in front of stores to solidarity demonstrations and blockage of foreign exports of the product. The strategic plan with implementing tactics and methods fills in the blanks, identifying which stores to picket, where and when to arrange demonstrations, what types of publicity to seek for promotion of the primary and secondary boycotts, and what groups to target for support in preventing exports of the product.

While method selection is involved here, some of these specific tasks may exist above the level of tactical planning, which—though part of the strategic plan—refers specifically to the concrete logistical and operational planning of each individual action within the campaign.

In short, the strategic plan is the overall operational guide for action. It is the plan for concrete application and implementation of the strategy. On a broad level, strategic plans normally include four phases:

- Preparation for the conflict
- Initiation of action to gain the objective(s)
- Development of the ongoing struggle
- After success, consolidation of the gains

Within each phase, the strategic plan should follow the campaign strategies to identify the specific tasks that need to be carried out on the various strategic levels, as well as the persons or groups who will be responsible for them. As previously mentioned, an important component of the strategic plan is the tactical plan, which should identify in detail the tasks required to implement successfully each individual action within a campaign.

Strategists should keep in mind that in complex struggles, including those against repressive regimes, prior to the initiation of conflict it is usually very difficult, and often impossible, to plan the concrete implementation of the grand strategy from the first campaign to the last. In these cases, the strategic plan should be as concrete and specific as possible for implementation of the strategy for the initial campaign, but will be necessarily vague for future campaigns. This is because the limited objectives of future campaigns, their strategies, timing, and tactical activities will be determined in large part by changes in the conflict situation that will occur during the first stage or stages of the struggle. Strategists will therefore need to keep a close eye on the progress of the struggle, and develop the concrete strategic plans for future campaigns accordingly, while the conflict is ongoing.

Further guidelines for responding and adapting to changes in the course of the conflict will be discussed in Chapter Thirty-seven. In the meantime, it is important to identify insights into strategic planning gained from past experience and analyses that can contribute to greater effectiveness in planning strategy for nonviolent struggle. This is the focus of the next chapter.

Chapter Thirty-seven

SOME STRATEGIC GUIDELINES

Careful attention required

Effective application of the technique of nonviolent struggle requires great care, much thought, skilled action, and strength. Careful attention is required to the elements discussed in this chapter about the development of wise strategies for effective future nonviolent struggles.

These guidelines and suggestions are based on an understanding of how nonviolent struggle works, on lessons from past applications of this technique, and on basic strategic principles.

Knowledge of nonviolent struggle

Perhaps the most important part of the understanding of nonviolent struggle is the analysis of the sources of political power, as we discussed in Chapter Two. In acute conflicts with repressive regimes, particular strategies can be developed to target, weaken and remove the sources of the opponents' power. This targeting can be a major factor in making nonviolent struggle effective against highly repressive regimes. This will be discussed more fully below.

The formulation of wise strategies and tactics for nonviolent struggles also requires a thorough understanding of the dynamics and mechanisms of nonviolent struggle, such as is presented in summary form in Chapters Twenty-nine to Thirty-four, and more fully in *The Politics of Nonviolent Action*.[1] This knowledge makes possible an understanding of several of the other elements in the effective practice of this technique, including the maintenance of nonviolent discipline.

Nonviolent struggle both requires, and tends to produce, a reduction of fear of the opponents and their violent repression. That control of fear, or its abandonment, is a key element in destroying the control by the opponents over the general population and potential resisters.

Another major characteristic of the operation of nonviolent struggle in many conflicts is that the power capacities of the two sides do not remain constant. The absolute and relative power of the resisting population and also of the opponents can vary widely during nonviolent struggles. As compared to variations of strength of the contenders in violent conflicts, these changes in the respective power of the opponents and resisters in nonviolent conflicts, when they occur, are likely to be more extreme, to take place more quickly, and to have more significant consequences.

This is because the wider strategies, tactics, specific methods, and behavior of the two groups are all likely to have effects far beyond the particular time and place in which they occur. Certain types of behavior—such as violence, destruction of property, or unwise provocative nonviolent acts—may have consequences that would not be expected or wanted. The number of resisters and the forms of their resistance can grow or shrink. At times, this happens slowly, but at other times it occurs rapidly and extremely. The opponents' power also may increase or decrease, again slowly or rapidly. The nonviolent group may by its actions and behavior help to control the increase or decrease in the power

---

[1] Gene Sharp, *The Politics of Nonviolent Action*, Boston, Massachusetts: Porter Sargent, 1973. Also issued in three volumes (paperback edition), *Power and Struggle*, *The Methods of Nonviolent Action*, and *The Dynamics of Nonviolent Action*.

of the opponent group, and this to a much greater degree than occurs in military conflicts.

In the preparation of strategies, it is necessary to be attentive to the selection of plans and actions that facilitate the operation of the dynamics and mechanisms of the technique. It is also necessary to remember the need to reject proposed actions that, if implemented, would disrupt the very factors that make this technique of struggle effective.

Self-reliance and third party[2] assistance

Essential to the planning of nonviolent struggle campaigns is a basic principle: plan your struggle so that the success of the conflict becomes possible by reliance on yourselves alone. This was Charles Stewart Parnell's message to Irish peasants during a rent strike of 1879-1880: "Rely on yourselves," and not on anyone else.[3]

Assuming that a strong nonviolent struggle is planned or already being waged, it is fine to seek limited and nonviolent assistance from others. However, calculations on how to win the struggle must be based only on capabilities and actions of one's own group. Then, if no one else helps, one still has a chance to succeed, assuming that the strategic planning has been sound and the resisters are strong. However, if the responsibility for success and failure has been given to others, when they do not come forward the struggle will fail. In any case, responsible external support is more likely to be forthcoming when a strong nonviolent struggle is being conducted by the aggrieved population, which is acting as though success or failure will be determined by its efforts alone.

Although it is dangerous to rely on support by third parties—for they have their own interests and objectives—their support can nevertheless be very useful at times. The motives for such external groups to assist may vary, sometimes relating to the resisters' objectives and to the choice of nonviolent struggle. At other

---

[2] Third parties are groups that are neither the nonviolent struggle group nor the opponent group. They may be parts of the overall society within which the conflict is occurring or may be groups from outside that society.
[3] Patrick Sarsfield O'Hegarty, *A History of Ireland Under the Union 1880-1922* (London: Methuen Press, 1952), pp. 490-491.

times, third parties may anticipate possible economic or political benefits after the nonviolent resisters have successfully ousted a repressive regime. (Of course, short-term economic benefits also may be a strong motive for third parties to side with the opponents and reject support for the resisters.)

The nonviolent resisters should cultivate third party assistance both in advance of the struggle and also while it is in progress. The kinds of help they may seek may include material resources, safe bases of operation, noninterference, and endorsement of the legitimacy of the objective and means used by the nonviolent resisters. Very supportive third parties may invoke economic sanctions and diplomatic pressures against the opponents, and even attempt to isolate the opponents internationally. However, the caution about depending on third party support remains valid. The resistance movement needs to be able to pursue the struggle effectively if this external assistance never develops or disappears.

A single struggle or several campaigns?

On the basis of the results of the strategic estimate, it is essential to determine whether or not the objective(s) of the conflict can be achieved as the result of a single all-out struggle. If the chances are high that a single struggle could succeed, then a sound strategy needs to be developed that may realistically achieve that objective.

This assessment of the potential for a single campaign to successfully achieve the objectives must be done carefully. It should include attention to both the characteristics and the requirements of nonviolent struggle, and also to an accurate strategic estimate of the capacities of the opponents and of the potential resisters, as we discussed in Chapter Thirty-six.

It must be recognized, however, that only rarely can the full objective(s) of a major conflict waged by nonviolent struggle against powerful opponents be achieved in a single effort.

The following is an incomplete list of the conditions that are likely to be prerequisites of a successful single struggle:

- The opponents have lost legitimacy on a wide scale—whether or not this loss has yet been openly expressed.

- The opponents are highly dependent, politically, economically, or in other ways, on a population that may wield noncooperation.

- The population already has, or is developing, groups and institutions that are outside the control of the opponent group.

- The groups and institutions that serve as "pillars of support" for the opponents, supplying their necessary sources of power, are unstable and lack full commitment to the opponent leadership.

- The current control over the general population by the opponents is less than fully effective.

- The general population—and especially the groups most likely to resist—have previously either had satisfactory experience in the use of nonviolent struggle or have received competent advice to develop resistance actions and an understanding of their roles.

- The issues on which attention is focused in the struggle have wide and deep support.

- A wise grand strategy has been developed for the struggle with supporting recommended specific resistance actions by particular population groups and institutions, including those that have served as pillars of support for the opponents.

- The opponents' bureaucracy and police and military forces include major portions whose loyalty and assistance to the opponents' leadership is uncertain at best.

In a large-scale conflict against a government or regime, efforts to remove the opponents' sources of power so that their regime collapses are unlikely to be within the capacity of the struggle group at the beginning of the conflict. However, if a single campaign is in fact attempted in order to achieve the objectives of a struggle, a contingency plan should be prepared in case such a campaign proves unsuccessful. If a single struggle is attempted and does not succeed, the opponents may not only survive institutionally but may also be relatively strengthened. The resisters will consequently have experienced a serious loss, in terms of both their morale and their resistance capacity.

It may, therefore, generally be wiser to prepare initially for a few campaigns with limited objectives. These will need to be ones that are compatible with the larger major objective and will help to make its accomplishment possible. This is not a case of being moderate in one's objectives, but instead an instance of concentrating one's strength on the opponents' weaknesses in order to gain objectives that are within the capacity of the resisters to achieve. As limited objectives are gained and efforts are made to strengthen the grievance group and the resisting population, the capacity to wage effective nonviolent struggle will increase.

Determine the objectives

The objectives of the individual campaigns will need to be formulated carefully and must be compatible with the resisters' major objective(s) in the overall conflict. Each campaign for limited objectives will require wise specific strategies and skilled action to ensure that it contributes to achieving the larger major objectives, as we will discuss later.

The objectives of both the overall struggle and its component campaigns need to be formulated in terms that are clear, understandable, and widely accepted. The objectives should not be expressed as vague platitudes, such as "peace," "freedom," or "justice." Rather, they should be concrete and relatively specific, while always related to the general grievance. For example, although in the second quarter of the twentieth century the overall goal in the struggle of Indian nationalists against the British Empire was independence for India, the specific objectives of the 1930-1931 campaign as formulated by M. K. Gandhi were 11 limited and concrete demands that, he believed, if gained would bring India closer to self-governance.

The terminology used in stating objectives should not be subject to wide interpretations. Proper terminology will make it easier to measure whether or not the objective(s) of a particular campaign or the wider struggle have in fact been achieved. Nor should the objectives be excessively detailed: in some struggles a "freely elected parliament" might be a reasonable objective, but stating that the parliament should have 537 members would be too detailed.

For a limited campaign, it is wise to choose an issue that will be a suitable point of attack. The key is to select an issue that symbolizes the general grievance, or is a specific aspect of the general problem, that is least defensible by the opponents and is almost impossible to justify. The initial objective would then be one for which the nonviolent struggle group could receive maximum support. It should also be an objective that is either within the capacity of the opponents to yield, or within the power of the resisters to take.

A poor choice of an objective in a limited campaign shifts attention away from the major objective(s) of the grand strategy. A wise choice attracts support from the general population, third parties, and potentially even some individuals and groups among the opponents.

It is often very helpful if the objectives of such limited campaigns are ones that challenge deplorable specific expressions of the general grievance against which the resisters are fighting. For example, if all racial discrimination cannot be abolished in a single struggle, individual campaigns may be launched—as was done in the southern United States in the 1950s and 1960s—against specific practices of discrimination, such as segregated buses and lunch counter service, employment discrimination, and voting restrictions.

For another example, a single limited campaign in a struggle against a dictatorship could focus on defending an opposition publication that the regime wants to prohibit, defying censorship or violations of religious liberty, defending the independence of social or religious institutions, creating new independent organizations (such as a trade union), or campaigning against election fraud. Selective objectives may also focus on specific vital social, economic, or political issues, chosen because of their key role in keeping the social and political system out of the opponents' control, in blocking achievement of the opponents' objectives, or in undermining their pillars of support.

If the struggle is against a foreign military occupation, comparable strategies of selective resistance with specific objectives can be waged. The campaigns may be focused on rejection of the legitimacy of the occupation regime, or on noncooperation with some specific part of it. Blocking the establishment of effective occupation and control over the society would be a crucial part of such a struggle. Strategies of selective resistance may also be focused on denying to the attackers one or more of their specific objectives. For example, the resistance may be focused on blocking a specific type of economic gain to the attackers, or preventing their use of the educational system, newspapers, radio, or television to indoctrinate the population in their ideology.

Having chosen the point(s) for concentrated attack, the resisters must not allow themselves to become sidetracked on a lesser course of action or dead-end issues. Initial success on limited points will increase both the resisters' self-confidence and their ability to move forward effectively toward the fuller realization of their objectives.

The perceived validity of the issues and goals espoused by the nonviolent struggle group, as compared to those of the opponent group, are likely to contribute to the effectiveness of the coming nonviolent struggle. The stated issues and goals will influence the support for the resistance from the affected population, as well as, potentially, some people within the opponent group, and perhaps third parties. Clearly stated goals and identification of grievances should be maintained throughout the ebbs and flows of the struggle so long as the grievances remain intact and the goals are still relevant, justifiable, and attainable.

Strengthen the population and the resisters

Parallel with the weakening of the power of the opponents by noncooperation and disobedience is the mobilization of power capacity by the general population. These people and institutions may have previously been thought to be weak and helpless in the face of the opponents' organizational and repressive capacity. This mobilization of the power potential of the population affected by the grievances into effective power that can be used in struggle is of extreme importance to the outcome of the conflict.

From the resisters' position, both the grand strategy and individual strategies for campaigns should be designed so that the resisters and the general population become stronger during the struggle than they were previously. It is possible to calculate their power by determining if they have independent groups and organizations, if they are able to apply nonviolent struggle despite repression, and if they demonstrate skill in using this technique of conducting a conflict.

There is no substitute for genuine strength in the resisting population. If the participants are weak when they begin the struggle and remain so during the conflict, they will almost certainly lose. In a large-scale conflict, it is necessary to mobilize sufficient struggle capacity to overwhelm the opponents by massive resistance and by the removal of the opponents' sources of power.

At a minimum, the resisters need to be able to force the opponents into a compromise settlement on nonessential issues. This means that the resisters require the ability to direct and coordinate forces to enable them to press the struggle forward despite difficulties. Major efforts are required to strengthen the resisters and the general population so that the opponents can no longer dominate them.

A phased series of campaigns can be designed to strengthen the aggrieved population, as well as to weaken the opponents' regime. These phased campaigns can give the population experience in applying nonviolent struggle. If planned and conducted skillfully, this option can bring a series of successes to the resisting population. These may increase their skills in conducting this type of struggle, give experience in strategic planning, and increase the self-confidence of the population and the resisters.

Strengthen institutions

Commonly, political oppression occurs where civil society—meaning a society consisting of strong independent institutions—is weak. Oppressive regimes already in existence commonly seek to destroy the independence of social, economic, and political institutions outside the control of the State or party. Weakened or destroyed independent institutions make societal resistance very difficult to conduct. The strength or weakness of such institutions is important in planning strategy for nonviolent struggle. Social groups and institutions can be organizational bases for waging nonviolent struggle. Individuals can witness or participate, but only groups can resist effectively.

The institutions of civil society are generally composed of organized groups that are neither vertically controlled by, nor integrated into, that part of political society regulated by the State. Examples of civil society groups include sports clubs, gardening associations, certain labor unions and business associations, religious institutions, organized social movements, and all classes of nongovernmental organizations. They can exist at a local, regional, or national level.

Other important independent institutions may at times include small governmental bodies, including local town governments, schools, and legislative, executive, taxation, and judicial units. This can happen either when these institutions already exist and are controlled by independent forces, or when new such bodies are created to replace those controlled by the opponent group.

Consequently, preserving and strengthening existing independent groups and institutions and creating new ones are important contributions to the capacity to wage effective future resistance. The condition of these bodies must be carefully considered by strategic planners, as they are important in determining the ability of the populace to wage nonviolent struggle successfully.

If such independent social groups and institutions are weak or largely absent, it may be necessary to create new groups or organizations in order to prepare for future strong resistance. Or, it may be possible to turn certain existing groups or institutions that have not been fully independent into ones with more independence of action, groups capable of playing major roles in future struggles. The creation and the strengthening of such institutions can significantly increase the future capacity for nonviolent struggle and can expand its effectiveness.

The role of leadership

Leaders have been defined as those who make the most important decisions for the conduct of the conflict and also those who personally serve as rallying points for supporters in the struggle.

It is important for planners of future resistance to review different models of leadership, from highly centralized and charismatic ones to committee structures with full group participation. The merits and disadvantages of different models in differing circumstances need to be considered. Leaders are always vulnerable to attack, discrediting, seizure, or assassination. Therefore, replacements and lines of succession of leaders need to be prepared.

It should also be noted that in some predominantly nonviolent struggles, such as the Russian 1905 Revolution, it was often difficult or impossible at various stages to identify who the leaders were, if indeed there were any, except locally and temporarily.

Analysis is required of the possibility that wide diffusion of knowledge of nonviolent struggle, including its dynamics and requirements, may greatly reduce the need for identifiable leadership in actual struggles.

Steps will need to be prepared to mitigate damage to the movement that would be caused by removal of resistance leaders by the opponents. Such measures should include spreading widely the plan of operations for the struggle throughout the resisting population well before the conflict begins. At times, setting up a more decentralized structure for the nonviolent struggle (as was done in Serbia in 2000) may also help.

Certain qualities should be taken into account when selecting leaders. Leaders should set the example, know their people and look out for their welfare, be technically and tactically proficient, seek out and accept responsibility, let others get credit for success, observe loyalty to superiors and subordinates, know the opponents, learn from the experience of one's own group and others as well, maximize and challenge the abilities of subordinates, and pick the right people for the right positions.

Very importantly, the leaders should either have significant knowledge of nonviolent struggle and be capable of wise strategic planning or have the judgment and humility to rely on other persons with those qualities for strategic direction.

Ensure access to critical material resources

Various material resources will be needed by the resisters and the population during the struggle. It is important to identify and secure access to them in advance of open conflict. Without material necessities, the conflict cannot be conducted effectively and the population may be unwilling to support the struggle.

There is a need to survey, for example, available supplies of food, clothing, energy, medical supplies, communications, and transportation, and to plan for secure future access to them.

Resistance strategists will need to answer such questions as these: What supplies will be needed? How may such supplies and access to them be affected during the struggle? What can the resisters and third parties do to ensure their availability? How can the resisters neutralize, or compensate for, the opponents' attempts to restrict or sever supplies of the materials the resisters need? Can supplies be decentralized in advance or during the struggle, therefore making the resisters less vulnerable to severance or seizure of these supplies? Can new ways be developed to produce these supplies and resources so that the opponents cannot easily defeat the resistance by controlling them? Are there other options or countermeasures open to the resistance to ensure access to material necessities?

Undermine the opponents' sources of power

In a serious conflict over important issues it is unrealistic to expect that the hearts and minds of the opponents will be changed because people are protesting and resisting nonviolently even in the face of the opponents' brutal repression. Some elements of conversion because of nonviolent suffering are possible on occasion for some people, as was discussed in Chapter Thirty-three. However, in a large-scale conflict about no-compromise issues and important power relationships, it is naïve to expect that the mechanism of conversion will resolve the conflict. Stronger action is required.

Nonviolent struggle is most effective when it is able to undermine or dislocate the opponents. This must be kept in mind in the planning of every strategic move. The strategy needs to be designed to concentrate the resisters' strengths against weak links in the opponents' policies or system of control.

The most efficient way to undermine the opponents' policy or system is to weaken or remove their sources of power. In relatively small campaigns over limited issues, this approach will be only partially required. For example, in a labor strike or a major economic boycott, the withdrawal of labor or halt to purchasing is designed to restrict the opponents' economic resources. In these conflicts, it normally is not necessary for the resisters to undermine other sources of the opponents' power.

However, in larger political struggles—such as attempts to repel a foreign occupation or dissolve a dictatorship—strategists of nonviolent struggle would be wise to attempt to weaken and remove as many of these sources of power as possible. This requires that the weapons of nonviolent struggle be applied against crucial targets, primarily the "pillars of support" of the opponents that are determined to be most vulnerable.

Resisters facing acute conflicts about no-compromise issues and serious power relationships will have a strategic option to attempt to restrict or sever the supply of the sources of power of their opponents through symbolic protests, forms of noncooperation, or disruptive intervention. Such action becomes especially powerful when it involves defiance and noncooperation by organizations and institutions. The impact of their resistance will vary with the degree of the opponents' dependence on them.

Often it will be wise to target specific sources of the opponents' power in a sequence of priorities. This sequence may be selected on the basis of certain criteria, including at times both their vulnerability and their importance to the opponents.

One of the most important sources of power, as we discussed in Chapter Two, is authority, or legitimacy. The undermining of this source of power was exceptionally important in Serbia in October 2000. Without authority, the provision of the other sources of power is unstable. Loss of authority can set in motion the disintegration of a regime's power.[4] As we noted earlier, all governments depend upon the cooperation and assistance of their subjects, of the groups and organizations of the society, and of the branches of the government. When these bodies do not sufficiently supply the several needed sources of power, or when they carry out the regime's wishes and orders slowly or inefficiently—or even flatly refuse to assist and obey—the power of the regime is weakened.

Governments may attempt to restore obedience and cooperation by imposing sanctions, or punishments. However, even sanctions will be inadequate to enforce obedience and cooperation as long as acceptance of the regime's authority is limited. If popular disobedience and noncooperation continue—or even grow—despite such sanctions, the power of the opponents will shrink or dissolve. This effect is heightened when police and soldiers refuse to obey orders. Another key source of power—sanctions—will then have been removed.

In some conflicts, specific actions can be undertaken with a view of undermining the morale and the reliability of the opponents' military forces and functionaries. Sometimes, such efforts

---

[4] For this analysis, we have assumed that the opponents either are the established regime or have the backing of the established regime.

may have little or no impact. Troops facing nonviolent resisters have sometimes perpetrated brutalities, as in China in 1989 and Burma in 1988. At other times, efforts to undermine troops have been extremely influential, as in Russia in 1991 and the Philippines in 1986. The general situation of a population resisting nonviolently, so as not to threaten the lives of members of the military forces, will sometimes suffice to create serious morale problems among soldiers and police. This can lead to laxity in repression, and occasionally, although rarely, to disobedience of orders and mutiny. While it is wise not to depend on such military disobedience, special efforts to influence troops, police, and functionaries can prove to be important.

If the acceptance of the regime, cooperation with it, and obedience to it are ended, the regime must weaken and collapse. This explains the phenomenon of "people power," and the collapse of dictatorships when confronted by the strong use of this technique.

Concentrate strength against weakness

To be most effective, nonviolent action needs to be concentrated against crucial targets. These targets need to be selected after careful consideration of one's own strengths, overall objectives, and campaign objectives; the objectives and position of the opponents, including their weaknesses; and the importance of the issues at stake themselves. Napoleon's maxim that it is impossible to be too strong at the decisive point applies here as well.

Campaign strategies need to be designed to utilize the strengths of the resisters to expose and attack the opponents' vulnerabilities and weaknesses, while avoiding engagement of the opponents at their strongest and most defensible points. This applies to both the selection of campaign objectives and the choice of tactical targets for attack within those campaigns.

However, it should also be recognized that some struggles may be launched against policies or governments that have wide popular support. In such cases, the struggles will often be about no-compromise issues, and both the struggle and the campaign objectives may not initially find wide acceptance among the population as a whole. If so, campaigns and actions should be designed to strengthen the resisters and chip away at the support for the opponents or their policies. These struggles will usually take significantly longer to win, and the external conditions will be unfavorable for the resisters.

Generally, however, when choosing points of attack for particular actions within the campaign strategy, it is wise for the nonviolent struggle strategists to target weak or particularly vulnerable supports of the opponents, their policies, or both. We have already noted the need to focus the resisters' capabilities against vital "pillars of support," defined as the groups or institutions that support and provide the opponents' various sources of power. However, it would be unwise initially to target those pillars of support that are the strongest and most defensible by the opponents. For example, if internal solidarity, morale, and cohesion of the military forces are among the opponents' greatest strengths, then at the beginning of the struggle it would probably not be wise to attempt to induce disaffection among rank-and-file soldiers as a primary campaign tactic.

In contrast, if the opponents are heavily dependent on the sale of mineral resources produced at mines that have been unionized by supporters or members of the nonviolent struggle group, then a key weakness of the opponents—and an important strength of the resisters—has been revealed. A wise campaign might then include application of economic pressures against the opponents through strikes, slowdowns, or other such measures at these facilities. The key, again, is to target the vulnerable sources of power of the opponents by concentrating strength against their weakest pillars of support.

Concentration of strength is vital. Activities and pressures should be selected that allow the nonviolent struggle group to apply its strengths, not expose its weaknesses. Without support of labor unions (as well as internal discipline within those unions), it is unlikely that many forms of economic pressure, including those in the example just given, will have much effect. On the other hand, if labor union support and solidarity with the nonviolent struggle group is one of the resisters' great strengths, then such strikes might prove effective if targeted against a key pillar of support of the opponent group. As another example, if the resisters enjoy the full backing of popular religious institutions, it would be wise to employ them in the struggle. If the religious institutions support the opponents, however, it would be unwise to plan activities that require their participation in resistance against the opponents.

This same principle holds for selection of methods. Methods of nonviolent action that require certain preparation or capabilities on the part of the resisters should be selected only if those capabilities exist. Demonstrations should not be called unless organizers are confident that turnout will be sufficient to achieve the identified purposes of such actions within the campaign. A hunger strike should not be launched if the resisters who volunteer to apply the method are not willing to continue it for the full declared duration. Consumers boycotts should not be launched without the capacity to apply them.

However, the above methods become viable if (a) the resisters have the strength to carry them out and to maintain them despite the opponents' countermeasures; and (b) the methods fit within a selected campaign strategy to target vulnerable pillars of support of the opponents. In all cases, the selected methods should be part of a strategic plan that will apply the strengths of the resisters against the weaknesses of the opponents, concentrating heavily on vulnerable pillars of support. To do otherwise is to ignore opportunities to advance in the struggle, while exposing potentially vital weaknesses of one's own side that the opponents will eagerly exploit.

Keep the opponents off balance

The resistance movement needs to keep the opponents off balance, and it must strike where the opponents are unprepared to deal with the attack. Timing and speed can be important here. Unlike what is sometimes true in military struggles, however, nonviolent resisters generally do *not* have to rely on surprise attacks in order to be effective.

The timing of implementation of the resisters' tactics can be very important. It is essential for the resistance strategists and leaders to be able to judge when people are willing to resist. Sometimes action may be timed to coincide with a significant day or special occasion. Where a combination of actions involving several groups is planned, the precise time at which each group is to act will be important. Timing of resistance actions is also important at the various stages of a struggle. It is important to determine the right time to shift from symbolic actions to massive noncooperation, for example, or to begin a new campaign within the overall grand strategy.

Prompt defensive actions may be required in response to an aggressive attack by the opponents. For example, if the opponents are attempting to seize control of the whole country, as by an invasion or a coup d'état, resistance should be initiated before the attackers have established effective control of the State. Similarly, resistance is important at the point when an oppressive regime is attempting to control or abolish the independent groups and institutions of the society in order to expand its control of the governmental apparatus and society. Defense of these groups and institutions is necessary in order to maintain both their freedom of action and their future ability to resist.

Block control by the opponents

In all large-scale conflicts, the resisters need to make efforts to block the establishment or maintenance of control by the opponents. Resistance should continue as long as required to achieve the goal, or as long as the nonviolent struggle group is willing to withstand the expected repression and to continue other aspects of the struggle. This is done principally in three ways:

(1) The resisters and the general population they represent should (a) disobey defiantly and withhold cooperation from the opponents, thereby denying the opponents control over them and also weakening the opponents' power, and (b) disperse resistance widely throughout the population and society. At times, this dispersal of resistance can include applying relatively mild delaying tactics and feigning incompetence among certain sectors of the populace. At other times, it may require applying stronger methods of defiance and noncooperation. Geographic dispersal of resistance is often necessary as well, although there will likely be physical focal points (such as important cities or industrial zones) where concentrated resistance may at times produce a stronger impact.

(2) Specifically, in cases of reaction to invasion or coup d'état, the resisters need to prevent, undermine, and make ineffective any collaboration with the opponents. Denying the attackers a group

of collaborators is an important specific application of the general policy of disobeying and noncooperating with opponents.

(3) The resisters should make efforts to undermine the effectiveness of the troops, police, and functionaries of the opponents. This is done by alienating their loyalty to their leaders and attempting, when feasible, to induce disaffection, mutiny, or desertion.

Defy the opponents' violent repression

Nonviolent struggle can pose grave problems for many opponents. Naturally, opponents whose power, privilege, and control are threatened will be disturbed. When this occurs, powerful opponents are likely to resort to violent repression. Resisters may be beaten, imprisoned, attacked, kidnapped, wounded, tortured, or killed.

Such repression is not a sign that the nonviolent struggle has failed. Indeed, this repression is a tribute to the degree to which nonviolent struggle has upset the oppressors. Casualties are not a sign of defeat in nonviolent struggle, any more than they are in military conflicts. Casualties are the expected human cost of waging an acute conflict with opponents willing and able to wound and kill in order to establish or maintain their control.

The degree to which the opponents' reactions will be crude and brutal, or refined and sophisticated with very little violence, will vary. However, strong responses from the opponents need to be anticipated. The opponents' reactions should be no surprise and the resisters should be prepared for them.

Some resisters in past movements assumed that they were defeated when their opponents applied strong repression against them. If resisters believe they have been defeated, then they have been. However, defeat is not a necessary consequence of repression. Grave repression may instead lead to increased resistance, increased third party support, and on occasion even sympathy and support from members of the opponent group.

If repression is not understood, and if wise responses to it are not applied, the opponents' violence can produce destruction, induce terror, and demoralize a population. People may become less willing to risk these consequences as the price of resistance. Some persons, angry at the brutality of the repression and at the suffering and death of friends and family, may wish to strike out in retaliation with their own acts of violence. This counter-violence, however, will not strengthen the resistance. It does not serve a strategic purpose, and it will almost certainly be counter-productive, helping to undermine the effectiveness of the nonvio-lent struggle, as we discussed in Chapter Thirty-one.

In the long run, the most effective response to violent repres-sion is to demonstrate that it does not produce submission, but instead increases resistance. Continued nonviolent resistance in the face of severe repression may at times also produce both un-rest among the opponents' own population and opposition to the opponents among third parties. For this to occur, however, there will likely be a time of suffering until the opponents' leadership recognizes that brutalities are counterproductive, or until the op-ponents' regime weakens and falls apart through political starva-tion due to the severance of its sources of power.

Resisters can take steps to weaken the impact of repression on the resisters and the population. Less provocative methods of re-sistance may at times be chosen. For example, people may be urged to stay off the streets where they can easily be shot and to remain in their homes where they are less obvious targets. Some-times, "lightning" actions may be taken, with participants rapidly assembling for an event and then dispersing extremely quickly be-fore police or troops have time to respond.

A shift of strategy and tactics, such as to use less risky methods that are still defiant, may be appropriate to reduce the impact of repression. At times, a temporary retreat may be wise, with the resistance taking a different turn. Intensified efforts may be launched to subvert the opponents' police and troops, and the population. Wherever possible, it is important to provide support for the victims of the repression and their families, through such means as medical assistance, psychological support, financial as-sistance, and similar measures. Fundamentally, the resisters need to maintain their solidarity and determination to resist through nonviolent struggle.

Harsh repression can also be countered by increasing the cost to the opponents for its use. If extremely violent repression is in-evitable, then some strategists have advised that one should at-tempt to ensure that the brutalities are committed in the open where they can be seen by the public, observers, and journalists.

News of the brutalities should be publicized so that they may alienate members and allies of the opponents' group, including decision makers, agents, the general population, and, also, members of third parties. The opponents' collaborators who become alienated by the violence of the repression may as a result even switch sides at times. In some cases, extreme repression can result in international economic sanctions and diplomatic pressures against the regime that inflicted the brutalities.

Maintain persistent nonviolent discipline

Nonviolent struggle can be waged effectively against opponents with massive capacity for military and police action precisely because it does not attempt to confront that type of power directly. Instead, the struggle is pursued by nonviolent means, which is more difficult for the opponents to control. Even limited violence by resisters, or on their behalf, including in response to brutalities, can be counterproductive. Resistance violence in the midst of a nonviolent struggle reinforces the opponents' ability to use repression effectively against nonviolent resisters.

In contrast, the maintenance of nonviolent discipline against violent opponents facilitates the workings of the mechanisms of nonviolent struggle, including the occasionally applicable process of political ju-jitsu, which was discussed in Chapter Thirty-two. This is a process in some nonviolent struggles in which the contrast between the opponents' brutal violence and the resisters' persistent nonviolent resistance tends to increase support for, and participation in, the nonviolent struggle, and to reduce support for the opponents.

It is important to note that such reactions in support of the resistance are by no means guaranteed and often do not occur. However, this process is greatly facilitated by the maintenance of nonviolent discipline on the part of the resisters.

Nonviolent discipline consists of two components: (1) adhering to the strategic plans for the struggle and (2) refraining from violence. Failure of the resisters to adhere to the strategic plan can produce confusion and can deflect strength away from the points at which it needs to be concentrated. The breakdown of nonviolent discipline and the outbreak of violence can have disastrous effects on a nonviolent struggle and can assist the opponents.

If the resisters become overly enthusiastic about participation and take action that is not a part of the original strategic plan, or decide not to carry out the actions prescribed in that plan, this often can be very harmful to the effectiveness of the struggle. Although there may be times at which innovation can be helpful, it can also be dangerous. Resisters need to discipline themselves to implement carefully developed plans designed to bring them success.

The general population and all resisters must understand the need for commitment to participate in the current campaign. Methods for dealing with fear should also be developed. Knowledge of disciplined responses to serious repression, and the rationale for maintaining nonviolent resistance despite provocations and repression, need to be understood and accepted.

The grand strategy for the overall conflict needs to provide for means to carry the struggle to successful completion by nonviolent forms of action. It must exclude the possible introduction of violence at a later stage, when resistance violence would be of great assistance to the opponents. Resistance violence would allow them to justify even harsher repression against the resistance group and to assist efforts to discredit the resisters as really terrorists in attempted disguise. Allowance for possible later use of violence can cause abandonment of the development of forms of action that are needed in critical stages of the conflict to achieve success. Resistance violence can also strengthen the opponents' internal support from their population, police, and troops. A struggle that is almost successful should continue to rely on the strengths that have brought the conflict that far. Otherwise, the course of the conflict may be reversed and the opponents may prevail after all.

The negative consequences of resisters turning to violence may include reduced participation in resistance, increased repression, higher casualties, increased solidarity within the opponent group, enhanced morale among the opponents' troops and police while conducting repression, loss by the resisters of the "moral high ground," and reduced or lost international sympathy and support.

Means of promoting nonviolent discipline may include spoken and written instructions and appeals; pledges and oaths; use of "marshals" to assist order during demonstrations; the design of challenging nonviolent activities to keep the initiative; avoidance of activities that are especially likely to turn violent; exertion of pressures on participants who have earlier pledged to remain nonviolent; holding "socio-drama" sessions to act out in advance anticipated actions and repression in serious conflict situations; and various efforts to raise morale for participation in the non-violent activities. Participants in demonstrations may be barred from bringing such items as weapons, alcohol, and drugs to demonstrations.

From guidelines to action

The above guidelines are extremely important in making non-violent struggle effective. However, to have an impact on the outcome, plans based on them must, if possible, be prepared in advance of the struggle and then be applied during the conflict.

The course of a strategically planned and well-prepared non-violent struggle will be a dynamic one. It will require wise responses and skilled action in the face of the many changes and problems that will be encountered, in order to bring the conflict to a successful conclusion.

Chapter Thirty-eight

CONDUCTING THE STRUGGLE

The role of a strategic plan

The diverse cases of nonviolent struggle described in earlier chapters of this book started in various ways. Almost without exception, they did so without a strategic plan for the impending major conflict. The closest to a strategic plan was the case of India in 1930-1931, although elements of planning were also present in Serbia in 2000.

The approach that is presented in this book is a more deliberate one. It envisages careful analysis and strategic development before the struggle begins. The deliberate initiation of the struggle with advance planning will likely increase the chances of the struggle being successful. Advance planning may also reduce, but not eliminate, the possibility of extreme casualties.

Once the struggle has begun, it will not remain static. Power relationships will change, sometimes rapidly. Although the nonviolent struggle group should always try to maintain initiative in the conflict, momentum may be periodically gained or lost. Unanticipated problems and setbacks may, and probably will, occur.

Strategic planners and leaders of the nonviolent struggle group should try to anticipate changes in the conflict situation and be prepared to take them into account over the course of the struggle. Such changes may result in a need to alter tactical plans for the implementation of the existing campaign strategies. Changes in the conflict situation will also be important in the continued development of the strategic plans for imminent future campaigns within the grand strategy. On rare occasions, the strategies for existing campaigns may need to be altered if it is determined conclusively that setbacks in the struggle are due to poor strategic planning rather than inadequate implementation.

In this chapter, we will offer some thoughts that may help to guide the resisters in these matters as the struggle develops.

Preparing the population for struggle

The effectiveness of nonviolent struggle can be significantly increased if certain activities are undertaken before the conflict begins. These can include improving the social context for the coming action, spreading the understanding of nonviolent struggle among potential participants, strengthening independent groups and institutions, and increasing the resisters' capacity to apply the technique skillfully.

An important initial step in preparing the general population for later struggle is the spreading of the simple concept of noncooperation, and some basic understanding of the technique of nonviolent struggle. It will be important to determine how deep and widespread the knowledge of nonviolent struggle is among the population of potential resisters. For some sections of the population, fuller explanations of nonviolent struggle may be required. For example, this may include additional emphasis on the role of noncooperation and the recognition that violence has no role in this struggle and must be excluded. Various means of communication may be used for these purposes, including radio, audio- and videocassettes, leaflets, booklets, books, cartoons, and stories.

It will be important also to assess what skills will be needed during future individual campaigns, and whether these skills are already present among expected resisters. If not, then preparations to develop these skills will be a necessary task.

It will also be important to spread the idea of phased campaigns with limited objectives, conducted both to gain those objectives and to strengthen the subordinated population and society, while weakening the controls of the oppressive regime. The population needs to become accustomed to the need for making repeated and continued efforts and not to expect instant success.

In well-prepared campaigns, clear instructions will be issued to the general population and to particular groups that are asked to carry out specific acts of resistance and defiance in disciplined ways. Guidelines for specific types of resistance behavior can also be determined in advance of a crisis (such as a coup d'état), with instructions for contingencies. These instructions may include the resistance roles of various groups in the population and various institutions in the society.

Experience also establishes that, even under the most extreme totalitarian systems, it has been impossible for the dictators to sever completely all communication among resisters and the general population. Illegal news sheets, pamphlets, and even books were published and circulated under Nazi occupations and Communist rule.

Facing problems: barriers or challenges?

It must be expected that problems will be encountered during the course of the conflict. How the resisters regard these problems and respond to them is very important. Both the resisters and their leaders need to regard identified problems as challenges, not insurmountable barriers. Unless this attitude is present, it will be impossible to move beyond such difficulties.

It is therefore very important to learn how to examine serious problems and how to develop effective ways to solve them. In that way, the problems can be overcome, bypassed, or removed, and the struggle can proceed toward achieving its objectives. It is wise to try to anticipate such problems throughout the course of the struggle and to seek solutions for them before they occur.

Maintaining momentum and initiative

It is very important that the resistance movement maintain the initiative and strong momentum during the conflict in order that the application of the adopted strategies can proceed with vigor and effectiveness. Failure to do so seriously weakens the movement. For example, a brave, disciplined, and imaginative demonstration may occur on a given day that attracts significant interest, attention, and support. However, if during the following weeks and months no new acts of resistance are carried out, the public focus will be on the period of silence and passivity, not on the earlier demonstration. Its impact will be largely lost. On the other hand, maintaining the initiative and the progressive advancement of the resistance movement by new acts of protest or resistance according to the planned strategy will strengthen the struggle and contribute to the movement's success.

The nonviolent struggle movement needs to conduct primarily offensive actions, taking and maintaining the initiative as much as possible. If the movement retains its capacity to resist but does not take the initiative, there is a serious danger that the movement will become primarily reactive. The choice of what to do and how to do it would then be determined by the opponents' initiatives, thereby giving them great advantages. Defensive operations should be limited to those taken to block advances by the opponents while offensive operations are being prepared. Keeping the planned strategy in mind, leaders and strategists will need to consider what their options are for taking the initiative in the next steps of the conflict.

Even in the case of a basically defensive struggle, such as one opposing a foreign occupation or a coup d'état, the defenders need to take the initiative to turn the struggle into one in which they are the driving force. The defenders will need to plan what offensive actions they can take to protect their institutional bases, principles, and ability to act to force the collapse or withdrawal of the attackers.

A wise grand strategy, as well as particular strategies for individual campaigns, should include plans for developing a progressively more powerful and successful movement.

A long-term struggle operating under a grand strategy may include several campaigns for limited objectives. Effectiveness of the long-term struggle is likely to be increased, and momentum is maintained, if both the campaign goals and the population groups required to bear the brunt of the responsibility for waging the struggle are varied between the successive campaigns.

In some long-term struggles, campaign strategies might focus on economic issues at one time, on freedom of expression issues at another, and on religious issues at still another. Quite different methods of action might be used in each of these campaigns. Each campaign may also call for differing degrees of both involvement and risk for different sectors of the resistance. For example, teachers may bear the brunt of the responsibility and the repression for a while. For other periods, the clergy, rail workers, journalists, judges, or students may hold prime responsibility for carrying out certain actions to gain specific objectives. Later, the group primarily responsible for resistance during one period may be given rest time, as the specific issue shifts or a different occupational or geographical group is required to assume a more active role in a new campaign.

If such a plan for developing an increasingly strong resistance movement has been made, then it is important to monitor the course of the struggle to determine whether or not the movement has indeed been growing more powerful. If the movement has become primarily reactive or has been acting largely defensively, a change to more aggressive action is needed. Decisions must be taken and implemented to make the struggle increase its drive, initiative, and force toward greater capacity to achieve its objective(s).

Monitoring the course of the conflict

During the course of the conflict, many important changes are likely to occur among both the opponents and the resisters, in their relationships to each other, and in their relationships to third parties. Very importantly, the degree and type of support that each of the contending parties receives from its own "pillars of support" may increase or decrease. The result is likely to be shifts in the overall conflict situation that was earlier assessed during the preparation of the strategic estimate, as we discussed in Chapter Thirty-six. The original situation will not remain static. Various factors will intervene as the resisters attempt to apply a chosen strategic or tactical plan and as the opponents react. Therefore, it is important to know how the support for each side has changed, how it is currently changing, and whether and how well plans for the nonviolent struggle are actually being applied.

Larger indicators of the impact of the struggle should be monitored. These will include developments among the resisting groups, the general population, the opponents, and third parties. A variety of important questions needs to be asked. What are the favorable developments? What are the unfavorable ones? How are the views, morale, and reliability of the opponents' troops, officials, and population being affected by the conflict? How has the tenacity of the resisters been affected thus far in the conflict, and are their numbers growing or shrinking? What has happened during the conflict to the opponents' ability to control the conflict situation and the resisting population?

It is important to identify the reasons why the changes in power relationships have occurred, on both sides. What are the trends? What factors have contributed to these changes? Are the events providing evidence that the original strategic plan was sound, or that it needs to be revised? Were the opponents' countermeasures anticipated, and therefore responses prepared, or are new actions by the resisters now required? What does this say about the possible benefits of initiating changes in the tactics and the methods to be employed, or even in evaluating the selected strategy during a future review? Additional information may also be gathered about other relevant and changing factors in the conflict situation, including the use of propaganda, intelligence agents and informers, movements of key opponent personnel, and other factors.

One of the most important tasks in the evaluation of the ongoing struggle is to assess how effectively the specific tactics and methods of resistance are being applied. This is especially the case when methods have been selected that require participation of large numbers of resisters. Examples of these methods include economic boycotts, labor strikes, various forms of political noncooperation, and even some symbolic actions such as protest marches or the public display of certain colors or symbols. If such methods are being applied by large numbers of people, that fact alone communicates a great deal, and can have a major impact on the conflict. On the other hand, if a call for the use of methods that require many participants receives a very small response, a weakness in the resistance is exposed that may have very negative consequences for the future of the struggle.

The strategists and leaders will need ways to monitor the strengths and weaknesses of their ongoing campaign in order to assess what, if any, new steps may be needed to increase its effectiveness and its chances of success. That assessment may make it possible to take steps (1) to prevent, correct, or compensate for certain negative developments, or (2) to take new initiatives to increase the power of their struggle, strengthen the struggle group, weaken the opponents, and gain increased third party support.

Shifts in tactics and methods

A wise strategy that has been prepared to guide the main course of the conflict by the nonviolent struggle group should not be regarded as easily disposable in favor of another. However, the plans that implement the adopted strategy can be subject to change when opportunities arise to accelerate momentum, or when unanticipated serious opposition is encountered.

As the situation changes and the conflict proceeds, opportunities may arise for the resisters to take steps that were earlier envisaged but not scheduled for that particular time. If, after assessment, the proposed new actions are deemed to be wise, the movement needs to be prepared to take advantage of the unexpected opportunities. However, these steps must be compatible with the adopted grand strategy and the strategy of the current campaign.

The movement must also be careful not to be distracted into focussing on side issues and undertaking activities that are not central to the basic strategy of the struggle.

Within a given campaign, shifts may at times be made in which population groups are relied upon to conduct particular applications of protest, noncooperation, or intervention. Other changes may also be made in the choice of specific methods to be applied in the short term. Such changes in methods, or groups of methods, can be used to shift responsibilities and dangers from one group of resisters to another that is perhaps less exhausted or more disciplined. Shifts in methods may also be made to change the kind of pressures applied to the opponents or to compensate for weaknesses in the nonviolent struggle group. Variation in tactics and methods may also add variety and interest—and often newsworthiness—to the campaign.

Retrenchment or acceleration?

If the course of the struggle has revealed that the necessary strength and ability of the resisters to persist in the face of punishments and suffering do not exist, that fact must be recognized. Ways must be sought to correct the weaknesses while continuing the struggle.

On the other hand, if significant weaknesses in the opponents are exposed, or if the nonviolent resisters are stronger than expected, it may be wise to accelerate the resistance and the implementation of the planned strategy.

The implementation of strategy and tactics requires sensitivity to the developing conflict situation. If a given tactical action succeeds, then what? If a given tactical action fails, what then? If there is partial success for that limited action, what follows? The capacity to respond to unforeseen, or unforeseeable, events must be acutely developed. It is especially important to conserve the morale of the nonviolent resisters and potential supporters and to continue their resistance actions. If a tactical action is not succeeding, plans must be altered. Under some conditions, a temporary retreat might be called in order to prepare for a stronger future effort.

Several additional important questions may need to be asked. When is it wise to continue current actions to increase the power of the resistance, or instead to modify those actions? When is it wise to initiate new activities and toward what specific limited objectives should the new action be aimed? When is it wise, despite a tactical setback, to attempt to strengthen the resisters and to persist with the chosen strategy? How does one determine whether it is wise to reassess and revise strategies already adopted?

Making gains despite setbacks

Not all struggles will proceed smoothly. Resistance leaders and strategists need to be prepared to offer guidance in situations in which the opponents have gained important ground and have won some or all of their objectives despite the resistance.

Setbacks are not permanent defeats. Without anticipation of such contingencies, and without preparations by the resisters to deal with them, setbacks and defeats in specific campaigns within an overall grand strategy may result in demoralization, confusion, and a collapse of the resistance campaign. On the other hand, with proper anticipation and preparations, the resisters may be able to handle setbacks and reverse them before they turn into debacles.

Lessons should be learned from setbacks. These may include ways to improve the development of strategies, increase the solidarity of the resisters, maintain discipline, improve their skill in applying resistance actions, and increase their capacity to continue resistance despite repression and other problems.

It is important to determine, on the basis of the examination of developments in the movement and careful analysis of events, whether the causes of a setback have been in the choice of the objectives and the strategy. If this was not the case, and the objective was wisely chosen and the strategy to achieve it was well developed and planned, then the objective and the strategy should not be lightly abandoned or replaced.

Difficulties on the tactical level are not necessarily grounds for abandoning the strategy. Changes may, instead, be appropriate on the tactical level. The general population and the resisting group may have been weak and thus needed strengthening. The implementation of the strategy and the tactics may have been poorly conducted. There may have been organizational and leadership problems. The resisters may have lacked effective means to counter the opponents' strengths and moves. In all cases, the precise nature of weaknesses in the resistance needs to be identified, and corrections need to be made on the proper levels.

In those cases where the objectives of individual campaigns have been achieved, those gains need to be recognized and the resisters given credit for their achievements. This recognition and credit will help the resisters to follow up their successes with further gains in the next stages of the conflict.

Bringing the conflict to an end

No technique of struggle, violent or nonviolent, can be guaranteed to succeed in all circumstances, irrespective of the conditions, the strengths and skills of the resisters, and the nature and actions of the opponents. Full consideration certainly needs to be given to the external conditions of the conflict and to the nature and capacities of the opponents. However, other important factors in determining the outcome of the struggle that are often neglected are the skill, preparation, bravery, strategies, and persistence shown by the resisters. If these qualities are weak or absent, then it is most likely that the struggle will fail. But if such capacities are present and can be fortified, the resisters stand a chance of winning against even ruthless opponents.

There are three basic ways in which a conflict may end: defeat, mixed results, or success. Conflicts involving the use of nonviolent struggle are no exception.

Defeat

The nature of defeat may range from simple failure to achieve the declared objectives of the struggle to full collapse of the resistance movement. This is similar to defeat in military warfare, except that this evaluation of nonviolent struggle is measured by an additional standard that is not usually applied to wars, namely, whether the vowed objectives have in fact been gained.

Defeat may occur because of insufficient strength, or weakness in organization, perseverance, or strategy. As we said earlier, there is no substitute for genuine strength in nonviolent struggle.

The consequences of defeat will vary. At times, there may be physical suffering, loss of life, mental anguish, economic losses, worsened conditions, or new legal restrictions. If there is demoralization and loss of confidence in nonviolent struggle, the chances of using this technique again may be small.

If defeat of a nonviolent struggle appears nearly certain, or at least very likely, the nonviolent leaders and strategists will need to make very careful calculations as to how to handle the situation.

Even if the struggle group is unable to achieve its objectives at the time, it does not have to abandon them or otherwise surrender legitimacy to the opponents. Deliberate steps should be taken to ensure the possibility of resuming the struggle after major regrouping, internal strengthening, and new strategic analysis and preparations.

A movement that has proved to be too weak to stand up to the opponents and has simply disintegrated will have very little capacity at that time to salvage anything from the debacle.

However, if the defeat has not been extreme, and yet the resisters and the broader population are incapable at the time of regrouping after losses, then a temporary halt to the action should be called. An effort can be made to salvage as much as possible from the crisis. It is important to know how to withdraw in an orderly fashion to a tenable position. What that position may be will vary widely with the particular situation and the strengths of the contending groups.

If a given struggle has been defeated, it is important to analyze what factors contributed to the failure. When those are identified, it will be necessary to examine them to see why they occurred, whether they can be corrected in the future, and, if so, how. That analysis must be done carefully and without simplistic explanations, such as "the opponents were too brutal."

An attempt will need to be made to turn the difficult situation into a period of regrouping and new preparations. If some spirit of resistance survives among the resisters and the population, it will be important to maintain at least some small symbolic means of protest and to continue some limited organizational work. This is what Norwegian philosopher Arne Næss has called "micro-resistance."[1] As conditions improve, surviving resistance leaders and strategists will need to conduct preparations for future nonviolent resistance, encourage people to take small, low-risk actions, and later even to initiate limited local protest and resistance activities for small objectives.

---

[1] Arne Næss defined micro-resistance as "resistance by individuals and tiny, temporary groups carried out in such a way that exposure and annihilation of larger organizations do not affect it, at least not directly." See Adam Roberts, ed., *Civilian Resistance as a National Defense,* Harrisburg, Pennsylvania: Stackpole Books, 1967 and *The Strategy of Civilian Defence* (London: Faber & Faber, 1967), pp. 252 and 270n. Several examples are offered.

Not all defeats are total and permanent. Even if the resisters appear to be defeated, the opponents' power, despite their victory, may actually have been significantly weakened. In military warfare, this is known as a "Pyrrhic victory." Even at times when objectives have not been achieved, the resisters may grow in organizational strength and skill in resisting. Such gains can be the basis for later increased strength and effectiveness. A fundamental reassessment of the situation is likely to be required, however, including a new strategic estimate.

Mixed results

In practice, of course, the end results of conflicts are often neither a complete success nor a complete defeat, but a mixture of both. In such cases, the nonviolent struggle group will need to reassess the situation and determine what needs to be done to achieve the full objectives of the campaign as originally intended.

Limited gains must be accurately reported and understood. They are not the same as defeats, but neither are they full successes. Nevertheless, in a situation of limited gains for the nonviolent struggle group, it is possible that the opponents also may have experienced comparable setbacks. They may lose self-assurance and become weakened and less able to deny the resisters' objectives in the future.

If the gains from the struggle have been less than desired by the resisters but no fundamental questions have arisen challenging the validity of the chosen strategy, then it is important to continue applying that same strategy, perhaps in a new way. However, if serious problems have been discovered in the earlier resistance, problems that can be identified as factors impeding other gains in the future, the previous strategic plan may need to be reconsidered.

Not all major changes can be achieved in a single struggle, and negotiated conclusions may be wise in some campaigns. Sometimes, the very fact of negotiating for gains—not losses—is a victory, for it reflects an improved power relationship. At times, a truce or interim settlement may be produced without formal negotiations and agreements.

The nonviolent resisters may compromise on secondary, nonessential matters, but ought not compromise on essentials or give up fundamental principles or demands. The resisters need to know the difference and ought not claim secondary issues as fundamental principles or major objectives. The full achievement of fundamental principles or demands may be postponed, but they must not be renounced.

The period following a truce or interim settlement will be difficult. It could be used by the resisters to regroup, strengthen positions, or consolidate gains. One should not continue along the same line that led to the truce. The new strategy and tactics are very important. The first actions after losing a battle should be brief, but one should never allow the opponents to dictate the resisters' future actions. The nonviolent struggle group should not allow itself to become completely passive and to return to submission. Periods of retreat and even defeat must be turned into opportunities for the recovery of strength and preparations for more favorable action. When limited successes have been won by producing basic changes in attitudes, power positions, and relationships, these successes are likely to be genuine and lasting, not easily taken away.

Strategists and leaders will need to assess how their struggle can be strengthened to enable them to proceed from a campaign or a struggle that concluded with mixed results, toward a new campaign capable of attaining their full objectives. How can they recover from losses, regroup, strengthen their people, and prepare to resume a new phase of the struggle? Do they need to focus on a more vulnerable specific objective? Or do they need to expand their objectives to capitalize on their newly identified strengths and opportunities? The strategy and tactics during such a period of regrouping and regaining strength will be of particular importance.

Success

Success in a limited campaign, or in a major nonviolent struggle operating on the basis of a grand strategy, needs to be precisely understood. Success in nonviolent struggles is defined as the achievement of the substantive objectives of the struggle group. Have the resisters' goals been gained? This is all that is necessary for victory to be declared, even if the opponents have not explicitly acknowledged the changed situation.

As we just discussed, some nonviolent struggles may produce results that are mixtures of success and failure. But a struggle cannot be called fully successful if only the morale of the resisters has improved, if only the general population has become better organized and skilled in resistance, or if the opponent group has merely been weakened. Those situations are indeed gains, but they are something less than full successes.

When there have been significant advances and victory is in sight, one has to be careful. This is a crucial and dangerous period. The nonviolent struggle group may become overconfident and careless. At this point, the opponents can make a supreme effort to avoid capitulating. The nonviolent struggle group's final effort is the most important and most difficult. Campaigns may be successfully concluded in different ways. These include negotiations, the opponents granting the demands, and the collapse of the opponents' regime.

On some occasions, a negotiated agreement between the contending sides may include the goals gained by the nonviolent struggle group. Sometimes, the goals may be formalized by a decision imposed by an institution, such as a court, that has not been a party to the conflict, as occurred at the conclusion of the Montgomery, Alabama, bus boycott in 1956. Examination is then needed of the degree to which that decision was directly or indirectly influenced by the nonviolent resistance. In extreme cases, such as a nonviolent uprising to end an extreme dictatorship, success may be produced by the disintegration of the oppressive system. This disintegration may result from the shrinking or the severance of the regime's sources of power due to widespread and focused noncooperation by the regime's previous pillars of support.

Often, opponents will firmly deny that the gaining of the resisters' objectives was in any way influenced by their resistance. Opponents who have been defeated will sometimes do the best they can to save face. It may also be the case that strong opponents rarely want opposition groups and the general population to become aware that their power potential could, by wise strategy and action, be turned into effective power. Some other explanation of the change may be offered. Perhaps, it may be claimed by the opponents that their views or policies had been misunderstood, the grievances had been the result of poor administration or wrong doing by underlings, or the change had been planned all along. It may even be claimed that the change had in fact been delayed by the actions of the nonviolent struggle group.

The ways success is implemented will vary with the chosen objectives, the scale of the conflict, and the nature of the opponent group. In a large conflict against a powerful dictatorship willing to apply ruthless repression, the dictatorship could be undermined by the withdrawal of authority and submission by the general population, massive shut-downs of the society, general strikes, mass stay-at-homes, defiant marches, loss of control of the economy, the transportation system, and communications, slowdowns and defiance by the civil service and the police, disguised disobedience or outright mutiny by soldiers, or other activities. As a consequence of such defiance and noncooperation, executed wisely and with mass participation in resistance over time, even dictators would become powerless. The democratic forces would, without violence, triumph.

Of course, this is not the typical situation in which nonviolent struggle is practiced. Most cases are far less difficult than facing an extreme dictatorship. Against a powerful dictatorship, the resistance most likely would require several campaigns and considerable time to succeed. However, in some situations in which conditions are favorable and much groundwork has been laid, the collapse of a dictatorship may occur extremely rapidly, as occurred in Czechoslovakia and East Germany in 1989.

Handling the transition skillfully

Nonviolent strategists and leaders should early on provide resisters with insights to help them to face and solve problems they may encounter when the movement is on the verge of success or has accomplished its objective. Such problems may include attempts by the opponents to disrupt the movement, to promote claims that the success credited to the resisters was really gained by some other group, or they may even attempt to seize the State in a coup d'état.

In the past, several nonviolent struggles that were mostly or completely successful in achieving an objective were met with hostile intervention and disruption that damaged the achieved results or produced a new oppressive regime. For example, the successful anti-tsarist Russian Revolution of February/March 1917 was followed within a few months by the Bolshevik seizure of the State in October/November. Another example is the predominantly nonviolent Iranian revolution of 1979, which was followed by the establishment of the clerical dictatorship. Such events can be made less likely if they are anticipated and plans are prepared in advance to prevent and to counter these dangers.

If the struggle is a major one that aims to disintegrate an established dictatorship and that aim is gained, a period of political uncertainty is likely to follow. The resisters should calculate in advance how the transition from the dictatorship to the new interim government is to be handled at the end of the struggle in order to establish a viable and improved political system. The path should be blocked to any persons or group that would like to become the new dictators, while they of course deny that intention.

It is very important for nonviolent struggle strategists and leaders to assess the situation accurately. They will also need to consolidate the victory and decide how best to prevent and defeat possible hostile attacks. These may include international attacks, such as military aggression or activities of foreign intelligence services and their collaborators. Particular attention needs to be paid to preparing plans to defeat coups d'état,[2] and any other efforts to establish a new dictatorship. Attention will also need to be given to planning how to face the dangers of the transition between dictatorship and the new regime, and to the importance of building a free society with capacity to withstand possible new threats.

Short-term issues that merit attention during the transitional period include how to consolidate and strengthen newly established democratic and popular rule, how to induce the military and the police to shift loyalties and to accept the new system, and how to resist attempted seizures of the State.

It is wise to recognize that the social and political situation following the collapse of a dictatorship will not be the ideal society desired by all persons and groups. Major additional objectives

---

[2] See Gene Sharp and Bruce Jenkins, *The Anti-Coup*, Boston, Massachusetts: Albert Einstein Institution, 2003, and Gene Sharp, *Civilian-Based Defense*, Princeton, New Jersey: Princeton University Press, 1990.

will remain to be achieved in the future. These include creating and enriching the forms of democratic control, political freedom, popular participation, and social and economic justice. At this point, these will be at best imperfectly achieved and at worst will still be serious problems requiring major attention. The reality will be, however, that a grave form of oppression in the form of the old political order will have been effectively removed as the result of the wise and courageous nonviolent struggle by the population. This success opens the way for additional effective steps in improving and enriching human society.

Expanding future potential

In a world of many acute conflicts, widespread oppression, and great violence, the technique of nonviolent struggle has considerable potential to be applied with greater success than ever before in a wide range of situations. Strategic analysis, planning, and action can significantly increase the effectiveness of its future use.

The insights into the importance and the wise development of strategic nonviolent struggle here are not the final word. Nor are they the only studies of strategy in nonviolent struggles that strategic planners and leaders should examine. A very important additional analysis has been offered by Dr. Peter Ackerman and Dr. Christopher Kruegler in their book *Strategic Nonviolent Conflict: The Dynamics of People Power in the Twentieth Century*.[3] They offer detailed analyses of 12 general principles of strategic nonviolent conflict.

Another very important study is Robert Helvey, *On Strategic Nonviolent Conflict*.[4] It offers both a review of basic insights into this technique of struggle and more advanced analyses of several elements of the application of this technique. These include the strategic estimate, psychological operations, strategic analysis, fear, leadership, contaminants, and consultations.

It is now urgent that major attention and resources be devoted to the task of refining nonviolent struggle, expanding the skilled

---

[3] Peter Ackerman and Christopher Kruegler, *Strategic Nonviolent Conflict: The Dynamics of People Power in the Twentieth Century* (Westport, Connecticut and London: Praeger, 1994), Chapter Two, pp. 21-53.
[4] Robert Helvey, *On Strategic Nonviolent Conflict: Thinking About the Fundamentals,* Boston: Albert Einstein Institution, 2004.

strategic uses of this technique in place of violence, and exploring the types of conflict situations in which it can be applied in place of both passivity and violence.

Chapter Thirty-nine

APPLICATIONS OF NONVIOLENT STRUGGLE IN THE MODERN WORLD

Surveying a technique of empowerment

This book has thus far been an examination of the nature of a very important technique of struggle, a way to conduct conflicts. This technique has been widely practiced for centuries in many societies and cultures, and under diverse political circumstances. This technique is not magic. At times the people using it have been defeated, and at times the use of nonviolent struggle has achieved major successes. In light of the many acute conflicts of our world, the seriousness of oppression and extreme dictatorships, the dangers of passive submission, and the frequent gravity

---

This discussion draws on Gene Sharp and Bruce Jenkins, "The Power Potential of Nonviolent Struggle," in L. Astra and Grazina Miniotaite, *Nonviolence and Tolerance in Changing Eastern and Central Europe* (Vilnius, Lithuania: Logos Publishers, 1996), pp. 126-135.

of the use of violence in these conflicts, this underdeveloped technique of nonviolent struggle merits serious attention.

As many past improvised cases demonstrate, it has at times wielded great power. It clearly has already served as a replacement for violence when passivity has rightly been rejected. The cases of the use of this technique that were recounted in Part Two demonstrate that it has been used in improvised forms in struggles for diverse purposes.

These include efforts to achieve social and political liberation, block coups d'état, end racial segregation, achieve independence, save victims from genocide, bring down dictatorships, oppose foreign occupation, increase economic justice, find political prisoners, achieve self-organization, right particular wrongs, and correct electoral fraud.

Methods of nonviolent action have also been applied for purposes that most democrats and supporters of social justice would reject.[1] The results of these conflicts have lacked the moral and political appeal of the issues in the recounted cases, and have often been negative. However, the predictable consequences of the use of violence for those same purposes would have been far more unfortunate.

We have already surveyed earlier in this Part the possibilities of increasing the future effectiveness of this nonviolent technique of conflict by learning how to apply it more skillfully through the development and the implementation of wise strategies.

We began the book by observing in Part One that many of the social, economic, and political problems of our conflict-filled world are related to some groups having vastly more power than other groups. The more powerful groups often use this excess power for purposes that cause less powerful groups to feel threatened, injured, or oppressed. Usually, the excess power is applied with the threat or the use of organized violence, as well as bureaucratic and economic pressures.

If the members of the weaker population are not to submit passively, and if they are not to respond with violence, what are they to do? Not all conflicts in which fundamental issues are at

---

[1] For example, at certain points the Nazis organized economic boycotts of Jewish businesses, and segregationists in the U.S. South called in bank loans and refused to sell gasoline to known civil rights workers.

stake can be settled by compromise. Some issues are, or are at least believed to be, too important for that. Nonviolent struggle is a technique for waging conflict in such situations.

We have surveyed in Part Three the basic characteristics of nonviolent struggle, protest, noncooperation, and intervention using psychological, social, economic, and political methods. We have argued that this technique can be practical for waging conflict for groups that believe they are oppressed, dominated, or exploited by a more powerful group. Through the wise application of these methods, the previously weaker groups can mobilize their power potential into effective power to defend and advance their principles and objectives.

The primary rationale for use of nonviolent struggle has nothing to do with an ethical or religious rejection of violence. Nevertheless, we have shown that the dynamics of the technique operate in such a way that a resort to violence needs to be rejected because it can damage or destroy the effectiveness of a nonviolent struggle.

Various false preconceptions and stereotypes exist about this technique. Many people believe that nonviolent struggle requires a tie to strong religious or ethical systems, or must be led by charismatic personalities, or can only be applied against relatively humane political systems, or can only be used by resisters who have achieved an advanced moral condition. The 23 cases of application of this technique in the twentieth century that we reviewed in Part Two demonstrate that these preconceptions are mostly untrue.

Skillful action required

This is not a simple technique, however. It is a complex type of struggle that has been applied against ruthless dictatorships, as well as in relatively democratic societies. Because oppressors often prefer to be resisted by violence, they will often do their best to provoke resisters to shift to violence, with which they are well equipped to deal. Contrary to some opinions, nonviolent struggle almost never succeeds by melting the hearts of opponents. More often, this technique causes enough difficulties that opponents must at least compromise. In more extreme cases, the opponents' power is disintegrated—whatever they may prefer to do—just because the sources of their power have been so undermined and dissolved by noncooperation and defiance that the opponents no longer have control.

A very important change, one that often goes unrecognized, can occur in nonviolent struggles that are conducted reasonably competently. A population that has previously been weak, and therefore subordinated by a more powerful group, becomes empowered. This results from developing the capacity to work together and to conduct protests, boycotts, noncooperation, and intervention. The members of the formerly weaker group are able to transform their undeveloped power potential into mobilized power capacity. This also contributes in a significant way to the change in power relationships between the contending groups.

While there are various ways that can potentially make a given application of nonviolent struggle more effective, one of the most important appears to be the development and the application of a wise strategy. This can make possible the application of the strengths of the nonviolent struggle group against the weaknesses of the opponent group, in order to weaken the power of the opponents and to help to achieve the objectives of the struggle group.

Strategy has been mentioned during certain past conflicts. However, serious strategic planning has been quite rare. Strategic wisdom is not common, and there has been no guide to help struggle leaders to make the action as effective as possible. In the concluding chapters of this book, some perspectives and insights into strategic planning have been offered. It is hoped that these may assist groups in future struggles to make their activities more successful. Greater success in future struggles will not only increase the chances of social and political changes that will improve human life in the future. Such successes will also likely increase the likelihood of the use of nonviolent struggle instead of violence in future conflicts.

Deliberate applications of nonviolent struggle

With increased knowledge of nonviolent struggle in a world of major conflicts, we can now contemplate the deliberate adoption of this technique for particular purposes instead of some type of violence.

There are several general types of conflict situations that involve issues of great importance for which nonviolent struggle can be adapted, adopted, and applied with advantage. This should come as no surprise. As the cases in Part Two show, even without serious planning and preparations, this technique of struggle has been used to undermine dictatorships, defeat coups d'état, resist foreign occupations, and uproot social oppression. Nonviolent struggle has also been applied in grave ethnic conflicts, in many economic conflicts, and in struggles for social and religious liberties.

Although some important work has already been done in exploring the future deliberate application of this technique in certain of these types of conflict situations, much more effort is required. We are now at the beginning of a new stage in the development and the practice of nonviolent struggle. We have already begun to move beyond historical practice. Let us, therefore, introduce some potential applications of this technique.

Dismantling dictatorships

Nonviolent struggle has considerable capacity and great potential for destroying dictatorships and facilitating the transition to democratic political structures. Dictatorships have weaknesses and internal problems that, over time, contribute to their weakening, decline, and collapse.[2] These can be deliberately aggravated by targeted applications of nonviolent struggle.

There is significant historical experience in the use of improvised nonviolent struggle against severe dictatorships. This includes anti-Nazi resistance in Norway, Denmark, and The Netherlands—and even Berlin—as well as in liberation struggles against Communist tyranny in Poland, Estonia, Latvia, Lithuania, East Germany, and Czechoslovakia. The struggle in October 2000 to bring down the Milosevic regime in Serbia is another example. These cases clearly show that nonviolent struggle can play a significant role in the disintegration of dictatorships and in democratic replacement.

---

[2] See Karl W. Deutsch, "Cracks in the Monolith," in Carl J. Friedrich, ed., *Totalitarianism* (Cambridge, Massachusetts: Harvard University Press, 1954), esp. pp. 313-314; Gene Sharp, "Facing Dictatorships with Confidence," in *Social Power and Political Freedom* (Boston, Massachusetts: Porter Sargent, 1980), pp. 91-112.

Nonviolent struggle may have even more potential for bringing down dictatorships than does violent resistance. It may also do so with far less loss in human life, social destruction, international risks, and future political dangers. It is only reasonable to explore this option very seriously. Development of this option requires that we (1) learn how to identify and aggravate weaknesses of dictatorships; (2) learn how to sever their sources of power; (3) extract important lessons from past experience with resistance and uprisings; (4) make careful strategic analyses of how to accomplish the change in specific countries; and (5) make careful plans and preparations.[3]

Blocking coups d'état

Many dictatorships have come to power by seizing control of the State apparatus through coups d'état, which include executive usurpations. In such cases there is usually no legal remedy, since constitutional and legal barriers have already failed. Also, there is often no serious military option to oppose the coup, because the army itself frequently conducts or backs the coup, and a hopeless civil war against one's own army is an undesirable remedy.

There are a few examples of improvised noncooperation and defiance to defeat attempted coups in the twentieth century, such as the case of Germany in 1920 against the Kapp *Putsch,* and that of France in 1961 against the Algiers generals' coup, as we have seen. The popular resistance movements in Estonia, Latvia, and Lithuania, before and during the Moscow coup in 1991, are also very relevant, especially as they involved government planning with deep popular support and unfavorable circumstances.

A major issue therefore is how nonviolent struggle can be made more effective for this purpose and how this defense can be prepared and incorporated into societies and political systems.

---

[3] See Gene Sharp, *From Dictatorship to Democracy: A Conceptual Framework for Liberation,* Bangkok: Committee for the Restoration of Democracy in Burma, 1993 and Boston, Massachusetts: Albert Einstein Institution, 2002 and 2003.

For bibliographical references to resistance to dictatorships, see Ronald M. McCarthy and Gene Sharp, eds., *Nonviolent Action: A Research Guide* (New York and London: Garland Publishing, 1997), pp. 337-342, 350-357, 359-364, 372-374, 387-395, 447-465, and 476-490.

These suggestions do not imply that constitutional democratic polities are perfect and need no improvements, but only that they are far better than dictatorships.

Planned and legally obligated noncooperation by a nation's population, civil servants, police, and military personnel has great potential for creating serious obstacles to the consolidation of control and effective rule by usurpers, even if government offices are temporarily occupied.

This support for democratic government by nonviolent struggle against internal attackers has begun to receive serious governmental attention. The new 1997 constitution of Thailand assures the right of the citizenry to resist coups nonviolently. The Thai constitution is a historic first, but plans to prepare and implement this defense remain to be developed. Much additional work is merited and required to develop serious consideration and concrete implementation of such a defense capacity against coups. Preparations for widespread noncooperation and defiance may also deter future attempted coups.[4]

Increasing defense against foreign aggression and occupations

Instances of feared foreign military aggression and continued foreign occupations remain grave problems for many countries. The usual military superiority of aggressors and the desire to avoid immense casualties and vast destruction during a hopeless attempt at military resistance are well grounded reasons to explore seriously viable supplements or alternatives to military resistance and guerrilla warfare in defense.

The policy of "civilian-based defense" has been developed to build on improvised experience with nonviolent struggle against aggression and occupations, such as in the Ruhr in Germany in 1923, Czechoslovakia in 1968-1969, and the Baltic countries in 1990-1991. This policy requires careful advance planning, preparations, and training, in order to go beyond past experience and to increase future effectiveness of this type of defense.

Advance consideration of such a policy requires attention to potential attackers and their likely objectives, the capacity of various sections of the threatened society to deny to the attackers

---

[4] For more extensive discussion of the potential of prepared noncooperation and defiance to defeat coups d'état, see Gene Sharp and Bruce Jenkins, *The Anti-Coup*, Boston, Massachusetts: Albert Einstein Institution, 2003. For other references, see McCarthy and Sharp, eds., *Nonviolent Action*, pp. 652-654.

their objectives, appropriate types of noncooperation and defiance, means of organization, responses to likely brutalities, means to undermine the attackers' regime, and ways to mobilize international assistance, as well as other elements.

Civilian-based defense has significant potential for small states that wish to remain independent and as a supplementary policy for countries that need to strengthen their total defense capacity beyond that possible by military means. For example, Lithuania in late 2000 formally added a nonviolent resistance component as part of its official defense policy. Several other governments had done so earlier with only limited implementation. However, the Lithuanian decision appears to be a more serious effort. Careful consideration, advance planning, and phased introduction of preparations for civilian-based resistance are usually recommended for a credible limited defense component or as small steps toward full adoption.[5]

Lifting oppression of ethnic, religious, and racial groups

Many societies experience various types of ethnic, religious, or racial conflicts. The specific issues vary widely and are often perceived differently by the contending groups. The issues may be seen by grievance groups to be social justice, religious liberty, racial equality, autonomy, political independence, full integration, and respectful treatment. The violence that is applied by the oppressing group—and sometimes also by the oppressed group—can escalate to catastrophic levels.

Nonviolent struggle may provide an alternative means of action for groups that would otherwise rely on forms of violence, such as terrorism or guerrilla warfare. Nonviolent action may provide ethnic, religious, or racial minorities with an effective means of pressuring unresponsive governments, third parties, or

---

[5] On civilian-based defense, see Gene Sharp, *Civilian-Based Defense: A Post-Military Weapons System*, Princeton, New Jersey: Princeton University Press, 1990; Adam Roberts, ed., *The Strategy of Civilian Defence*, London: Faber and Faber, 1967 and Harmondsworth, Middlesex, England and Baltimore, Maryland: Penguin, 1969; also issued as *Civilian Resistance as a National Defense*, Harrisburg, Pennsylvania: Stackpole, 1968; and Johan Jörgen Holst, "Civilian-Based Defense in a New Era," Cambridge, Massachusetts: Albert Einstein Institution, 1990. For references to other literature, see McCarthy and Sharp, eds., *Nonviolent Action*, pp. 577-582.

even the dominant group to address their grievances. Such non-violent pressures could potentially lead to the deeper incorporation of an ethnic group into the political system of the country in which they live, as the United States civil rights movement did to a certain degree. The choice of nonviolent means in that case not only was powerful in breaking down segregation, but also was beneficial to the whole society. Such incorporation may provide a more stable framework for addressing the grievances of a dominated group.

On the other hand, some groups may be committed to autonomy or independence rather than integration, and may apply nonviolent struggle to that end. Deliberate, planned nonviolent struggle can offer significant advantages to such groups seeking independence. While majority groups in dominant positions rarely are enamored with nonviolent independence movements, it can be argued that the choice of nonviolent means of struggle by the pro-independence groups is, in the long run, beneficial to all concerned.[6]

Lifting social and economic injustices

Populations that see themselves as suffering from social and economic injustices commonly are weaker than the groups and institutions that have imposed the wrongs against them. Under those conditions, it is not surprising that members or supporters of the group believed to be victimized sometimes resort to violence in the forms of rioting, terrorism, or guerrilla warfare in order to right the wrongs. In other cases, they may seek to win the favor of the government, or gain control of the State through elections or other means, in order to use its superior power to change the structural situation.

Nonviolent struggle by the subordinate group can provide an alternative to both such violence and the growth of State power.[7]

---

[6] For references to the use of nonviolent action in the U.S. civil rights movement, see McCarthy and Sharp, eds., *Nonviolent Action,* pp. 191-228. For a discussion of the use of nonviolent struggle in ethnic conflicts, see Gene Sharp, "Nonviolent Action in Acute Interethnic Conflicts" in Eugene Weiner, *The Handbook of Interethnic Coexistence* (New York: Continuum, 1998), pp. 371-381.

[7] For bibliographical references to the use of labor strikes in the U.S. and Canada, see McCarthy and Sharp, eds., *Nonviolent Action,* pp. 155-189, for Britain, see pp. 406-418, and for the use of economic boycotts, see pp. 508-510. For references to theo-

In fact, various forms of nonviolent action, such as labor strikes and economic boycotts, have historically been used to win higher wages and improved working conditions, and continue to do so. Only rarely have these methods been used to gain restructuring of economic ownership and controls, however. Careful consideration is needed of the potential role of nonviolent struggle for effecting changes in economic ownership or in altering global economic policies or conditions.

The use of nonviolent struggle can contribute significantly to the empowerment of people who have lacked effective capacity to help shape their lives and may also contribute to a more equitable distribution of power in the society.

Preserving and extending democratic practices and human rights

Nonviolent action can provide a powerful corrective to tendencies in all societies to centralize political power and ignore or give inadequate attention to human rights, civil liberties, and democratic practices. Societies with only the formal trappings of democratic rule, but not the substance, may provide no recourse for the disadvantaged or weaker sections of the population who feel aggrieved.

It is easy to violate human rights when the population is too weak to offer serious resistance. Recognition and practice of human rights will be undeniable when the population is strong and skilled in forms of action to ensure they can assert and defend their rights against all threats and attacks.

Popular empowerment through nonviolent action may place a check on the centralization of power and may provide groups constructive avenues of social action. While such organized resistance may be seen as an immediate threat to power-holders, nonviolent action for human rights, civil liberties, or increased political participation can actually strengthen the democratic fiber of a society and contribute to greater stability.[8]

---

retical discussions on nonviolent revolution, see pp. 582-583, and on broader examinations of revolutions, see pp. 646-652.

[8] For references to the woman suffrage movement in the U.S., see McCarthy and Sharp, eds., *Nonviolent Action,* pp. 132-138, and in Britain see pp. 401-494. For references to diverse other cases of actions to preserve and extend democratic practices

Dictatorship prevention

In past decades, it was common to assert that nonviolent struggle could be effective only when confronting a democratic opponent and rarely, if ever, when facing a dictatorial regime. This objection has not been heard so often in recent years. More has been learned about nonviolent resistance under Nazi rule, against military regimes, and about the nonviolent struggles in Communist-ruled Central and Eastern European countries. It is undeniable that effective struggles under such harsh political conditions are much more difficult than those occurring under relatively benign political systems. Nevertheless, nonviolent struggles in Poland, East Germany, Czechoslovakia, Estonia, Latvia, Lithuania, and the Soviet Union (against the 1991 coup), and Serbia (in October 2000) have changed the political map of Europe.

Most people understandably wish to prevent their societies from being ruled by dictatorships in the first place. However, they do not see that preparations for nonviolent struggle will have a preventive, or deterrent, effect. Major attention is needed to the potential role of prepared nonviolent struggle in a wider comprehensive program of dictatorship prevention. Such a program of dictatorship prevention should have as a prominent component plans to block future coups d'état, which constitute a major way in which dictatorships are initially established.[9]

Genocide

In light of the various attempts by governments to conduct massive slaughters and commit genocide, many people assume that nonviolent struggle is helpless against attempted genocide. This contention, too, is rarely examined critically, especially in comparison to the effects of passive submission or of violent resistance against the capacity of a State or a group to inflict genocide. Genocide-prone regimes are dependent in some cases not only on

---

and human rights, see *Nonviolent Action,* passim. For a theoretical analysis of such uses, see Gene Sharp, "Popular Empowerment," in *Social Power and Political Freedom,* pp. 309–378.
[9] See Gene Sharp and Bruce Jenkins, *The Anti-Coup,* for recommendations on preparations to block coups that could be taken by governments and by nongovernmental organizations.

the submission of their victims, but on the obedience and cooperation of their own populations and aides, such as the bureaucracy and the police and military forces. Their behavior may in
turn be affected by the behavior of the targeted population.

Not all attempts to perpetrate genocide have been equally successful. Nazi attempts to deport Jews for extermination did not
have the same effects in all occupied countries. While in some
countries the proportion deported to the camps was high, the
proportion was markedly low in others, such as Norway, Denmark, France, Italy, and Bulgaria. This was because some groups
whose cooperation was required to assist the deportations refused
to help. Sometimes it was the intended victims themselves who refused cooperation, and sometimes it was the general population,
collaborating governments, or even German officials. There is
also suggestive evidence from the Nazi period that wartime conditions significantly facilitated the implementation of the Nazi desire to exterminate Jews.[10]

Major historical and social research is needed into past resistance of various types against attempts to impose genocide, and
to the effects of this resistance on the actions of the genocidal regimes. It is important to identify the key points at which it has
been possible to frustrate genocidal efforts and to identify how
those blockages were accomplished. Further study is also required
into the effectiveness of different forms of struggle that may be
carried out by the intended victims of genocide.

Preservation of indigenous peoples and cultures

Indigenous people in various parts of the world face constant
serious conflicts because other societies, often with major political, economic, and military power, converge on them. Counter-
violence by the indigenous populations can facilitate supposedly

---

[10] See Gerald Reitlinger, *The Final Solution: The Attempt to Exterminate the Jews of
Europe 1939-1945,* New York: A. S. Barnes & Co., 1961 (1953); Raul Hilberg, *The
Destruction of the European Jews,* Chicago, Illinois: Quadrangle Books, 1961; Nora
Levin, *The Holocaust: The Destruction of European Jewry 1933-1945,* New York:
Schoken Books, 1973; Louis P. Lochner, ed. and transl., *The Goebbels Diaries 1942-
1943* (Garden City, New York: Doubleday & Co., 1948), pp. 148 and 116; Hannah
Arendt, *Eichmann in Jerusalem: A Report on the Banality of Evil, New* York: Viking
Press, 1963; and Gene Sharp, *Social Power and Political Freedom* (Boston: Porter Sar-
gent, 1980), Chapter 3, "The Lesson of Eichmann," pp. 69-90.

defensive extreme violent repression of the resisting population by the intruding society. This violent repression will contribute, slowly or rapidly, to annihilation and genocide of the population.

However, the methods of noncooperation (as distinct from other methods of nonviolent struggle) are not of obvious effectiveness when the intruding society has little or no need for the cooperation of the indigenous population. At times, this is similar to the situation faced by intended victims of genocide. What kind of strategy of nonviolent struggle or other action is relevant in those situations?

Noncooperation with the intruding society may be required in attempts to preserve as much as possible of the original culture and society of the indigenous population. However, without dependence on the indigenous society, noncooperation with the intruders cannot be a very effective means of resisting the intrusion itself. Other types of methods are likely to be required that are targeted to secure the support of sections of the intruding society or of potentially influential international groups that could assist the defending indigenous society.

Attempts to apply nonviolent struggle, including noncooperation, can be used along with other peaceful means to help to preserve as best as possible the original society. The objectives of these efforts can include preservation of identity, language, custom, culture, and social structure. Attention is also required on how to arouse support from the international community—and even the population of the intruding country. Much can potentially be learned from study of significant cases of cultural survival even during centuries of foreign occupation. In some cases, not only have the language and identity survived, but nations have been reborn centuries after the names of their countries have been erased from the maps.

Nonviolent struggle in the midst of violent conflict

In some situations in which a major struggle is already under way and in which both sides are already relying on violence, it is very difficult to determine how the use of nonviolent struggle can be helpfully introduced. The situation itself is exceptionally difficult, and potentially tragic. Innovative strategic analyses are needed to explore what might be done in such situations to increase effectiveness and reduce dependence on violence.

Some problems and objections

Considerable skepticism about the future potential of nonviolent struggle as a substitute for violence continues to be widespread despite the extensive, albeit improvised, past use of this technique in conflicts. Some of the main problems are those that pertain to the feasibility and effectiveness of applying this technique to particular types of conflicts. Other problems include questions of timing, issues at stake, and types of opponents. We need to identify some of these general problems and issues and also to discuss them briefly.

Standards of evaluation

Perhaps the most common problem in popular acceptance of this technique is that the potential, merits, problems, and weaknesses of nonviolent struggle and of violent struggle, as well as their successes and failures, are rarely examined and evaluated by use of the same standards and criteria.

Nonviolent struggles are commonly held to much higher standards than violent ones. There seems to be a widespread simple belief in the superior efficacy of violence in acute conflicts, which is not always the result of rational and critical examination of evidence.

"Success" in a nonviolent struggle is often measured not only by whether the objective of the conflict was achieved, but by whether different important issues and conditions that were not in contention in that specific conflict existed after the initial conflict had ended. For example, the achievements of the Indian nonviolent struggles that contributed to independence are sometimes deprecated because, after independence, communal tensions and poverty still exist in the subcontinent. However, in a violent conflict when the goals of the struggle were *not* achieved, but major destruction, injury, and death were inflicted on the opponent group, that violent conflict is often regarded as a success. It is important to establish careful standards for evaluating success and failure in conflicts and to apply these standards in a balanced way to both nonviolent and violent struggles.

Additional concerns for future study

There are other problems and questions as well that require significant attention by both researchers and practitioners of nonviolent struggle.

Nonviolent struggles can be decentralized to a much greater degree than most violent struggles. If widespread decentralization is characteristic of a particular struggle, it will be important to examine how the conflict can nevertheless be conducted in a disciplined manner. To what degree are decentralization and discipline compatible when implementing a strategic plan?

If the issues in a conflict are not political, but instead economic, how can nonviolent struggle best be applied? The impact and potential of domestic resistance on economic issues is seriously weakened by the globalization of economic activity and controls. What is the potential role for nonviolent struggle against international economic institutions or policies? The dynamics and the operation of nonviolent struggle will likely be more complex in such conflicts and are worthy of further study.

A new stage of development

At the beginning of the twenty-first century, we have reached a new stage in the development of nonviolent struggle. It is now possible to refine this technique, to make it more effective, to increase the chances of success while reducing casualties, and to adapt it for use in meeting the types of acute conflicts that we have identified.

A great deal more research, analysis, policy development, and planning is still required to explore and develop the potential of nonviolent struggle to address acute conflicts of our time. These efforts will require going beyond, and often against, important established trends of modern society and powerful national and international forces. The centralization of power, the militarization of interstate politics, and the hegemony of traditional methods of problem-solving. These and other factors work against reasoned consideration of the potential relevance of nonviolent struggle.

However, such consideration is likely to reveal realistic possibilities that have not previously been adequately explored.

The extent to which we can increase the effectiveness of non-violent struggle for these purposes will to a very high degree determine the extent to which violent sanctions will be replaced with nonviolent forms of struggle. Expanded applications of non-violent struggle in the future will not only contribute to the reduction of major violence but to the expansion of democratic practices, political freedom, and social justice. The choice is ours.

Appendix A

PREPARING A STRATEGIC ESTIMATE FOR NONVIOLENT STRUGGLE

Before attempting to plan an overall grand strategy for a long-term phased nonviolent struggle, or limited strategies for individual campaigns within that struggle, it is necessary first to gather and analyze much information about the context in which the impending conflict will occur.

It is insufficient simply to be familiar with the technique of nonviolent struggle and understand how it operates, although this is a vital prerequisite. Rather, in order to make the application of nonviolent struggle as effective as possible in a given set of circumstances, strategic planning is also essential.

It is impossible to develop a wise strategy for the conduct of a particular struggle if the planners are not intimately familiar with the "conflict situation," or the context in which the struggle will take place. It is essential to know and compare the characteristics, strengths, and weaknesses (actual and potential) of the groups that will be contending in the future conflict, as well as of those groups that will not initially be directly involved. Geographic, social, economic, political, cultural, climatological, and other factors also need to be examined.

The preparation of a strategic estimate can provide this needed knowledge. This, in turn, will increase the ability of strategists of the nonviolent struggle to prepare a wise strategy that will maximize the chances of achieving their objective.

The aim of this essay is to provide guidelines for preparing this strategic estimate. We will first explain what the strategic estimate is. Then, we will survey factors that need to be taken into consideration when gathering relevant information and preparing that analysis. Finally, we will comment on the role of the strategic estimate, its uses and limitations.

This appendix is based on the work of Robert Helvey, President of the Albert Einstein Institution.

The importance of a strategic estimate

Military planners usually prepare a strategic estimate prior to developing plans for their campaigns. The information produced by this process is extremely useful for nonviolent struggles as well. So far as is known, however, a deliberate and thorough examination of the conflict situation of the type required for preparing a strategic estimate has never been done in preparation for past nonviolent struggles. Instead, past nonviolent struggle leaders have, at best, relied on less rigorous impressions of the impending conflict situation. Past struggle groups have therefore often been less prepared than they could have been for developing a course of action to increase their chances of success. The proper use of a strategic estimate can help to prepare them more adequately, as well as to reduce the likelihood that they will overlook important facts in planning a nonviolent struggle.

At its most basic level, a strategic estimate is a calculation and comparison of the strengths and the weaknesses of the nonviolent struggle group and of that group's opponents, whom we shall call the "opponent group." In some conflicts, the opponent group may be the government itself or a specific part of the ruling regime. In other cases, the opponent group could be a nongovernmental body, such as an educational institution, an economic organization, a religious body, a transportation system, or some other type of institution. A nongovernmental opponent group may have the backing of the current government, with its means of control and repression, or it may not. The proper identification of such relationships is, in fact, one of the first tasks in preparing a strategic estimate.

Of particular value to those involved in strategy development would be the sections that contain analyses regarding the pillars of support of both the opponent group and the nonviolent struggle group, as well as other political considerations. Also, those responsible for propaganda would find demographic considerations quite useful. Information regarding military units, such as locations and capabilities, would be quite useful to operational planners in anticipating military responses to applications of nonviolent resistance. Other components of the strategic estimate will be relevant to other elements of the chosen strategy.

In order to gain the relevant information for the strategic estimate, however, it will take time and energy. While this information can be very valuable, strategic planners must also remember that the strategic estimate is not the only important factor in developing strategies and supporting plans for a future struggle. Therefore, it needs to be kept in perspective. Strategic planners need to avoid becoming bogged down in the minutiae of the situation and need to keep the strategic estimate within the context of other important elements in the development of strategies and the formulation of plans for their implementation. In this regard, one should be mindful of the advice given by Carl von Clausewitz that "strategy forms the theory of using battle for the purposes of war." In other words, using in part the analysis of information gathered for the strategic estimate, the strategist determines objectives, times and places for campaigns, while those who will wage these battles prepare their own supporting plans.[1] They, in turn, may draw upon the strategic estimate to complete their own estimate of the situation. The emphasis placed upon some portions of the strategic estimate provides an indication of the importance to the planners in determining both the strategy and also how this information should influence supporting plans.

The strategic estimate of the conflict situation is perhaps the most fundamental document on which a strategic planner relies. It is the product of intense, structured, and focused intellectual scrutiny that contributes to greater understanding of the situation in which the struggle will be waged, and the selection of the most effective courses of action to achieve the objectives of the conflict. Since the strategic operational plan is based heavily on the strategic estimate, both the quantity of information analyzed and the quality of the analysis itself help to determine the quality of the developed strategy. Ideally, this document should be critically reviewed in draft form, so that others can challenge the accuracy of facts and the quality of analyses.

Inaccurate or unrealistic views of the strengths, the weaknesses, and the capacities of the contending parties will produce unwise strategies and will likely spell defeat. Although it may at

---

[1] *Neue Bellona 9 (1805)*, p. 271. Quoted from Peter Paret, ed., *Makers of Modern Strategy: From Machiavelli to the Nuclear Age* (Princeton, New Jersey: Princeton University Press, 1986), p. 190.

times be necessary to make assumptions about the contending parties when facts cannot be obtained, no assumption is as good as a fact. So it is important to make as few assumptions as possible. If assumptions are used, extra care should be taken to ensure their probable validity. Of course, it is far better to use facts wherever possible.

Needed information

There are seven subject areas about which the persons preparing the strategic estimate should seek solid information. These are:

1. The general conflict situation
2. The issues at stake and the objectives of both parties to the conflict
3. The opponent group
4. The nonviolent struggle group (and the wider grievance group)
5. Third parties (friendly, hostile, and neutral or uncommitted)
6. Dependency balances

On the basis of the information and the understanding produced by such an examination, the nonviolent struggle group will be better equipped to prepare wise strategies to guide the conduct of the conflict.

The strategic estimate serves multiple purposes. The strategic estimate process will greatly assist in identifying strategy options. Additionally, it becomes an important reference document for developing supporting plans to implement the chosen strategies. The strategic estimate is also useful when developing policies and responding to crises, and for providing organizations with a source of sound and thoughtful analysis and factual data.

As you review the following information requirements contained in a strategic estimate, it may appear quite daunting—and it is, indeed. But rather than visualizing one person attempting to gather and analyze all this information, you should be thinking, Who knows about this particular topic and can that person or persons provide information to me? Once information is received from subject experts, that which is directly relevant to the estimating process can be included in the strategic estimate.

1. The general conflict situation

It is useful to list here in some detail some of the many categories of information about the general conflict situation in which the nonviolent struggle will be conducted. These may provide extensive and in-depth knowledge of the conflict situation. It is highly desirable to be familiar with all factors that could have a conceivable impact either on the opponent group or on the nonviolent struggle group. These include, but are not limited to, the following:

- **Terrain and geography**
  (including land forms and waterways, and how they may assist or impede one or the other side in the conflict)

- **Transportation**
  (including all available means of transportation for either side in the conflict, local and national transportation infrastructure, alternative routes, and how these might impact the capabilities of either side)

- **Communications**
  (all types, access, extent of controls, surveillance, issues of privacy, etc.)

- **Climate and weather**
  (including seasonal variations and their possible impact on transportation, communications, food and agriculture, and activities of either side)

- **Political system and governing regime**
  (including their characteristics and capacities on various levels, from the top echelons down to small units; any variations in central control or local initiatives; and who controls the State and the roles or functions of the State, political parties, and controlled subordinate organizations)

- **Economic system**
  (including both type and condition of the economy, strength and degree of independence of unions and business sectors, and degree of State intervention in the economy)

- **Judicial system**
  (especially the degree to that this remains independent of the control of the State or of the opponent group)

- **Demographics**
  (information about both the total population and the segment of the population related to the conflict, including statistical breakdowns by age groups, gender, population growth and death rates, population densities in varying locations, and literacy rates)

- **Population strata**
  (including socioeconomic classes, ethnicities, religion, language, culture, status of indigenous and immigrant populations, etc.; geographical distribution of such; any variations or differences in these groups in satisfaction, loyalties, or economic interests; and also any conflicts between or among different population groups, whether or not the reasons for such conflicts are related to the nonviolent struggle)

- **Control of economic resources and life support**
  (fuel, food, water, etc., and consequences for dependency of one side on the other)

- **Status of civil society**
  (extent and condition of nongovernmental organizations and social life, including degree of organization and autonomy from the State; and status of other aspects of social life and organization that lie outside control of the political system and/or the regime)

In addition, it is important to examine the immediate general political situation. Are special controls, such as martial law or other means of serious repression, in effect? What are the current political and economic currents and trends?

2. The issues and objectives of the contending groups

It is very important to identify or develop accurate and clear statements of the issues at stake in the conflict from the perspectives of both the opponent group and the prospective nonviolent struggle group. These statements may often be based on declarations by each group, but sometimes additional information from other sources, independent observers, or other groups may be required.

Also, it is important to identify and recognize the differing objectives of the two groups. To what degree are these objectives compatible or incompatible? The stated objectives are not always the full story. Both groups may have not only short-term objectives but also long-term goals that may not be avowed at the time. Both types are significant in preparing strategies for the nonviolent struggle group.

Clear objectives for the nonviolent struggle group are prerequisites for developing strategies and supporting plans for their implementation. If objectives have not been stated at the time the strategic estimate is being prepared, it would be appropriate to make very careful assessments about the aims of both the opponent group and the struggle group.

The issues and objectives of the two contending groups, and how fundamental each side believes them to be, are likely to have important consequences on the actions of both sides during the conflict. These issues and objectives will likely influence the degree to which the opponent group is determined to resist or repress the resistance. The issues and objectives will also likely influence the tenacity of the nonviolent struggle group to persist in the struggle despite repression. Additionally, the degree to which third parties or the general population are willing to side with the nonviolent struggle group will often also depend partly on how such sectors view the issues at stake in the conflict.

3. The opponent group

Full and detailed knowledge of the opponent group that the nonviolent struggle group will face in the pending conflict is extremely important. Such knowledge should focus on the opponents' capabilities rather than on their statements of intent or on assumptions about their interests or intentions. Detailed responses to the following questions about the opponent group are required:

- What is their political system?
- What is their social and cultural system?
- What is their economic system?

- Are these systems independent of each other, or closely interrelated? Are they dependent in any way on the political, social, or economic systems of the potential nonviolent struggle group?

- To what degree are these respective systems controlled by the State structure?

- What is the nature and importance of any religious, moral, ideological, or other doctrinal beliefs and commitments of the opponent group?

- What are the demographics of the opponent group? (age, gender, birth and death rates, literacy, educational standards, and geographical distribution, etc.)

- What is the degree of support for the opponent group's system or regime among the general population and institutions?

- What is the ideological situation (the degree of doctrinal support for the opponent group and/or regime, or for the resistance to its policies and controls)?

- To what degree does the opponent group rely on each of its potential sources of power?
  - Authority or legitimacy
  - Human resources
  - Particular skills or knowledge
  - Psychological or ideological factors
  - Material resources
  - Ability to apply sanctions

- What are the pillars of support of the opponent group (people, groups, and institutions) that supply the needed sources of power? Some of these pillars will require detailed examination. The pillars may include, but are not limited to, the following:
  - Moral and religious leaders and groups
  - Labor groups
  - Business and investment groups
  - Civil servants and bureaucrats
  - Administrators
  - Technicians
  - Police
  - Prisons

- Military forces
- Intelligence services
- Media
- Foreign investors
- Particular classes or ethnic groups

- To what extent are the pillars of support influenced, or actually or potentially controlled, by the opponent group itself? Are any influenced or controlled by the broad grievance group or the potential nonviolent struggle group? Which pillars are the strongest and most durable? Which pillars are the weakest and most vulnerable?

- Who are the opponent group's internal (domestic) allies, and what is their extent and reliability?

- Who are the opponent group's external (foreign) allies and what is their extent and reliability?

- Can any of these be considered "natural allies" of the opponent group? (If the opponent is a government or a regime, these might include the army, intelligence services, civil servants, the business community, settlers, foreign governments, certain political parties, etc.)

- Who are the "natural enemies" of the opponent group? (Examples may include repressed minorities, disaffected youth, the unemployed, workers, political parties, the lower, middle, or upper classes, etc.)

- Is there any potential or actual support or sympathy for the nonviolent struggle group from within sectors of the opponent group itself?

- What is the organizational structure of the opponent group (administration, organizational branches, complexity, efficiency, reliability, degree of initiative, degree of centralized controls, etc.)?

- What is the opponent group's military capacity? Necessary information includes the following:
  - Strength, number, size, structure, and types of units
  - Locations of units
  - Opponents' military capabilities to counter resistance, impose repression and restore control, including their capacity and willingness to inflict brutalities

- The speed with which the military forces can arrive at specific locations where quick demonstrations might occur
- Commanders of the important units and their characteristics
- Personality profiles of select officials and commanders
- Efficiency, reliability, and morale among troops
- General profile of military personnel, including education, class, religion, politics, motivation, ethnic group, age range, and possible reasons for disaffection
- Logistics of troop movements and operations, location of supply lines, and means of re-supply

- What is the opponent group's police capacity? (The same type of information obtained about military forces—as described above—needs to be obtained for police and other security forces as well.)

- What intelligence organizations, if any, does the opponent group have at its disposal? What are their characteristics, including their known activities and their resources?

- What is the level of the opponent group's strategic skill?

- To what degree does the opponent group have competent leadership?

- What means of nonmilitary control are wielded by the opponent group? Examples may include the following:
  - Censorship
  - Ownership of radio, television, and print media
  - Control of education
  - Financial means to influence behavior
  - Control of private industry or State enterprises
  - International recognition
  - Control of communications technology
  - Control of the judiciary

- What are the political fissures, internal conflicts, and other weaknesses in the opponent group, such as within the leadership group and supporting organizations, institutions, or population groups?

- Are there any organizations or institutions that normally support the opponent group but might be targeted for transfer of loyalties or for organizational destruction?

- Is the present leadership of the opponent group disputed or contested from within, through rivalries, power struggles, or other reasons?

- What other vulnerabilities and weaknesses of the opponents can be identified? These may include, but are not limited to, the following:
  - Vulnerabilities and internal conflicts
  - Incompetent leadership or governing ability
  - Being despised by, or leaving a generally unfavorable impression on, the population
  - Lack of trained strategists
  - Ideological bankruptcy
  - Economic crisis
  - Corruption
  - Lack of ability to withstand foreign diplomatic or economic pressure
  - Overreliance on repression or military means as a means of control

4. The nonviolent struggle group (and the wider grievance group)

Full and detailed knowledge of the nonviolent struggle group and the "grievance group" (defined as the wider population that suffers from policies and actions of the opponent group) and other potential or actual sympathizers is just as important as knowledge about the opponent group. The interests and intentions of the nonviolent struggle group are not very useful for this part of the strategic estimate (though they should be recorded when examining the issues and stake and objectives of the contending sides, as described above). Rather, attention should be focused here only on the group's actual condition and capabilities.

Detailed responses to the following questions about the nonviolent struggle group are therefore required:

- What are the demographics of the nonviolent struggle group and its potential or actual sympathizers, including the general grievance group (age, gender, geographical distribution, literacy rates, and educational levels, etc.)?

- What is their political system?

- What is their social and cultural system?

- What is their economic system?

- Do these systems operate independently of each other, or are they closely interrelated? To what extent are they identical to, integrated with, or independent of, the political, social, or economic systems of the opponent group?

- To what degree are these respective systems controlled by the State structure?

- What is the nature and importance of any religious, moral, ideological, or other doctrinal beliefs or commitments of the grievance group and the nonviolent struggle group?

- What is the broad ideological situation (the degree of doctrinal support for the nonviolent struggle group, and its ideas, positions, or platforms)?

- What is the actual and potential degree of support for the nonviolent struggle group from the general grievance population, specific groups, institutions, and contact networks? Which groups can really help?

- What sectors of the population are most or least likely to provide support or sympathy to the nonviolent struggle group over the course of the conflict?

- What is the actual and potential degree of support for resistance from third parties or previously "neutral" sectors?

- Who are the "natural allies" of the nonviolent struggle group? (e.g., students or youth, political parties and associations, religious, ethnic, or minority groups, etc.)

- Who are the nonviolent struggle group's current and potential internal and external allies?

- What are the internal conflicts, rivalries, or power struggles within both the grievance group and the nonviolent struggle group (e.g., groups with differing ideological positions or long-term objectives)? Are there any rivalries between important sectors of the grievance group and the nonviolent struggle group?

- Is there any potential or actual support or sympathy for the opponent group from within sectors of the general grievance group or the nonviolent struggle group?

- What are the operative or potential sources of power of the nonviolent struggle group? What are the operative or potential sources of power of the general grievance group?
  - Authority or legitimacy
  - Human resources
  - Particular skills or knowledge
  - Psychological or ideological factors
  - Material resources
  - Ability to apply sanctions

- What are the pillars of support (people, groups, and institutions) that serve to supply those sources of power? Some of these pillars will require detailed examination. Examples may include
  - Moral and religious leaders and groups
  - Labor groups
  - Business and investment groups
  - Civil servants and bureaucrats
  - Administrators
  - Technicians
  - Media
  - Dominated classes or ethnic groups
  - Youth and/or student organizations
  - Other societal institutions

- To what extent are such pillars of support for the grievance group or the nonviolent struggle group influenced, or actually or potentially controlled by, the nonviolent struggle group, or by the opponent group?

- Which pillars are suitable for use in resistance activities? Which ones need to be strengthened? Do any new ones need to be created?

- What other vulnerabilities and weaknesses can be identified? Can any of these be rectified through deliberate efforts?

- Does the nonviolent struggle group currently exist as a coherent movement or organization? If so, what is its organizational structure (administration, organizational branches, complexity, efficiency, reliability, degree of initiative, degree of centralized controls, etc.)? Does it have capable and competent leadership?

- What is the strategic skill level of the nonviolent struggle group and its leaders?

- Who among the nonviolent struggle group has knowledge of the theory, methods, and practical dynamics of nonviolent struggle?

- Does the grievance group as a whole, parts of that group, or the nonviolent struggle group have prior experience in using nonviolent struggle?
  - Where has it occurred in the past?
  - What population sectors were involved?
  - How competently were such struggles carried out?
  - What were the results?
  - What lessons can those past struggles bring to the present situation?
  - Is the recollection of such struggles remembered reasonably accurately, or has a mythology about them been perpetuated? What are the consequences of this?

- What preparations have already been made for the application of nonviolent struggle in this conflict?

- What means of nonmilitary control, if any, are already wielded by the nonviolent struggle group or its sympathizers? Examples may include the following:
  - Ownership of radio, television, and print media
  - Ownership or control of electronic media sources
  - Control of education (through school administration, teachers, professors, alternate schooling, etc.)
  - Control of private industry
  - International recognition of legitimacy

- What is the information and intelligence capacity of the nonviolent struggle group?

- What economic resources are at the disposal of the nonviolent struggle group?

- What are the communications capacities of the resisters?
  - How are communications transmitted?
  - How secure are these means?

It is necessary, finally, to provide a general assessment of the struggle capacity of both the nonviolent struggle group and the general grievance group, based largely on the above information. Wise strategists will not plan a campaign that requires a struggle capacity beyond the current abilities of the nonviolent struggle group. If an expanded struggle capacity is needed, attention must be devoted to the means required to develop this increased strength.

5. Third parties

It is very important to assess the potential roles of third parties on behalf of either of the two sides over the course of a conflict. "Third parties" are defined here as any group, institution, or sector, internal or external, that is not initially a direct party to the conflict. Third party roles may include, but are not limited to, the following:

- Assisting public relations (for either side)
- Providing diplomatic assistance or exerting diplomatic pressures (for either side)
- Supplying financial assistance (for either side)
- Providing police and military assistance (for the opponent group); (police or military action intended to assist the nonviolent struggle can instead undermine it)
- Providing educational and technical assistance (for either side)
- Providing safe areas (usually for the resisters but sometimes for the opponent group)
- Applying economic pressures (on either side)
- Providing knowledge about nonviolent struggle (primarily to the resisters)

It is also necessary to assess which third parties could potentially provide such assistance to either side, and also to determine which groups already serve as pillars of support to one side or the other. Strategists will later need to determine which third parties should be courted for possible future assistance and which groups should be undermined.

6. Dependency balances

In the development of strategies for the struggle, it is important to determine which of the two contending sides is dependent on the other, in what ways and to what degree. These calculations should include the following:

- The degree of dependency of the opponent group on the resisting population and on the wider grievance group for meeting identified needs

- The degree of dependency of the resisting population and the grievance group on the opponent group for meeting identified needs

- The degree of actual and potential independence of the opponent group from the resisting population and general grievance group for meeting identified needs

- The degree of actual and potential independence of the resisting population and grievance group from the opponent group for meeting identified needs

Conclusion

After preparing a strategic estimate, it will be necessary to update it as changes occur in the conflict situation. A strategic estimate for a specific conflict that has been well prepared on the basis of accurate and complete information will make it possible to think clearly and make wise decisions about how to act, even in the face of serious pressures and difficult circumstances. This document, with a structured format, allows the reader to find information quickly that is both general and detailed.

This estimate will be of great assistance when choosing specific types of methods for use during the conflict. For example, if the opponent group is heavily dependent on the grievance group for meeting certain needs, methods of noncooperation may prove to be highly effective. However, if there is no such dependence, noncooperation is unlikely to be useful.

If the strategic estimate reveals that the nonviolent struggle group is weaker than required for a major struggle with the prospective opponent group, then the former should not at that time launch a struggle that requires great strength. There is no substitute for, or shortcut to, strength in a movement of nonviolent struggle. If the group is weaker than needed, the action should initially take only limited forms, perhaps symbolic ones, that can make some impact without great strength. More ambitious action should at the time be postponed until effective means have been taken to strengthen the nonviolent struggle group relative to the opponent group. Clearly, major efforts should in this situation be placed into strengthening the population and the institutions that are primarily affected by the grievances and into developing the group's capacity to wage stronger nonviolent struggle in the future.

Additional factors also require attention before focusing on specific steps that may be helpful in preparing a strategy for the coming struggle. One of the most important factors, of course, is knowledge of the technique of nonviolent action that is to be used. Deliberate steps can be taken to gain and disseminate that knowledge.

Once that knowledge is obtained, however, it is the development and implementation of wise strategies, not simply the use of nonviolent methods, that will allow the nonviolent struggle to become as effective as possible. The ability to develop such strategies rests on an adequate understanding of the whole context within which the struggle is to be conducted. The primary purpose of the strategic estimate is to provide this understanding.

With much detailed information readily at hand, planning can be accomplished quickly to exploit new opportunities that may arise during campaigns.

Appendix B

GLOSSARY

ACCOMMODATION: A mechanism of change in nonviolent action in which the opponents resolve—while they still have a choice—to agree to a compromise and to grant certain demands of the nonviolent resisters. Accommodation occurs when the opponents have neither changed their views nor been nonviolently coerced, but have concluded that a compromise settlement is desirable.

The accommodation may result from influences that, if continued, might have led to the conversion, nonviolent coercion, or disintegration of the opponents' system or regime.

AUTHORITY: The quality that leads the judgments, decisions, recommendations, and orders of certain individuals and institutions to be accepted voluntarily as right, and therefore to be implemented by others through obedience or cooperation. Authority is a main source of political power, but is not identical with it.

BOYCOTT: Noncooperation, either socially, economically, or politically.

CIVIC ABSTENTION: A synonym for acts of political noncooperation.

CIVIC ACTION: A synonym for nonviolent action conducted for political purposes.

CIVIC DEFIANCE: Assertive acts of nonviolent protest, resistance or intervention conducted for political purposes.

CIVIC RESISTANCE: A synonym for nonviolent resistance with a political objective.

CIVIC STRIKE: An economic shutdown conducted for political reasons. It is important to note that not only may workers go on strike, but also students, professionals, shopkeepers, white-collar workers (including government employees), and members of upper classes, may participate in strikes or other non-cooperation.

CIVIL DISOBEDIENCE: A deliberate peaceful violation of particular laws, decrees, regulations, ordinances, military or police orders, and the like.

These are usually laws that are regarded as inherently immoral, unjust, or tyrannical. Sometimes, however, laws of a largely regulatory or morally neutral character may be disobeyed as a symbol of opposition to wider policies of the government.

CIVILIAN STRUGGLE: Social, economic, or political conflict waged by the civilian population by means of the technique of nonviolent action.

CONVERSION: A change of viewpoint by the opponents against whom nonviolent action has been waged, such that they come to believe it is right to accept the objectives of the nonviolent group. This is one of four mechanisms of change in nonviolent action.

COUP D'ÉTAT: Seizure by action of a small group of physical and political control of the State machinery. Coups d'état initially target the prime governmental centers of command, decision, and administration, and later the whole State apparatus. The seizure of the State is seen as the key step to gaining control of the whole country.

DICTATORSHIP: A political system in which the position of ruler is occupied by a person or group that claims the right to control the political system and society without respect for constitutional limits, division of powers, or opportunities for the population to select, as in elections, who shall be the officials. Basic civil liberties do not exist and opposition is dealt with by repression.

DISINTEGRATION: The fourth mechanism of change in nonviolent action, in which the opponents are not simply coerced, but their system or government is disintegrated, and falls apart as a result of massive noncooperation and defiance. The sources of power are restricted or severed by the noncooperation to such an extreme degree that the opponents' system or government simply dissolves. This is one of the four mechanisms of change in nonviolent action.

DYNAMICS (OF NONVIOLENT ACTION): The extremely complex general process of the workings of nonviolent struggle to achieve the objectives for which it is applied. This involves the clash of forces with the opponents, and the application by the nonviolent resisters of the various leverages at their disposal (psychological, social, ideational, economic, political, and physical). These leverages may be applied in many possible ways to confront the opponents' means of control and repression. These dynamics in successful cases tend to produce change by four mechanisms: conversion, accommodation, nonviolent coercion, and disintegration.

ECONOMIC SHUTDOWN: A suspension of the economic activities of a city, area, or country on a sufficient scale to produce economic paralysis. The motives are usually political.

This may be achieved by means of a general strike by workers, while also management, business, commercial institutions, and small shopkeepers close their establishments and halt their economic activities.

FAILURE: The situation in a nonviolent struggle when the conflict has ended without achieving the resisters' objectives.

FAST: Deliberate abstention from certain or all food. A fast may be undertaken for personal reasons (health, religion, penance, self-purification) or in order to achieve social or political objectives. Fasts may be conducted for specific limited time periods or for unlimited periods.

FREEDOM (POLITICAL): A political condition that permits freedom of choice and action for individuals and also for individuals and groups to participate in the decisions and operation of the society and the political system.

GRAND STRATEGY: The broadest conception of how an objective is to be attained in a conflict by a chosen course of action. The grand strategy serves to coordinate and direct all appropriate and available resources (human, political, economic, moral, etc.) of the group to attain its objectives in a conflict.

Several more limited strategies may be applied within a grand strategy to achieve particular objectives in subordinate phases of the overall struggle.

GRIEVANCE GROUP: The general population group whose grievances are issues in the conflict, and are being championed by the nonviolent resisters.

HUMAN RESOURCES: The number of persons and groups who obey "the rulers" (meaning the ruling group in command of the State), cooperate with them, or assist them in implementing their will. This includes the proportion of such persons and groups in the general population, and the extent, forms, and independence of their organizations.

A ruler's power is affected by the availability of these human resources, which constitute one of the sources of political power.

LEGITIMACY: Validity because of being in accord with the society's accepted sources, criteria, and standards of authority.

MATERIAL RESOURCES: This is another source of political power. The term refers to property, natural resources, financial resources, the economic system, means of communication, and modes of transportation. The degree to which the ruler controls or does not control these resources helps to determine the extent or limits of the ruler's power.

MECHANISMS OF CHANGE: The processes by which change is achieved in successful cases of nonviolent struggle. The four mechanisms are conversion, accommodation, nonviolent coercion, and disintegration.

METHODS: The specific means of action within the technique of nonviolent action. Nearly 200 specific methods have thus far been identified. They are classed under three main classes of nonviolent protest and persuasion, noncooperation (social, economic, and political), and nonviolent intervention.

NONCOOPERATION: A large class of methods of nonviolent action that involve deliberate restriction, discontinuance, or withholding of social, economic, or political cooperation (or a combination of these) with a disapproved person, activity, institution, or regime.

The methods of noncooperation are classified in the subcategories of social noncooperation, economic noncooperation (economic boycotts and labor strikes), and political noncooperation.

NONVIOLENCE (RELIGIOUS OR ETHICAL): Beliefs and behavior of several types in which violent acts are prohibited on religious or ethical grounds.

In some belief systems, not only is physical violence barred, but also hostile thoughts and words, and the idea of conflict itself may be rejected. Certain belief systems additionally enjoin positive attitudes and behavior toward opponents, or even a rejection of the concept of opponents.

Such believers often may participate in nonviolent struggles with people practicing nonviolent struggle for pragmatic reasons, or may choose not to do so.

NONVIOLENT ACTION: A general technique of conducting protest, resistance, and intervention without physical violence. The term "nonviolent struggle" can be used as a synonym.

Such action may be conducted by (a) acts of omission—that is, the participants refuse to perform acts that they usually perform, are expected by custom to perform, or are required by law or regulation to perform; (b) acts of commission—that is, the participants perform acts that they usually do not perform, are not expected by custom to perform, or are forbidden by law or regulation from performing; or (c) a combination of both.

The technique includes a multitude of specific methods that are grouped into three main classes: nonviolent protest and persuasion, noncooperation, and nonviolent intervention.

NONVIOLENT COERCION: A mechanism of change in nonviolent action in which demands are achieved against the will of the opponents because effective control of the situation has been taken away from them by widespread noncooperation and defiance. However, the opponents still remain in their official positions and the regime has not yet disintegrated.

NONVIOLENT INSURRECTION: A popular political uprising against an established regime regarded as oppressive by the use of massive noncooperation and defiance.

NONVIOLENT INTERVENTION: A large class of methods of nonviolent action that in a conflict situation directly interfere by nonviolent means with the opponents' activities and operation of their system. These methods are distinguished from both symbolic protests and noncooperation. The disruptive intervention is most often physical (as in a sit-in), but may also be psychological, social, economic, or political.

NONVIOLENT PROTEST AND PERSUASION: A large class of methods of nonviolent action that are symbolic acts expressing opposition opinions or attempting persuasion (as vigils, marches, or picketing). These acts extend beyond verbal expressions of opinion but stop short of noncooperation (as in a strike) and nonviolent intervention (as in a sit-in).

NONVIOLENT STRUGGLE: A synonym for nonviolent action. This term especially connotes the waging of strong forms of nonviolent action against determined opponents who are prepared to impose serious repression.

NONVIOLENT WEAPONS: The specific methods of nonviolent action.

OBEDIENCE: Compliance with, or submission to, a command or law. Obedience may arise from either free consent or fear of punishments.

OPPONENTS: The adversaries in a conflict, whether they function as a group, institution, regime, or invader.

PILLARS OF SUPPORT: The institutions and sections of the society that supply the existing regime with the needed sources of power to maintain and expand its power capacity.

Examples are the police, prisons, and military forces supplying sanctions, moral and religious leaders supplying authority (legitimacy), labor groups and business and investment groups supplying economic resources.

POLITICAL DEFIANCE: The strategic application of nonviolent struggle in order to disintegrate a dictatorship and to replace it with a democratic system.

This resistance by noncooperation and defiance mobilizes the power of the oppressed population in order to restrict and cut off the sources of the dictatorship's power. These sources are provided by groups and institutions called "pillars of support."

When political defiance is used successfully, it can make a country ungovernable by any dictatorship and therefore able to preserve a democratic system against possible new threats.

POLITICAL JU-JITSU: A special process that may operate during a nonviolent struggle to change power relationships. In political ju-jitsu negative reactions to the opponents' violent repression against nonviolent resisters is turned to operate politically against the opponents, weakening their power position and strengthening the power capacity of the nonviolent resisters.

Political ju-jitsu can operate only when violent repression is met with continued nonviolent defiance, not with violence or surrender. The opponents' repression is then seen in the worst possible light.

Resulting shifts of opinion are likely to occur among third parties, the general grievance group, and even the opponents' usual supporters. These shifts may produce both withdrawal of support for the opponents and increased support for the nonviolent resisters. The result may be widespread condemnation of the opponents, internal opposition among the opponents, and increased resistance. These changes can at times produce major shifts in power relationships in favor of the nonviolent struggle group.

Political ju-jitsu does not operate in all cases of nonviolent struggle. When it is absent, the shift of power relationships depends greatly on the extent of noncooperation.

POLITICAL NONCOOPERATION: A withdrawal of usual political cooperation, obedience, or other participation in the political system, or a specific part of it, under existing conditions. The action may be aimed against a specific regulation, law, policy, usurping group, regime, or even a foreign government.

POLITICAL POWER: The totality of influences and pressures available for use to implement, change, or oppose official policies for a society. Political power may be wielded by the institutions of government, or in opposition to the government by dissident groups and organizations. Political power may be directly applied in a conflict, or it may be held as a reserve capacity for possible later use.

RESISTANCE MOVEMENT: A widespread and usually informally interrelated network of individuals, informal groups, institutions, and resistance groups engaged in planned or spontaneous resistance against an established government, political system, usurpation regime, or military occupation administration.

SANCTIONS: Punishments or reprisals, violent or nonviolent, imposed either because people have failed to act in the expected or desired manner or because people have acted in an unexpected or prohibited manner.

Nonviolent sanctions are less likely than violent ones to be simple reprisals for disobedience and are more likely to be intended to achieve a given objective. Sanctions are a source of political power.

SELF-RELIANCE: The capacity to manage one's own affairs, make one's own judgments, and provide for oneself, one's group or organization, independence, self-determination, and self-sufficiency, including the capacity to act and resist.

SKILLS AND KNOWLEDGE: These constitute a source of political power. The ruler's power is supported by the skills, knowledge, and abilities that are provided by persons and groups in the society (human resources) and the relation of those available skills, knowledge, and abilities to the ruler's needs for them.

SOURCES OF POWER: These are origins of political power. They include authority, human resources, skills and knowledge, intangible factors, material resources, and sanctions. These derive from the society. Each of these sources is closely associated with, and dependent upon, the acceptance, cooperation, and obedience of the population and the society's institutions. With strong supply of these sources, the rulers will be powerful. As the supply of the sources of power is reduced or severed, the rulers' power will weaken or collapse.

STRATEGIC NONVIOLENT STRUGGLE: Nonviolent struggle that is applied according to a strategic plan that has been prepared on the basis of analysis of the conflict situation, the strengths and weaknesses of the contending groups, the nature, capacities, and requirements of the technique of nonviolent action, and especially the strategic principles of that type of struggle. See also grand strategy, strategy, tactics, and methods.

STRATEGIC PLAN: The concrete blueprint for the implementation of a strategy. The plan should answer the questions of who, what, when, where, and how for the strategic components of each campaign.

In small or extremely limited struggles, this strategic plan might exist realistically only on the tactical level. In such a case, the preparation of the strategic plan will not necessarily be a separate step from the planning involved in selecting tactics and methods for the implementation of the campaign strategy.

In a broader and more complex struggle, however, the strategic plan may exist on multiple levels. The plan will contain a variety of specific, more limited, tactical plans to gain smaller objectives that contribute to accomplishing the overall objective of the selected strategy. In rare struggles in which it is possible to plan concretely for multiple campaigns to operate simultaneously or in short sequence, the strategic plan should specify the order of those campaigns and the timing when each is to begin, based on the strategic relationship between them. It will also identify any subdivisions within the campaigns themselves.

STRATEGY: A plan for the conduct of a major phase, or campaign, within a grand strategy for the overall conflict. A strategy is the basic idea of how the struggle of a specific campaign shall develop, and how its separate components shall be fitted together most advantageously to achieve its objectives.

Strategy operates within the scope of the grand strategy. Tactics and specific methods of action are used in smaller-scale operations to implement the strategy for a specific campaign.

STRIKE: A deliberate restriction or suspension of work, usually temporary, to put pressure on employers to achieve an economic objective or, sometimes, on the government in order to achieve a political objective.

SUCCESS: The achievement by a party to a conflict of its substantive objectives. Success and failure are therefore both always related to goals.

TACTIC: A limited plan of action in a nonviolent struggle based on a conception of how, in a restricted phase of a conflict, to use effectively the available means of action to achieve a specific limited objective. Tactics are intended for use in implementing a wider strategy in a phase of the overall conflict.

VIOLENCE: Physical violence against other human beings that results in injury or death, or threatens to cause injury or death, or any act dependent on such infliction or threat.

In contrast to this understanding, believers in some types of religious or ethical nonviolence conceive of violence much more broadly. They may use the term to express a moral or political judgment, not to describe behavior. In contrast, the definition of nonviolent action and nonviolent struggle offered here permit the participation in the struggle of persons and groups that do not share a belief in some type of moral nonviolence, but who are prepared on pragmatic grounds to practice nonviolent struggle.

Appendix C

PREPARING TRANSLATIONS ON NONVIOLENT STRUGGLE

The need for translations

Although nonviolent struggle has been widely practiced in improvised forms, and has produced significant successes, it has remained little known. Knowledge of how to wield it effectively has been highly limited, and solid literature about its operation has been unavailable in most languages.

We know from experience that improved understanding of nonviolent struggle gained from published studies can be very helpful to groups that are considering using this technique or are preparing to apply it in a future conflict.

Knowledge of the nature and use of nonviolent struggle is power potential. Knowledge of how to act, how to organize, and how skillfully to transform their power potential into effective power can enable even previously weak people to participate in the determination of their own lives and society.

Without knowledge of nonviolent struggle, however, it is unlikely that this technique will be chosen instead of violence. If it is applied without much knowledge, the chances of it being successful are greatly reduced.

Various important studies on nonviolent struggle have been published in recent years. Sometimes, individuals with English language skills whose people face severe conflicts have found that the insights in this newer literature in English can be very helpful. Some of these people have therefore recommended that certain publications be translated into their own language.

The quality and clarity of those translations will often determine whether the concepts and phenomena discussed in an English language text are accurately conveyed and understood by

---

These notes on translations draw heavily on the experience and insights of Bruce Jenkins, Jamila Raqib, and Hardy Merriman of the Albert Einstein Institution.

readers of the translated text. Accurate and understandable translations enable readers to understand correctly the information, conceptions, and analyses conveyed by the original writer. On the other hand, inaccurate translations can have disastrous consequences. This is especially true in this field, because it has been so inadequately known and often confused with other phenomena. Therefore, it is important to offer some guidelines to assist with the preparation and conduct of future translations of writings about nonviolent struggle.[1]

The following tasks and steps in these translations will be explained in more detail shortly.

Steps in preparing for a translation

- Select a suitable text for translation, keeping in mind the situation for which it is needed and the available resources for making and disseminating the translation.

- Determine whether permission is required to make and distribute a translation, and if so secure such permission. Whenever possible, notify the author before beginning the translation.

- Anticipate how to publish and disseminate the final translation.

- Ensure that no alterations to the text are made during the translation.

- Consider issues with terminology. Make sure that the terminology used in the translation conveys the original meaning of the text.

- Assemble the translation team. Select competent persons to be the project manager, the translator, and the evaluator.

- Prepare contracts, if desired.

- Be prepared for problems in the work and be determined to overcome them.

---

[1] To assist with translations from English into another language, the Albert Einstein Institution has developed a set of standard procedures. These procedures were developed originally by Bruce Jenkins. The recommendations here closely follow those procedures.

- Proceed with the translation, the evaluations, and the revisions.

- Publish and disseminate the translation.

Step 1: Select a suitable text for translation, keeping in mind the situation for which it is needed and the available resources for making and disseminating the translation.

The choice of which publication to translate and publish should be done after careful evaluation. Serious errors in this choice can be made if one is not careful.

Sometimes in the past, the initial selection of the text to be translated has been made simply on the basis that an English language publication has been well known. However, the selected book may have a broad focus, may be extremely long and difficult to translate, and/or may not be especially relevant to the specific situation. The translation and publication of an excessively long book might require so much time to translate that it is never finished or is completed and published only long after the political crisis that aroused the interest in nonviolent struggle has ended. However, translation of an extremely lengthy book that is a classic in the field can be fully justified if there is no time urgency and if sufficient resources and institutional sponsorship are available.

The possibility of translating a much shorter and simpler publication that is focused on the type of problem that is being faced should always be seriously considered. The translation can be more rapid, less expensive to make, cheaper to print, and easier to distribute. It will also more likely be read.

Step 2: Determine whether permission is required, and if so secure such permission. Notify the author whenever possible.

Individuals and groups wishing to translate specific literature on nonviolent struggle are advised to contact the original author, or the publisher, before starting the translation. In order to prevent alterations of the text, the publication may already be copyrighted, and therefore translation and publication rights may require permission of the author or the publisher. Also, in some cases, advance checking will avoid duplication of efforts. Perhaps the text has already been translated or a translation is already in an advanced stage of preparation.

Step 3: Anticipate how to publish and disseminate the final translation

Quality translations require a great deal of time, knowledge, and skill. The time that the preparation of a translation requires depends on the original text, its length, the density and difficulty of the writing, the time available for the work by the translator and the evaluator, and their working habits and ability to concentrate on the work, despite pressures and distractions. Skilled supervision can shorten the time required for a completed translation.

Early in the work, planning is required for publication and dissemination of the translation. This may be possible within the given country with little or no difficulties. Options for publishing include pamphlets, books, cassettes, radio broadcasts, or placement on web sites. Dissemination may be possible even under repressive conditions, just as illegal publications were possible in The Netherlands and Norway during the Second World War and in the Soviet Union when repression was severe.

In some of the most severe cases, it may be necessary to print the publication in another country, or to put it on a foreign web site. At times, it may be possible to find creative ways to get the publication printed externally and then transported and distributed inside the country for which it is intended. All these efforts may require additional financial support. Under severe repression, the resistance groups will often lack sufficient funds to pay the costs of printing when that is possible, and external financial assistance may be helpful.

Early anticipation of the usefulness of a specific translation and prompt action to make it available can help to avoid experiences like the one a midlevel leader of the Tiananmen Square protest had. Years later, after reading a new publication in English on nonviolent struggle against dictatorships, he said, "Why didn't we know this in 1989?"

Sometimes, preparation of translations can be conducted by exiles and external allies. Dissidents and resisters inside the country are often preoccupied with their immediate situations. Translations, whether prepared inside the country or externally, may then be made available to people living in the extreme situation.

We know from much experience that even after a good translation has been prepared, for which there is great practical need, sometimes it may be impossible to get it printed without financial assistance to the publisher. Publications on nonviolent struggle are often needed in countries with economic problems, as well as political and social ones, and willing publishers can lack cash reserves to take the financial risk. Well in advance of completion of the translation, someone should have given attention to how the final text is to be printed or otherwise distributed. Often, of course, without a completed translation to offer, both solid financial assistance for printing and firm publication arrangements are impossible to make.

It must be remembered, however, that in the past, in very difficult circumstances, resisters have found ways to publish and distribute resistance news and even newspapers without external financial assistance, as in several Nazi-occupied countries.

Step 4: Ensure that no alterations to the text are made

Accuracy in translations requires that no changes be made in the text, neither additions nor deletions. Also, great care must be taken to preserve the exact original meaning of the text.[2]

Step 5: Consider issues with terminology

Quality translations of new literature on nonviolent struggle are very important as the carriers of concepts, knowledge, and insights that have not been previously familiar or easily shared. Careful translations may therefore facilitate consideration of what type of action the group will undertake and may also assist in its planning for such action.

---

[2] Rarely, however, certain statistics in the original text that have become outdated by the time of the translation of the work may be corrected, provided that permission is secured from the original author or publisher. In no case should wider changes be made to the text, nor should the original text be rearranged.

No matter the conditions in which translation work is conducted, the translation itself is likely to be difficult. A primary reason for this is because the general phenomenon of waging conflict by means other than violence has rarely been the focus of in-depth study and analysis. That type of exploration requires development of a specialized vocabulary for the field. Careful consideration must be given to how appropriate and important terms and concepts from English literature are to be translated into the new language so that their meanings will be understood accurately by new readers.

The terminology for the important concepts, ideas, and types of action of this technique is rarely, if ever, well-developed in the target language. Prior to the 1950s, this was also true in English, in which there have been significant terminological improvements in recent decades.[3] Even now, significant room still exists in English for improving the terminology and clarifying the concepts for this field.

Some of the English terms in this field do not translate readily into other languages. Other terms in this technique may be assumed at times to have exact foreign equivalents but those may not actually be accurate. For example, some persons have incorrectly translated the term "nonviolent action" into the target language as the equivalent of "passive resistance" although nonviolent action can be extremely active. Also, "nonviolent action" has often been translated as the equivalent of "nonviolence," which also is inappropriate because "nonviolence" may be understood to involve ethical, moral, or religious beliefs (when the reality is that nonviolent action has been widely practiced by nonbelievers for pragmatic reasons). The widespread confusion between nonviolent action (or nonviolent struggle) and "nonviolence" is potentially very serious. Those beliefs in "nonviolence" may have their merits, but they are a different phenomenon than pragmatic nonviolent struggle. When the term for nonviolent action is mistranslated in this way, this technique may be summarily rejected by persons and groups that regard themselves as realists. All persons working on translations need to understand these differences very well.

---

[3] This development of an improved vocabulary has begun in certain other languages in recent decades, such as in German and French.

There are additional issues with terminology as well. Direct equivalents for "nonviolent action" and related terms may not already be in standard usage or may not even exist in the target language. New terms may need to be coined and introduced in some translations. For example, in Burma the term "political defiance" was coined because anything called "nonviolent" had connotations of passivity and naïveté.[4]

In particular, experience has demonstrated that some confusion is especially likely to arise during the translation of the English terms for specific methods of nonviolent action, such as fasts and forms of noncooperation. The confusion arises from efforts to translate the words literally that have been used in English to identify each of the 198 specific methods. (Of course, many additional methods beyond the 198 exist.)

Some of the names of specific methods have been incorporated from earlier literature, such as studies of labor strikes or economic boycotts that identify particular types of these classes of methods. Comparable names for the exact same specific forms of action may already exist in the target language, and if so they should be used in translations.

However, the names of some other methods in the English text may have been newly coined and may make no sense in literal translations. Examples are "lightning strike," "mill-in," and "Lysistratic nonaction." The form of action may have been earlier practiced, but an attempt to produce a literal translation of the English term may be fruitless. The translation should then be made from the definition of the form of action (or in other cases from the concept), not from the literal English name.[5]

Step 6: Assemble the translation team

Many people assume that translations of texts on nonviolent struggle from English into whatever language are simply a matter of handing the task to a bilingual person (preferably with transla-

---

[4] The term was coined by Robert Helvey in Burma in the Karen resistance headquarters at Manerplaw.
[5] These problems illustrate that translations of names of methods should never be made from simple lists of methods. Instead, the translator should always consult the definition and description of the specific method that are included in Gene Sharp, *The Politics of Nonviolent Action,* Part Two, *The Methods of Nonviolent Action,* Boston: Porter Sargent, 1973 and later editions.

tion experience) and accepting the translation provided. That is not true in this case.

Experience also shows that a given text should never be divided up among more than one translator and one evaluator. Doing so can appear to save time, but can easily result in a translation of poor quality that contains different vocabularies and different writing styles. Costly translations have had to be discarded in the past because of these problems.

The project manager

Quality translations require a great deal of time, knowledge, and skill. Not everyone can prepare a quality translation in this field without considerable orientation and supervision. This means that direction and supervision by a competent project manager are needed. For such a person, not only is considerable understanding of nonviolent struggle required, but also previous experience in managing translations, or at least in translating, is highly recommended. Knowledge of at least one additional language other than English and the target language is a great plus, but is not essential, for the project manager. The project manager need not be competent in the target language.

The right project manager can greatly assist with the successful completion of the translation by helping to select the translator and the evaluator.

The project manager also oversees the exchanges of draft translations and evaluation comments and helps to keep the translation process moving ahead at a reasonable speed.

The translator

Of course, translators (even experienced ones) are not all equally skilled in doing translations for this particular field. Therefore, candidates for the positions of translator and evaluator who have not worked successfully on translations about nonviolent struggle previously will need to be tested and evaluated prior to selection. Experience in translating writings on moral or religious nonviolence is definitely not a plus. This is because the focus in those writings has been on beliefs, while the focus on literature on nonviolent struggle is on forms of action in conflicts.

The concepts and terminology of the two are different. Failure to reflect this in the translation can lead to confusion and serious problems.

With extremely few exceptions, the translator should always translate into his or her native language. For example, a native English speaker should not translate a text into Arabic even if the person is fluent. Only a native speaker of the language of the translation, with very few exceptions, can really understand the language's idiosyncrasies and subtleties.

Candidates need to be evaluated on their fluency in both English and the language into which the work will be translated. Candidates may also be evaluated on their general knowledge surrounding the subject area and their understanding of the terms and concepts present in the chosen text.

One way that testing and evaluation of possible translators and evaluators can be done is by having two or three qualified candidates translate into the new language a few relevant pages of the intended text and also about 25-40 key terms as a trial. These key terms should convey concepts in nonviolent action and should also be present in the work to be translated. These test translations are then evaluated and compared by someone who is very competent but unavailable for making the translation itself. This initial sample translation arrangement is additional work for the project director and the candidates, but it reduces problems later.[6]

The evaluator

An evaluator can be selected by a similar process as the translator that tests the prospective evaluator's skill, both in translating and evaluating a draft translation prepared by another person. The evaluator should be a person who is capable of producing a good translation and who might well have been selected as the initial translator under different circumstances.

The evaluator's primary responsibility is to review thoroughly the draft translation and to provide feedback and criticism for the

---

[6] For a list of potential key terms for translations, see the attachment to this appendix. Some key terms will vary, depending on which text is translated. However, the core concepts of nonviolent action, noncooperation, and various other elements will be relevant to all translations.

translator. In addition to general comments, the evaluator may offer identification of specific problems and may recommend revisions to the translator. The evaluation should be in writing, and this may be supplemented in conversations with the project manager.

Experience indicates that there are advantages to keeping the identities of the translator and the evaluator unknown to each other. The translation and the evaluations should be passed through the project manager. At a bare minimum, the translator and the evaluator should not be collaborating directly. The reason for having an evaluator is that that person is independent of the translator, and therefore able to evaluate more objectively the drafts of the proposed translation.

Step 7: Prepare contracts, if desired

In some cases, the translation process can be facilitated by formal contracts between the sponsoring body and the translator and the evaluator that cover the preparation and completion of a quality translation of a specified text. The contract provisions should be clear and relevant for the specific task. Contracts may include projected completion dates for parts of the planned translation and evaluation of the draft translation, the responsibility of the translator to consider the evaluator's recommendations, the need to cooperate with the project manager, mention of conditions under which the translator or the evaluator can be terminated, and the intended financial arrangement.

Contracts for translators and evaluators should have clauses that provide financial incentives to encourage both quality and speed of the translation. If the draft translation turns out to be of poor quality or is unduly delayed, financial penalties are appropriate and the contract can be cancelled.

Sometimes, a high quality translator and an evaluator may volunteer to work without financial compensation. Volunteers to prepare the translation and to evaluate drafts of it can be extremely helpful provided that the volunteers are skilled, firmly committed to the project, and able to act without undue delays.

Experience has shown that the financial cost of securing a good translation of the same text differs widely by language, situation, and individuals concerned.

Step 8: Be prepared for problems in the work and be determined to overcome them

Step 9: Proceed with the translation, evaluations, and revisions

Once the translator and the evaluator are selected, the translation begins. This work is under the general supervision of the project manager.

The translator starts with an initial major section or a chapter of the text.

This draft translation is submitted to the project manager, who subsequently passes it to the evaluator.

The evaluator reviews this initial translation and presents feedback to the project manager to be passed on to the translator. The project manager then consults with the translator concerning the evaluation. The translator then carefully reviews the evaluation. The translator should seriously consider the evaluator's suggestions and incorporate the proposed changes that are accepted as valid, and should then discuss the evaluation with the project manager.

If major problems exist between the translator's initial translation and the evaluator's report, and these cannot be resolved with the aid of the project manager, then either the translator or the evaluator may be replaced, depending upon the judgment of the project manager. If this was to be a paid translation, the terminated translator or evaluator may be given a fair and modest payment for the past effort. A new person will then be sought for the task. If minor problems exist, the translator proceeds with the full translation of the text, keeping in mind the comments of the evaluator. In the case of such minor disagreements, the translator's determination will stand.

If available, the author of the English text may at times provide needed clarification and/or suggestions during the translation project.

Once the entire text is translated, the evaluator reviews the full text in the new language and gives additional feedback for the translator to the project manager.

Once the translator has considered this feedback and made any necessary changes, the final version of the text is complete and the translated article or book is considered to be final and ready to be printed or otherwise distributed.

Step 10: Publish and disseminate the translation

After the translation has been put into the final form, it is ready for publication in any of the various forms that were mentioned in Step 3. Dissemination is the next step.

Congratulations

High quality translations can be very important in contributing to effective practice of nonviolent struggles. They merit our attention and assistance. The preparation of a quality translation makes this possible.

Attachment One

POTENTIAL KEY TERMS FOR TRANSLATIONS

- Accommodation
- Authority
- Boycott
- Civil disobedience
- Civilian struggle
- Coup d'état
- Dictatorship
- Dynamics (of nonviolent action)
- Disintegration
- Failure
- Fast
- Freedom (political)
- Grand strategy
- Legitimacy
- Mechanisms of change
- Methods
- Noncooperation
- Nonviolent action
- Nonviolent coercion
- Nonviolence (religious, etc.)
- Nonviolent intervention
- Nonviolent protest and persuasion
- Nonviolent struggle
- Nonviolent weapons

For definitions of these key terms, see Appendix B, Glossary.

- Obedience
- Opponents
- Pillars of support
- Political defiance
- Political ju-jitsu
- Political noncooperation
- Political power
- Resistance movement
- Sanctions
- Self-reliance
- Sources of power
- Strategic nonviolent struggle
- Strategic plan
- Strategy
- Strike
- Success
- Tactic
- Violence

Appendix D

SOURCES FOR FURTHER READING

The following short list of sources can assist in the planning of strategic nonviolent struggle.

Books

Peter Ackerman and Jack DuVall, *A Force More Powerful,* New York: St. Martin's Press, 2000.

Peter Ackerman and Christopher Kruegler, *Strategic Nonviolent Conflict: The Dynamics of People Power in the Twentieth Century,* Westport, Connecticut, and London: Praeger, 1994.

Robert Helvey, *On Strategic Nonviolent Conflict: Thinking About the Fundamentals,* Boston, Massachusetts: The Albert Einstein Institution, 2004.

Gene Sharp, with Bruce Jenkins, *Civilian-Based Defense: A Post-Military Weapons System,* Princeton, New Jersey, and London: Princeton University Press, 1990. Out of print.

Gene Sharp, *The Politics of Nonviolent Action,* Boston, Massachusetts: Porter Sargent, 1973. Available in three paperback volumes only: *Power and Struggle, The Methods of Nonviolent Action,* and *The Dynamics of Nonviolent Action.*

Gene Sharp, *Social Power and Political Freedom,* Boston, Massachusetts: Porter Sargent, 1980.

Monographs

Gene Sharp and Bruce Jenkins, *The Anti-Coup,* Boston, Massachusetts: The Albert Einstein Institution, 2003 (64 pp.).

Gene Sharp, *From Dictatorship to Democracy,* Bangkok, Thailand: Committee for the Restoration of Democracy in Burma, 1993, and Boston: The Albert Einstein Institution, 2002 (77 pp.) and 2003 (88 pp.).

Gene Sharp, *There Are Realistic Alternatives,* Boston, Massachusetts: The Albert Einstein Institution, 2003 (54 pp.).

Research guides

Ronald McCarthy and Gene Sharp, with Brad Bennett, *Nonviolent Action: A Research Guide,* New York: Garland Publishing, 1994.

Roger S. Powers and William B. Vogele (eds.), *Protest, Power, and Change,* New York and London: Garland Publishing, 1997.

Encyclopedia articles

Gene Sharp, "Civil Disobedience" and "Nonviolent Action," in Joel Krieger (ed.), *The Oxford Companion to the Politics of the World,* Second Edition (Oxford and New York: Oxford University Press, 2001), pp. 137-138, and 603-605.

Gene Sharp, "Nonviolent Action," in Lester Kurtz (ed.), *The Encyclopedia of Violence, Peace, and Conflict,* Vol. 2.   San Diego: Academic Press, 1999.

Gene Sharp, "Nonviolent Struggle and the Media," in the *Encyclopedia of International Media and Communication,* vol. 3 (San Diego, California: Academic Press, Elsevier Science [USA], 2003), pp. 363-370.

INDEX

Prepared by Hardy Merriman

A Library for a
More Hopeful Future

Esteemed educational and social critic Porter Sargent founded this publishing house in 1914 "to bring new concepts and ideas outside the usual range of the educator's vision."

F. Porter Sargent established Extending Horizons Books in 1955, expanding his father's mission to include other authors. He chose to first publish a new edition of Kropotkin's classic, *Mutual Aid,* to ensure its availability would not be subject to capricious trends in social thought.

Today, Extending Horizons Books continues to provide a unique forum for timeless ideas.

A full list of available titles, including such Gene Sharp classics as *Politics of Nonviolent Action, Social Power and Political Freedom,* and *Gandhi as a Political Strategist,* is available at www.extendinghorizons.com, or by contacting the publisher.

Additional copies of this book, as well as other Extending Horizons Books, may be purchased from most booksellers and distributors or by contacting our customer service center:

Extending Horizons Books

PORTER SARGENT PUBLISHERS INC.
300 Bedford St., Ste. 213, Manchester, NH 03101 USA

Tel: 800-342-7470 (US/Canada) +1-603-647-4383 (worldwide)
Fax: 603-669-7945   Email: orders@portersargent.com

www.extendinghorizons.com

Other Available Extending Horizons Books

Author	Title	Price
Barbour, Floyd B.	*The Black Power Revolt*	$5.95
Briffault, R.	*Marriage Past and Present*	$3.95
Dasgupta, Sugata	*Social Work and Social Change*	$6.95
Kropotkin, Petr	*Mutual Aid*	$9.95
Lindenfeld, Frank	*Workplace Democracy and Social Change*	$20.00
Long, Priscilla	*The New Left: A Collection of Essays*	$6.00
Mattick, Paul	*Marx & Keynes*	$6.95
Melko, Matthew	*The Nature of Civilizations*	$4.95
Montagu, Ashley	*Toynbee and History*	$7.00
Morgan, Arthur E.	*Dams and Other Disasters*	$7.50
Sharp, Gene	*The Politics of Nonviolent Action*, 3 parts (package)	$29.95
Sharp, Gene	*Part One: Power and Struggle*	$7.95
Sharp, Gene	*Part Two: The Methods of Nonviolent Action*	$10.95
Sharp, Gene	*Part Three: The Dynamics of Nonviolent Action*	$13.95
Sharp, Gene	*Gandhi as a Political Strategist*	$14.95
Sharp, Gene	*Social Power and Political Freedom*	$15.95
Sorokin, Pitirim A.	*Social and Cultural Dynamics*	$10.00
Templin, Ralph T.	*Democracy and Nonviolence*	$4.00

Order Tel: 800-342-7470 (US/Canada)
+1-603-647-4383 (worldwide)
or
www.extendinghorizons.com